P.O.W
Prisoners of War

AUSTRALIANS UNDER NIPPON

Hank Nelson

From the ABC OOO Radio series

CHRONOLOGY

September 3 1939 Australia declares war on Germany
January 1940 Troops of the 2nd AIF sail for the Middle East
December 1940 Australians in battle in North Africa
February 1941 22nd Brigade and attached troops of the 8 Division sail for Singapore and Malaya
March-April! 1941 Lark Force (2/22nd Battalion) arrives in Rabaul
April 1941 Australians fighting in Tobruk and Greece
August 1941 27th Brigade and attached troops of the 8 Division arrive in Singapore
December 7-8 1941 Japanese attack Pearl Harbor, Philippines and Malaya
December 12 1941 Sparrow Force (2/40 Battalion) arrives in Timor
December 17 1941 Gull Force (2/21 Battalion) arrives in Ambon
January 14 1942 Australians in battle at Gemas and Muar, Malaya
January 23 1942 Japanese land at Rabaul
January 30 1942 Japanese land on Ambon
February 14 1942 *Vyner Brooke* carrying sixty-five Australian nurses sunk in Banka Strait
February 15 1942 British Forces on Singapore surrender
February 19 1942 Units of 7 Division land in Java and become part of Blackforce
February 19 1942 First Japanese bombing of Darwin
February 19 1942 Japanese land on Timor
February 28 1942 Japanese land on Java
February 28 1942 *Perth* and *Houston* sunk in Sunda Strait
May 1942 POWs in A Force sail from Singapore to Burma
June 1942 US forces defeat Japanese in battle of Midway
July 1942 *Montevideo Maru* sunk off the Philippines and over 1000 service and civilian prisoners captured in New Guinea killed or drowned.
July 1942 Australian officers and nurses captured in Rabaul sail to Japan
July 1942 B Force sails from Singapore to North Borneo
August 1942 Senior officer POWs sail from Singapore to Taiwan and eventually to Korea and Manchuria
September 1942 Australians inflict first land defeat on Japanese at Milne Bay
October 1942 500 Dutch and Australian POWs on Ambon sail to Hainan
January 1943 Dunlop Force sail from Java to Singapore and Thailand
January 1943 Japanese forces defeated in Papua
March 1943 D Force travels by train from Singapore to Thailand. F and H Forces follow
March 1943 E Force sail from Singapore to North Borneo
June 1943 Eight Australians escape from Borneo and reach the Philippines
September 1943 Allies recapture Lae and Salamaua in New Guinea
October 1943 Burma and Thai ends of railway joined at Konkoita
December 1943 Survivors of F Force return to Singapore
June 1944 Allied Forces land in Normandy
July 1944 *Byoki Maru* with over 1200 POWs leaves Singapore on ten-week voyage to Japan
September 1944 *Rokyu Maru* carrying 1250 Australian and British POWs sunk and 141 men rescued by USA submarines
October 1944 Americans return in force to the Philippines
November 1944 Acting Prime Minister, Frank Forde, makes public statement on the treatment of POWs in Singapore and on Burma-Thailand railway
January 1945 First Sandakan-Ranau death march
April 1945 Americans land in Okinawa
May 7 1945 Germany surrenders
May-June 1945 Second Sandakan-Ranau death march
August 6 1945 Atomic bomb dropped on Hiroshima
August 9 1945 Atomic bomb dropped on Nagasaki
August 15 1945 Ceasefire against Japan
September 2 1945 Japanese sign surrender documents on USS *Missouri* in Tokyo Bay

---

Published by ABC Enterprises for the
AUSTRALIAN BROADCASTING CORPORATION
Box 9994 GPO Sydney NSW 2001
145 Elizabeth Street Sydney NSW

Copyright © 1985 Australian Broadcasting Corporation

First published 1985

All rights reserved. No part of this publication may be reproduced, stored in a retrieval system or transmitted in any form or by any means electronic, mechanical, photocopying, recording or otherwise, without the prior written permission of the Australian Broadcasting Corporation.

National Library of Australia
Cataloguing-in-Publication entry
Nelson, Hank.
 P.O.W., prisoners of war.
 Includes index.
 ISBN 0 642 52736 9.
 1. World War, 1939–1945 — Prisoners and prisons, Japanese. 2. World War, 1939–1945– — Personal narratives, Australian. I. Australian Broadcasting Corporation. II. Title.
 940.54′72′52

Illustrated by Don Moore
Edited by Helen Findlay and Nina Riemer
Designed by Leigh Nankervis
Set in 11/12 Goudy by Caxtons Pty Ltd, Adelaide
Printed and bound in Australia by The Griffin Press, Adelaide

COVER
Australian prisoners-of-war eating their rice ration in Selarang Barracks, Changi Peninsula, Singapore, 1942. Photograph by George Aspinall. Originally published in Changi Photographer *by Tim Bowden, ABC Enterprises/Collins, 1984.*

CONTENTS

	Introduction	4
1	You'll Be Sorry	7
2	You'll Never Get Off the Island	24
3	Travelling to Slavery	35
4	Nippon Very Sorry, Many Men Must Die	46
5	Changi Was Like Heaven	58
6	An Ordinary Bunch of Women	69
7	The Long Carry	84
8	You Could Feel Yourself Dying	98
9	To Escape Was to Live	110
10	Long Odds to Liberty	125
11	Travelling in Captivity	138
12	From Timor to Manchuria	151
13	Outram Road	164
14	Rice Now for Rice Later	177
15	Are We Free?	191
16	Lost Years and Wounded Minds	206
	Bibliography	219
	Acknowledgments	221
	Index	222

INTRODUCTION

Within three months of the Japanese entering World War II on December 8, 1941 over 22 000 Australians had become prisoners-of-war. They went into camps in Timor, Ambon, New Britain, Java, Sumatra, Borneo, Singapore and Malaya, and a few were scattered to other points in what was briefly part of the Japanese empire. Later most of the prisoners were to be shifted further north into South-east Asia, Formosa, Korea, Manchuria and Japan itself. They were captives within lands and cultures and to experiences alien to those known to all other Australians. At the end of the war in August 1945, 14 315 servicemen and thirty service women were alive to put on new, loose-fitting uniforms and go home. One in three of the prisoners had died. That is, nearly half of the deaths suffered by Australians in the war in the Pacific were among men and women who had surrendered. Another 8174 Australians had been captured in the fighting in Europe, the Middle East and North Africa: but of these men only 265 died as a result of wounds, disease or execution.

By any quantitative measure the imprisonment of so many Australians is a major event in Australian history. For many soldiers it was living—and dying—in captivity which made World War II different from that of World War I. But the prisoners have received no permanent place in Australian history. Their story is not immediately recalled on celebratory occasions. In a general history of the nation in which a chapter is given to the war the prisoners might be mentioned in a sentence, or part of a sentence. Where the horror, stoicism and gallantry of Gallipoli have become part of a common tradition shared by all Australians, the ex-prisoners are granted just the horror. The public may be sympathetic; but the horror is for the prisoners alone. To make another comparison: in five months of fighting on the Kokoda Trail in 1942 the Australians lost 625 dead, less than the number who died on Ambon. Yet the events on Ambon are unknown to most Australians. There were no reporters or cameramen on Ambon and,

INTRODUCTION

South-east Asia. The men of the 8th Division were unconscious pioneers in the first major encounter with the lands and peoples of South-east Asia.

for the 309 who defended Ambon's Laha airfield, no survivors. How many of them died in battle or died as prisoners will never be known. But there are more than just practical reasons why the record of the prisoners of war is so slight and uneven in the general knowledge of Australians. They have not tried to find out. No historian has written a book to cover the range of camps and experiences, and only in specialist medical publications has anyone investigated the impact of prison life on subsequent physical and mental health. The complexity of the experience and its impact on particular lives have not been expressed in a way to give them significance for other Australians.

All ex-prisoners are aware of the gap between their own memories and popular knowledge. On one occasion a very well-intentioned lady told a group of ex-prisoners that the reason they looked so well was because they had lived for a long time without rich fatty foods. The ex-prisoners had all seen men die appalling deaths with their bodies bloated and covered in sores, and at each reunion they spoke of the recent dead. But now none of them made any comment. They were all well-practised in techniques for gaining a quick escape from conversations full of misconceptions and embarrassment.

The ex-prisoners themselves are still trying to find meaning in the experiences which so dominate their lives. They have written over thirty published autobiographies. Some of those published early by Rohan Rivett and Russell Braddon caught the immediate postwar curiosity; but many have been written more recently. After forty years the authors are still expressing an incredulity that they could have passed through such events. After forty years the ex-prisoners are still wondering what it all meant; and they are more willing to talk.

The men who surrendered to the Japanese came from all parts of Australia. By the way that units were formed, men from particular areas tended to serve together. The 2/40th Battalion, which was to go to Timor, was established and began its training in Tasmania; and the 2/19th Battalion was, Gilbert Mant says, 'to all intents and purposes a Riverina battalion' made up of men who talked of sheep and cocky farmers. Men from the 20th Light Horse, a militia unit in Victoria, transferred to the 4th Anti-Tank Regiment, and as a result twelve men from the one northern town of Numurkah went into the same unit, and into captivity in Singapore. Ten of them returned. They say that they 'did it hard' and are proud of their record of survival. The 2/4th Machine Gun Battalion was formed in Western Australia, and throughout the war Evelyn Facey from her home in north Perth wrote regularly to her son Barney in Singapore. He had in fact been killed on the day of the surrender. The gunners of the 2/10th Field Regiment were Queenslanders with most of the men coming from the Darling Downs and the southwest. One of them wrote in 1941:

> And the moleskins and the leggings,
> That were sweaty, old, and torn,
> Are discarded now entirely,
> And a khaki suit is worn.

The twenty-four bandsmen of the 2/22nd Battalion enlisted as a group. All were Salvation Army musicians, half from the Brunswick Corps and the Melbourne Salvation Army Staff Band. Within the battalion they trained as stretcher-bearers as well as musicians. One of them survived. A characteristic of being a prisoner was a levelling of experience; once the surrender had taken place it did not matter much whether a man was from the navy, the artillery, the infantry, the Q store or divisional postal unit. The men and women who talk in the following chapters were in civilian life lawyers and carpenters, dental mechanics, bank tellers, railway workers, farmers, nurses, fishermen and unemployed. In the services they were privates, gunners, able seamen, NCOs, lieutenants and senior officers. Such were the fortunes of prisoners that the most extraordinary events were as likely to entangle a butcher in the service corps as they were an officer in an elite unit.

THE ILLUSTRATOR
VX37051 Sergeant Don Moore of the 4th Anti-Tank was captured in Singapore, worked with D Force on the Burma-Thailand railway, sailed in the Byoki Maru *to the dockyards and coalmines of Japan, and returned to be a soldier settler and school teacher. He has transformed memories into illustrations.*

CHAPTER ONE

YOU'LL BE SORRY

Australians would continue to look to Europe as the centre of great events . . . but were about to change their perception of their place in the world.

The soldiers of the 2nd AIF did not go innocently to war. Many had fathers and uncles in the lst AIF. Stan Arneil, whose father had died of war wounds in 1938, felt that the feats of the Anzacs were 'a tradition bred into me'. Tom Morris, the son of a First War soldier, went to a nearby town to enlist under-age; and it was not long before his father had joined up again. In fact in nearly every unit there were men entitled to wear the ribbons of the Great War. The two men in the 2/3rd Reserve Motor Transport who had served in the Boer War had apparently been able to tell plausible stories to the recruiting officers about their lack of youth.

Familiarity with the experiences of men in the First War ensured that the recruits did not go into camp with the naive eagerness of contestants going to a great sporting match. But they did expect to excel. Like the men of the lst AIF they would win international esteem on the battlefields of Europe and the Middle East. To go to war with expectations of excellence could be a heavy burden.

The soldiers of other wars and the schoolboys who had been just too young to enlist in 1918 were now the 'old and the bold' or the 'toothless and ruthless'. They were balanced by the youths. Private Frank Robinson landed in Singapore as a reinforcement in January 1942:

> I was sixteen when I enlisted. And I see kids today the age that I was then, and I think to myself I should have had my bottom kicked from here to Wynyard. When we were transported to Singapore there were Lascars on the ship, and they were big fellows. They looked at me and several others, and you could see them chatting among themselves and laughing. When one looked at me and made a rocking motion as if rocking a baby, I knew exactly what he meant. That's when I told him to get stuffed and walked away.

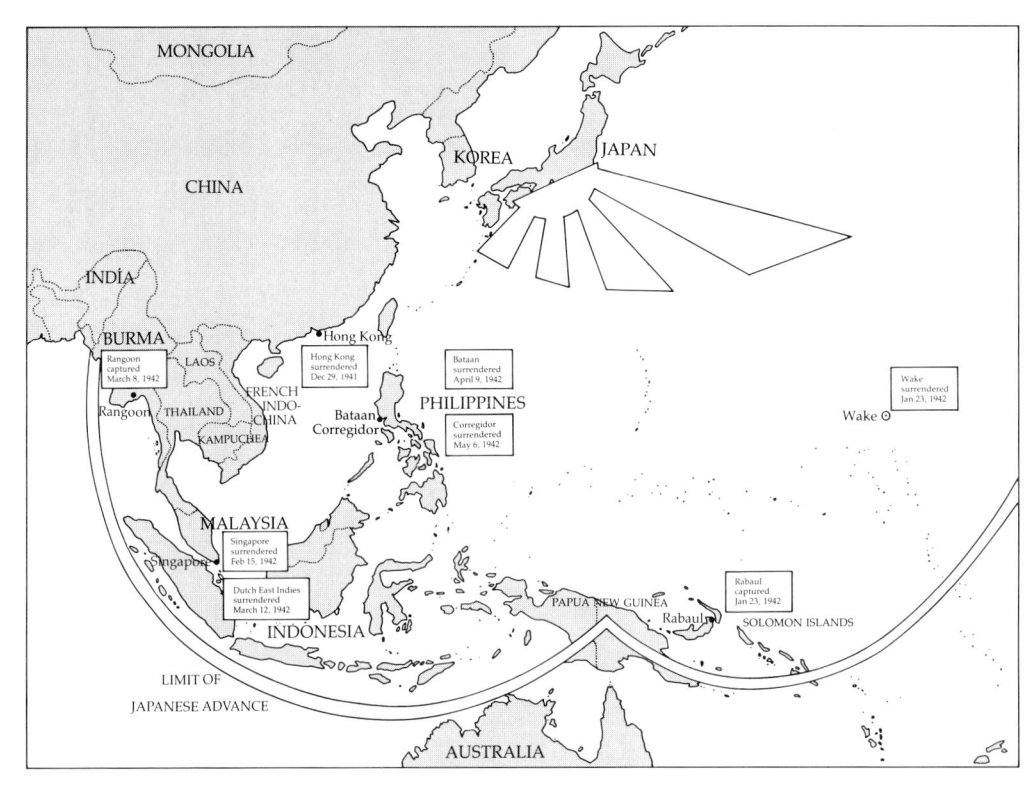

The Japanese did not move steadily south, but in sudden thrusts were among and around the defenders.

David Runge 'from up north at Murwillumbah' was another who was seventeen when he arrived in Singapore, 'but Danny Johnson had his twenty-first birthday when he got home'. The average age of the 2/10th Field Regiment on its formation in 1940 was twenty-one, and that of the infantry battalions was probably slightly higher.

All the recruits had lived through the economic depression of the 1930s, but they had not suffered equally. Many cannot talk of themselves in the prewar without seeing a young man in relation to tough times. Frank Robinson grew up in northern Tasmania: 'At the age of eight and nine years of age I used to go out with a shotgun and shoot rabbits. I used to go fishing.' The detail is implied in Snow Peat's laconic summary: 'I was in the gardening game. Things was crook then and if you had a job you was lucky.' Although most of the young men at university in the 1930s were from families with sufficient income to cushion them from economic stringency, Glyn White worked on the Melbourne wharf lumping frozen mutton during vacations and on Tuesday nights to pay his way through the early years of his medical course. Sir Edward Dunlop spent his first year at university 'pinned down to nothing but study and saving footwear'. In later years he won scholarships to support him—and give him time for sport.

The depression was an apprenticeship in survival. Men recall their physical toughness: 'my feet were so hard they were like leather'. And a man who rides a bike twelve kilometres and swings a pick day after day is confident of his capacity to work beyond the point where the new chums fall with exhaustion. It was, an English prisoner on Sumatra says, 'a punishing experience to find oneself working with an Australian';

they did, the Englishman remembers, explain that they needed to keep in trim if they wanted to hold a job on their return home.

Nearly all the troops that met the first southward thrust of the Japanese were in units of the 8th Division, formed after the fall of France. If the men of the First War had taught them that war was not joyous, the news now told them that the battles in Europe would be neither short nor easy. Adventure and the chance to participate in great events were still motives for enlistment. George Williamson: 'Before the war I was a butcher living in Northcote. I just thought I'd like to join the army and see what it was all about.' The sense of duty was still strong. Jack Panaotie compressed the events and the motives of his generation: 'I was a poulterer. I was on the dole before that. And the war came and I enlisted. I just wouldn't be able to live with myself if I hadn't.' Doctors who go to war to repair and not to destroy have a coming together of patriotic and professional duty; and they competed for positions in the AIF. One remembers being 'burnt up to go'. War, he saw, as a 'marvellous alternative' to 'grind and respectability'.

The men trained in the belief that they would follow the 6th and 9th Divisions to north Africa and the Middle East. In January 1941 the Australians of the 6th Division were in battle at Bardia, long columns of Italian prisoners were trudging east, and the British forces were advancing west towards Tobruk and Benghazi. In February the troop trains carrying units of the 22nd Brigade of the 8th Division to Sydney were decorated with the chalked slogans, 'Berlin or Bust' and 'Look out Adolf'. Those enlisting in the 8th Division had entered camp to the cries of 'You'll be sorry' from the recruits of a day earlier, and now as they went on board the imposing bulk of the *Queen Mary* lying at anchor off Taronga Park Zoo again there were the familiar cries from the men already leaning on the railings, 'You'll be sorry!' The greeting of the old hands to the new had become the sardonic salute of the 2nd AIF; and it was prophetic for the men going north.

The 22nd Brigade were the first troops to embark in shorts. As the ships pulled away to cheers, cooees, the Maori Farewell, Auld Lang Syne and a fleet of small craft, Singapore had shortened sharply in the odds for those wanting to bet on their destination. West Africa was still a long shot, although no one could say why Australians might need to be posted there. Off Fremantle the issue was finally decided. The men were told that they were on their way to Malaya; and the announcement was confirmed by pageantry at sea. In a manoeuvre which was impressive then, and remains significant now, the old *Queen* pulled out of the convoy, circled, and with a display of stately speed, charged past the rest of the fleet. Again cheers and band music bounced across wave and wake. The *Queen Mary* and her escort went north, and the rest of the convoy carrying Australian and New Zealand troops continued west across the Indian ocean following what had become the traditional route of young Australians going to war. Australians would continue to look to Europe as the centre of great events, but as the *Queen Mary* turned northward carrying 5750 troops, Australians were about to change their perception of their place in the world. For the first time the near north of Pacific islands and South-east Asia was to be of crucial importance to Australians. But the troops themselves felt cheated. Sir Adrian Curlewis, a captain with the headquarters of the 8th Division, said:

> We had enlisted for active service and we had thought until we sailed that we were going to the Middle East. It was such a disappointment. We felt that if people asked us, 'What did you do in the great war, Daddy?' then we'd feel a bit ashamed that we were only garrison troops in Malaya.

Soldiers began applying for transfers to the 'real war'.

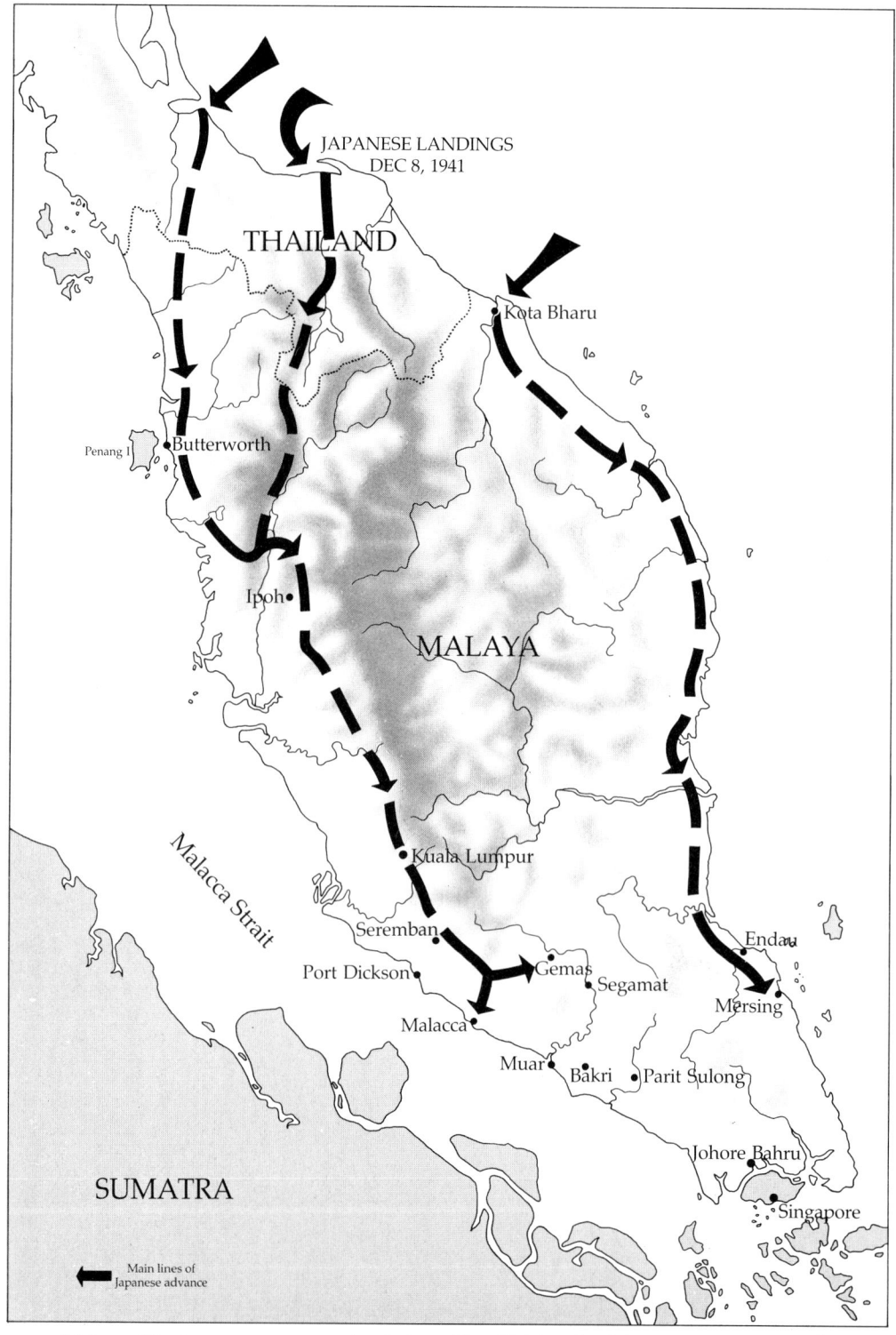

Malaya. The Japanese came overland, travelling light and seizing every enemy truck and village bicycle.

The men of the 8th Division were unconscious pioneers in the first major encounter between Australians and the lands and peoples of South-east Asia. They were little prepared for the meeting. The only places with which they had even a nominal acquaintance were those fellow members of the British Empire, those marked in the familiar British red on schoolroom maps. As they came into Keppel Harbour men looked for, and believed that they saw, the fortifications and armaments which were supposed to make Singapore an impregnable British base; but they responded more to their sensual perceptions of an exotic land. Private George Aspinall remembers arriving on the second convoy with the 27th Brigade:

> The first thing that struck us was the heat and the smells. We disembarked in a very heavy downpour, and we were like half drowned rats when we were standing beside the ship wondering and waiting to see what was going to happen next. It was all very bewildering as many of us were only overgrown boys.

George was seventeen when he arrived in Singapore. In scenes reminiscent of their fathers' meetings with peoples in Ceylon and in Egypt, men threw pennies to watch the scramble on the wharf until 'some bloke got bloody smart and started to heat the pennies and throw down hot coins'.

Thatched roofs, palms, rain forest and rice paddies were all extraordinary. And as they were 'all young blokes', they thought 'maybe some women and all this sort of thing'. They tried the local beer, trained, dug gun pits, received the *Sporting Globe* and *Bulletin* from Australia, played cricket and Australian rules on tropical *padangs*, wired defence positions, went to the pictures in Malacca, and had occasional 'grouse nights' in Singapore at the Lulu Cafe and the Happy World fun park. They met English and Scottish regulars and men from the Indian regiments. Having entered outposts of old empires which were still almost untouched by the war in Europe, they had time to observe the white-suited and sun-helmeted *mastas* (in pidgin English), the *taubadas* (in the Motu language of Port Moresby) or the *tuan besar* (in Malay). But nearly all remained outside the society of the residency, long drinks on cane chairs, overhead fans and a hierarchy of servants to cut grass, wash clothes and serve food.

Even in the Australian Territory of Papua the troops that came to man the guns on Port Moresby's Paga Hill disturbed the conventions of the local white community by unloading their own goods from the ship and carrying them down the wharf. What, the long-term residents asked, will the natives think when they see white men behaving like labourers! In Malaya the Australian commanding officer, General Gordon Bennett, refused to allow Australian troops to be used against striking plantation workers although senior British officers told him it was his duty to do so. At Seremban Australian soldiers patronised the Negri Sembilan Club with its Indian and Malay membership, and were quietly told that they were lowering white prestige. Compared to other armies the Australians were egalitarian among themselves and refreshingly casual and curious in their meetings with local peoples; and they did not like the cosy, privileged style of life of the planting and administering groups which seemed to take no account of war. Australian soldiers had not volunteered to leave their own homes to give security to people who still took long siestas and dressed for dinner. As one said, 'Either we were crazy or they were crazy'. But some of the Australian antipathy to the society of the resident white communities sprang from their exclusion from it; ordinary soldiers were plainly not welcome in Raffles Hotel in Singapore or in many of the clubs. And, inevitably, the Australians had carried racial prejudices with them. Don Moore remembers admiring the Malay people, learning a little of their language, and spending time as their guests at a festival; but he was 'criticised by my fellow Australians "You'll go wog"'. Cuthbert de Souza of Portuguese and Asian heritage implies that local communities simply responded to the obvious loneliness of young men separated from their own families:

> Usually every evening these Australian boys used to pass down the road. My nephews were playing football, and they kicked the ball over the gate. The Australians took the ball and lobbed it into the garden. A little nephew of mine just thanked them. But the Australians came up to the gate, looked through at the two little fellows playing, and one of them had tears in his eyes. My dad then came down and invited them into the house. They behaved very well and asked if they could come more often. My dad said certainly, you are welcome provided you respect our women folk. After two or three visits we were so friendly with them that we started giving them beer, and we found that they were real gentlemen.

The Australian camps were notorious for the numerous brown-bodied boys saluting and calling 'Hello Joe'.

The cross-cultural exchanges were extended by market forces. Men on leave, Sergeant Don Moore says,

> were asking for sausages, for steaks. The shopkeepers didn't understand. We'd give them a description. Next thing we'd see in Malacca 'Australian Steak and Eggs Cafe' written rather crudely under the Chinese characters. And 'Australian Cafe, fish and chips served'.

The unit magazines of the Australians are still sprinkled with Malay words—*tid apa, makan, lagi*—evidence of nostalgia and of the unexpected cultural transfer.

The open curiosity with which many of the troops approached the local communities was not extended to their potential enemy. The Japanese were 'the yellow peril' long feared by Australians. Towards the end of 1941 the threat of a sudden Japanese attack had brought close to reality the Australian nightmare of covetous Asiatic hordes pouring southward. Prejudice replaced military intelligence. The Japanese, Stan Arneil remembers being told, were

> all half blind of course. And there was this brigade major who lectured us how the Japanese set off crackers at night time, and we wouldn't be frightened of that. We said, no, we wouldn't be frightened of crackers.

Cliff Moss heard the comforting story that 'their rifles were no good. You could squeeze the bullets out like blackheads.' That is if the myopic Japanese were ever able to hit anyone. The reputation of the Japanese as the copiers of the tinsel and the tinny from the West precluded their being taken seriously as an enemy of the full might of the British Empire and the United States. It was only among a few of the senior officers and the more perceptive of the lower ranks that men were conscious of the efficiency of the Japanese, and of their own vulnerability.

By early 1942 Australian forces with the deceptively gentle names of Sparrow, Gull and Lark occupied spots across Australia's north on Timor, Ambon and at Rabaul. The 2/22nd Battalion and the attached troops of Lark Force numbering 1400 men had been in the Rabaul area of New Britain for ten months; Sparrow Force of 1400 men and Gull Force of 1100 had sailed from Darwin in December 1941. 'There was no man', Roy Harris of Gull Force says, 'who didn't want to go.' They had all enlisted to fight overseas, and 'there had been a bit of strife' trying to control men bored by garrison duties in

Darwin. Further north, the hastily assembled units of Blackforce totalling 3500 assorted troops had arrived in Java just ahead of the Japanese. Some had come from Malaya, some were reinforcements from Australia originally on their way to Singapore, and most of the force had sailed on the *Orcades* with the 7th Division returning from the fighting in the Middle East. Included on board, Bob Wallace found when he went to the hold, was a stowaway who was under the mistaken impression that the troops were on their way back to Australia. Most of the Division was, but the stowaway had chosen the wrong boat. In Malaya and Singapore over 15 000 Australians waited for the advancing Japanese. Ships of the Australian Navy and units of the airforce, trying to co-ordinate with sections of British, Dutch and American forces, were scattered widely through the region. Most of the 25 000 Australians in the near north were deployed to be ineffective in their own and in Australia's defence.

Flying from bases on the east coast of Malaya, RAAF crews saw, between monsoonal fronts, the Japanese convoys preparing to make the opening strike of the war in the Pacific. The next day, December 8, 1941, Flight Lieutenant C H (Spud) Spurgeon was in action against the Japanese landing:

> We got to Kota Bharu about 6 o'clock in the morning. It was a squally day with low cloud about a mile and a half off the coast. The only thing I saw was one ship that appeared to be burning; it was smoking anyway, and it had obviously run on the beach or was about to. A whole bunch of barges were disappearing into the rain squall offshore where the other ships were. I remember strafing a barge. I can't remember whether it was on the first strike on the barge or on a subsequent one, but I got hit in the starboard main plane. I can remember a considerable note of surprise, somebody was actually shooting back. It frightened me too, a hell of a bang. Fortunately it didn't penetrate the tank. I suppose we ran around strafing barges for twenty minutes. Anyway I decided to belt my bombs into the ship that looked as though it was on the beach, which I did, and of course in my anxiety and haste forgot all about the fusing. We let them go, and got the bloody lot back. I can remember looking with surprise as a gun barrel bent back to me. The shrapnel came straight through the aeroplane. There were no hydraulics, all the gauges disappeared off the clock. The airfield was a mile and a half away. I flung the thing on the airfield very very quickly, doing stupid things like selecting flaps because it says in the book you put flaps down, and not thinking about no hydraulics. I didn't get any flaps, I didn't get any undercarriage, it just landed on its guts. We finished up in the ditch down at the other end of the airfield.

Flight-Lieutenant D A Dowie, the lone survivor of another Hudson, was plucked out of the sea by the Japanese and became a prisoner-of-war. Spurgeon survived the first day to see some 'pretty damned magnificent' flying, and to join in the withdrawal from Kota Bharu in the evening. He was 'back on the job again in a couple of days' sometimes flying a 'clay pigeon run' where enemy fighters were thick and sometimes making the long droning 'milk runs'. On January 24, 1942 he was piloting one of two Hudsons suddenly confronted by a group of fighters, and both made for the cloud, 'balls to the wall'. When Spurgeon emerged a fighter was waiting. The opening burst of gun fire came over Spurgeon's shoulder killing the wireless operator, and Spurgeon was forced to put the smoking aircraft on the sea, 'along the swell like the man says'. Spurgeon was the only one of the crew of four to survive the strafing, the emergency landing and a night in the water to reach a small island off the east coast of Malaya. Some Chinese tilemakers took him by *prau* to the mainland, but the Japanese had made another landing cutting him off from the Allied forces further south. Near Mersing Spurgeon was captured and tied on the outside of a car. With his feet on the running board and his arms through the window Spud Spurgeon was driven into captivity.

Ship's crest of HMAS Perth, sunk on March 1, 1942, with the loss of 350 men.

The cruiser HMAS *Perth*, after a gentle war in the West Indies and hectic conditions in the Mediterranean, returned to Australia in mid-1941. Early in 1942 the 680 men of the *Perth* were back in action with new allies and against a new enemy. On February 27 the *Perth* and the American cruiser, the *Houston*, survived the battle of the Java Sea in which two British and three Dutch ships were sunk. After refuelling and making a futile search for ammunition around the confused and damaged docks of Tanjong Priok, the port for Batavia, the two cruisers sailed on the evening of February 28. Ross Glover from Arkansas was a twenty-year-old loader on one of the *Houston*'s anti-aircraft guns:

> We proceeded to Sunda Strait following the *Perth*, and about midnight we ran into the big convoy that was approaching the Strait. At that time we could just see the silhouettes of them. I think we fired the first shot, as their signals didn't jibe and we knew it was the enemy. The Jap destroyers came in on us. They turned on searchlights and the machine gunners put out the lights. They were close enough where you could hear the hissing from the stacks; the air that forces the smoke up the stacks. They were right on us when they torpedoed us. The *Perth* went down first.

Yeoman of signals, Petty Officer Jack Willis, was one of the long-term seamen on the *Perth*. He had enlisted in 1929, and had been with the *Perth* from her commissioning in the Australian navy:

> Then the order went out, abandon ship. So I dived over and as I was going through the air I thought to myself how bloody silly that was because I could have dived on somebody who'd gone over forward. Anyway, I got in the water safely. But for one awful moment I thought I might have mistaken the order, hadn't heard it, because I couldn't see or hear anybody else in the water. I thought, Good God, surely there was the order. As the ship, still under way, went past and left us I could hear voices in the water, and I realised that I'd done the right thing in a true seaman-like manner and abandoned ship when I was told to. The *Houston* was still firing and ablaze.

With a final explosion the *Houston* followed the *Perth* down. The two cruisers had run into the Japanese fleet assembled for the invasion of Java. Half of the men on the *Perth* and the *Houston* died in action or were drowned in Sunda Strait. The rest struggled ashore through the oil and debris of battle. Jack Willis was one of ten seamen who salvaged a small boat, charcoalled the name *Anzac* on the bow, and attempted to sail to Australia. They were captured at Tjilatjap on southern Java. Over 300 men from the *Perth* became prisoners; they were the largest group of Australian sailors to endure the war under Japanese guards.

After their initial attacks on December 8 the Japanese did not move steadily south, but in sudden thrusts were suddenly among and around the defenders. The first major Australian land force to be captured surrendered on Australian administered territory. Within hours of the Japanese landing at Rabaul on January 23, 1942 all effective resistance had ended, and eventually 800 men, six army nurses and many of the civil administering and planting community went into prison camps. After epic journeys by foot and small boat 400 of the troops in Rabaul escaped south; but Lark Force had been destroyed. Disaster followed disaster as the Japanese captured Gull Force on Ambon and attacked in strength on Timor. Don Noble was a lance-corporal in the signals with Sparrow Force:

> I may have been the first person to see the Japanese paratroops land. It was a most incredible sight. If you can imagine the Koepang end of Timor as almost a flat plain, a coastal plain, and then you've got a great bastion of hills which would have been a wonderful thing to defend if we'd been up there, but we were not. The planes came below the ridge line of the hills, and the Japanese dropped from a very low height on to the plain. I can still remember the different coloured parachutes, obviously food, ammunition, men, different colours for different things. Of course it was full alert. Colonel Leggatt realised that the drome at Penfui was indefensible. The best way to defend, according to Colonel Leggatt, was attack, and attack he did. To see the 2/40th going into a bayonet charge was a bit of a thrill. They had to go up the side of a hill, it was almost bare, and to see them going in open order and taking that hill from the Japs who were entrenched on the top was just something worth seeing.

In a series of attacks through the maize crops by the village of Babau and at Usau the 2/40th inflicted heavy losses on the paratroopers. But several thousand more Japanese landed on the coast and after three days of fighting the Australians tried to force their way east. Over one hundred wounded were on trucks in the centre of the column.

Harry Medlin: We woke up in the morning and found ourselves surrounded by Japanese who were all very friendly. There was even verbal contact between them and us. They came around the road corner behind the column with about a dozen or so tanks waving white flags. It was even said by some of our less perceptive members that it looked as though the Japanese wanted to surrender. But the truth was quickly discovered. The first reaction of the CO was to say that he would never surrender, and it was put to him that the troops should be given some say. There was a half hour period of grace, and the collective decision was that we should surrender.

Nearly 250 Australians, separated from the main force, escaped east to join the 2/2nd Independent Company then fighting a successful guerilla campaign in Portuguese Timor. Just before the Japanese landings on Timor the men of Sparrow Force had learnt of an intense air raid on Darwin. They now went into prison camp on the shores of Koepang Bay or continued to fight from mountain camps uncertain what was happening in the rest of the world, and particularly in their homeland. It was another two months before the guerillas had salvaged enough radio parts to send a weak signal to Darwin informing surprised senior officers that there was still a section of the Australian army at war on Timor.

In a confusion of movement and counter-movement the men of Blackforce under overall Dutch command fought sharp skirmishes in central Java. On March 8, 1942 the Australians learnt that the Dutch had capitulated, and without capacity for independent action the British, Australian and American troops joined the general surrender. News of the call to lay down their arms reached the main force of Australians when they were caught in 'the muck and mire' of mountainous north Java with all their trucks bogged. By pushing every second truck over the road edge they made space to turn the other vehicles around and went back to Leles, 'a nice little town'. Between arguments on whether or not they should 'shoot through' and games of baseball played with a pick handle and a tennis ball, they spent a relaxed fortnight waiting for the Japanese to appear. 'In all our experience through the Middle East', an engineer sergeant said, 'our VD had been one per cent, but it jumped up in place like Leles.' A sensuous fortnight was small compensation for men who had fought with distinction in the Middle East and whose last battle was in what Roy Bulcock called the 'Black Farce'.

The Japanese who had been advancing down the Malayan Peninsula did not clash with the main Australian land forces until the middle of January. By then the Japanese were numerous and confident. The cyclists, their rifles slung on their backs, rode into the ambush set for them by the 2/30th Battalion at Gemas. Further east near Muar the 2/29th Battalion and supporting gunners were soon in action. After coming under attack from probing patrols and artillery in the night the Australians took up positions just forward of Bakri where the road curved through a cutting.

Lieutenant Ben Hackney: I was first wounded on the morning of 18 January 1942. On that occasion many Japanese tanks came right into the battalion headquarters' position. Because of the outstanding performance of Sergeant Clarrie Thornton of the 4th Anti-tank Regiment, instead of firing away at the first tank that came into sight, he waited until the first five tanks came into view before he started to fire. According to Clarrie Thornton these were followed by three, very soon afterwards, making a total of eight tanks that were destroyed.

Thornton was hit in the hip with shrapnel, and that, he now thinks, was 'a winning stroke'. The 'number two bloke took over swinging the gun' and with 'me still hobbling around that gave us two observers', essential with some tanks having gone past the gun position and others still coming into sight. The detail of the action is still vivid with Thornton:

I was giving a lot of orders in respect of which target to go onto: 'Can you front him, Brownie? Can you pick him up?' Or I'd sing out to Ray Cooper, 'Ray, keep your eye on that bloke on the right.' He said, 'I've been watching him. He's OK at the moment.' That sort of talk was going on all the time. And there was a hell of a din. Other tanks were firing, shells were exploding and we were banging them off. Our gun could fire sixty rounds a minute.

When we'd finished Claudie Brown just sat back, he was older than us, he'd be seven or eight years older than me, and he said, 'Well, Thorny, I feel a very proud man. We have done our job. We knew we could do it if we got the chance, and luck went with us. And', he said, 'we've upheld the name of the old diggers.' We often wondered how we'd go. The old blokes had it on the record and we had to put it there. As Captain Bill Bowring said, 'My God, they've upheld the old diggers' name today, haven't they.'

Before they had gone into action Thornton's crew had won an efficiency test. Claude Brown, the gun layer, said, 'That's bad. When the blue starts we'll be pushed right up the front.' He was right. He had been on the most forward gun. Now, with more Japanese coming forward and Japanese already behind them, the Australians were trapped against the river, the Parit Sulong. Abandoning guns and trucks the last of the fit men of the 2/19th and 2/29th Battalions and the gunners struggled through swamp and bush to join the general retreat. Of the crew of six on the forward anti-tank gun only two survived. Sergeant Thornton and Keith Fletcher were taken prisoner, Claude Brown died of head wounds early in the withdrawal, and the other three were last seen in a desperate race to evade capture.

At Gemas, Muar and at Mersing on the west the Australians had been able to win brief victories, but they were moments in long days of retreating, preparing positions, and retreating again. At the end of January 1942 the last of the British troops crossed the causeway to Singapore island; they could go no further. In seven weeks the Japanese had advanced 600 miles from Kota Bharu to the Straits of Johore.

Fresh British, Indian and Australian troops arriving by ship added to the defence and to the congestion on Singapore. Major SAF Pond was allocated 500 of the new men to reinforce the depleted 2/29th Battalion:

> I found that some of the men had been in the army for one month. They had had a week getting outfitted in Australia, they'd had another week's pre-embarkation leave, they'd had a fortnight on the ship going to Singapore, and they'd been two days in Malaya. I took the bull by the horns and had myself paraded before General Bennett and told him what the situation was. I made it quite clear that I would do what I was told, but that I didn't think the battalion as organised would be of any use at all. He told me to take them away and train them for as long as was possible. So we had the interesting experience of the troops learning to fire their rifles on the Bukit Timah rifle range with the Japanese planes overhead.

It was a brief training. The Japanese landed on Singapore a fortnight after the recruits.

The Australian 22nd brigade, spread thinly on the north-west of the island, was battered by bombing, shelling and strafing, and then faced the main assault on February 8, 1942.

Private Stan Davis: It's still very vivid in my mind. Just bombardment all night.
> Frightening it was. The sky was alight practically continuously, the heavy guns were roaring, it's turning your stomach out, the mortars were firing, and we're in little holes. I was brought up a Catholic. A lot of blokes that never said their hailies said them that night. And it's amazing how much of your body you thought you got under your steel helmet. A few men got hit, and some were killed.

The 2/29th with its new recruits moved forward in support on the first night and was in action on February 9. After a week of heavy fighting the defenders were forced back into a perimeter on the edge of Singapore city. Medical teams occupied whatever large buildings were available—St Patrick's school, the Cathay cinema and St Andrew's cathedral—and attempted to treat the mass of military and civilian wounded.

Dr Des Brennan: We were in the cathedral. The smoke was going up all over the place.
> You could see the huge oil fires burning. There were lots of people running around and lots of people killed. I think about 12 o'clock the adjutant called me in and he said, 'Look at this.' And there's a message: 'Destroy all heavy equipment by 4 o'clock.' I said, 'God, it must be the surrender.' So we got to work very busily doing all sorts of destruction, or they did, I was pretty busy trying to do some surgery. I spent half my day giving anaesthetics on the baptismal font.

George McNeilly followed the traditions of other YMCA officers in trying to elevate the minds of men:

> The bombing became so intense that bombs came through the cathedral and over the altar. Then the whole building began to shake and we thought it was the very end. So I then said, if it's the end, we're going out singing! I went up to the grand organ and played the old hymns. We had spirit!

In the streets soldiers of various nationalities searched for their units, or for personal safety. For one soldier the sight of an old Chinese woman tottering on her tiny feet between shell bursts, 'panic stricken and aimless', has remained a visual summary of Singapore under siege. A minority of the troops decided that flight and the chance of a charge of desertion were preferable to staying on Singapore. At Keppel Harbour, Patrick Levy says, 'we were chasing men who were running into the water and throwing their weapons away. They were panicking, trying to commandeer boats.' At the wharves Dr Albert Coates found that his rising sun badge of the AIF placed him under suspicion. A group of Australians, displaying the independence and aggression which in other circumstances made them great soldiers, had forced their way at gun point on to one of the last boats taking out civilians.

On February 15 the British commander, General A E Percival, surrendered unconditionally. For some soldiers the first indication that the battle had ended was the sound of cheering among the Japanese, and the stopping of the screech and roar of shells. After a week of constant bombardment the silence was disturbing; it increased the sense of bewilderment among the physically exhausted men. Cliff Moss who had been manning an anti-tank gun mounted on a cut-down truck remembers 'a fair amount of despondency mixed up with relief. But anyway we had a bottle of gin and some condensed milk and we celebrated the event. Tasted beautiful.' Others, with the thought of drunken Japanese troops raping and killing in the streets of Nanking, were smashing the bottles of liquor which could not be immediately consumed.

Nearly all Australians were surprised by the surrender. Captain Ray Steele who had been with the artillery at Muar:

> We were absolutely flabbergasted. All of us. I can remember the reactions from the various fellows: some of them just swore, some of them threw things about, some of them were just silent and shocked. We just didn't want it. We felt that we were capable of fighting on.

All the soldiers had thought about the chances of being killed or wounded; but few had considered being taken prisoner. To the very end many had clung to the idea of fighting the 'last glorious battle', or holding the enemy at bay through a long siege as at Tobruk, or taking part in face-saving withdrawal as at Gallipoli or Dunkirk, or being saved by the arrival of air support and fresh troops. But there was just defeat. They would have no further chance to excel in battle. All now had to pass through the change in expectations, as they themselves changed their nominal identity from being soldiers to being prisoners.

In the fighting on Malaya and Singapore the Australians had lost 2178 killed or missing and presumed dead. It had been one of the hardest campaigns fought by the AIF in World War II. Many of the ex-servicemen of Malaya and Singapore regret that they have been received in Australia almost exclusively as ex-prisoners; their experiences after surrender have subsumed their identity as ex-soldiers.

Most of the captives waiting to meet their captors were apprehensive. They were right to worry for they were impotent and Japanese behaviour was to vary greatly at that first meeting. There was mutual curiosity.

Sergeant Jack Sloane: It wasn't until the next day that we actually saw our first Japanese. What impressed me was that we were looked on as curios, and we were somewhat interested in what they looked like. They seemed like ruffians. But the front line Japanese appeared to me to be a fellow who realised that like himself we were just doing a job.

Many of the Australians saw the Japanese in terms of the stereotype which they carried with them: the Japanese were 'monkey-men' who were unsoldierly in their baggy uniforms. The defeated men knew that contrary to appearances the Japanese had been well-equipped and trained for war in South-east Asia; but many Australians never lost their repugnance at the very sight of the Japanese.

Japanese were soon moving among the dispirited troops looking for spoils. Corporal Tom Morris lost a cheap watch he had bought recently in Singapore for fifteen shillings: 'The little Jap already had about half a dozen on his wrist'. Charles Almond watched while 'a little bloke commandeered a big Harley Davidson motor bike. He could not get it started so one of our blokes started it for him and sat him on it. He finished up on his face just around the corner.' The full savouring of such incidents was circumspectly delayed. On Sumatra Frank Robinson learnt another cultural compromise:

> We were treated reasonably well by the Japanese for a start, except for the fact that we had to bow to the Japanese when we met them. This was a little bit below our dignity. We didn't like the idea of bowing to a Jap, and much to our sorrow many of us were bashed about it. We decided in the finish we'd better forget our dignity and bow to them. We realised later that to bow, and they'd bow back, was to salute them. It was just their way of life.

But few Australians could ever bow easily.

Other prisoners had more violent early encounters. Dick Ryan from military transport was recovering from a broken leg when the sector was overrun by the Japanese:

> I was in hospital in Singapore when the Japanese came in, the day before the surrender. I was sitting up rolling a cigarette. I didn't want to take any notice of them, but a Japanese stood at the end of my bed and when I finished he said, 'Gimme.' I licked the thing along and gave it to him. He got me to make three more for the three other blokes that were with him. They said how lovely they were. Of course they were made of Australian tobacco. They sent me in three packets of Japanese cigarettes. That was all right. But that same day Japs came in and murdered one doctor in the ward, killed the bloke on the table and wounded another doctor. Can you understand that sort of business?

It is now thought that some Indian soldiers retreating through the hospital grounds had fired on the Japanese. Assuming that the British had used the red cross to protect fighting troops, the Japanese took savage revenge.

There were no mitigating circumstances to excuse the behaviour of the Japanese described by Ben Hackney:

> Try and imagine a gorilla gone berserk, and that sums up the treatment of the Japanese. They had no care whatsoever for anything. Bayonets, rifle butts, anything used anywhere.

Captured at Parit Sulong the wounded Hackney was among 110 Australians and fifty Indians who were bashed and bayonetted. Hackney, pretending to be dead even as his boots were dragged off him, was left while those bodies still with life in them were piled, machine-gunned and burnt. Equally brutal killings of groups of newly surrendered men had taken place at Tol plantation on New Britain, at Laha on Ambon and on Singapore when Australian bren gun carrier drivers were shot. News of some of the acts of savagery spread quickly among the troops, adding to the general tension, and increasing the incentive to flee.

Men wanting to escape faced practical and moral barriers. Captain Adrian Curlewis, president of the Surf Life Saving Association before he left his law practice in Sydney to volunteer for service overseas, was told four days before the surrender that his legal and swimming skills might be needed in a plan to get General Bennett to Australia:

> I didn't think it was ethical for a general to leave his troops. But the general made up his own mind. I wasn't asked for my opinion and I didn't give it at the time. I didn't quite know whether it was an order or a request that I should join his party to do some swimming through mangrove swamps to get a boat. Then when I went away from the original invitation I started to think it over: would the men feel that they had been let down by the officers? I made up my mind then that I wouldn't go, and two or three others joined me.

Officers had conflicting duties: to escape and to continue to take responsibility for the welfare of the men. In the event Bennett and two other officers, Major Charles Moses and Lieutenant Gordon Walker, escaped immediately after the formal surrender. Another officer who was invited, and declined, to go, Captain Harry Jessup, wrote in his prison diary two years later that he still did not know if he had made the right decision.

Although a few of the ordinary soldiers escaped after the cease-fire, the chances of success were slight, as signaller Chris Neilson found:

> There was a mate of mine called Frank Thomas, a New Guinea bloke. We straight away said, 'Right, we'll go'. I buried two pistols I had in a latrine. I broke my rifle, a good sniper's rifle. I broke it round a tree, and threw it in the river. And I said to this Frank Thomas, 'What about it?' He said, 'Yeah, fair enough'. So we went looking for a boat, but the Malays had put holes in all the canoes. We couldn't find one. We got spotted running out through a coconut plantation near a cemetery. And a bullet hit Frank. I said, 'Hit the ground!' But he grabbed a coconut tree, the worst thing he could have done because they put a machine gun on him and cut him in half. I dived round the cemetery and got back.

Nearly all the men who did get away from Singapore in small boats were picked up in Sumatra or on other islands; at great risk they had gained a few days of freedom.

For weeks after the fighting on the Malayan peninsula hundreds of Allied soldiers evaded Japanese patrols, scrounged for food in plantations and villages, and searched for an escape route. A few, guided by courageous Chinese, went from the west coast across the Straits of Malacca to Sumatra. Others, given up for lost, rejoined their units on Singapore—in time to surrender. And some men joined the Communist Chinese and served for another three and a half years as guerillas behind the Japanese lines. But most of the men cut off after the fighting at Gemas and Muar were either killed or went into the old civil gaol of Pudu in Kuala Lumpur. The men in Pudu started prison life heavily handicapped. They were all physically exhausted and hungry, and many were wounded. Hackney had lost five stones from his strong frame by the time he entered Pudu two months after he was first wounded. Few of the men had any money, mess gear or spare clothes. And with its concrete walls, iron bars, aggressive guards and overcrowding Pudu was a tough gaol.

Gunner Russell Braddon: Pudu was a black time. We were straight in at the deep end. There were no cushy jobs there; everyone worked, food was short, disease was rife and men died. That didn't start in Changi for a year later.

Another who was lucky to escape execution was Clarrie Thornton, and he survived disease in Pudu: 'Dysentery broke out. They called it the three-day shits; if you got it you were dead in three days.'

There was one saving factor for the Australians in Pudu.

Russell Braddon: From the very beginning officers postulated their entire behaviour on the fact that they were responsible for their men. They would not eat until their men had eaten. It was military etiquette to the nth degree in favour of those who were less privileged. And it was magnificent. We were looked after by our sirs. And we needed to be looked after because life was grim.

Among those in Pudu were Spud Spurgeon, one of two from the RAAF, and four escapers from Changi who had crossed the Straits of Johore and been recaptured on the mainland. All the Pudu inmates were transferred by train to Singapore in October 1942. In spite of the harsh conditions, only five had died out of 185 in the Australian wing, and another three had been executed.

The survivors of the *Perth* went into captivity with fewer possessions than even the Pudu men. Able Seaman Arthur Bancroft entered his first prison, a converted theatre, in Serang on north Java:

We had nothing. I was standing there in all my glory. Black, I've never been so black in my life. I sunburn easily. So I was a blackman with a money belt around me. Well, they issued us with their little G strings so that covered up our modesty. I think the Japs were very curious to see what we looked like. So that's how we started our life for the next few years, virtually in the nude. And with nothing else.

The Serang compound, with 500 prisoners, one pit toilet and well water which had to be boiled, offered no comforts and the likelihood of disease.

In all camps a crucial early question was whether the structure of the units and the systems of command would continue after the surrender. The issue was decided quickly among the men from the *Perth* when the senior surviving officer addressed them on the sort of behaviour he expected.

Bancroft: One of our old seamen, an old three badgeman, was Joe Deegan, a great character. Most of us were only lads. We were only twenty or nineteen, some were only seventeen, and Joe would have been one of the old ones. I suppose he might have been thirty. He was just lounging on the floor, back to the wall. The nickname for Lieutenant Commander Lowe was Pusser which is the navy term for very correct and all that. So Joey said, 'That's all right about you Pusser. But you're in this just as much as we are. If you think we're going to take any notice of you you've got another think coming.' So Pusser turns around and says, 'I say, Deegan, would you please stand up when you address me?' And before Joe knew what he was doing he was up. That broke us up right away. We all laughed, and that brought Joe down to earth. From there on I don't think we had any real problems. I think we all appreciated the need for some type of discipline to keep us as a body together.

But there was, Bancroft explains, a 'marrying' of the naval system with leadership which emerged from among the ratings. With varying degrees of enthusiasm Australian servicemen generally accepted the authority of their officers.

Two days after the surrender on Singapore nearly 15 000 Australians and 35 000 British prisoners were ordered to march to Changi on the eastern end of the island. The apparently endless columns of men dramatised the enormity of the defeat, and the transformation of the white man, the *tuan*, from guardian of empire to prisoner of the Japanese. Don Moore marched on his twenty-second birthday:

> You could see a mass of our fellows marching forward, and when you came up a long hill you'd just see this long line of humanity at the back of you. There seemed to be thousands and thousands and thousands of us. It made us puzzled, why couldn't we have done something? Look at us!

Uncertain what their captors would provide at the other end of the march, men carried as much food, clothing and bedding as they could.

Ray Steele: It was more a kind of amble or a shambles. It was a bit like refugees, fellows carrying everything they possibly could. As the march got long and hot they tossed stuff aside until in the end some of them arrived with very little.

There was a strong incentive to keep going.

Cliff Moss: The story was that if we fell by the wayside we'd be shot. That didn't happen, but it made a lot of people keep on walking when they would have preferred to lie down. It got pretty tough, and the people along the way, the Chinese, helped us. They'd watch out for the Japs. They were flying Japanese flags on their houses, but they were running out with drinks and this sort of thing for us. Without that we probably wouldn't have made it.

George Aspinall noticed Japanese movie and still photographers along the way and decided that most of the Japanese flags had been distributed for propaganda. But not all the civilians were sympathetic to the prisoners, and the occasional jeer added to the anger and humiliation of the marchers.

With so many troops on the road, the last units did not step off until the evening.

Don Moore: Darkness started to descend. The *kampongs*, the villages, were a bit more spaced. And when we were feeling a little low, the piper started up. Then it was really good. We knew he must have been as exhausted and depressed as what we were, and yet up he sounded.

The piper was Jimmy Oliver, and he was to carry a set of pipes into the work camps.

The march had been about twenty-nine kilometres, not far for fit men, but the prisoners were exhausted by battle, ill-fed and depressed by defeat. At Changi they lay on ground or concrete. Gunner Frank Christie wrote in his diary: 'all rooted, slept where we could'. The Japanese had forced other prisoners to march in Hong Kong, Manila and Batavia; there could be no doubting who were the new masters in South-east Asia.

Changi, with its rolling hills, lush vegetation, views of the sea and modern barracks, was one of the best of the British garrison bases. But now Changi had been through a battle. 'Everything', Snow Peat said, 'was upside down and the place was blown to buggery.' Selerang Barracks, once the home of 900 Gordon Highlanders, was crowded with Australians whose immediate concern was food. For the first few days they lived on the rapidly diminishing stores which they had carried with them.

Don Moore: We went on to some very tight rations. There was just one biscuit with bully beef pasted over it for the midday meal. In the evening there was another meagre ration, some tinned vegetables smeared over a biscuit. Things were a little tough.

We were asking, 'Can't the cooks use a little bit of imagination? Can't we get some more stuff?' 'Well, look', said the major, 'we've got quite a few bags of rice here. It has been coming here for the past few weeks. Would you eat that?' 'Oh Jesus! What do you think you're coming at? Of course, yes, yes, we'll eat the damned stuff!'

They had rice; but as Snow Peat says, 'No bugger knew how to cook it. We weren't used to the boong type of cooking with kwalies and things like that.' The prisoners had to go further in their cultural and physiological adaptation. The process was slow: the cooks, often working with weevil-infested, unhusked rice 'took months to learn how to separate the grains and keep it fluffy'. There had to be a change in army priorities. The men in the kitchen and hygiene squads, Dr Rowley Richards saw, now had to come from the most capable men in the camp. Even so, he says, it was some time before all the cooks accepted that 'rice was a vegetable rather than a milk pudding'. In the end, the war artist Murray Griffin claims, the cooks 'could make rice almost sit up and beg. It was coloured bright green, orange, pink, red, and just plain white. But it was all rice, and some men could not take it.'

With the change in diet men's body weight fell away, and prisoners found themselves blacking out when they stood up. There were other consequences: 'At first it was just boiled rice, and watery rice, and watery rice, and watery rice. And we urinated, and we urinated and we urinated.' The excess in fluids was balanced by an initial deficit in solids:

> Every POW gets hung up on bowels. Our stomach had the impact of sudden starvation placed on it, and it was painful. Some fellows went fourteen days, myself eleven days, without having a motion. When you did have a motion the strain and the pain of it was something you won't forget.

Soon, Jim Richardson found, dysentery was rife and 'your backside looked like the tail light on a vehicle; it just burnt your tail off'. Some men started to run then and, 'I tell you, kept running right through the jungle, and only stopped a couple of years ago'.

As the army engineers went to work and repaired the plumbing and electricity Changi became, in Geoff O'Connor's term, 'a resort'. Men could take a shower and read or play cards by electric light in the evenings. And 'we didn't see the Japs at all. Even though we weren't eating well, we sort of had peace of mind'. But apart from the perpetual concerns with food and bowels, there was one constant problem: when would they be free? They were prisoners of indeterminate sentence. Stan Arneil, on the explicit authority of his battalion commander, believed that

> we would be rescued in six or seven weeks by an Allied landing on the Peninsula. And six weeks later we knew that perhaps he was a little bit out in his timing, it would be another three months, and so on.

So firm was the belief in a swift deliverance that it was difficult to persuade men to build, store and plan for the long term. At the combined British and Australian hospital where there were 2600 patients in March 1942 Glyn White began husbanding scarce resources on the assumption of a four-year stay with reserves set aside for catastrophe. Such practical pessimism did not spread into the wards and beyond to the compound. 'Home for Christmas' had such an appeal that as imagined details were added to fantasy, men began to pack for home at the end of 1942. 'Then 42 got to 43, and 43 to 44...'

CHAPTER TWO

YOU'LL NEVER GET OFF THE ISLAND

'You're soldiers, and when I march you out of this camp I'm going to march you out as soldiers.'

Gunner Frank Christie wrote on his second day in Changi, 'no dinner, water scarce and filthy, played a game of footy, 13th Battery won 13-9 to 10-8'. On his first Sunday in Changi he slept, read, played majong, went to church parade and did an hour's squad drill. Except for the poverty of the food, he could have been in one of many previous army camps. Changi had no confining wall or fence—until the prisoners themselves were ordered to build one—and few Japanese entered the area. 'That', Rod Wells says, 'was mutually beneficial. We could maintain our own sort of discipline and the Japanese could release their first line to continue the war.' The early days in Changi gave the prisoners few signs of how the Japanese would act as gaolers or how they themselves would endure. The prisoners' immediate problems were with material comfort and morale. The sense of relief that came with the end of the violence of battle, the despondency of defeat and inadequate food led quickly to lethargy and recriminations. The men had just taken part in the biggest failure in the history of British arms. Many soldiers wanted to excuse themselves and blame others. 'Everybody was blaming everybody right up the line. Morale was bad' Geoff Boreham remembers. The torpor had to be broken.

Officers assembled units to maintain group strength and to begin functioning along military lines. One problem was to find something for the men to do. Some tasks were obviously to the common good; clearing the drains to prevent the breeding of malaria-carrying mosquitoes, obtaining salt water from the beach, pushing the motor-less trucks on 'trailer parties' to obtain wood for the cooking fires, and digging latrines. An answer to a basic sanitary need was provided by teams of men walking round and round behind a crossbar driving a thirty-centimetre auger three or four metres into the ground. Topped by a latrine box the shaft impeded the spread of disease and added to the prisoners' vocabulary: a 'borehole' became the Changi term for a rumour. But there were limits to the tasks the men would undertake. Tom Morris was one of a group who decided that

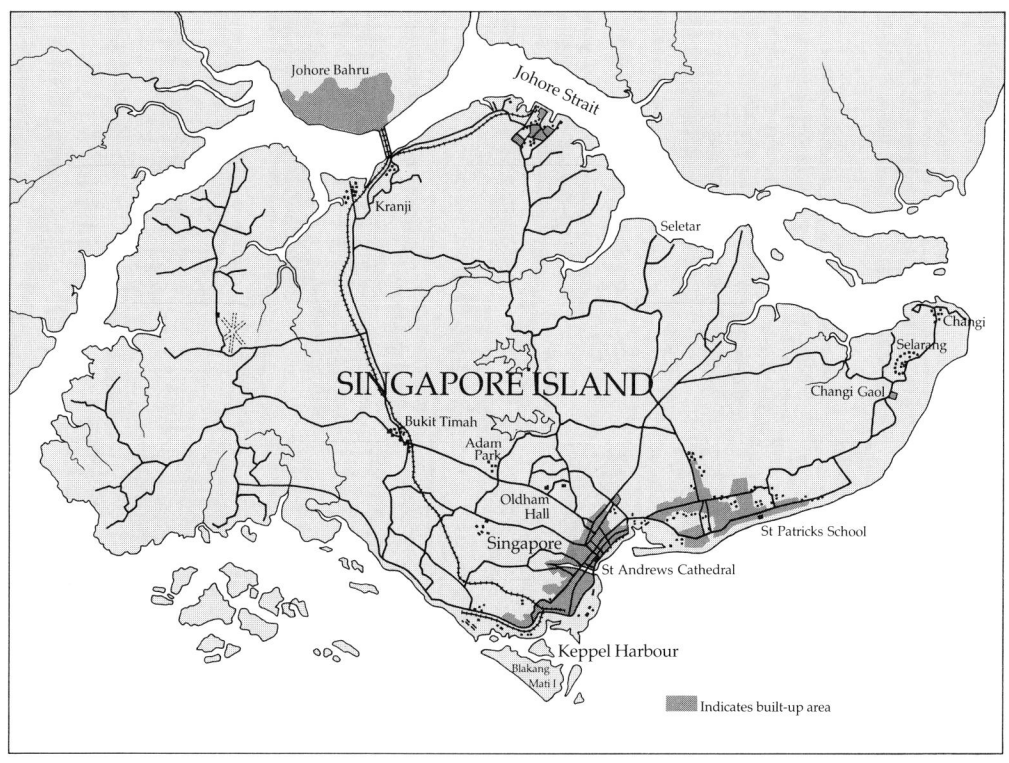

Singapore Island, Britain's impregnable base in the Far East

they would rather face a charge of disobeying a lawful command than build a separate officers' mess. After stating their case the men accepted the arguments of an officer with a fine record of leadership: they cut palm leaves and roofed the mess. And many men, such as George Aspinall, found themselves 'marching around and doing exercises'. The parade ground drill was resented by those with feet still blistered from the march into Changi and many of the troops thought it absurd to be concerned with ceremonial training while in an enemy prison camp. They certainly did not want to practise for the 'gloat parades' when they were forced to turn out for high-ranking Japanese visitors. In spite of the touch of military madness on the parade ground the malaise of the first days of defeat was cured; men became active and units regained cohesion.

There was another reason for insisting that the men should work and sweat. Warrant-officer Eric Bailey was with one of the early work forces to leave Changi:

> Although sex wasn't talked about in later years, obviously in the early stages it was very much thought of because it was cut off very suddenly. The boys were still very healthy. One of my jobs was to go round at night because certain couples were known to be going to particular spots and indulging in homosexuality. I was supposed to break it up, tell them to get back to their separate bunks. On one occasion it seemed to be getting so bad that the officers went to the Japanese and asked them would they give the soldiers some long trenches to dig. And so they dug those, and nobody was told what they were for. In actual fact they worked just to get rid of some of their energy. Others had to fill the trenches within a week or so, and then the men had to dig more of them. If the boys worked hard and long enough, other urges just didn't come so frequently.

Other prisoners have said that in three and a half years of living within a congested, exclusively male society they never saw any overt homosexuality. In any case malnutrition quickly drove even the thought of sex from the minds of the prisoners. Soon all sensuous dreams and conversations of gratification were about food.

Among men of reduced virility boredom was still a problem, and in the early days of Changi the prisoners were optimistic enough to put forward constructive and ambitious solutions. They founded the University of Changi.

Sir Adrian Curlewis: Within four days of the capitulation Brigadier H B Taylor was appointed as the 'chancellor' of the university and I was appointed dean of the faculty of law and general organiser. It was amazing the response we got from the troops; they all wanted to learn. We had representatives who could lecture on Tutankhamen in Egypt, on history, languages, mathematics, engineering and art. I personally took up the Malayan language and motor engineering. We had plenty of what we called bomb-happy vehicles to pull to pieces. But the paper shortage was simply terrific. We made blackboards, and used clay from a nearby pit for chalk.

Tom Morris was just one of 1900 who enrolled for business principles. There were also many, as George McNeilly explains, who did not have the basic education to benefit from most of the courses, and they were given the chance to acquire primary school skills. 'We even found men who couldn't read and write, so we taught over 400.'

Russell Braddon is incredulous of his own memory of one of the classes in self-improvement:

Alec Downer [later Sir Alec and a member of the Australian Parliament] suddenly decided that he really couldn't bear any longer the way Australians spoke. He assembled a class of hairy, uncouth, pig-headed, very volatile Australian privates. They were thieves of the first water, and they'd survived because of their daring and recklessness. They used to sit on logs in front of Alec Downer while he conducted a litany of elocution, 'How now brown cow . . .' It was magnificent! Nobody sent them up. Nor did they send up Alec. But it was weird.

For those who wanted a more private path to advancement there was a library of 20 000 books. Men who in other circumstances would never have had the chance or inclination to read, made their way through classical, romantic and travel literature. Colonel Edward Dunlop encouraged each man leaving Batavia to carry a book in his pack, and the Java men travelled in the holds of ships and crowded railway carriages with their own circulating library.

Many prisoners remember the pleasure of listening to recorded music in Changi's warm evenings.

Men sat on the grass all round the huts. For some of the concerts, when I played jazz records for instance, I had an audience of ten thousand. The music seemed to just float over the air into the night, and the boys really loved it.

George McNeilly, a professional singer, had started his collection of records by walking around the camp appealing for loans. Some British officers had classical records as Singapore had been their home base, and other prisoners had salvaged records on the correct assumption that either they took them or they became a prize of war for the Japanese. Then, in an unexplained act of international propriety, the Japanese agreed to obtain more records, and eventually packages of books and records arrived by courtesy of the YMCA in Geneva. Further additions were made by prisoners who went through the wire to scrounge anything that could be eaten, sold or used. In the end McNeilly had several hundred records including all Beethoven's sonatas and concertos. The men built a special hut to house the records and the gramophone, and there McNeilly held appreciation courses.

The mass audiences were given more than a recorded concert.

Stan Arneil: Before each record George or another prisoner would explain the music, and if it was an opera he would explain everything about it. We became quite expert. These are labourers and truck drivers I'm talking about. We could at one stage give you a rundown on lots of operas. It was great fun.

Up to 3000 men came to the classical concerts. Their enjoyment was heightened by the exchanges between McNeilly and his audience.

George Sprod: The troops all wanted swing records. Every time George would announce a record he'd put on his priestly voice and say, 'It don't mean a thing if you ain't got swing!' And the troops would sing out, 'Rubbish, rubbish!' George would then announce, 'Now as a special treat you're going to have the Christmas Oratorio by Johann Sebastian Bach'.

By the second day in Changi the Australian concert party had begun rehearsals. The first shows were held in the natural light of the late evening with a succession of individual artists putting on acts. But soon the concert party of about thirty members became full-time entertainers and moved into a huge open-sided, steel-framed garage. Planks on coconut palm stumps provided the seating, and, drawing on the vast range of technical skills among the thousands of prisoners, footlights, floods and dimmers were fitted 'just like the Tivoli'. The coloured clays taken at various depths from the boreholes were used to paint backdrops of such vividness that they competed with the actors for the attention of the audience. Demand for seats was so great that each unit had to be allocated a quota. With paper scarce no tickets could be used. The Dutch and English prisoners were given quotas and the Japanese guards made sure that they had some of the best seats in the 'house'. Keith Stevens, immediately recognisable to everyone in Changi as 'Dizzy', the female comic under a red mop-head wig, was one of those who went through the wire to the former British submarine base to 'borrow' a piano. Twelve men lugged a Morrison upright one and a half kilometres through the night. The concert party had such affection for their piano that they brought it back with them on a troopship to Sydney in 1945.

Happy Harry Smith of the concert party gave the men a slogan that was both sardonic and defiant: 'You'll never get off the island!' Stevens says that you would hear a 'fellow down the road yell it out' and prisoners would 'laugh their heads off, as much as to say, "Balls, we'll get off the island".' The concert party also gave the men their own popular songs; the hit parade rankings were determined by the frequency with which various tunes were being whistled. Composers, such as Slim de Grey, were rightly proud of their capacity to create folk culture. Like most popular lyrics, the Changi songs were based in reality and given a romantic gloss—songs such as 'Waiting for Something to Happen' and

> I'll always remember the day
> The moments before you sailed away.
> I feel sad and lonely
> But I think of you only
> While I'm waiting and praying for you.

> I'm waiting and praying for you.
> I still hear you saying, 'I love you'.
> Knowing you will be coming back to me soon
> . . .

Before the Japanese finally closed down the stage shows early in 1945 the concert party had put on several original shows made up of co-ordinated review and musical material.

The lack of women to play female roles was obviously a handicap.

Slim de Grey: All army concert parties had female impersonators and they were a big joke. I mean every time a guy came on in a dress the audience would yell and say, 'Ho ho, look at him!' But as time went by in Changi the female impersonators became more and more conscientious about their make-up and they would not burlesque their roles. After a while you looked upon them as women. You knew that they weren't, but in the particular show you'd accept them. You'd say, well that's the girl. You wouldn't laugh at her and she would look rather attractive.

The 'women actors' were given permission to grow their hair long. Keith Stevens was an exception: he kept to the comic role of the digger pretending to be a dumb sheila.

In 1983 eight members of the Changi concert party reassembled in Sydney: Berry Arthur, Jack Boardman, Fred Brightwell, Slim de Grey, Syd Piddington, Keith Stevens, Fred Stringer and Ray Tullipan. With its inscription, 'This piano belongs to the history of World War 2' the Morrison upright rests in the Sydney headquarters of the Ex-Prisoners-of-War Association.

The Japanese had signed but not ratified the Geneva Convention of 1929. Under the Convention nations had the right to compel prisoners from the ranks to work; officers were not to be forced to join the labour gangs. The work for the men was not to be excessively heavy, dangerous, or directly concerned with the war. The Japanese were quick to exploit the massive potential work force of Allied prisoners; and the prisoners soon found that international conventions had nothing to do with their working conditions. The type of job, the hours and the attitudes of the guards were all part of the lottery of prison life. Within weeks of the surrender thousands of men from Changi were dispersed to work camps throughout Singapore. Before the end of 1942 so many prisoners had left Changi that most of the educational courses had been cancelled or closed down. The University of Changi had flourished briefly.

At Bukit Timah just north of Singapore town the prisoners shifted the top of a hill to clear a site for a memorial to the Japanese victory. The prisoners had one compensating satisfaction: 'the Queenslanders located some termites and brought them in matchboxes' to place in the wooden base of the shrine. The Bukit Timah workers had been housed in what had recently been village shops but Hugh Clarke's group occupied stranger quarters:

> About 500 of us were taken into the Great World, one of three massive amusement parks, the New World, the Happy World and the Great World. The guards said, 'Right, there's your home', so we just spread around and I ended up in a beauty parlour with three other blokes; in fact I slept in one of the showcases. There was a beer garden nearby, there was a theatre with a projection room. And of course we spread out like rats into every corner. We had a few electricians amongst us so very soon the camp was geared to electricity. I think we would have been using as much electricity as the rest of the city. From there we went to work the wharves.

Much of the electricity disappeared into the crude immersion heaters, cookers and cigarette lighters which the men attached to any exposed points in the wiring.

Private Keith Botterill had a gentle introduction to life beyond Changi. Sent to the islet of Pulau Bukum just off Singapore to clear the rubble around a refinery and fuel depot, the prisoners came under the care of solicitous gaolers:

> The guard on duty came round of a night with his torch. He would check to see if your mosquito net was tucked in properly. If it wasn't he would tuck it in and make sure you were protected.

Botterill was to know the absolute extremes of Japanese behaviour.

Men were keen to go on work parties. They escaped the boredom of Changi, they gained opportunities to loot, and they were still naive enough to believe that most other places would be better.

Sergeant Frank Baker: There was an enormous amount of food on the wharves which the Japanese were taking away to Japan. They took loads and loads of beer—and they took a lot of empty bottles incidentally—from those wharves. We made hay while the sun shone. But one day there was something like eight heads of various Asian thieves displayed around Singapore. They were there as a warning to the population. To make sure we knew, they marched us past the head that was at Singapore railway station, just opposite the wharf gates. Strangely, that day probably more stuff went out than on any other day. I think most of the fellows worked on the assumption that the Japs wouldn't bother to search; they would reckon we would be too scared.

The Australians became noted as audacious thieves, and prisoners of other nationalities thought that they stole with untroubled daring. In fact many of them came from homes, churches and schools which made even stealing from the enemy a troubled first step. But they learnt quickly as they pierced the tins of condensed milk at Nestle's House and encouraged each other with the cry, 'Get the vitamins into you!'

The innovative scroungers of the Singapore work parties were responsible for some of the most frequently told prisoner-of-war stories. Alex Drummond claims to have been present when a prisoner persuaded a guard that laxettes were number one *makan* (food) and induced him to finish off a tin full. George Aspinall witnessed the event that gave rise to the best known of the looting yarns:

> For a long time the Japanese didn't wake up that you could get quite a number of packets of cigarettes into the sweat band inside your hat. Often when we finished work the Japanese used to line us up ready for a search. Now we had one particular Japanese lieutenant who had just enough English to get himself into bother. He decided that he was going to address us about scrounging cigarettes and food. First of all he got a digger's slouch hat, put a tin of condensed milk on the ground and covered it with the hat. Then he mounted a box and started to talk to us: 'Now you Australian soldier you think we know fuck nothing that's going on here. You are wrong, we know fuck all!' He got down and said, 'You have your hat there and under it you are stealing things.' He went to pick up the hat and show the tin of condensed milk; but the tin was gone. Somebody had picked it up before he got there!

Donald Wise, then a young British officer, watched a high ranking Japanese officer and his interpreter, Hank the Yank, arrive to abuse Australian prisoners who were stealing petrol and selling it to the Chinese. In his American English Hank warned, 'Well, Jeez, you guys he's really mad at you this time. You've been flogging petrol, and he says he'll behead two prisoners every day until it stops.' Satisfied that he had put the fear of death into the prisoners the Japanese officer got into his flag-bedecked car and drove off—for thirty metres. His car had been milked of petrol.

Looting, or scrounging as the prisoners called it, was essential to survival, and the stories of triumphant looting sustained morale.

Conditions in the Singapore work camps were generally better than the prisoners were to find elsewhere. On Blakang Mati island where Leon De Castres rolled fuel drums the Japanese made a permanent camp, and out of 1000 men only four died in over three years. But on most of the work parties there were frequent slaps, and when the work was heavy and the guards were constantly driving and goading the prisoners, more savage violence was likely. Sergeant Stan Arneil was with a group of men lumping bags of wet salt on the wharf. Enraged by a guard who slashed at each passing man with a lump of wood, Arneil rushed at the tormentor and chased him from the shed. At lunch time the Japanese separated the six foot six inch Arneil from the rest of the labour gang.

Arneil: I knew what they wanted. They wanted me to stand to attention in the Japanese style, and of course I wouldn't because I wasn't a Japanese; I was an Australian soldier and I stood to attention like an Australian soldier with my fingers clenched and down the side of my leg. So they started on me with billets of wood and knocked me down. The first thing I remember I was on the ground. How in the hell did I get on the ground? I got up again and was on the ground before I knew where I was. Then they started on me properly with their billets of wood and broke my wrist. It didn't matter then about standing to attention because I couldn't use my wrists anyway. By this time dirt was in my eyes and mouth and I was too proud to wipe it out. I was like a nigger because I was sweating badly in the sun. At the end it was very difficult to get up off the ground because of my wrists, and I was pushing myself up with my elbows. It eventually finished and I was bleeding a little from the face and nose. They stood me on a pile of timber, and I stayed there all afternoon. But my knees swelled up which was a real problem because I was still trying to stand like a soldier, not like a craven coward. I would topple off the damn thing because my knees were locked. But I got back again. In the afternoon when it was all over, it must have been about 4 o'clock, they helped me down from the timber on which I was standing, repeated the whole grisly performance until I was unconscious, so it didn't matter anyway, and threw me into a truck.

After a week in hospital Arneil returned to the work parties. The men who had watched were almost as distressed as Arneil.

The men at the work camps heard rumours and intermittent reports of a tense confrontation between the Japanese and the prisoners still in Changi. The incident arose when the Japanese demanded that the prisoners sign an agreement: 'I, the undersigned, hereby solemnly swear on my honour that I will not, under any circumstances, attempt escape.' As all prisoners have a duty to escape, a confrontation between prisoners and guards was inevitable. At Gloegoer camp in Sumatra when the Dutch, English and Australian prisoners refused to sign they were crowded into barracks and the doors and shutters closed. The men sat without food in heat and stench. Those with malaria and dysentery suffered the most. On the third day the prisoners agreed to sign. At all the camps the prisoners tried to take their objection to the point where they had established that they were signing under duress; but without forcing the sick to pay with their lives. The most dramatic confrontation took place in the Selarang barracks.

The incident began on August 31 when the Japanese presented senior British and Australian officers with the no-escape agreement. At the end of two hours of argument the officers had not signed and the Japanese were adamant that every prisoner would do so. Suddenly on the night of September 1 the Japanese ordered that every prisoner assemble in Selarang barrack square. The 15 400 men remaining in Changi, carrying their personal gear, cooking utensils and kitchen stores, filed into an area 240 by 120 metres. The square was serviced by two water taps.

Fred Stringer: It was men upon men upon men. Practically every square inch of the ground was covered with fellows and makeshift tents. Those who happened to be under cover were lucky.

Gangs of men dug latrines through the asphalt and a temporary hospital was erected.

While the prisoners were moving into Selarang Lieutenant-Colonel Fred Galleghan, the senior Australian, and other Allied officers were instructed to go to Changi beach. On arrival they found that they were to witness an execution. Either out of perversity or nervous indecision the Japanese kept shifting the position of the victims, the firing squad and the spectators. At last Lieutenant Okasaka was satisfied. The four men facing the rifles included two Australians, Corporal R E Breavington and Private V L Gale. Both had attempted to escape, suffered extreme deprivation, been recaptured, and returned to Changi. The men refused to be blindfolded. Breavington turned to Galleghan and said, 'Goodbye, sir, good luck'; and Lieutenant Okasaka signalled to the Indian riflemen to fire by waving his handkerchief. But the macabre drama was not over. At the first volley at least three of the men were wounded only. After another five or six shots Breavington shouted, 'For God's sake shoot me through the head and kill me'. The Indians fired another ten shots before Okasaka ordered them to stop. Through an interpreter a Japanese colonel said, 'The Japanese army does not like to put to death prisoners but unless you obey our orders you must be put to death.' The Allied officers were ordered into trucks and driven back to Selarang.

'Coralled up like cattle waiting to be slaughtered' the men in the square queued endlessly for water through Thursday, September 2. Syd Piddington was suddenly given more to think about than mere survival:

Black Jack Galleghan came to me and said, 'We'll put on a concert tonight.' I said, 'Where?' He said, 'In the middle of the square.' So we built a platform out of bits of wood and things and we put on this concert to the largest audience we ever played to, 15 400. They couldn't get away! By this time the Japanese had machine guns and mortars surrounding the square in case there was any attempt to break out. At the end of the concert Black Jack walked up to me, I was then the stage manager, and he said, 'Play the King'. So the orchestra struck up the King and over 15 000 sang God Save the King. I think it was one of the most moving moments I can remember in Changi. It stunned the Japanese.

The undemonstrative Captain David Nelson who had served in the Singapore Volunteer Corps conceded in his diary that 'the Australians [had] put on a jolly good concert'.

With an increasing chance of the men being decimated by an epidemic, the Allied officers agreed to sign. They had secured one subtle concession: the Japanese agreed to make it clear that they were ordering the prisoners to sign. 'Some people', Aspinall says, 'wrote fictitious names. Names like Bob Menzies came to light, Jack Lang, and the old favourite Ned Kelly was mentioned many times.' On September 5 the men returned to their former areas. One unexpected result of the Selarang Barracks incident was an immediate lift in morale. Other ranks and officers, British and Australian prisoners, had been united. Normally so conscious of their own ineffectiveness, all had been invigorated by the chance to make a gesture of defiance against the enemy.

The men went back to worrying about getting enough to eat, and with more than a passing concern about their virility.

Alex Drummond: A doctor gave a lecture early in the piece on the fact the prisoners might lose their fertility if they were long enough on the diet they were getting. After the lecture he asked, 'Has anybody got any questions?' One bloke said, 'Would you know of anything around the Changi area that would give us the vitamins to ward this off?' The doctor thought about it, and he said, 'Well there's the hibiscus hedge around the camp. If you eat the leaves, that would help.' The next day it looked as though a plague of locusts had been through the hedge.

Modern Girls, 'two-faced and no guts'

But eating hibiscus leaves was not easy. The most inventive cooking produced 'a sticky oily mess'. The 'only thing to do', Murray Griffin says, 'was to eat them raw'.

By comparison with other camps and Changi in later days, Selarang in the early months was a 'strange scrounging show'. Many of the men still had money, and it was in currencies valued above the 'banana dollars' issued by the Japanese. Patrick Levy remembers 'the traders, mainly Indians, some Chinese, who would come round the wire and sell Chinese brandy, tins of sardines which were very good, and fruit'. There was little to stop adventurous men going through the wire at night 'to flog things to the boongs down the village'. Australian officers tried to curb the independent trading because they believed it increased thieving within the camp. Under a free trading system every object, a watch, a blanket or a light globe, could be converted into food, and the temptation for hungry men was high. But trading could not be totally eliminated. Soon the men who had the initiative to go outside the camp were operating in a crowded central area known as 'Change Alley': 'Bully two bucks, modern girls a buck'. (Modern girls were small dried fish with a stench to flavour rice, or anything else.) The attempts to suppress the free market were not likely to succeed while the men were not convinced of its immorality and some of the officers were the wealthiest and keenest customers.

Prisoners coming back to camp from work parties were constantly supplementing their own diet and that of their mates. Out of necessity they became adept at smuggling goods through the searches at the work site and at the camp gates. The penalty, a severe bashing, was high, but it was offset, Snow Peat found, by the fact that the Japanese would often allow the victim to keep his stolen goods. The height of the smuggler's art was reached by those who could conceal bulky goods while dressed only in a G string. They were the experts in 'crutching'. 'One man', Lloyd Cahill says, 'distinguished himself by crutching a live chook'. Peat's achievement was as great, but the cost was higher:

> I got this small-sized pineapple. I pushed it right down into my crutch, in between my legs. Anyway we marched back home and I was bow-legged all the way, ripped raw and sore. I got me pineapple home, and six of us had a feed out of it, just added it to the rice. It was most delicious. It was well worth the effort.

Peat had endured the rough end, and earned his feed.

Conditions in Changi intensified a persistent conflict within all Australian units: the clash between privileged and order-giving officers and other ranks who believed that they were carriers of an egalitarian and independent tradition. A soldier who served in both wars, Gunner Victor Jelliman, wrote to his brother that bitterness in the ranks in the early days in Changi was greatest against those officers who had performed badly in battle. Where other Australian units had replaced ineffective officers after their first test in battle, the troops who met the Japanese in South-east Asia went from battle to captivity without a chance to promote the deserving or transfer those whose peace-time diligence was inadequate against the demands of war. Resentment amongst the ranks was increased by the privileges given to the officers: they did not have to do the exhausting work in the labour gangs, they had more chance to move around, even after they had paid levies to support the sick they had much more pay in hand than could be earned by a private in a work party, and they had slightly better accommodation. George McNeilly extends his disappointment with some of the officers to the padres: 'half were not suited' to camp life. They became absorbed in their own survival, 'just trying to scrounge things to eat, collecting snails, catching birds' and neglecting everything else.

Resentment against officers was not universal. Colin Brien decided that 'if they got things a little better than us, well good luck to them'. Many of the other ranks also recognised that given the chance they would have acted in the same way. And some soldiers were determined to be seen as members of disciplined and efficient military units. They wanted to preserve an identity as good soldiers in the face of defeat. If that meant that they had to accept officers who assumed privileges, then that was just part of the price the other ranks would have to pay.

In August 1942 the Japanese removed officers of the rank of full colonel and above from Changi. Most were to survive the war in isolated camps in Manchuria. The senior officers then remaining in Changi were the Englishman, Lieutenant-Colonel Holmes, and Lieutenant-Colonel F G Galleghan. One officer now assumed a dominant position among the Australians, and when other ranks are talking about their attitudes towards their officers in Changi they may have just one man in mind. Galleghan, later to be Sir Frederick, but always 'Black Jack' or the 'Old Man' to the troops, was a sergeant in the First AIF and he had commanded the 2/30th Battalion in Malaya and Singapore. He demanded fitness and efficiency, and he responded with almost tribal loyalty to 'his boys'. But men from other units could be more aware of Galleghan's posturing than of his aggressive leadership. Whenever the Changi survivors talk of Black Jack someone is certain to use the term 'a man among men'. Arneil, a member of the 2/30th and later to be Galleghan's biographer, says he was a 'focal point, he was the one who seemed to be there protecting, succouring'.

Russell Braddon who was transferred from Pudu to Changi was conscious of the insulation of Changi from the worst of the conditions in other camps:

> In the fancy dress days of Changi when it was a holiday camp with its university courses and everything else, Galleghan went so far as to issue an order that other ranks who had walking shoes would surrender them to officers; they were suitable garb for officers only. Officers must have two pairs of short pants, two pairs of long pants—I can't remember the exact numbers—but it was a handsome wardrobe. Ostensibly it was so that they would appear to be properly dressed as officers and gentlemen. Those clothes had to come from other ranks who had carried them seventeen miles into Changi. They were confiscated; there was no question of being able to hide them.
>
> Galleghan was as sincere as he was conceited and vain. He was like the monarch at the trooping of the colour. He became quite hysterical if he were denied by anyone, even officers, the military courtesies. He was in many ways egomaniacal, and although brave and conscientious, destructive. And yet that same man, and I have little to say about him that's flattering, was the one who did the most valuable thing of all for the men who came back from Thailand. We were a whinging mob then. Cholera has a side effect which is a kind of melancholy. We all had it in a way. We had been more ill done by than any other group of men in the world, and we wouldn't let those who had not been north forget it. Suddenly Black Jack got the majority of us together and said that he knew we'd had a rough time, and we knew we'd had a rough time, and it was time to forget it and stop whinging. It was extraordinarily salutary. But whilst that is a plus, there are many minuses.

There is another concession that Galleghan's critics make. Some officers notorious for their parade ground aggression were timid when confronted by the Japanese. But Galleghan was as belligerent with the Japanese as he was with everyone else. To the discomfort of his fellow officers who feared a beheading, Galleghan would thump the table and he even chased one bewildered Japanese with his cane. Whatever privileges the Australian commander took, not many were in the form of food: Galleghan's weight dropped from fifteen stone on his entry to Changi to just over nine stone on his release.

Before his death in 1971 Black Jack recorded his own defence:

> We were able to continue in all the years to run Changi as an army. I know that that got criticised. You've got Russell Braddon who wrote *The Naked Island*. Russell Braddon's idea of how to run that camp was that it was to be like a town council, of which the mayor would be elected and all the rest of it. After all Russell Braddon was a private. I ran it totally differently. I ran it as if we were still in the army. I remember I used to say to the troops as often as I could, 'You're soldiers, and when I march you out of this camp I'm going to march you out as soldiers. I'm not going to march you out as a mob. You'll still be soldiers on the day it's over.'

Indeed Galleghan's farewell message of September 9, 1945 to 'All AIF troops in Singapore' had claimed: 'You finish your prisoner period as disciplined soldiers whom this Jap could not break'. That had been his consistent aim.

CHAPTER THREE

TRAVELLING TO SLAVERY

To travel in ignorance was part of the impotence of being a prisoner.

From mid-1942 the Japanese began moving Allied prisoners-of war from the main camps on Singapore and Java. By the end of 1943 nearly 15 000 Australians had left by boat and train as members of various Japanese controlled 'forces'. They were uncertain of their destination and of what they were to do when they got there. To travel in ignorance was part of the impotence of being a prisoner.

The prisoners were not reluctant to leave Changi. They thought that at worst they might work harder and eat better. That had been the experience of the earlier groups who had been shifted from Changi. And, as always, there were rumours of better times. As the first group, A Force, including 3000 Australians, left Changi the most persistent borehole speculation was that the men were to be exchanged by the Japanese for bales of Australian wool. Someone added the apparently confirming detail that the exchange was to take place in the neutral port of Lorenco Marques in Mozambique. The prisoners' first sight of the two ships that were to carry them from Keppel Harbour destroyed any romantic illusions. The *Tohohashi Maru* and the *Celebes Maru* were small, rusty and dirty. The Japanese guards seemed indifferent not only to human comfort but to the laws of physics as they forced more and more men into the crowded holds. Men were still being bullied onboard while those clinging to the ladders had nowhere to go. On the shelving installed between the decks, Ray Myors crouched in a space forty-five centimetres wide, a metre long and with a metre of head room. The men could neither stand nor lie; they were stowed like sitting sardines.

Jim Richardson: When we were stationary it was hot. The perspiration just welled out on your body and face, and it even ran into your ears. I never thought it was possible to have anything like it. Diarrhoea was pretty rife, and if you wanted to relieve yourself you had to go up a vertical ladder and get out over the side. Of course a lot

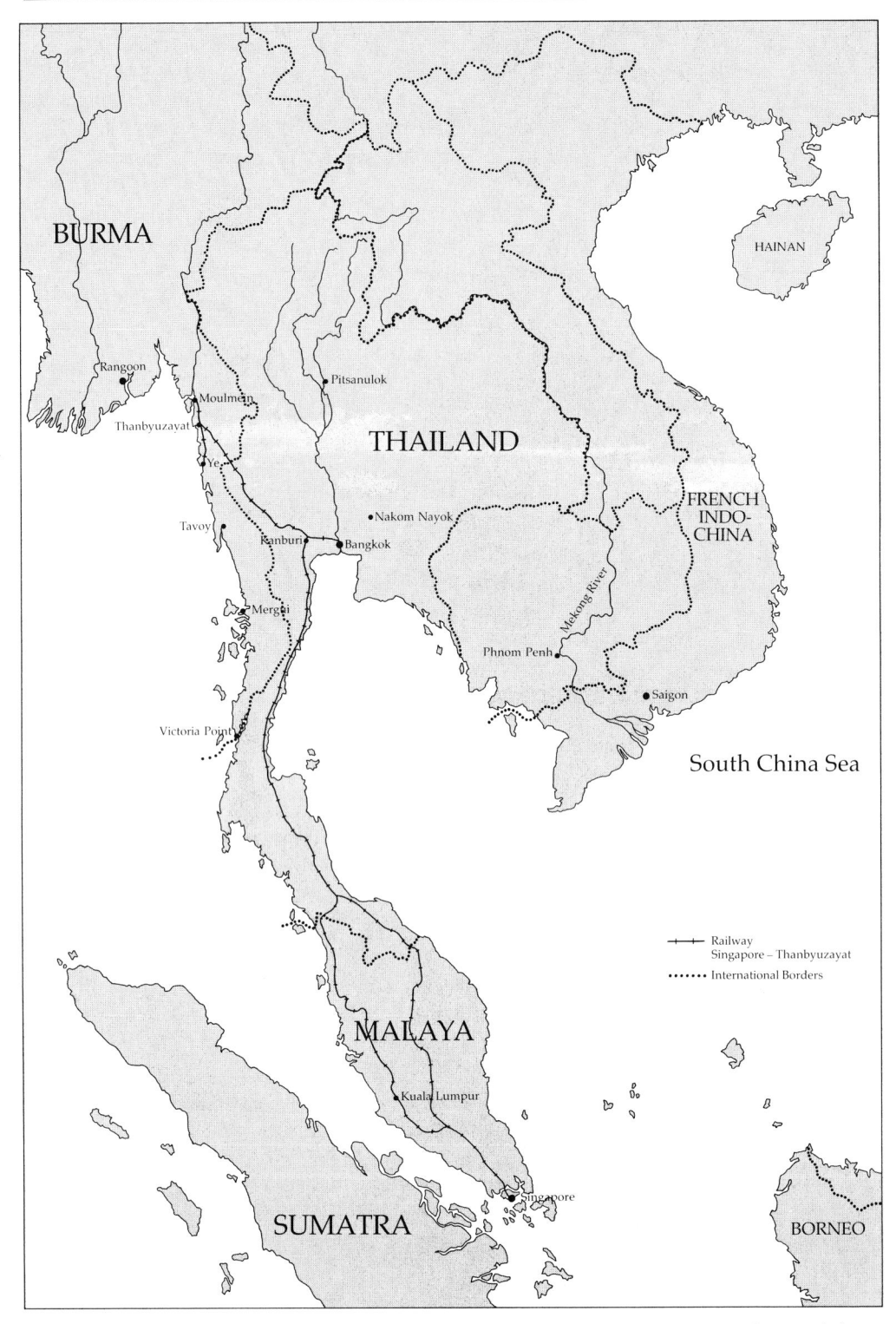

By ship, train, barge and foot, the prisoners scattered to workcamps in South-east Asia.

of the time you didn't make about the tenth rung, and down she'd come. You kept going and left the lot behind. Shocking it was.

After a day in the harbour the ships pulled away and turned north; there would be no quick trip home.

The men were given only a quarter of an hour on deck each day. At night sleep was almost impossible. Any man who moved buffeted and jolted everyone in his path, and 'rats the size of cats were running all over you'.

Eddie Henderson: There was a little fellow called Bernie Cavanagh. We were all pretty glum and down once, and he let out a yell: 'Don't let it get you down, boys! Three cheers for Australia!' We all let fly. Then we started singing, and the tension was broken.

There was a minor consolation on the *Tohohasi Maru*: the cooks working on the open deck served 'the first properly cooked rice' that the men had had since the surrender.

Some prisoners were unloaded at Victoria Point in the extreme south of Burma; the rest went ashore further north at Mergui and Tavoy. The men taken by lighters to Tavoy had spent twelve days of cramped inactivity, and their decline in physical fitness was immediately apparent as they struggled to complete the forty-kilometre walk to their camp. All of A Force was instructed to level ground for airfields. Once the supply system and cooking had been organised the basic living conditions were adequate, and the work demanded by the guards was within the capacity of the prisoners. The men had time to watch the water buffaloes being driven around the paddy fields churning the mud before the rice seedlings were planted; they traded with the Burmese for curry powder, tumeric and cooking oil so they could vary their diet; they looked at the numerous Buddhist temples; and in the distance they could see the terraced fields on the foothills backed by the mountainous central spine of the peninsula. They still had the freshness of mind to look with curiosity on scenes they had glimpsed in travel books or on postcards. To the Australians one of the most memorable characteristics of their environment was the drenching monsoonal rain. It fell with such an intensity that a man seen in the distance at the end of the drome would be bent at forty-five degrees; he would be leaning against the deluge trying to push his way through the driving rain.

With British forces on the northern border of Burma and the apparent slackness of the guards, the prisoners began talking about escape.

Roy Whitecross: A couple of friends and I discussed the possibility of hiding up in the hills; the Burmese people would look after us, the Allies would re-take Burma, and that was it. But before our particular plan could be put into effect eight men did escape. They simply walked out of camp. The help of the natives was such that they were given away, and the Japanese rounded them up the next day.

The men who had attempted to escape were all Victorians from the 4th Anti-Tank Regiment; their leader was Warrant Officer M W Quittendon.

Jim Richardson was one of a gang directed by the Japanese to dig eight holes just off the end of the Tavoy aerodrome. The guards, talking and laughing amongst themselves, gave no indication of the purpose of the excavations; but Richardson remembers wondering if they were digging graves, and if so, were they themselves about to be shot, or were the graves for some other bodies already cold. When they were stopped after gouging shallow holes only a metre by a metre, they decided that their digging must be for some other reason. Their fears returned when they had to drive a heavy stake into the ground at the head of each pit. At the sound of approaching vehicles the prisoners were hunted off to the edge of the clearing. From there they watched the Japanese take eight chained men from the back of a truck and tie them to the stakes. Scraps of uniform showed that the men were Australians. The condemned prisoners shouted cheerios to each other and died in a burst of gunfire. With cries of 'speedo speedo' from the guards, the men in the labour gang were brought forward to cut the bloody bodies from the stakes, force them into the graves, and bury them. The Japanese, anxious to finish before the monsoon rain fell, kept yelling and threatening anyone working at less than fever pitch, but one prisoner knelt down and covered a face with a piece of cloth before they shovelled dirt over the crumpled corpse. As a torrent of rain swept across the clearing the Japanese ordered the prisoners to pick up their tools and leave. With his last look at the graves Richardson saw the flooding surface water already about to wash away the thin cover of earth they had tossed across the bodies.

By September the men of A Force had finished work on the airfields and been moved further up the Burmese coast. At Thanbyuzayat they were organised into work gangs and each man was issued with a wooden tag on which was inscribed his prisoner-of-war number. More troops, Dutch, British, Australian and American, began arriving, and soon there were over 9000 prisoners in camps south of Moulmein.

Other groups had been leaving Changi: B and E Forces went to Borneo, and early in 1943 men were assembled for somewhere 'upcountry'. Dunlop Force left in January, then D Force, F Force, H Force and other smaller groups followed throughout the year. Again there were rumours of better times. Geoff O'Connor who was on D Force says, 'All we knew was that they wanted a work party to go to Thailand. It was going to be a land of milk and honey, plenty of food and very little to do.' Dr Kevin Fagan followed on H Force with illusions fostered by the Japanese: 'We were told we were going to a holiday camp, good food, bring the old pianos and musical instruments'. At Singapore station the men had little chance to conform to the prisoners' ethic of taking every opportunity to loot and loaf as they were crowded into freight trucks. Each train took about 600 men, and over ten successive trains were needed to move the largest forces.

The men travelled north with uncertainty; but the Japanese knew exactly what they wanted the prisoners to do. They had a large army in Burma which had to be supplied and reinforced. The sea route around the Malayan peninsula was long and exposed. The only effective alternative was to build a railway from Bampong in Thailand northwest, crossing the border at the Three Pagodas Pass, and joining the Burma rail system at Thanbyuzayat. The railway, 420 kilometres long, was to be built by Allied prisoners-of-war and Asian labourers who were either tricked or compelled into offering their services.

For the first two days on the train the men travelled through country in which they had trained, taken recreational leave, and fought. When they saw the strange scrawled writing on the station name plates and the different grey and green uniforms of the soldiers, they knew they had crossed the border into Thailand. With twenty-five to thirty men in each steel-sided truck it was another 'eyeball job' for the men crowded together. By using every available piece of cord or strapping, all gear and packs were hung in a swaying curtain above the mass of heads, bodies and limbs. During the day the airless steel carriages were intensely hot, but at night they cooled quickly, and the fleshless men had the unusual experience of suffering from cold. The prisoners made the best of their conditions by changing positions so that all had equal time in the breeze from the sliding door, and by taking shifts at standing to allow some men to stretch out on the floor. The food that they had taken with them was rancid within a few hours of leaving Singapore, and little was issued on the way. One section of F Force went forty hours without a meal. When food did appear it was likely to be a bucket of rice swarming with flies. Excretion was as difficult as ingestion.

Stan Arneil: There were no toilet facilities whatsoever. Now you may not believe it in these modern days, but the average Australian is a very modest person. So without toilet facilities they had to be held out from the side of the truck.

Two strong men braced themselves and took an arm each while the straining operator prayed that he would not be paraded past a platform of bewildered Thais or whipped by branches. Most prisoners waited in hope for a moment of greater comfort.

Don Moore: As soon as the train would stop they'd come out and you'd see thousands of bare bottoms as they'd go down. There'd be a blast of the whistle and some fellows used to shout out mockingly, 'Cut it short! Cut it short!' They'd come back pulling up their trousers and attending to their necessary hygienic arrangements while racing for the train. I felt sure that some would be left behind. God knows what would have happened to them.

Cleanliness was sought and savoured whatever the risk.

Snow Peat: One of the best pleasures I had was when we got to a place called Ipoh and they refuelled. We were in the truck second from the engine. Water was pouring out of the overhead tank. Righto, we dropped the tweeds and underneath we went. It was absolutely beautiful just to get the sweat and stink out of you. One of the Nip guards grabbed a number nine shovel and got stuck in amongst us. A couple of us got a good whack across the arse, and one bloke's arm was cut. But other than that it was fantastic. Just the pleasure of being clean; or partially clean.

After five days the trains reached Bampong, the railhead town for the branch line to Burma. The men, stretching with relief as they left the trains, stepped into varying experiences. Some were directed into the mud and fouled ground of old camp sites while others found eager traders among the Thais. Frank Christie bought twenty bananas; he was suddenly an affluent prisoner. And Hugh Clarke was one of a group from D Force taken to a site close to the nearby town of Kanchanaburi and abandoned:

> Our guards disappeared. We waited and nothing happened. Other Japanese there took no notice of us. We thought, maybe they can't feed us and they're letting us loose. So we went down to the river which was about a mile away, and got water and stole some chooks. I remember one fellow, Hughie Tulley, eating twelve eggs in one hit.

Captain Reg Newton, one of the senior Australian officers with the D Force: It was heaven. There were no Japs. We had odd bits of tents so we made our camp, and all the Thai traders from the city and surrounding villages arrived. They set up market stalls. It was Paddy's Market all over again. They wanted to buy everything in sight and our blokes were prepared to sell anything they had.

Clarke: At this stage some of the fellows had watches, fountain pens, things like that.

Newton: They were selling their clothing, their shorts, and souvenirs they had picked up in Singapore. One chap I caught selling a sixteen inch long by twelve inch wide and two inch thick marble desk set with penholders. He'd carried it all the way from Singapore. When I asked him why, he said, 'Well, it's my souvenir. I want to get it home.' And I said, 'You're a bloody idiot. Sell it, get rid of it.' So he sold it and bought food.

Clarke: Some of the fellows got a little more adventurous, went into town and came back full. A couple of the ladies of pleasure set up business in an old hut. They got some patrons. I think that most of us were a bit frightened. For one thing you weren't in any condition to play around, and there was this dread of disease which had been hammered into us.

Eventually Japanese guards arrived to impose order on the marauding prisoners.

Newton: It took a full day to find them. We had the officers, NCOs and senior privates going around collecting them from the bush, the scrub, you name it. What they'd been up to I would not ask. But I was concerned that they could have contracted VD, so the next day I got David Hinder to carry out a short arm parade and it was all clear, thank God.

It had been, another prisoner remembers, 'rather a good week'.

In stark contrast to that interlude of freedom the 7000 men of F Force, made up equally of British and Australian prisoners, left Bampong on an horrific forced march. The prisoners on the last train had no chance to spell before the guards were shouting instructions, and as the men milled in confusion, the shouting turned to hysterical screaming. Exhausted men were slapped and kicked into conformity. The march began at 10.30 pm.

Arneil: We marched for 190 miles. The first night wasn't too bad: it was on a metalled road. The Thais were like scavengers buying things from us, and we were so exhausted we were selling everything we had, jumpers or anything like that, for a fraction of their worth. We marched all night and lay down like dogs in the morning alongside the river. We went into the river and out again. But of course the heat was well over 100 degrees and without shade there was very little possibility of sleeping. We repeated that night after night.

The men had covered nearly thirty kilometres on the first night, and they would keep going for another sixteen nights. In spite of angry clashes with the guards very few of the sick men were allowed to drop out. Early in the march the men might sing, but later there was just an exhausted procession spreading over a couple of kilometres. 'Then', Peat remembers, 'another bugger would be getting a dose of the wog or something. The boys would split his gear up amongst them and another couple would give him a helping hand. You didn't leave your mate for dead sort of set-up.' Some men were carried for hour after hour on stretchers.

George Aspinall: When the march got some three or four nights old and people weren't going too good Captain John Taylor, who was a medical officer with our unit, and Padre Paddy Walsh were continually helping any stragglers at the back, carrying their gear and doing everything possible to help them along.

Other officers eased their own way by paying men to carry their gear.

Although they marched at night the humidity was high, and the men were wet with sweat within the first hour. Dust rose in clouds settling on the marchers. Light showers were welcomed; but heavy rain turned the track to slippery mud.

Arneil: It was a waning moon which meant that we finished up in pitch black most of the night. I don't know how the guards found the way. The sandflies almost bit us to death. Men cut their hair off to keep them away, and most of us carried a piece of smoking bamboo and waved it around our heads; but they almost bit us to death.

Some of the daytime camps had no shelter and little shade; the men just lay on the open ground. At Wampo an Australian officer attempting to buy additional food approached a Thai woman; she found some sago and moistened it with her own breast milk. For most of the Australians the march ended in May 1943 at Songkurai, close to the Burma border.

The bridges were giant matchstick mazes of wood.

By mid 1943 over 12 000 Australian prisoners-of-war were scattered through camps in Thailand and Burma. They were just a part of the 61 000 Allied prisoners and 250 000 Asian labourers in the workforce. The Japanese had undertaken a massive engineering task; and almost the only energy they would use to clear, dig, bridge, ballast and lay tracks was human. The only incentive for the humans was that they would suffer more if they did not work. The first task for many of the prisoners was to build their own camp: the fortunate ones found tents and *atap* thatched huts to house half the force, and the rest started with a clearing in the jungle and their camp was what they could make.

Men worked in gangs. On the embankments some prisoners would be using the *chunkel*, the large Asian hoe, or the shovel; another group with wicker baskets or 'stretchers' made of rice bags slung between two bamboo poles carried the freshly dug earth; and a third gang would be levelling the soil when it was dumped on the pegged line of the railway. Creeks were bridged with tiers of sleepers laid in pairs across each other, effective giant match stick mazes of wood. On major rivers the men sank the main bridge supports into the mud with a primitive pile driver. Using a variation of the Japanese 'one, two, three', the men sang 'ichi, ni nessaiyo, send the bastard higho' as they heaved on a rope then let a weight crash down on the pile. Prisoners who prided themselves on their own capacity for hard work and ingenuity were constantly surprised at what the Japanese aimed to accomplish with little more than sweat, handtools and materials found on the site. As Hugh Clarke says, the men could not believe the Japanese engineer when he told them that they were going to dig and dynamite their way through the cutting which became known as Hellfire Pass. It was to be over 500 metres long and twenty-five metres deep. Before explosives could be used the hammer and tap men had to drill into the rock, one man holding the drill and twisting it after each blow, and the other man swinging the heavy eight-pound hammer. The hammer man could rest briefly while his partner scooped shattered rock dust from the drill hole with a piece of hooked metal. Donald Stuart, who had learnt a little of hard rock mining in his travels in Western Australia, deplored the waste of human energy and admired what could be achieved with primitive machinery:

> I've seen them when they were short of dynamite fill the drill hole with water, drive wooden rods into it, and leave it overnight. If you've got enough of the rods and they're close enough together, the swelling of the wood will bust the rock a bit. Then you get in with blunt picks and crowbars that bend like sticks of solder, and you niggle and you gouge. And gradually we got those damn cuttings through.

At some of the early camps the Japanese exhorted the men to work with signs: 'Work cheerful and work diligent'.

In Burma the men of A Force began pushing the railway south-east from Thanbyuzayat. At first the daily work targets were not excessive.

Arthur Bancroft: We fell for the three card trick fairly early in the piece. The Japs said you have one cubic metre of sand to dig, and when you've finished that you can go back to camp. Some of the energetic ones thought, this is good, let's get rid of the sand, we'll be back by noon. And of course it was a piece of cake. Our officers were saying, don't go rushing into this because they'll give you more to do. And that's exactly what they did. They just added and added and added. Eventually they got to the stage of staying out all night.

The men had one defence against the high daily quotas: when the guards were out of sight the prisoners shifted the pegs 'and in that way you'd save yourself a third of the job'.

To work hard the prisoners needed more and better food than when they were sitting around in base camps. But the distant work camps where conditions were harshest were the ones most likely to suffer from the Japanese store system that was faulty and sometimes criminally perverse. The longer the supplies had to be carried the more likely they were to be diverted, delayed or looted. Often the only 'livestock' available was the grubs in the rice, but any protein reaching the inland camps had to be eaten whatever its condition. 'Occasionally', Aspinall says, 'we'd get cases of prawns. But by the time they reached us the insides of the prawns would be eaten out by maggots.' The medical officers assured the men that it was better to boil and eat the seething mass than go without. The men had 'prawn soup', the maggots 'tasted like prawns because they had been living on prawns'. Boxes of yak meat were equally noisome, and the skinny, bone and leather live yaks provided little more than flavouring when they disappeared into the rice of 300 men. But, Lloyd Cahill claims:

> The worst feed I ever tackled was sun-dried porpoises' tongues. These were rotten and green, but we were so hungry that we cut the outside off and ate what we possibly could of those wretched tongues. They were like leather. Foul things.

Survival depended on the capacity of the prisoners to force their senses and stomachs to tolerate food that all previous conditioning had taught them to reject. Some men whose intellect told them that they had to eat stinking refuse still could not bring themselves to do so. One night Snow Peat came back late from working on the line to the comfort of fires burning and the sight of food being dished out:

> I said, 'Meat, you beauty!' There were maggots an inch long floating on the top of it. One bloke sitting alongside me said, 'Jeez, I can't eat that'. I said, 'Well tip her in here, mate, it's going to be my meal ticket home. You've got to eat it. You've got to give it a go. Think they're currants in the Christmas pudding. Think they're anything. You've got to get the tucker into you.'

The doctrine of consuming everything that was remotely edible was encapsulated by Albert Coates, the leading medical officer with A Force: 'You'll see your ticket home in the bottom of your dixie'.

After weeks on a diet of about half a kilo of rice a day and precious little else, prisoners began to gag on the gluey monotony of their food. Men searched desperately for something to add to their basic ration. 'Even if it was leaves off a tree' it might change the flavour of the rice and make it edible. Bob Yates remembers how the Dutch taught them to collect small wild tomatoes and make a sambal. Wild chillies, too, could be picked and ground; 'a spoonful on a plate of rice and it used to go down pretty good'.

Itinerant Burmese traders and Thai bargemen could not reach the men in the mountains near the Three Pagodas Pass; and in more accessible areas the Japanese sometimes restricted contact between the prisoners and local Asians. But in some camps, such as Tarsau, the Japanese allowed the prisoners to trade openly. The Thais brought barges full of duck eggs up the Menan Kwa Noi River. Gordon Maxwell:

> I think that there'd be something like 20 000 eggs in a barge load, packed loosely, just piled one on top of another. The unloading party used to eat the broken eggs on the spot, *au naturel*. The unloading party were also the sick blokes who weren't fit enough to work on the line, and they'd get this bonus of the broken eggs.

At the camps serviced by traders the men could invest their pay in food: 'You got ten cents a day and an egg cost ten cents. Theoretically after ten days you could buy yourself ten eggs and have a beano.'

The Australians were angered and many remain embittered by the apparent indifference of the Japanese to sick prisoners. The sick might be issued with no food or perhaps half rations. In extreme cases where the sick were lying shoulder to shoulder on bamboo platforms and only one third of the men were able to stagger to work, an equal distribution of food left everyone hungry. The Japanese attitude to the sick was consistent with their general ruthlessness in forcing as many men to work as possible, but the Japanese actions also reflected their different beliefs. Where the Westerners were inclined to see sickness as misfortune, the Japanese thought it was a sign of weakness. Sickness, they believed, was a result of a lack of will or 'right thinking'. If an individual soldier did not have the power within himself to overcome his weaknesses then his superiors had a duty to compel him to greater effort to secure his own well-being.

When men had lost one third of their body weight, were physically exhausted and suffered chronic illness, apparently minor factors could make a difference between life and death. Anything that would, even briefly, divert the prisoners' attention from their depressing environment was significant. While the men worked some of the talk was deliberately directed to topics that would engage and enliven their minds. 'Sydney blokes would be naming the railway stations from the city to Liverpool and one would say that Lewisham was before Summerhill and another bloke would say, "I live on that bloody line, I know"'. Sometimes questions would pass from group to group along the line, and the authoritative answer would pass back through the working gangs. Don Moore recalls putting on 'wireless shows' in the hut at night. Three or four of them would combine their memories and voices to put on well-known radio programs, 'a lot of it ad lib and a lot of it rubbish'.

More ambitious entertainment was attempted on days which in other parts of the world were times of celebration.

Geoff O'Connor: At a place called Kinsayok they had a stage built up about three foot. They had big bamboo fires around it, that was our lighting. And it's amazing what you can find when you get a thousand blokes together. There were Englishmen, and some Welsh, and they sang Christmas carols. The concert went on for a couple of hours. The Japs came. There was a chair for the camp commandant; he came and we all stood up and bowed, and he bowed back. The Japanese enjoyed it because they were as bored as we were, stuck in the middle of nowhere. We had to be half queer to enjoy it, but it was Christmas and everybody was singing his head off, some of them shaking with malaria. But they were all in it. They thought, well, it might be their bloody last.

Variations on popular songs helped sustain the morale of the prisoners, especially when the Japanese joined the chorus of 'Go home you mugs, go home' sung to the tune of 'Should Old Acquaintance be Forgot', or

> They'll be dropping thousand pounders when they come,
> They'll be dropping thousand pounders when they come,
> They'll be dropping thousand pounders, they'll be dropping thousand pounders,
> They'll be dropping thousand pounders when they come.

The guards would sometimes ask the prisoners to sing the 'Kai yai yippee song'.

There was a great celebratory day for the Australians in Burma in 1943.

Arthur Bancroft: I think it was at the 105 kilo camp. Melbourne Cup Day was coming up so they decided they'd ask the Japanese for a day off. A few of them got together, they organised a committee to arrange a track and encouraged as many as they could to do themselves up for the day. Some of the fellows got dressed up as girls. They got rice bags and made themselves dresses, and some of those who were in the concert party made up stuff. The Japs used to love to see these fellows dressed up as girls; I think they used to get a bit serious at times! The committee licensed bookmakers who had to show the colour of about twenty rupees. Besides having Phar Lap, Peter Pan, Hall Mark, Rivette, Second Wind, The Trump and Shadow King, they also had horses like White Slave, and that was out of Camp by Daybreak; POW, out of Luck by Cripes; Yak, out of Jungle by Shotgun; and Eggs, out of Canteen by Japanese. They had men lined up with the old hobby horse type of thing for the event. The race didn't really end up as the caller had it; there was quite a bit of confusion. But as the call was done you would have sworn you were listening to a Melbourne Cup broadcast. It sounded so real it was crazy. The Japanese thought it was magnificent.

The guards, indifferent to the significance of the first Tuesday in November and their army's demand for a railway, were ready to have another race meeting the next day.

Relationships between the prisoners and the Japanese rarely reached the benevolence of Cup Day in Burma. The guards were constantly shouting. 'They shouted at each other, they shouted at you. An order sounded like a mad yell.' Men who in 'normal trim' might have been indifferent to the shouting were vulnerable just to the noise. All the regular guards were known by nicknames: the BB or the Boy Bastard, the BBC was the Boy Bastard's Cobber, Gold Tooth, Babe Ruth who wore his hat pulled down like a baseball player, and Poxy Paws who had his hands bandaged.

Hugh Clarke: At Konyu there was Mussolini who obviously looked like Mussolini; there was one Korean they used to call AIF Joe who was quite friendly. Then there were others like the Mad Mongrel who used to get drunk and come down to the camp at night looking for people to beat up. Dr Death was a medical corporal. The only medical implement I ever saw him with was a wooden sword. If you paraded sick, he'd thump you with it.

The immediate barrier between prisoners and guards was language. A guard would shout, a prisoner would respond and suddenly find himself being buffeted by an enraged guard for unwittingly moving in the wrong direction. The cultural gap between the two sides was so great that even a smile or hand gesture was equally likely to be misinterpreted.

The prisoners were always conscious that the Imperial Japanese Army operated on immediate physical punishments. But that did little to ameliorate the pain of the prisoner who was bashed.

Patrick Levy: They beat each other. A Japanese first class private had the right to beat a second or third class private. When I was interpreting I heard a Japanese sergeant sort of backchat a Japanese officer in a hut where I was trying to get eggs and food for the men. He was promptly kicked to death on the floor in front of me. He never made a sound. There were four of us standing there to attention; we couldn't move an eyelid or we'd have joined him.

The difficulties of the prisoners were increased because so many of the guards were Koreans. They were at the bottom of the rigidly hierarchical and brutal Japanese army system. They themselves suffered the harsh discipline, and as outsiders they had to be more aggressive than ordinary Japanese to gain acceptance within the Nipponese army. Ray Parkin thought that as a group the Japanese peasants made more humane guards: 'there was one little bloke we called Smiler, Happy was another'. Their loyalties, Parkin believes, were to the Japanese countryside and not to a jingoistic military code; they were 'just the same as our country blokes'.

With little interaction between the various groups of prisoners on the railway the Australians at the base camps had slight knowledge of what was happening at the work sites further up the line. But occasionally a prisoner who had been delayed by illness would go forward and bring the eyes of an outsider to measure the deterioration of the men. In mid 1943 George Moss rejoined his old group from D Force at Konyu:

> The blokes that were left there wouldn't talk to you, they'd got beyond that, and there was only a handful of blokes out of the 500 left working. One of them was George Dickie who came from the same home town. George enlisted with me. He was still working and he could still talk, old George. He was a big man, a heavy built bloke, and he was like a drought stricken horse. You could hang a hat on him anywhere.

When large numbers of sick men were evacuated by barge the Australians at the camps lower down the river confronted the starved and shrunken remains of their former comrades.

Don Moore: Probably one of the most horrific experiences I had was to see friends of mine. I knew by the colour flash on their hats that they were Anti-Tank and part of my mob, but I couldn't recognise them because they were skeletons. The whites of their eyes were grey. Their eyes, like broken eggs, were dilated; just a splodge in the middle of the grey. They had no stare, no focus. And I'm afraid some of them did die. They collapsed and died walking up to the hospital. I realised how fortunate I had been at Tarsau.

These remnants of fit young men were the evidence of the terrible conditions in the higher camps; and there was worse to come.

NIPPON VERY SORRY, MANY MEN MUST DIE

'. . . the railways must be completed; Nippon very sorry, many men must die.'

Early in 1943 the Japanese were becoming increasingly worried about the vulnerability of their army in Burma. After a review of the Burma Area Army's position, Imperial General Headquarters decided that their troops could not survive if they waited to be attacked: the Japanese in Burma must go on the offensive against the British poised on the northern border. In 1943 the Burma front was one of the few places where the Japanese could still hope to advance; perhaps the aggressive General Mutaguchi could yet thrust deep into British India. But the success of the Japanese offensive depended on the Burma Area Army being reinforced and better equipped in time to campaign in the coming dry season. The overland supply route, the Burma–Thailand railway, would have to be completed ahead of time. The tactical decisions taken by the Japanese had profound effects on the Allied prisoners-of-war and the Asian labourers who were the tools of Japanese policy. If the railway was to be built more quickly, then the prisoners and labourers would have to work harder and longer, wet or dry, sick or well, fed or starved. It was true that the Japanese had some elephants but, as one prisoner observed, the elephants were better than men at demonstrating that if they did not eat they did not work.

The difficulties of the prisoners had already increased when the wet season set in. The rain came as a 'waterfall'. Kevin Fagan remembers it as continuous, penetrating everything, squelching underfoot and rattling down the back of his neck. The sky was a mass of cloud sitting at bamboo-top.

Hugh Clarke: The ground turned to mud, your clothes rotted away, your boots, if you had any boots at that stage, rotted off. The six-foot latrine pits which we had dug filled up with water and in no time the whole camp area was crawling with maggots. In the cemetery the graves filled up with water and the bodies came to the top. But

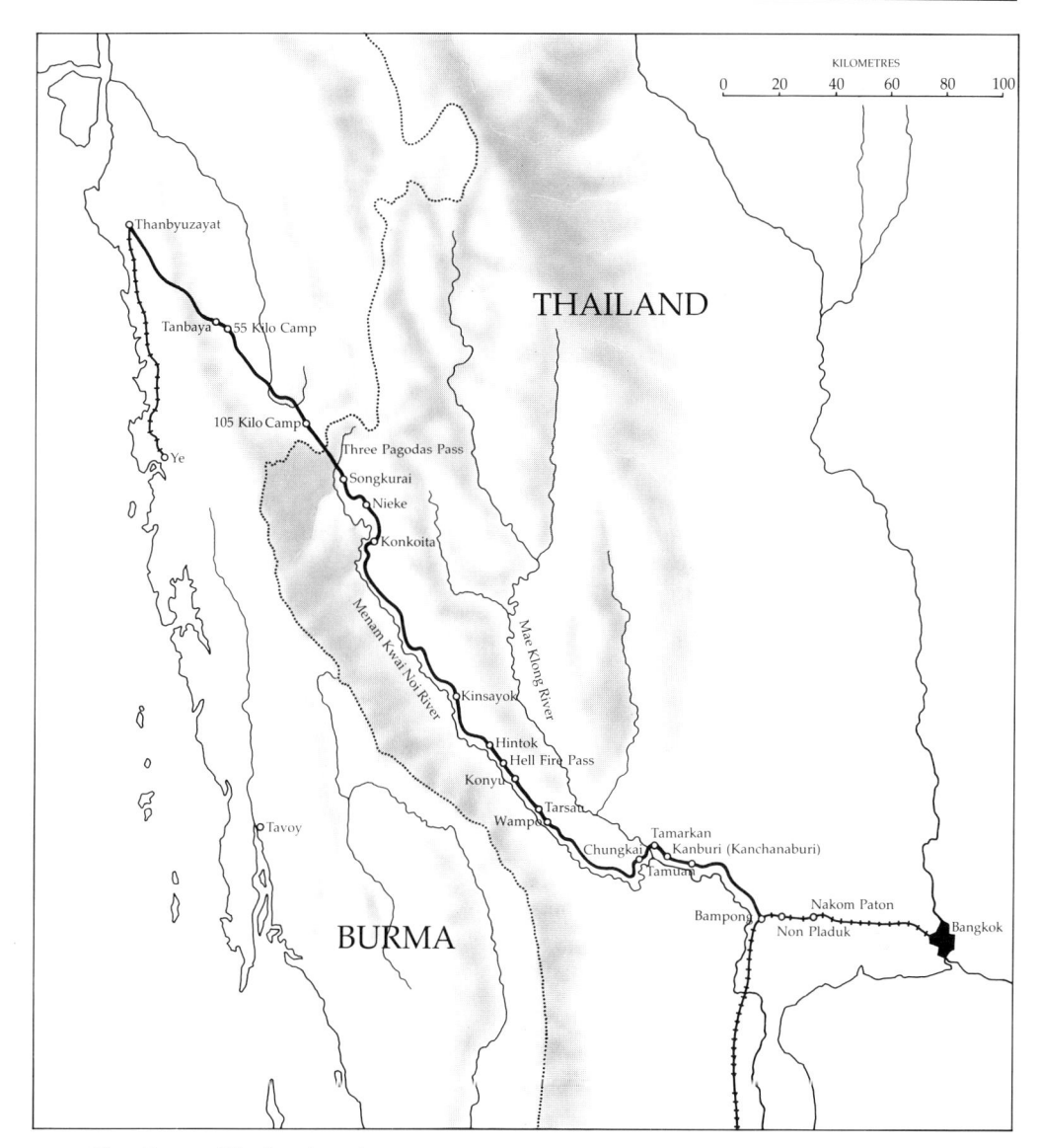

The Burma-Thailand railway linked Thanbyuzayat with Bampong across four hundred and twenty kilometres of jungle and mountain.

none of this affected the progress of the railway. You were just living in a watery world, and after a while it didn't occur to you that there was anything unusual about it being wet all the time.

The wet further disrupted the ration supplies: trucks bogged, the barge traffic was disrupted by floods, and even the yak carts were down to their axles in the mud.

One hope had persisted among the prisoners: the monsoon would eventually force the Japanese to suspend work. In fact with the rain came the demand that the railway be built with greater urgency. A Japanese officer transmitted the instructions of the Imperial General Headquarters in stark terms.

Ray Parkin: He gave a long speech and said we were doing a good job and the railway was progressing, but the railway must be completed; Nippon very sorry, many men must die. Well, that began at least 150 days without a day off.

The days of feverish haste were known as the 'speedo': 'it came to be called that because the Japanese were always calling "speedo, speedo" when they were hurrying us up'.

While the pressure was most intense Stan Arneil was at Songkurai:

> In one of the worst speedos we started at 5 o'clock in the morning and got home at 11 at night and we got home at one o'clock the next morning, and one o'clock the morning after that. This was just prior to the linking up of the railway. We'd leave in the dark. Paddy Walsh, the priest, would be at the front of the camp. We'd be in pouring rain of course, and he'd be there to see if anybody wanted to go to confession in case they died during the day. We would all have a pick or a shovel or both and be barefoot.

Ray Parkin was at Hintok and Kinsayok:

> A split bamboo has got an edge like a razor blade, and when it gets in the mud and you walk and you slip, you've got slices in your feet. There's nothing you can do about it; you just get absolutely fed up. This is when you're at your most vulnerable, both physically and mentally, and you wince at everything. Then you just go on and on for 150 days without a let-up. During that period it was just a matter of getting out to the job and getting back, and getting out and getting back; that was all. You went, and then you flopped on your bunk at night. I was in a tent at one stage with twenty-two others, and I couldn't have told you the names of three other people in that tent. We were like zombies although on the job we were conversing and all the rest of it; but we were single minded in just getting backwards and forwards. We were wrapped up in sheer survival.

At Hintok Parkin observed a 'wobbly tripod'; two malaria cases supporting a man with cholera. He turned it into a sketch of men co-operating in despair.

The Japanese engineers and guards, under great pressure themselves, tolerated no excuses for being absent from work.

Arneil: If they wanted 200 men they had to have 200 men. The guards would deliver 200 men even if perhaps thirty of them might be on the backs of their mates. In the rain. So when we got there, if the beriberi was excessive, you might have to lie some of them on their backs with their feet against the side of the embankment to keep the fluid flowing down through their legs into their bodies so their legs wouldn't burst. They couldn't work at all. We'd feed them at lunch time when we had a break. They were looked after, hats placed over their faces to keep the rain out, and they were talked to and joked to. They understood the position. We would carry them back at night. Usually one would die during the day.

Sometimes, Frank Baker says, men who were carried on stretchers to the work sites could hold a rock drill while another prisoner struck it with the hammer.

The Korean guards who were constantly rushing around driving the prisoners to greater effort did not always have the effect that they wanted. Men close to physical collapse were incapable of sustaining an increased pace for more than a moment, and, Arneil says,

> It's very difficult to keep Australians working when they shouldn't be working. The Korean guards were very few and far between, you might have only two or three. I remember once, it was quite amusing, a Korean guard running through the

embankment hitting everybody on the head with a stick. It was not very hard, but a sort of a whack. By the time he hit the next person the other person would have stopped, or got back to half pace. But speedo days were bad.

Prisoners no longer hoped for a 'smoko' and the man who asked to go to the *benjo* (toilet) might be bashed. 'It was nothing', Clarke remembers, 'to be hit on the head with a drill; whatever the guard had handy you got thumped with. Geoff Singer happened to get a bashing over the head, and he died the next day.' Reg Newton calculated that sixty-eight men were battered to death in the cutting of Hellfire Pass.

The prisoners, numbed and exhausted, were still able to record a vivid picture of the work scene.

Clarke: It looked like a scene out of Dante's Inferno. The Japs decided we would work twenty-four hours a day, two shifts, one was the day shift and one was the night shift. Lighting became a problem but they're a pretty resourceful people, and there's plenty of bamboo, so they formed a light party. Its job was to keep the fires burning all night. In addition to the bamboo fires which threw a fair bit of light, there were some bamboo containers with hessian wicks and a bit of dieseline, and there were a few carbide lights. If you stood on the top of the cutting you would see the burning fires at intervals of about twenty feet; you'd see the shadows of the Japanese with their Foreign Legion caps moving round with their sticks belting men. We still had our slouch hats so you could distinguish the prisoners by being naked under the slouch hats, moving rocks around, hammering and clearing. There was shouting and bellowing. And this went on all night.

It was, Adrian Curlewis says, a 'magnificent sight': the flaring fires, the movement and the noise combining in an intensely dramatic scene confined by the blackness of the surrounding jungle. 'Dante', Donald Stuart claims, 'knew less about infernos than we knew. We could have given him lessons.'

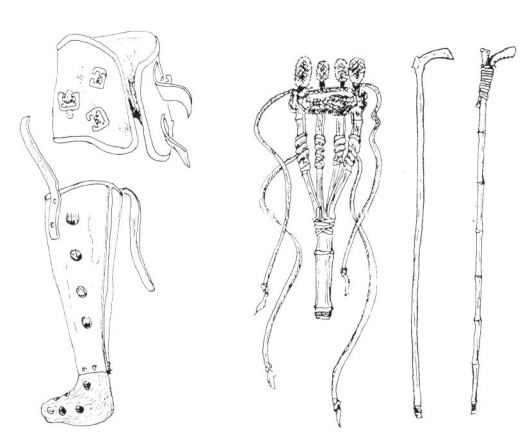

'You can have me left boot, Harry,' was a cry of bravado. But the ingenuity of surgeons and craftsmen could save few amputees.

When the British forces surrendered in Singapore over one hundred Australian doctors serving as medical officers had gone into captivity. Doctors and medical orderlies travelled with each group of prisoners sent to Burma and Thailand, but they carried little equipment and few drugs from Changi's limited stock. In some cases the Japanese told them they would be able to obtain medical supplies at their new camps. In fact in 1943 on the railway the medical workers faced their greatest task when they had their fewest resources. Sir Albert Coates later wrote that he probably did the best work of his life at the 55 kilo camp in Burma. At that time he had few medicines and little equipment that had not been available to the military surgeons who had sailed with the first convict fleets to Australia.

The medical officer was 'the buffer between the sick and the Japanese'. Confronted with huts crowded with sick and wasting prisoners, the guards would abuse the doctor, blaming him for failing to have at least eighty-five per cent of the men fit to work. 'Often', Ian Duncan remembers, 'the medical officer got beaten up every day because he had so many sick in the camp.' A guard inspecting the sick might kick men on sores or afflicted limbs to check the severity of the disability and to discourage everyone from seeking the shelter of the hospital huts. Other crude tests were applied.

> Kevin Fagan: There was one Korean guard whom we knew as Mephistopheles. He was a sort of pressure man. He wanted to know through the interpreter why we were seven men short that morning. I said the men were all sick. *Byoki* is the word we used to use. After a bit of chatter all those who were supposed to have dysentery—which they all did have—were formed up in a circle and made to squat down and pass a stool. If they didn't have any blood they got a kick in the back and were sent to form a parade separately from the others. Those who had blood were usually people who had piles and were not at all sick. It was a great saviour to have haemorrhoids that bled.

Even in Changi, Glyn White says, he met no Japanese with whom he could communicate as a fellow professional; the skilled doctors within the Japanese army were not seen by the doctors in captivity.

The prisoners reserve their highest praise for the medical officers: Lloyd Cahill, Albert Coates, Ian Duncan, Edward Dunlop, Kevin Fagan, David Hinder, Alan Hobbs, Bruce Hunt, Rowley Richards and many more. Doctors probably survived better than most prisoners. Their work did not engender moral doubts or a sense of futility; it was constant, sometimes professionally exciting, clearly beneficial and the other prisoners were immediately appreciative. Men who were themselves close to starvation would set aside food for the doctor; he was often the one resource they possessed to combat disease and the demands of the Japanese. Given the chance to employ their technical and human skills, the doctors won unqualified admiration from the prisoners who look cynically on nearly all who held positions of power or privilege. Ray Parkin travelled with Dunlop from Java through Changi to Thailand:

> Weary's one of the great figures. He's like Mount Everest. You don't really see him till you stand well away. Up in Hintok we used to parade in the morning in the wet season; sick men and all had to turn out except those actually bedded down in hospital. The Japanese would select work parties from the fit men, then they would go for the next people, the so-called 'light sick', and they'd possibly send most of those out, and then there were those that were doubtful. There was a huge log laid alongside the road, and the sick used to sit on it. We called it the wailing log. The Japanese would come along and they'd interrogate these blokes with a great '*kura*!'. Of course the first thing you did when you heard a *kura* was to stand straight up to attention. If these fellows happened to stand up they were fit enough to work. Weary told these men not to stand up in any circumstances: they were sick, and they couldn't get up. The Japanese would come along and say, '*kura*!' The men would remain. Weary would go and pick up a man in his arms like a baby, bring him over to Nippon, and say, 'This man, Nippon?' And then he would carry him back.

Even the most hardened Japanese found it difficult to accept a man proferred in Dunlop's arms as fit to labour on the railway. But, as Dunlop himself asserts, no organisation, no subtle appeals for compassion and no unlimited capacity to endure bashings could prevent the destruction of a third of the men: the Japanese 'just sent the fitter men back and back and back to a relentless grindstone'.

The reason why most men died is simple: they starved. The greatest atrocity committed by the Japanese against the prisoners was that they did not feed them. The Australian army ration of 1941 had given the men a daily intake of 4220 calories; they could survive and do some work on 3000; in Changi they had been getting just over 2000 calories, and at that level they had been losing weight and suffering from deficiency diseases. On the railway the few grams of rice, watery vegetable stew and infrequent flavouring from meat and fish was often giving them less nourishment than they had been getting in Changi. The diet would not sustain men who were being forced to work at maximum effort. They were vulnerable to diseases which would not have killed, and perhaps not have afflicted, the prisoners had they been well fed.

Nearly all of the men had amoebic or bacillary dysentery, or both. Some had contracted it before they left Changi, and they were to have it in varying degrees of intensity throughout their imprisonment. Dysentery was enervating and demoralising. Men were attempting to stumble to muddy pit latrines twenty times in the one night. One young prisoner felt that he reached his most depressed point when he stood in a creek at night making a pathetic attempt to clean his soiled body and clothes. Nearly all the prisoners had malaria. Coates was later to say before the Tokyo War Crimes Trial that ninety-five per cent of the men in Burma suffered from malaria. Rowley Richards, who was also with A Force, observed the lethal effect of diseases in combination. A prisoner with malaria would go through the cycle of high temperature, sweating and shivering, and then while his resistance was lowered the dysentery would intensify:

> This just went on and on. Because during the attack of malaria one didn't eat very much, and during the dysentery one couldn't eat, the malnutrition exaggerated. And of course if the individuals were sent out to work they were burning up what little vitamin reserve they had. They were more prone to develop pellagra particularly, and also beriberi. It was a constant battle, and the supply of quinine with which we could have treated the malaria was almost non-existent. If we could have broken the cycle there, the dysentery wouldn't have presented anything like the problem.

At times the doctors had only crushed charcoal in water to offer patients dying of dysentery when they knew that a little emetine would have saved them. The doctors were always searching at the margins of their professional experience, recalling lectures on the history of surgery so they could resurrect the techniques used before the equipment and drugs of the 1940s became available, and pooling what they knew of the afflictions of poverty-stricken and congested populations in the tropics.

One form of insidious malnutrition worried the doctors. It was caused by a lack of niacin, one of the vitamin B group.

Richards: We remembered from our text books that pellagra was something which occurred in some deprived areas where they had famine on a yearly basis. The first year it would be characterised by skin rashes on the face, legs, and on the scrotum. Next year the condition would manifest itself as diarrhoea. The third year as dementia preceding death. And we went through the stages of recognising the pellagra rashes and then the diarrhoea, and because there was no improvement in rations it became progressive. When we had a few cases of dementia we were facing the incredible spectacle of half the men going mad. In addition to the pellagra problem we also had cerebral malaria which gave people hallucinations. It was a frightening concept.

The men were brought back from the work camps to better supplied bases in Thailand before they manifested the most terrible effects of prolonged malnutrition.

The prisoners were more conscious of another deficiency disease, beriberi. In 'wet' beriberi the body accumulated fluid until it was distended and grotesque. Men limped along with a leg swollen from knee to ankle, a puffed elephant boot.

Arneil: I remember there was one case of a chap called Butcher Smith. He was lying there like a hippopotamus. His testicles were so large they were just a little bigger than a normal soccer ball. My mate Doug Blanchard used to hold them in his hands and lift them up so that we could turn Butcher Smith to wash him and wipe him. He had no neck, just a head sitting on shoulders. He died; they all died with that type of thing.

In 'dry' beriberi there was no deformation, but death could be sudden. 'You'd be talking to a chap, he'd be sitting up, and he'd just suddenly fall; and he would have died of cardiac arrest.' The husk on the rice—had it been available—contained enough vitamin B1 (thiamine) to combat beriberi.

Any scratch or splinter that broke the skin was likely to become a tropical ulcer. It was a type of local gangrene, a bacterial infection. Among the ill-fed prisoners who rarely had any soap, disinfectants or bandages, the ulcers had intense virulence: disfiguring, disabling and killing. They were most common on the lower leg, sometimes spreading from knee to ankle. Bones and tendons would be exposed. The prisoners had no effective treatment.

Donald Stuart: We tried everything. We tried hot foments, we tried rock salt pounded up to powder, heated in a mess tin to cracking point and then poured in. There were no sulpha drugs and no ointments, no bloody nothing.

If all the infected flesh was cut away the sore might begin to heal; but fresh infection was also likely. Gouging ulcers with a sharpened spoon and no anaesthetic was extremely painful. Two men held the patient while a third dug into the rotted flesh: 'I can still hear the fellows now,' Rusty O'Brien says, 'screaming when that spoon would go into their ulcer.' Maggots penetrated the open sores, but as they fed off the infected flesh they probably did more good than harm. With advanced ulcers the only course open to the doctors was amputation. The pain of the ulcers was such that some men would actually say, 'For Christ sake, cut my leg off.'

Alf Michell was an ulcer patient in Burma:

They'd made a base hospital in one of the old camps back at the 55 kilo, open huts of bamboo slats and *atap* roofs. We were all lying there with our ulcers and our dysentery and malaria and everything—no medicine, nothing at all. At the end of the hut you could see the Colonel [Coates] operating. With the help of the Dutchman [C J van Boxtel] they made a drug and they used to stick it in the back of your spine. The orderlies held your head and bent your back right over and stuck it in, which would paralyse you from the chest down. You could go there and watch. And the soldier paralysed from the chest down could see his own operation. The

Colonel would cut right around the flesh and he'd grip the arteries and that to stop the blood from flying out. He had a sort of tenon saw to cut through the bone and snap it off. He was taking six legs a day off there.

In the meantime some more doctors joined us. One of them was Major Alan Hobbs. He said to me and a couple of others after he looked at my foot, 'Lean on one another and hobble down to the river and let the fish eat that bad flesh out.' So we walked into the river and the small fish, they were tiddlies, ate away at your foot, and all you could feel was a slight little bumping all the time. The fish ate all the black flesh that was turning into gangrene. When we looked at our wounds they were nice and clean. You could see the red flesh. My foot was up like a balloon and it had what looked like a crater in it. We just went back and lay there. The Colonel, well, he didn't get my leg.

Other limbs were saved by the scavenging, cleansing fish; but a total of 120 amputations was performed at the 55 kilo hospital.

Captain van Boxtel was a brilliant improvisor, a chemist able to apply his craft while separated from all laboratory equipment. He had made the spinal injections from cocaine tablets, and he also manufactured a little of the precious emetine by using sodium carbonate and alcohol to free it from ipecacuanha. The alcohol was distilled from Burmese brandy. In Thailand, Lloyd Cahill explains,

> We actually did a few blood transfusions. We used to get a few coves and you can match blood crudely by getting the donor and comparing his with that of the recipient. But you have to spin the blood and we had no centrifuge. So we just used to tie a little vase on to the back wheel of the Jap bicycle and spin it hard. Eventually you could separate it out.

The doctors encouraged the men to collect scraps of metal, glass and thread, anything that might be converted into a medical instrument.

Cholera was the most feared disease. It was sudden and random: it took weak and strong. 'The boys used to say cholera makes dysentery look like an attack of constipation.'

Ray Parkin: One of the symptoms of cholera is a white stool. And I remember one day out on the line, I was sitting having my bit of rice up on the topside when a fellow came along and he squatted down just on the other side of the railway line to me. There was no false modesty out there, it was quite natural, in fact we were all very clinical. This fellow looked down and saw a milk-white motion; and he saw that I saw it. He just gave me a look and it went right through me; it was the look of a condemned man. He knew he had it. He was dead the next morning.

Cholera is dramatic in its onset. There are intense cramps, the voice fades and fluid flows from every orifice. The eyes sink and the cheeks fall in as the dehydrated body 'shrivels up like a walnut'.

Arneil: We could tell within five minutes whether they had cholera. We would place a bamboo identification disc around their wrists with their regimental number and name on it because in four hours it was not possible to recognise a man who had contracted cholera.

Medical officers instructed the men to do what little they could to protect themselves from infection. All water was boiled and the men tried while standing in mud to keep their mess gear clean and the flies away.

Cholera is a disease of one symptom. If the fluid and salts expelled by the body can be replaced then the patient has a fair chance of living. It was essential to make a saline drip.

Richards: We used stethoscope tubing. We'd boil that up. When the needles became blunt we used copper tubing which we acquired from Japanese vehicles. We sharpened it and used it. Remembering we had seen gramophones that used to operate on bamboo needles, we got a very fine bore bamboo. That went into the veins quite effectively.

In four hours it was not possible to recognise a man with cholera.

At Hintok Dunlop organised men to distil water and to re-crystallise rough salt several times to procure the materials for the saline solution. Approximately forty per cent of the cholera patients were to die; a low mortality rate considering the weakness of the men and the appalling conditions in which the medical teams worked.

F Force was the hardest hit by cholera; 600 of them died with its rapid wasting of their bodies. But this was less than the total deaths from the combined effects of malnutrition, malaria and dysentery. Forty-four per cent of the 7000 British and Australian troops in F Force died.

When the first deaths occurred on the railway the prisoners held simple and effective burial services; a bugler played the last post, the padre or another serviceman read a service, and a proper grave was dug and left with an appropriate marker. But as deaths became numerous and the Japanese demands for workers became more insistent, the men had neither the time nor the energy to dig graves or attend funerals, and bodies had to be disposed of quickly to prevent the spread of infection. On the worst day at Tanbaya nineteen men died. Geoff O'Connor was working near the Thai-Burma border:

One of my jobs was burning the dead. They'd have two logs. The teak wood would burn very well. You would get those and put them about two or three feet apart and put kindling in between. We got the fire going and lowered the home-made bamboo stretcher on top of it. It wasn't too good. You'd take off! You couldn't just wait there because when the bodies start to burn they sit up. Well, it's a bit unnerving burning people, particularly your friends.

Where possible ashes were placed in bamboo tubes and preserved. At the end of the war the remains of 1362 Australians were reburied at Kanchanaburi in Thailand and 1348 at Thanbyuzayat in Burma.

In their daily confrontations with the Japanese the doctors had a simple aim: to prevent as many sick as possible from being forced to work. But sometimes the doctors were in the invidious position of selecting men for work camps where the chances of survival were slight. By August 1943 H Force had passed through the cholera epidemic and a cruel 'speedo', and better rations were starting to come through.

Kevin Fagan: The worst experience I had was the job of choosing 100 of the survivors of the holocaust to go further up into Thailand to a place called Konkoita to help with a cutting which was behind schedule. There were about 300 of us left out of about 600. From that group, none of whom were well, all of whom had malaria, were malnourished, and some of them were shivering on parade, dressed in a laplap or a pair of shorts, rarely any boots, I had to choose 100 men to march another 100 miles into the unknown, certainly to worse and not to better. I never saw any of those men again. I felt that I had come to the end at that stage because these were the fellows whom I had nursed through difficult times and there was a bond of affection between us. I would have understood if they'd cursed me, turned on their heels and walked away. Instead of that they came and shook hands with me and wished me good luck. And I found it necessary to walk into the jungle and weep for a while. It was the most terrible thing I've had to do. If I hadn't done it, then the Japanese would have taken the first 100 they found, and they would all have died. Some of these men had a chance of surviving. None of them should have been asked to do any more. Later on that day the Japanese medical officer came by, a pompous fellow who could speak quite good English. I said to him, 'Unless you change your treatment of these prisoners they will all die.' He said, 'That would be a very good thing; it would save the Japanese army much rice.'

Just under thirty per cent of the men in H Force died; it was the second most harshly treated, and its experience had been most compressed. H Force had not arrived in Thailand until May 1943 and it began moving to the base camps in September.

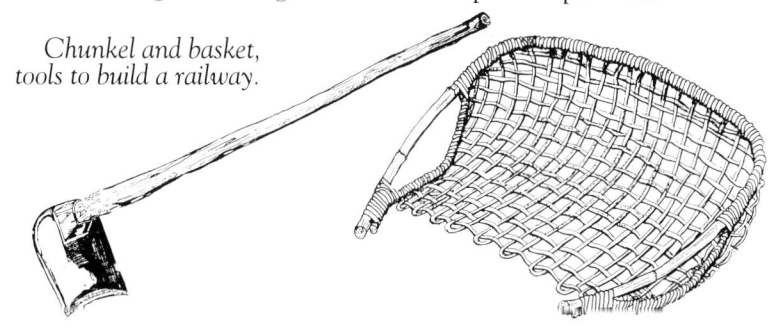

Chunkel and basket, tools to build a railway.

'Dying', one prisoner said, 'was easy. It was living that was hard.' But why were some men better able to keep on living than others? It is a question which has never left the survivors. Chance was always a factor. A man might be standing next to a suddenly enraged guard and be beaten to death; he could be one of the thirty-one killed in accidental falls from the Pack of Cards bridge at Hintock; and he might be lucky and miss the draft for a distant cholera camp. Age, build and being accustomed to hard work were also important. 'The big men,' Ian Duncan says, 'died first. There was just not enough food to keep them going.'

Rowley Richards adds: We expected that these young bronzed Aussie surfers and footballers would be the ones who would survive best. In fact that did not occur. Those who survived best were the twenty-five to thirty or thirty-five age group, the next group would be say twenty or twenty-five, and then the thirty-five to forty group. Among the worst would be the below twenty, the eighteen-year-olds who hadn't sufficient experience in coping with difficult situations. They were completely lost. And of course the older people, the over fifties, certainly fared very badly.

But to all these generalisations there were exceptions. Some big men, men under twenty and men over forty were among the survivors.

Factors less easily measured than age and size were also significant. One was the capacity of the prisoners to form mutually supporting groups. Prisoners from other nationalities noticed the strength of Australian groups, and the Australians themselves took a pride in their ability to keep each other alive by sharing, encouraging and abusing.

Hugh Clarke: No one would ever be on his own without support. The groups were usually small, they might range from just two men to four or five, and these men scrounged and shared. If one was sick the others would look after him. This wasn't so important in Changi, but once things got bad on the railway it was vital. Malaria could recur say every ten days, and when you had malaria you couldn't eat so your mates would eat what you couldn't, and then of course your turn would come.

Snow Peat: When we'd get back and have some tucker we'd go and see how Mick is, how Curly is, how Bluey is and wake him up and say, 'How're you going, Bluey?' Prop him up and make sure his bed sore was all right and do what you could. You couldn't do bloody much, just make sure he had water, get him talking, get him interested.

George Sprod: Well you'd joined up together and if the bloke wouldn't eat you'd say, 'If you aren't going to eat that I'm going to ram it down your neck'. You knew the bloke, you'd had good times with him, drinking and going on leave.

Duncan: It's a lot to give away even a spoonful of food when you're starving. It really is a lot. When every grain of rice is counted, to actually give away part of your ration to someone is a sacrifice that is to me rather wonderful.

There is repeated testimony of a practical application of mateship to help the living and the dying.

Arneil: It's difficult for any person in Australia today to understand the depth of the bond. Difficult to understand death, for example. In Australia one dies in a sterile hospital bed. If the doctors are quick enough they might have the relatives there, but many times the patient is dead before the next of kin get there. In Thailand when a man died, he died in an aura of love and brotherhood which is not available now possibly anywhere in the world. You died with your head in the lap of a mate, with somebody holding your hand, with somebody with a hand on your forehead saying a little prayer, and people actually sorry to see you die. That's a bond which you just cannot obtain now. Many of the people who were there became closer to their friends than to their families.

Some men did die making petty accusations against everyone around them; the surprising thing is that the dying so rarely went in acrimony.

Sometimes a man such as Warrant Officer Eric Bailey would have responsibility for selecting men for particular tasks, and he would be able to switch those who were in need of a spell to softer jobs: on a river barge, working in a cook house or on camp duties. Tom Morris is one who believes that his survival partly depended on the fact that Bailey sent him to cook in the canteen and travel on the barges to Bampong, including a memorable trip when they filled their water bottles with Thai whisky. Having picked up weight, Morris volunteered, as Bailey expected, to go back up the line. But the number in need of special consideration was always greater than the positions available. Men with the responsibility of selecting work parties were in a constant dilemma. When a prisoner was deteriorating more quickly than the rest of his group a mate might sell something or steal eggs to help sustain his ailing companion. Always the practical assistance that could be given was slight: its significance often lay in what it expressed rather than in what it did.

Few prisoners decided that death was preferable to life in such appalling conditions. The prisoners demonstrated an exceptional power to remain optimistic and to cling to life. Roy Whitecross who was in Burma:

> Out of my particular force of over 1000 men to my knowledge there was one who decided that to battle on was quite useless, and he one day sat with his rice from the midday meal and said, 'Anybody want any rice?' I said to him, 'What's the matter? Have you got malaria, are you crook?' He said, 'No, but do you want my rice?' I said, 'You eat it.' 'No,' he said, 'no point. You battle on today and you're dead tomorrow. You battle on today and tomorrow, and you're dead the next day. It's no bloody good.' Two or three of us got to him and we argued and we talked and we cajoled. We threatened to thump him, but it didn't do any good. He had just simply given up. About a week later he got a bit of a cold, it wasn't even influenza, it certainly wasn't malaria, and he promptly died. The rest of us never had any doubts that in the foreseeable future, a few months, we would be out. And that's what carried us through.

The senior officers with F Force classed with certainty only two deaths among the Australians as suicides.

Men needed a specific motive to keep on living.

Peat: Well, I had a wife and a little girl. And the will to live. I said, 'I'm not dying in this bloody place, and that's all there is to it'.

Parkin: At the back of my mind I could visualise myself as an old bloke somewhere. Whether this was seeing into the future or not I don't know. But I'd just imagine myself as an old bloke, and I thought if I'm going to be an old bloke I'll have to see this lot out.

O'Connor: I hated their guts, and I wanted to get home. Perhaps I was a determined, irritable, cranky sort of bugger, and the more they did to me, the more it made me spark a bit. I never ever believed we wouldn't win.

Ray Myors: Determination. I reckoned the bastards weren't going to kill me. Confidence that somehow you were going to live, and a strong emotion, hate or love, could help get men on the boat home.

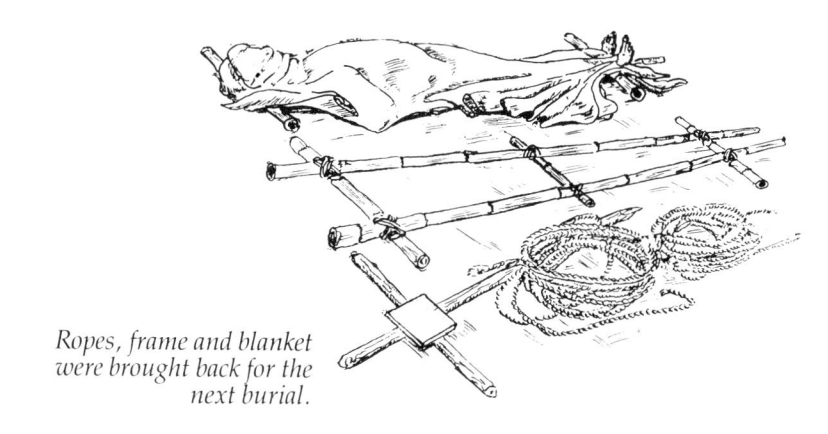

Ropes, frame and blanket were brought back for the next burial.

CHANGI WAS LIKE HEAVEN

'We got out of the trucks . . . We were not ashamed because we were soldiers, and we wanted to look like soldiers. The people from Changi stood back and uttered not a word.'

In October 1943 the prisoners in two rail-laying gangs met just south-east of the Three Pagodas Pass; Burma and Thailand had been linked by railway. The 'speedo' had ended, the worst of the cholera epidemic had passed, and the monsoon rains were giving way to drier weather. At Kinsayok the Japanese dynamited the river and allowed the prisoners to celebrate with over one hundred kilograms of fish. At Songkurai where the men completed a final section of bridging and embanking with as little as three hours' rest at night the Japanese gave a 'presento': 200 cigarettes for those who had worked for forty days without a break, 150 for those who had worked thirty days and 100 for those who had managed twenty. Although there was still a lot of hard work to be done on repairing and strengthening the railway with its spongy foundation and flimsy bridges, most of the men had come through the time when there was only work, sickness and death.

All the prisoners on the railway had been deprived, but they had not been equal. The men themselves noticed that if a group of destitute prisoners arrived at a camp some would soon be obvious because of their better equipment or food supply; they would have a pair of new boots or a tin of curry powder. They might have been lucky in their scrounging, taken risks to go out at night to trade, or got their hands on negotiable currency. The money-making schemes, always known as 'rackets', were usually minor ventures into private enterprise: buying a *kati* of native tabacco, teasing, washing and drying it, and then selling it in small quantities; running a card game; or making a deal with another prisoner such as a truck driver to bring in scrounged goods. The opportunities were slight, but there was always someone ready to exploit every opening in the camp economy.

The conditions in Burma and Thailand exaggerated the differences between officers and men. The officers were worse off than they had been in Changi; but the men were suffering much more. There was now an observable difference. The officers might be two stone heavier than the men in the ranks, and the officers were likely to be standing in boots and uniform while the other prisoners, after weeks of working in all weathers, were barefoot and dressed in G strings and tattered shorts. The very appearance of the officers was sufficient to cause resentment amongst men who knew that they, or some of those standing alongside them, were within days of death. A soldier in D Force writing of his experiences for his family wondered whether the officers who 'were reverent and humble when they read the funeral services over our dead' ever realised how 'bitter, harsh and sour' the men felt towards them.

When the prisoners first began work on the railway many officers attempted to be protective foremen, the role they had sometimes played effectively in Singapore. And as Cliff Moss observed, 'It made an awful difference if you had officers that would have a go'. But at most of the railway work camps the Japanese would tolerate no interference.

Hugh Clarke: In my particular group which was T Battalion the officers were not permitted anywhere near the line. They were allowed to have nothing whatever to do with the work we were doing. I doubt if they saw the line. Their job was administration, such as it was, and making sure that the right quota of men were available for work.

Where officers could intervene they had to display courage and fine judgment. They took the chance of being humiliated and bashed; and an obtuse officer could always get the men into even greater trouble. Those officers, 'and there were few of them about', who were 'always having a go and always getting a belting were tremendously admired'. And the men saw a particular strength in officers who persisted in spite of an abhorrence of the violence and shouting.

Don Moore: There was one officer I knew who was dedicated to duty. He knew what was expected of him: he was an officer. He did have moral fibre. But he visibly shook when nervous: and he still did his job. Sometimes he was ineffectual; sometimes he made it. I remember him physically putting himself between the Japanese and some of the boys, realising that he could probably have stayed aloof. But he got into that situation, which meant he copped it. He would be visibly shaking; but he did it.

Inevitably, some officers began to avoid confrontations with the Japanese.

Snow Peat: They got a bloody hiding and they didn't come back for the next one and get bashed. They were right out of the firing line. Cringed like a mongrel dog. Just like some of the men couldn't take it.

Most of the other ranks accepted that it was only the exceptional officer who would have the presence, the command of language, and the tolerance of pain to keep pressing the men's case against the Japanese; their anger is not against the officers who merely avoided being battered and humiliated.

The men direct their resentment against privilege. Although some officers took off their badges of rank and took a turn in the work gangs to give sick men a spell, or the Japanese forced them into labouring at the height of the 'speedo', many of the other ranks feel that the officers could have worked harder around the camp to ease the lot of the men on the railway. But even more, the men resent the officers' access to better food.

Stan Arneil: There was a moral problem. Officers were paid about thirty dollars a month. Now they were in the same camps as we were. And they were not working. We were. They believed that that money belonged to them. We were paid about ten cents a day. Well, we weren't really paid. I had two payments on the line in nine months. One was a handful of native tobacco which I gave to my mate, and the other was a piece of soap which lasted one wash, I think, and I was very happy to get that. But the officers did receive money, in large lumps, and they had what they called a canteen. Prisoners-of-war, not officers, were sent down the line beyond the area where we were and they humped back what we called the canteen supplies to Songkurai.

The distribution of food reads like a fairy tale. Cooking oil was very precious to us. In that state you start to dream about oil and lumps of fat. The same with sugar. Officers could have as much oil as they could find containers to place it in. They had as much fish and eggs and that type of thing as they could have. And the troops, I think we got a pint and a half of oil between 100 men, or something like that. It was quite wrong really. The morality of it is argued on the fact that the money belonged to the officers. If that's their thinking, that's OK with me, but I didn't have that idea when I was there. We were most furious about it. I believe it might have been better if all the money had been put into a pool and we had shared it all. I am not too sure whether I would have done that had I been an officer. I can't tell, I was never tempted.

Officers did set aside some of their extra pay to provide medicines and stores for the general good, and they drew the same basic ration as the men. The amount of additional pay that the officers retained was slight; but relatively it was affluence. Officers also had more opportunities and more credit when they attempted to raise loans. Any advantage sufficient to supply an occasional egg or tin of sardines could make the difference between living and dying.

The other ranks take their criticisms further against two or three officers.

George Aspinall: There was one particular officer who was renowned for laying back all day doing nothing, issuing orders, and making life very hard for the rest of the men that were working. To some extent he was co-operating with the Japanese to our detriment. The men detested this particular person. Even today they don't talk about such things publicly; they prefer to let bygones be bygones. But when a group is talking privately some of these names come up and there's a real hate session. It did anger people. But we were supposed to be soldiers, we were supposed to take orders from our superior officers. We perhaps tried to live up to a code, something set by our forefathers in World War One.

Don Moore speaks of another case: There was one officer known as the White Jap. He was entirely dedicated to his own self-preservation. He was affluent by POW standards. He had money that he could lend where he'd be paid double or three times the price in English currency when he came back. This money had come from the proceeds of a canteen which he ran at a camp of which he was the commander. In this case it was a private enterprise purely and simply for himself. This fellow I speak of has never been back to any reunion that I know of.

One of the officers most condemned by his fellow prisoners displayed a peculiar courage in his complete indifference to the opinions of those around him.

The advantages of the officers, Stan Arneil argues, have continued into history: the officers wrote the reports from which much of the subsequent official history was written. But the private writings of the officers confirm some of the criticisms of the men. In his diary the British doctor Robert Hardie, who was in Thailand, wrote of being angered by the reluctance of his colonel to ask the Japanese to allow men to do life-saving hygiene work; he noted the number of officers who 'simply lie back and contribute nothing to the general welfare'; and he could not understand the refusal of a few officers to share with men who were obviously dying of want. An Australian officer wrote in his private memoir that there was always a minority holding the King's commission who 'collaborated' with the Japanese; and he thought that the one senior officer who secured his own survival by taking extra rations was guilty of 'bastardry'. An Australian captain listing in his diary the human and physical deficiencies revealed on the railway made an entry for 'the utter failure of certain senior officers'.

As prisoners the officers had choices denied to the other ranks, and in the exercise of those choices they had acted in ways which made them the most praised and the most abused prisoners. Kevin Fagan, a medical officer who was generous to his fellow men, makes the assessment:

> Officers too were sick. They were hungry. Most of them didn't have to work, and indeed it might have been better if more of them had offered to work, if they had, even for one day, given some sick other rank relief. The result of their not working was that to the other ranks they appeared to do nothing but eat and sleep and make lists of men fit for work. There were innumerable officers who behaved with exemplary compassion and consideration for their men. They did everything possible to lessen their misery. But I know also that there were a few who did nothing other than prepare lists of other ranks available for work, who appeared to take little part in the administration of the camp, and who did little to conceal their ambition, an ambition that we all shared, to survive. It's unfortunate that the indifference or timidity of a few gave the other ranks such an unhappy picture of the whole. One must realise too that other ranks and NCOs are by nature harsh critics of officers.

The irreverent men from the ranks see a special irony in the way some of the officers most ready to take public praise in the postwar were among those who were absent when the Japanese were most aggressive.

The statistics confirm the claim by the other ranks that as prisoners they did the dying. The 2/29th Battalion lost twelve officers and fifty-eight other ranks killed in action. Even when it is taken into account that many other ranks were classified as 'missing believed killed' the officers died in battle out of proportion to their numbers. But as prisoners two officers and 381 other ranks died. In H Force the death rate for British and Australian officers was six per cent; for the men it was over thirty per cent. Among the Australians in F Force three officers died in comparison with 1065 other ranks. On the *Perth* eighteen officers were killed in action or were drowned, but none died as prisoners of war: 331 ratings were killed or drowned and 104 died while prisoners. The battle conditions which made junior officers vulnerable were reversed when the Allies surrendered.

The privileges given to officers were set out in international agreements, and neither the Japanese who sometimes aknowledged them nor the officers who benefited were responsible for their drafting. The clauses granting better conditions to officers had their genesis in negotiations between European powers at a time when officers were drawn almost exclusively from upper classes and when officers did their soldiering in a manner sharply segregated from that of the ordinary soldier. The men who met to draw up the international agreements came from the same class as the officers. Both the Japanese and the Australians were being influenced by alien rules.

When asked why he survived, one private soldier gave the names of two officers: one was a doctor, David Hinder, and the other was Reginald Newton. An electrical engineer from Sydney, Newton at thirty-five in 1942 was older than most captains, and in Pudu he had experienced more direct contact with the Japanese than most of the officers who were imprisoned in Changi. Early in 1943 he learnt that he was to be in charge of a battalion of D Force to travel into Thailand:

> I selected officers who I knew could be rough and tough, and could handle the Nips, they had proven this in Singapore work parties. I did not select anybody who had been in Changi throughout because I knew they had not had Japanese experience. But above all they had to be of the rougher and tougher type who could handle themselves and handle troops. I was determined I would only take one officer per hundred; that still left back a number of younger ones who were very good lads. This was unfortunate, but I was determined I would not have a superabundance of officers and then be at the beck and call of all the Nips for having too many drones around the place.

Newton had a reputation for aggression on the parade ground. One of his sergeants says: 'We called him Roaring Reggie because he was Roaring Reggie. Christ, when he was on parade he made enough noise that he'd wake the dead.'

Cliff Moss: He was a tremendously strong character, in a sense a very overbearing personality. He could mete out some pretty rough justice too if he had to. I remember on one occasion there was a bloke caught stealing some watches and stuff. He lined us all up and said, 'Well, there he is. You can do what you like with him. If I've got to bury him tomorrow it won't hurt me.' That was the sort of fellow he was. They didn't kill the thief. But they straightened him out, well and truly. I don't think there was any more thieving for a long time, if ever.

Newton did not change character when he confronted Japanese guards who were shouting orders and grasping at their swords.

Geoff O'Connor had served with Newton in the 2/19th Battalion on the Malayan peninsula and saw him again in Thailand:

> He was a byword on the line. He fought the Japanese all the way and in lots of cases he blocked them. He wasn't frightened to get knocked over. He carried a wireless in his water bottle, and he could have been shot for that. He wanted boots for the men one time, they wouldn't give them to him and he performed. They gave him the treatment and stood him in front of the guard house, and he kept on demanding the boots and they kept him there. Eventually the Japs got sick of him; they couldn't shut him up. And the men got their boots.

Newton gave the men confidence 'that what could be done would be done'.

Newton's success in protecting U Battalion depended on the way he supplemented his persistence and courage with administrative skill and a readiness to negotiate with equally strong Japanese who could get things done. Newton formed an effective relationship with Sergeant-Major Aitaro Hiramatso, the Tiger, one of the most feared of the guards. It called for 'a lot of guts' to stand up to the Tiger, but Newton did, and, Hugh Clarke says, the Tiger 'would even oppose other Japanese guards or engineers if he thought that Newton's men were being unfairly treated'. Frank Baker also comments on Newton's capacity to use Hiramatso:

> I'd say there was mutual respect there. The Tiger used to respect Reggie because Reggie was a fellow who would stand up and bellow at everybody, and of course that

suited the Tiger down to the ground to think that we were being well disciplined by our own officers. And he did run a tight ship. So the Tiger respected him to the point where they could argue, negotiate, and not do too badly. U Battalion, because of that relationship, I believe suffered a lot less than some of the others.

Newton claims that 'the Nip' would always look upon the officer 'as the number one', but that it was up to the officer to ensure that he deserved to be looked upon as a leader. In the postwar Newton has continued to fight for 'his boys' against any public slight or bureaucratic ineptitude.

Given that the survival of prisoners could depend on the efficient and just dispersal of resources, the relationships between the various captive national groups could be crucial. About half of the 61 000 prisoners in Burma and Thailand were British. The next largest group of 18 000 were from the Dutch East Indies and they included Dutch, Eurasians and Indonesians. The 13 000 Australians were the third largest group. Only 700 Americans, nearly all from the *Houston* or the 131st American Field Artillery Regiment, worked on the line. The major forces on the railway were made up of troops drawn from different nationalities with overall command usually going to the senior officer from the dominant group. The Australian, Brigadier A L Varley, had responsibility for A Force and Dunlop Force took its name from 'Weary' Dunlop.

In most camps and at work sites the Japanese separated the national groups, but there was some mixing and many casual encounters.

Arthur Bancroft: There was a little rivalry between the British, Americans and Australians, and the Dutch, of course. At times it didn't get too friendly either. But as Australians we did our best to mark ourselves by saying, 'We're the Aussies', and the Americans were very keen to show that they were Yanks or Americans, and so were the British. The Dutch were a bit removed from us because there was the language barrier. They were the colonial type of Dutch who had been serving out in Java for some years and where they'd had all their whims looked after; they had servants. So they felt that they were a little above anybody else.

Many of the prisoners talk of moments of tension with Dutchmen. Some of the antagonism was expressed in different perceptions of recent events in the war. The Dutch said that they had been left vulnerable by the collapse of the British in Singapore, and the Australians countered that the Dutch navy had been brave but foolhardy, and the Dutch army in Java were 'Huns with their guts ripped out'. The prisoners captured in the East Indies balance their criticism of Dutchmen with admiration for the courage of Dutchwomen. Roy Bulcock has written of the women of Surabaya who used to ride past on bicycles and throw parcels of biscuits, cigarettes and fruit to the men in the work parties in spite of the threat—and the reality—of severe punishment from the guards. In Java all news was attributed to a 'Dutchwoman on a bicycle'; an acknowledgement of the persistence of the cyclists.

Many prisoners exclude particular Dutchmen from their criticism, and Geoff O'Connor isolates one group:

I'd just as soon talk to one of the black Dutch, say Good day mate, or something. He would talk to us as an equal; he respected us and we'd respect him. At different times on work parties I've sat in amongst them, and eaten with them. One time there when I was a bit crook one of the Eurasians brought me a meal. I ate it down and it was bloody lovely; I didn't know that it was goanna. But I mean, it's only white meat and I was as hungry as hell. I said, thank you very much. He said, that's all right. We didn't look down on them, we just called them Dutchie.

All prisoners were indebted to the Dutch for helping them exploit the edible resources of the tropics, and the Dutch doctors were more familiar with the infections and deficiency diseases of south-east Asia.

Australian prisoners comment on their inability to share jokes with the Dutch, but when the American Ross Glover was asked why he got on so well with the Australians he said that he shared the same sense of humour. Australians and Americans could express rivalry, even trade insults, and still laugh. The survivors of the *Houston* and the *Perth*, having gone into battle, the sea and captivity together, had a special bond, but on the railway Glover teamed with an Australian soldier, Doug Flaherty. The tall ex-farmboy from Arkansas was twenty years old in 1942. He explains:

> Doug used to have malaria and I used to get his chow and maybe come and wash him down in bed. Then I'd get the malaria. He and I would stagger it; I'd get it, and then I'd get over it and he'd get it. We got along good.

Later Glover and other Americans were sent to French Indo-China where they were separated from the Australians. Another of the sailors from the *Houston* tried to pass himself off as an Australian so that he could stay with his 'mates', but he was detected and sent back to his countrymen.

The rivalry between the 'Poms and the Aussies' was 'natural', Ray Parkin says, but 'it wasn't very deep'. It was expressed on the cricket ground in Changi; and the diggers had techniques, both subtle and brash, to make an English officer sharply aware of national differences.

> Donald Wise: At one stage in Thailand, when I was sick and left in a very small camp by the roadside, I found myself going out in charge of Australian working parties. That could have been a very difficult situation because there was no reason why any Australians should take orders from a Pom, especially where we had all been defeated, and they were bloody minded, depressed and sick. In those days I wore a big moustache and the first time I went on parade there were about fifty or sixty of these Australians lined up with their big hats, and stripped to the waist. I walked on parade. I didn't see anybody move his mouth, but a voice said, 'What is it?' and I thought, 'They're going to stand me up.' Another voice said, 'I don't know, never seen one like this before.' And then a third voice said, 'Jesus, do you reckon it fucks?' I thought well do I stamp my tiny lieutenant's foot and get angry or do I laugh or what the hell do I do? This was an impossible situation which I'd never learnt about in officers' school. Finally a voice said, 'Looks like a rat peering through a broom.' Now all this, I may say, was from men who apparently weren't moving their mouths. They were just talking like ventriloquists' dummies. But they were getting the stuff over. When he said, 'Looks like a rat peering through a broom', I just fell about laughing; I just roared. Of course it saved the day. If I'd started shaking my little finger at them I think all would have been lost. That was my opening gambit with Australian soldiers and from then on we got on fine.

Another Englishman has recorded that before leaving for the railway his troupe presented the play 'Journey's End', set in the First World War, to appreciative audiences. When they tried to perform in front of Australians they found aggressive theatre-goers who persisted with interjections and ended up barracking for the German prisoner. The national differences were apparent, but they are not easily explained.

The national groups who suffered most on the railway were nominally free: they were the Burmese, Chinese, Javanese, Malay, Tamil and Thai labourers. The most disadvantaged were those so far from their homes that they could not easily escape. Some men had even taken their families to enjoy what they hoped were high wages and good conditions.

Kevin Fagan: They signed a contract for six months. Very few of them got back. They were the real victims of the railway. We were badly treated, but these poor devils had no organisation, and no medical services. They got paid in the depths of the jungle a pittance which they couldn't spend on anything, and they were treated with the same lack of regard as our men. And they really suffered terribly. There was a stream running through our camp which of course was dangerous to the men if they drank from it because there was cholera everywhere. I came across a young Tamil, a very pleasant man who spoke good English and he was about to drink from this stream. I said to him, 'Look, please don't drink that water, it's almost certainly contaminated with cholera.' He said, 'Don't worry about me. If I drink this water I might get cholera, I mightn't. And if I get cholera I might die, and I mightn't.' Fate. Well, I saw him a week or so later and he gave me a patronising grin and said, 'I didn't get cholera and I didn't die.' That was their attitude to hygiene.

The young Tamil may not have died but 70 000 of the other Asian labourers, and perhaps many more, perished on the railway. About one third of the Asians died, a higher death rate than in all the prisoner groups except F Force.

The Australian prisoners gained a heightened sense of their own nationality. One prisoner spoke of his relief as he came into a new camp and heard the drone of the accent, saw the blackened billies hanging up, and noticed the slouch hats with their faded unit colours slung on sleeping platforms. He might not be welcomed with any enthusiasm, but he was moving into a familiar environment; he would be able to throw his gear down, ask questions about what mob they were and whom they had seen, and feel at ease. The men who came back from the railway carried with them a pride in being Australian.

A feed for two hundred

They believe that they had demonstrated a capacity for survival in extreme conditions, and that some of their strength derived from their very Australian-ness.

Donald Stuart: I said to one British major, 'Why is it, that with 500 of your blokes and 500 of our blokes, we got about eighty deaths in the last month and you had about 400. We're on the same rations, the same work and the same conditions.' 'Well', he said, 'you Australians are well fed.' 'Christ no', I said, 'I was brought up in poverty.' 'No,' he said, 'you got meat at least once a day even if it was only scrag end. You got vegetables. You got good bread, you got a bit of butter on the table, all that sort of thing.' 'Well,' I said, 'you don't look too bad. You're a pretty muscular sort of bastard.' 'Yes', he said, 'I'm county family old boy. Everything of the best. But my men got up in the morning and had half a cup of black tea without sugar; that was

> their breakfast. White bread and margarine for lunch. Black tea again with no sugar. At night, well, they might get a vegetable soup. My men are real men, but they just haven't got the background.' He said, 'You can't starve them in the womb, then in infancy, boyhood and young manhood and expect them to stand up to these conditions as well as you people do. Don't sling off at my mob; they're a wonderful set of men.' 'Yeah,' I said, 'they're all going to die though.'

The conditions on the railway made no concessions to any man who started with a handicap.

There are few times when a fair comparison can be made between nationalities. The raw statistics of survival rates say little about the endurance of the different national groups. The prisoners rarely worked at the same location, did the same work over an equal length of time, and ate the same rations. If men were fit they were forced to work harder and longer. As a result in some camps the survivors were likely to come from men who were incapacitated early and so missed the protracted 'speedos' just before the line was completed. In the raw figures the Dutch have a superior survival rate, but that is partly because hardly any Dutch were allocated to F and H Forces. In both of these forces the British and Australian other ranks worked under broadly similar conditions. Lloyd Cahill, one of the doctors trying to sustain life in the patients on 'Cholera Hill' at Songkurai saw the worst of the camps in Thailand:

> I felt very sorry for the Brits upon the railway line because many of them had come on the last division to reach Singapore. They were Londoners who'd never been out in the bush or anywhere at all. This was where the Australians were so lucky because we had so many country coves with us. Some of them were quite extraordinary, and I'm sure that this accounted for the big difference in death rates between the British and the Australians. I always remember one fellow, Ringer Edwards, who appeared in 'A Town Like Alice'. Now the Ringer was on my crowd that went up on the railway. He was one of the most amazing men I've ever met. We'd be marching up at night and fellows would be falling over and breaking their arms in the pouring monsoon. You'd stop, and the Ringer would have a little fire going within about five minutes, and how he did it in the wet jungle I don't know. But he was a tower of strength there. If you've got a bunch of fellows like that around you, it doesn't matter what conditions you're living in, in the bush; you'll be OK. But the poor old Brits had a tough time; they did it the hard way. They had no idea how to set up a kitchen or set up latrines. Even when they were cremating people, they had no idea what to do. There was certainly not the communication between the officers and the men as there was with the Australians, and again I think that the officers had no idea. If you were lucky enough to be with a good bunch of Australians you could see most of it through.

By April 1944 in F Force 1060 Australians had died from a total of 3664; and 2037 British were dead out of 3336. The percentage death rates were twenty-nine for the Australians and sixty-one for the British. Although the British in Changi had been more inclined to listen to the blandishments of the Japanese and include 'light sick' to go to camps in 'pleasant and healthy surroundings', the difference in death rates is still very high. In H Force the death rate was twenty-five per cent for the Australians and thirty-four per cent for the British.

Better initial health and better practical skills certainly helped the Australians, but perhaps as important was their group strength.

Fagan: I felt that the Australian other ranks had a greater sense of group loyalty than the British. There was this terrible class thing in the British mind. It's horrible. I've seen British officers at the end of a long day's march as soon as they arrived at the camp just flop down on the ground. Someone would say, 'What about the men?' 'Oh, so-and-so the men. I can't do any more.' Whereas a fellow like Newton would be scrounging around trying to buy a few eggs for the sick, trying to organise the men to be together, finding out where everyone was, and whether anyone needed a doctor—and all this before he even thought of eating or sitting down.

Fagan also says that the ordinary Australians were exceptional in the way they would steal and lie for each other; and he sums up these qualities in a sentence of contrasting gentleness: 'they were kinder to each other'. Rowley Richards, another doctor, says that the cohesiveness of the Australians made them more 'highly disciplined' than other nationalities: they were not so destructively competitive or so careless of the weak. Hugh Clarke also emphasises the way the sense of being Australian linked the men together:

> I can't recall any Australian that was ever in a position where there was just himself. But I can recall plenty of occasions with, say, the Dutch or even the British, where a man would be dying and he wouldn't seem to have any mates. He would just die on his own. I don't recall a single Australian dying without somebody to look after him in some way.

The most convincing evidence of the cohesiveness and morale of the Australians comes from the outside; from the English officer sitting in the rain at night watching a group of Australians slogging back from work singing, and he asks, 'Just what is it that these Australians have?'

When conditions were at their toughest the men knew that it was only a matter of time before they all died. And the Japanese made it clear that they were expendable; the work was more important than life. Their only hope was to finish the job and get away. They had to complete an engineering task so great it seemed absurd for ill and emaciated men to even think about making the attempt. It was in these circumstances that men literally worked themselves to death; and it is these men whom the ex-prisoners feel have never had sufficient recognition from their countrymen.

Dunlop: It was a matter of ultimate pride to me that the Australians outworked, outsuffered and outlived every other national group on the Burma-Thailand railway. Now that I think is beyond question, and the Japanese recognised it. But the trouble was that if you were sinewy, indestructible, if you were a good workman, you got sent back and back and back on these terrible tasks with utterly inadequate food. You could see these magnificently strong men with great hearts who slowly went to pieces and died.

Courage on the battlefield is measured by a scale of medals, but there are no awards and little popular acclaim for the men who swung a hammer against a rock drill all day then turned to help others finish their set tasks. And kept doing it day after day, knowing that exhaustion was killing them. It was sustained and calculated bravery.

A strong sense of nationalism that embraced all Australians could have its cost. At Tarsau the British Lieutenant Colonel commanding the camp mounted a dais and addressed those men fit enough to leave their huts. An orderly, he explained, had been caught trading outside the camp with goods he had stolen from the dead. The Lieutenant Colonel hoped that the man would take stock and in future live up to the standards of the country from which he came. He ordered the man to come forward. As he came through the ranks the Australians saw the slouch hat. It was, one of the men standing on parade says, 'tough to take that one'.

From September 1943 the Japanese were moving prisoners from the work sites to base camps in Thailand. Vast hospitals at Tarsau, Kanchanaburi, Tamarkan, Chungkai and Tamuan sheltered many of the men. Over 15 000 prisoners were treated at Tarsau in the eighteen months of the hospital's existence, and 805 patients died there. Eventually the largest hospital was built at Nakom Paton where fifty vast thatched huts could each hold up to 200 men. In spite of the depressing conditions the men of F and H Forces put on weight in the month that they waited for transport back to Singapore.

Changi now seemed like home, 'almost in Australia'. For the men coming back from Thailand it was, Fred Stringer says, 'like heaven'. The first trains began arriving in November 1943; of course, Aspinall adds, 'it didn't take as many trains to bring the survivors back'. The men remember the return journey as less exhausting than the trip north, but the five cramped days cost them the condition they had gained in the base camps. They went by truck from Singapore station to Changi where they were met by those who had stayed behind. Snow Peat was helped from the trucks by men saying:

> 'How are you mate?' They just couldn't believe it. You know, we were six and a half, seven stone. It was unbelievable for them to see the bloody wrecks, and we were supposed to be the bloody fit men. One of the officers made a comment about the state we were in, and then when he saw some of the officers with us he wanted to know, 'What the bloody hell did you do to my men?' There were no beg pardons. You could see the difference between the condition the officers were in and the condition the men were in. 'What's bloody happened?' he said. That was the first time that they really knew what was going on.

The men from the railway kept together. Their memories confined them more closely than Changi's outer fence.

Stan Arneil arrived at Changi on December 21, 1943. He has no memory of getting from the train in Singapore station to Changi, but he has vivid recollection of his reception in Changi:

> It was a moonlight night and Changi with the tropical waters round the island was so beautiful. I can still hear the squeal of the brakes as the trucks lined up. The people from Changi knew we were coming, and they came over to see us, to look for old friends, and see how we were. We got out of the trucks, a couple were dead and we laid them on the ground, and we lined up on the road. We were not ashamed because we were soldiers, and we wanted to look like soldiers. The people from Changi stood back and uttered not a word. It was really quite strange. We lined up on the road as best we could and stood up as straight as we could. Those who couldn't stand up straight were on sticks. And those who couldn't stop shaking with malaria were held by their friends. We thought this was what we should do as soldiers to say that we were not beaten. The sergeant major dressed us off and we stood in a straight line as he went over and reported to Colonel Johnston. Johnston went over to Black Jack Galleghan and he said, 'Your 2/30th all present and correct, sir.' And Galleghan said, 'Where are the rest?' The major, he was a major then, said, 'They're all here, sir.' And we were. Black Jack Galleghan, the iron man, broke down and cried. It was an incredible scene. We wanted to show them we were soldiers.

AN ORDINARY BUNCH OF WOMEN

> *. . . they had come to work 'and if this was the end of the road, well we wanted to stay in the hospital and nurse the fellows'.*

Within weeks of the call for volunteers 4000 Australian nurses applied to serve overseas. To qualify the nurses had to be experienced and registered, over twenty-five and under thirty-five years of age (except for matrons), single, and medically fit. In January 1940 the first contingent of the Australian Army Nursing Service (AANS) sailed with troops of the 6th Division for the Middle East. A year later when the Australians went into action in north Africa the nurses in tented hospitals attended the wounded.

While one group of nurses worked through dust storms and twelve-hour shifts other members of the AANS were sailing to Singapore on the *Queen Mary*. 'It was,' one said, 'a grand way to go to war.' Matron O D Paschke extracted a promise from the nurses that they would be in their quarters at a respectable hour and agreed that they could dance. In a room where millionaires and aristocrats had competed in display, the band played and officers in formal rig and nurses in caps and capes stepped and swirled, foxtrotted and waltzed, clapped and bowed; and the watchers marvelled. Later more nurses sailed north with other 8th Division troops being posted to Malaya. On duty they wore the scarlet and grey of the nurses of the First War. The dress, a grey overall falling to within fourteen inches of the floor, was topped by a scarlet cloak. The white starched cuffs and collar and lisle stockings were ill-adapted for the tropics; but in peacetime Malaya they had breaks for sampan parties, chicken suppers at St John's Fort in Malacca, tennis on the courts next to the nurses' quarters, and even to take recreational leave at 'Frazer's', the hill station in the highlands beyond Kuala Lumpur.

The women who enlisted in the AANS were daughters of teachers, accountants and craftsmen; middle and lower middle class families. They had entered nursing when duty, idealism and self-denial were an implicit part of the calling. In training the nurses

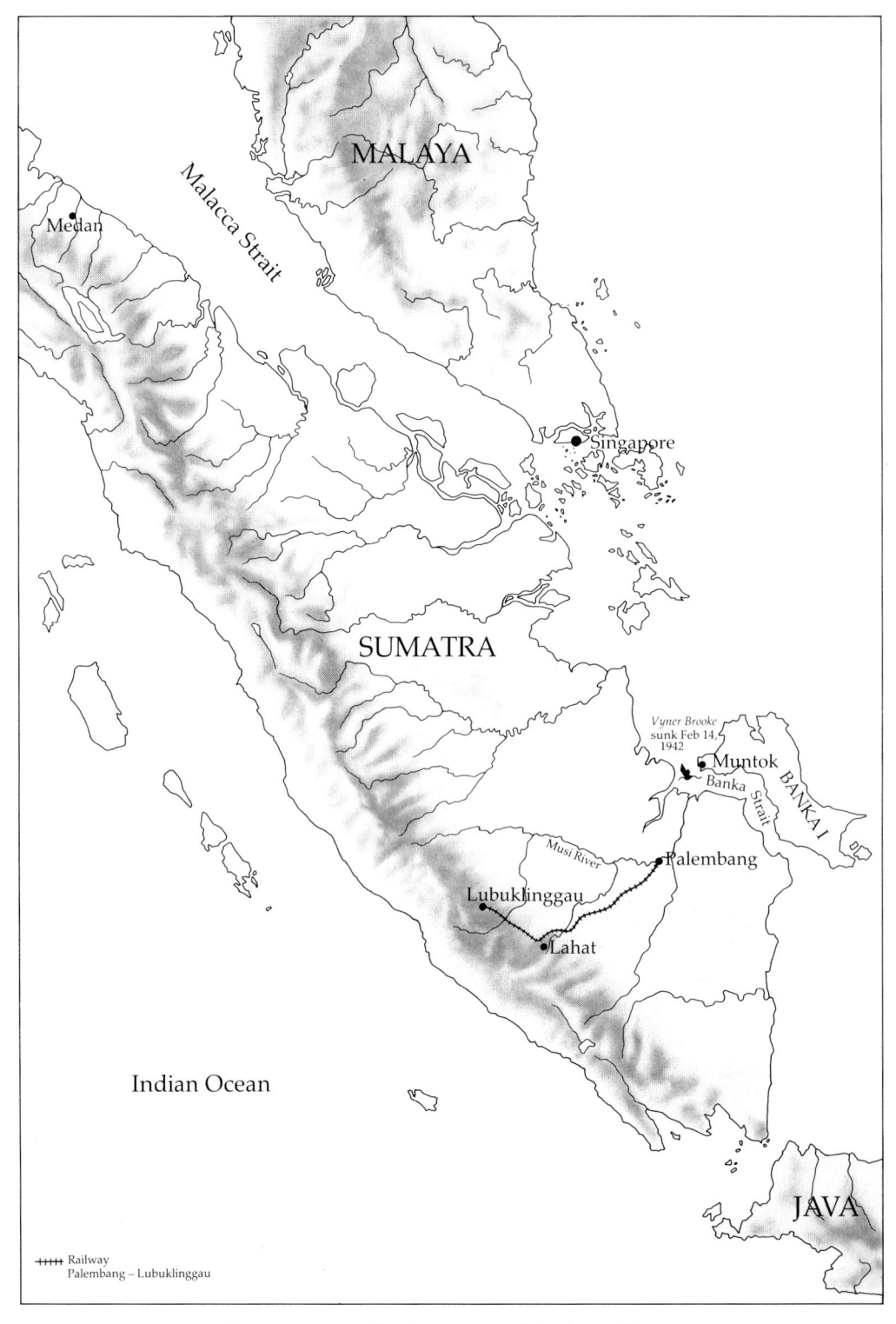

Southern Sumatra, showing camps of the Australian nurses

worked long hours for little pay, and the discipline was always strict: 'if a senior nurse said do this, you did it'. From the days of Florence Nightingale the war-time nurse was a special British heroine. In gifts to children the nurse's uniform was the female equivalent of the boys' lead and wooden soldiers. 'All my life I was going to be a nurse,' Sylvia Muir remembers, 'and go to the next war. I just trained for it. I was frightened the whole war would be over before I got there, and all my training would be wasted.' By contrast Vivian Bullwinkel at primary school in Adelaide and at high school in Broken Hill was more interested in sport; she was not concerned about planning a career. Something, she believed, 'would fall into her lap':

> It was in the depression years and my parents couldn't afford to keep me. My mother had always wanted to be a nurse, but she belonged to the generation that didn't work. She said, 'Well, what about nursing?' I sort of said yes. That's how I commenced my nursing.

Her mother, Bullwinkel concedes, knew her better than she knew herself.

The members of the AANS posted to Malaya came from all parts of Australia and, in spite of their common age and training, 'everyone was different'. Betty Jeffrey says it was as though they had been handpicked to be complementary, each having a particular temperament and interest. Sister Micky Syer's characterisation of them as 'just an ordinary bunch of women' is both true and an understatement.

Motivated by patriotism and an obligation to use their skills where they were most needed, the nurses also looked for adventure. They sailed with 'little apprehension and a lot of excitement'.

Sylvia Muir: It was all hush hush in those days; you sailed for a destination unknown. It was most exciting. Then we arrived in Malaya. I was sure no action would ever happen there. We were so far from the Middle East. It was quite a joke with me. They would say, 'Why did you join the army?' I'd say, 'To meet David Niven'. He was a major in the Middle East.

Like the men in the AIF they felt cheated by being diverted to garrison duties in a colourful backwater of Empire. On the eve of the Japanese attack 140 nurses were stationed with three units in southern Malaya: the 2/10th Australian General Hospital at Malacca, the 2/4th Casualty Clearing Station at Kluang and the 2/13th Australian General Hospital at Tampin.

Immediately the Japanese attacked in December 1941 the code word 'Raffles' was passed to all medical stations. The nurses had not gone to war; war had suddenly come to them. With the rapid advance of the Japanese the 2/10th AGH at Malacca was exposed and its staff and equipment for 600 beds had to be trucked to Oldham Hall, a school on the northern edge of Singapore city. As the Australians went into action in January the medical staffs prepared for the first rush of casualties. In a moment of anti-climax recalled by Betty Jeffrey the waiting surgical team received its first five soldiers; all were suffering from appendicitis. But soon the convoys of shattered men began arriving:

> All the wounded just kept coming and coming, one ambulance after the other, day and night; it just didn't let up. We never had enough beds. When the hospital was full after a few days we had to start taking the houses down the street. They were all evacuated, empty, and we just took them and took them and took them. So the hospital staff was very spread out. But somehow or other we just coped. No person went without care.

Civil casualties, distressed and confused, increased the demand on medical services.

In the optimism of peacetime, the medical units had planned how to keep up with advancing troops. In reality they were competing with other troops for space on trucks and roads as all units withdrew across the causeway. Wilma Oram was with the 2/13th AGH which trucked a 1200-bed hospital in less than two days into St Patrick's school. And the wounded kept coming:

> We had so many surgical casualties the mind just couldn't take it in. We were operating round the clock in the theatre and we still had them lined up outside. We could not get through them fast enough.

Between December 8 and February 15 the AIF alone suffered 405 killed, 111 dead from wounds and 1400 wounded in action.

From the first days of the fighting the nurses had witnessed air raids, but once the Japanese landed on Singapore aerial attacks increased and artillery fire was close and frequent. Oldham Hall, on the edge of the Allied perimeter, was bombed day and night. And, Nesta James says, the nearby British guns replied, adding to the confusion of sound.

Betty Jeffrey: You'd hear the shell coming. We all had our tin hats on, and as it went overhead we'd bend down, as if to keep our heads out of the way. I guess it was many feet up in the air, but you automatically did it. Then you just got on with it.

Shell fragments cut through the roofs of tents erected as temporary wards on grass tennis courts. When it rained the beds sank through the soft ground, and, Betty Jeffrey says, 'we were practically nursing on our knees'.

As early as January 20 Colonel Alfred Derham, the senior Australian medical officer, recommended that the nurses be evacuated. It is, Glyn White says, one of his blackest memories that they were unable to persuade the senior military officers to get the women away earlier. The nurses themselves were less worried. Vivian Bullwinkel remembers the rumours of impending evacuation and the determination of the nurses to stay: they had come to work 'and if this was the end of the road, well we wanted to stay in the hospital and nurse the fellows'. Even as all seemed to be falling around them the nurses shared the optimism of many of the troops. 'It didn't enter my head until about the last day,' Jeffrey says, 'that Singapore would fall. I just felt we'd win because the British always win in the end.' But on February 10 the first of the nurses left: six detailed to look after the wounded sailed on the *Wah Sui*. The next day half of the remaining nurses boarded the *Empire Star*. Two of them were decorated for attending the injured on the bombed deck of the *Empire Star* which eventually got through to Australia.

Another day later on February 12 the remaining nurses, taking letters pressed on them by soldiers anxious to get a last message home, set out for the harbour.

Sylvia Muir: We got onto the ambulances and drove through the city. It was bombed and burning, a real shambles. When we got to the wharf there was an air raid on and we had to shelter again.

Muir noticed Chinese women refugees carrying what she thought were 'pathetic little bundles' of possessions. For the next three and a half years she was to keep everything she owned in a similar 'pathetic' bundle.

In a pause in the raids the nurses left the wharf.

Vivian Bullwinkel: The senior medical men, Colonel Derham and Colonel Glyn White, were there to see us off. Some of the girls started to sing 'Now Is the Hour', which I have never liked since.

The nurses went by a small boat to a 'nasty little black ship', the *Vyner Brooke*. Crowded with 300 passengers, nearly all of them women and children, the *Vyner Brooke* survived another air raid before she got under way in the evening. The nurses, having had little rest for days, slept on the deck. The *Vyner Brooke* left harbour three days before the Allied forces on Singapore surrendered.

During daylight on February 13 the *Vyner Brooke* rode at anchor in the islets, hoping to escape being seen by Japanese aircraft. In deceptively lazy and peaceful conditions Matron Paschke called the nurses together and explained that they could not expect to get far on the *Vyner Brooke*. They carried very little food or water, they had too few life boats and attack from the air was almost certain. A strafing raid from a Japanese fighter confirmed the matron's assessment. The captain's plan to sail in the security of the night was frustrated by search lights constantly cutting through the darkness, and on Saturday, February 14, the *Vyner Brooke* was exposed on a flat sea. At about 2 o'clock in the afternoon the raid began: bombs fell, waterspouts rose from the near misses, and the *Vyner Brooke* zig-zagged. Finally, Iole Harper says, 'They dropped a bomb down the funnel which was clever of them.' Further hits followed.

Sylvia Muir: There was a lot of shrapnel, and the poor old fellow right beside me had his stomach ripped open. He was sitting there. I can still see him, hanging on and singing 'Britons never never will be slaves'. So it must be something we British, or ex-British, do. The girl beside me had her buttocks slashed open. With the impact of the bombing I was thrown over and I got my elbow cut. It seemed terrible. I looked down and my hand was full of blood; but it was nothing serious. That piece of shrapnel went in the girl beside me. I don't know if she's still got it; I must ask her one of these days. Then it was pure chaos.

The *Vyner Brooke* sank quickly. In the rush to abandon ship the nurses gave what first aid they could and helped get the aged and the children away. 'We were pretty sure,' Micky Syer says, 'that there was nobody left on the ship when it went down, and it went down in a quarter of an hour after being hit.' Iole Harper found that as the ship listed she could 'walk half way down to the water' and then jump. But Betty Jeffrey, with the self-effacing humour that helped her survive, remembers:

> I was an idiot. The ship lurched very suddenly so I grabbed a rope and slid down with my bare hands. It was a cranky thing to do because I skinned my fingers and the palms of my hands. Did that hurt! I landed in the water with all of them.

Jeffrey claims that when her head emerged from the sea she was still wearing her tin hat. The nurses were in calm, warm sea strewn with debris and struggling survivors.

Sylvia Muir: You look around and there's all these people, some of them dead. Then the boat just turned over and disappeared. Away in the distance was a little grey speck, it looked about an inch long. One of the men near me said, 'That's land. It's ten to fifteen miles away.' I'm bobbing around there, and a Chinaman grabbed me. He pulled me down, and I couldn't get away from him. It was panic. But Sister Tweddell came over, slapped him in the face, and he let me go. We had about sixteen or seventeen hours in the water.

Only two life boats were serviceable, and the rest of the passengers were dependent on hard, ungainly life jackets which kept pushing up under their chins. There was also, Micky Syer says, 'salvage from the ship, such as bits of rail, which we could hold on to. Though it didn't support us, it was a great morale booster'.

In the night one of the nurses felt the need to relieve herself:

> I decided, well, if there was one thing in the world I could do, I could do that. So I did. Of course in those days you never mentioned these things; it wasn't nice. The man behind me said, 'I think we're getting somewhere, I feel a hot current. (Later the nurse was to learn that other women had deliberately relieved themselves so they could experience the brief warmth around their numbed feet. But in the tropical sea the desire for sleep was more dangerous than cold.)

Micky Syer: You knew that you must not sleep. But I used to say, 'Please God just let me sleep for half a minute.' But you'd let go. This is why so many people drowned, I think. One of our girls had a little sleep. I saw this body drifting past, and I thought, 'Oh dear, someone has just died.' It wouldn't have been thirty seconds after that I heard, 'Oh, here! Wait, wait! Wait for me! You've left me! I fell asleep! Wait on!' She was terrified that we'd get right away from her.

Betty Jeffrey was swimming behind Iole Harper. Although handicapped by her burnt hands Jeffrey knew she 'would make it; just give me time'. After they had been swimming for several hours Harper looked back and said, 'By the way what's your name?' They exchanged names and home addresses in a mid-ocean introduction; and went on swimming. Harper was sitting in a mangrove tree on the shore line of Banka Island when Jeffrey's steady strokes finally brought her to land. On their second day in the water one group of women was picked up by Japanese landing craft, but most of the scattered swimmers were left to their own luck and energy. Two nurses, separated from the others, survived seventy-two hours in the water. Another group kept struggling teasingly close to land.

Beryl Woodbridge: We would almost touch it, and then we'd be swept out again. That upset us. We thought, 'Why can't we land?' Well, had we landed in that particular spot we'd have met with the same fate as Vivian Bullwinkel and the lasses who were with her.

Vivian Bullwinkel, clinging to the side of a life boat, came ashore on Radji beach, Banka Island. Soon twenty-two nurses and other passengers from the *Vyner Brooke* were joined by twenty British soldiers who had escaped from another boat sunk in Banka Strait. Ten or twelve people who were wounded lay on improvised stretchers at the edge of the beach. A deputation that walked to a nearby village returned with depressing news: the people refused to give any help, the island was occupied by the Japanese, and all foreigners should give themselves up. After discussing their plight the survivors decided that with so many wounded and children they would have to surrender. An officer from the *Vyner Brooke* left to walk to the town of Muntok on the north of the island and report to the Japanese. Matron I M Drummond organised the civilian women and children into a group, and under the care of a Chinese doctor they set out for Muntok and captivity. At mid morning on Monday, February 16, the ship's officer returned with a Japanese officer and a troop of fifteen soldiers.

Vivian Bullwinkel: They ordered the men up, and marched them off at rifle and bayonet point around into another cove. They came back and we knew what had happened. We'd heard no shots, but they came back wiping their bayonets. We realised what was going to happen. I can remember one of the girls saying, 'Two things that I hate most, the sea and the Japs, and I've got them both'. We were all sitting down, and we were ordered up, and then told to march into the sea. Which we did. As we got to about waist level they started machine gunning from behind. I was hit just at the side of the back. The bullet came though, but I wasn't aware of it at the time. I thought that once you were shot you'd had it. What with the force of the bullet and the waves I was knocked over into the water. And in doing so I swallowed a lot of water. I became violently ill, and as I stood I realised I was very much alive. Next thing I thought, they'll see me heaving. I tried to stop and I just lay there. I wouldn't know how long. When I did venture to sit up, there was nothing. All my colleagues had been swept away, and there were no Japs on the beach. There was nothing. Just me. I got up, crossed the beach, and went into the jungle.

Either unconscious or asleep Bullwinkel lay in the vegetation on the edge of the beach. She woke and it was dark. When she awoke again it was well into the next day. Everything was quiet, but her eyes caught movement. From her prone position she saw a line of helmets and bayonets disappearing down the track to the beach. The Japanese soldiers had already passed close to her. Not daring to move she waited until they came back and, she says, 'I swear I looked into every pair of eyes that went past'. Desperately thirsty Bullwinkel went towards the beach to find drinking water. Suddenly an English voice said, 'Where have you been, nurse?' The sound hit her almost with the impact of another bullet.

The man who had spoken was Private Kingsley. Taken ashore wounded, he had been bayoneted as he lay on a stretcher. They decided to combine their injured resources, but immediately, Bullwinkel says, they had their first difference of opinion. He had crawled to shelter in a fisherman's hut built over the water; she had her haven on the edge of the jungle; and both felt an urge to return to their own place of refuge. They went together into the jungle. Bullwinkel carried bottles and life jackets collected from the beach. With the life jackets she made a bed for Kingsley and using coconut fibre she wrapped a gaping wound on his upper arm. When she had time to investigate the bullet wound in her own body she found clean entry and exit wounds just above the hip, and with each day she felt stronger. Bullwinkel had been one of the party which had walked to the village before the massacre, and now in even greater need she asked again for help. Again the head men refused, but as she reached the edge of the village the women pressed food upon her. The same rejection by the men and compassion from the women were repeated on two later visits.

Ten days after the killings on Radji beach Bullwinkel said to Kingsley:

> We can't go on like this. We're not going to die as quickly as we thought. I think the only thing we can do is to give ourselves up and hope they do a better job. He agreed. 'But,' he said, 'do you mind if we leave it for another twenty-four hours because I'll be thirty-nine tomorrow, and I'd like to think I had my thirty-ninth birthday free.' I said, 'Well, time's no object.' So we had another twenty-four hours out there while he had his thirty-ninth birthday in freedom.

On the road into Muntok they were picked up by a car carrying a Japanese soldier and a naval officer. Bullwinkel concealed her wound with a water bottle, and Kingsley had taken a shirt from one of the bodies on the beach to cover his injuries.

As they came into Muntok Bullwinkel's confidence rose:

> We turned the corner and I saw a line of European servicemen. I thought, 'They are taking prisoners.' There was much shouting as the car drew up. I was told to get out, I went into a building, and an Englishman came forward and said, 'Nice to see you, Sister. Can I have your name, number, and unit?' Down at the far end all I could see was a mass of faces. So quite calmly I started telling him my name and my number. Then somebody said, 'It's Bullwinkel!' That was the end. Somebody there knew

me! I went blindly towards the voice with the Englishman saying, 'But I've only got two or three more questions to ask you.' I said, 'I don't care! Somebody knows me!' And I howled happily. It was two of the girls from the 10th Australian General Hospital. They grabbed me, took me over, and I met up with those who'd already been taken prisoner. I'd made up my mind that I was not going to say anything about what had happened on the beach or who the girls were. But of course everyone they asked me about was one of the girls on the beach. For about the first six I said, 'No, I don't know what happened. I don't know.' Then I broke down, and I said, 'Yes, I do know what happened.' And I told them. Of course they were just appalled. Our senior nurse, Sister James, said I must go and tell the intelligence fellows, they'd got to know. They said, 'Well for God's sake don't talk about it. Don't say anything. Just forget about it. If an inkling of it gets out to the Japanese you'll all be taken out and killed.' From that day until we got home the girls were marvellous. Those who weren't there at the time I was telling the story never asked me anything further about it.

The fate of their comrades on Radji beach was constantly in the minds of the nurses, but even when a group of them were alone they did not talk of the incident. Of the sixty-five nurses on the *Vyner Brooke* twelve had drowned, twenty-one had been killed on the beach, and thirty-two had gone into prison. Private Kingsley died a few days after he arrived in Muntok.

In the Australian Mandated Territory of New Guinea another six nurses with the 2/10th Field Ambulance were in the path of the advancing Japanese. In March 1941 they had been posted to Rabaul on New Britain to serve with the 2/22nd Battalion and other units of Lark Force. Japanese bombs fell intermittently, and the dust and ash of volcanoes fell frequently before the hospital was shifted east along the coast to Kokopo. The nurses made the journey on the eve of invasion. In the night they heard the sounds of battle and at daylight on January 23 they 'counted forty-nine boats' of the Japanese attack force stretching away to their left. Padre John May of the Church of England went forward carrying a white handkerchief to meet the Japanese:

> At about ten to eleven we heard people shouting. There was a line of Japanese coming up the grass in front of the hospital, fixed bayonets and all at the ready, making a terrific din as they did, shouting to keep their courage up. We had some Red Cross bed covers which we'd hung up to show that we were a hospital. They came up and took charge of us and established a guard in the middle of the hospital verandah. The nurses were naturally worried and Sister Parker, who was the senior, had a tiny pistol which she carried in her handbag. She wanted to keep it. But when we decided we'd better lock up the rifles she agreed that she'd better hand it over.

All the army doctors and orderlies, except two men, had left earlier, joining the general retreat of Lark Force. Civil and mission nurses had stayed with the army nurses and over one hundred sick and wounded.

Sister Tootie McPherson: The Japanese said that as we had no doctors we were not nurses at all: we were there for the use of the troops. They got their Tommy guns, put a gun on each of us, and we had to stand there with our arms up surrendering for an eternity.

At last the Japanese declared, 'You will not be shot today'. The confrontation had been more than dramatic intimidation. About twenty of the patients were taken away, executed and buried in a mass grave.

In their first days of captivity the nurses lived in constant fear, sometimes sleeping under the patients' beds in the hope of finding somewhere secure. They suffered some violence.

McPherson: I got the most fearful whack and I was knocked down and got a few kicks because I didn't bow deep enough. I did bow my head, very begrudgingly; but from then on I did bow deeply. Some of the Japanese were so dreadful, and they thought we were just big jokes. Many's the time they chased us trying to urinate on us while the rest of them just stayed back and screamed with laughter. It was nothing for them to take their trousers off and things like that. We just had to put up with it.

As Mavis Cullen explains, the nurses had a last resort:

The only plan if things got too bad and we felt we couldn't cope was that we each had a tube of morphine in our uniform pocket. We carried that until we discarded it when we got to Japan. It was just something to hang on to if things got too bad.

The nurses took some satisfaction from never letting the Japanese see them weep; but they cried in private. They also found themselves in the ironical position of having to comfort some Japanese soldiers; they were boys of fourteen who were lonely and bewildered.

The nurses were separated from their patients and in July they were suddenly told that they were to be shifted. The six army, seven civilian and four Methodist mission nurses and two other women were taken by small boat to the *Naruto Maru* and sailed for Japan. Also on board were the officers from the Rabaul force. Nearly all of the other ranks and the men of the civil administration of New Guinea had already sailed for Japan on the *Montevideo Maru*. No prisoners from the *Montevideo Maru* were seen again. The most probable explanation is that the 1000 Australians on board were drowned when the *Montevideo Maru* was torpedoed off the coast of the Philippines by an American submarine. The nurses and officers on the *Naruto Maru* were among the first Australian prisoners to be imprisoned in the Japanese homeland.

On Banka Island the nurses stayed in the unsanitary stench of the Muntok coolie gaol for a fortnight before they were shipped across Banka Strait, and up the Musi River to Palembang in southern Sumatra. Standing on the backs of trucks they were driven through sporadic jeers to temporary residence in a school. The next day they were shifted to houses.

Sylvia Muir: Most of them had two bedrooms, a lounge-dining room, a kitchen outside, a bathroom and a garage. They'd put up to twenty-eight people into these. They ran barbed wire around you, and that was the perimeter of your camp. We got up to what we called breakfast. We just boiled so much of the rice. We would get into 'congsies' [from the Chinese word for company], so many to a small group. It was easier. You'd pool so much rice, and you boiled it and boiled it until it was just a gluey, thin mess. That was breakfast and you had tea or your coffee if you were lucky. Then your rations would come. We had cigarette or Klim tins for our measure. You can't believe what it is not to have food. You always had to hold some food back in case you didn't have anything to eat. That was one of the frightening parts. Even your rice ration mightn't turn up. Then they'd bring in carrots or something. But by this time we were probably up to 600 women, and you'd have one sugar bag of carrots. We used to cut all the tops up one day and serve them. The next day we'd cut the bottoms up. You might only get three very very thin slices.

Women moving from one group of prisoners to another found that the topic of conversation had not changed; it was always food. They described meals, talked of cooking techniques, exchanged recipes and, Iole Harper says, 'every picture was something to do with food. We had one in the house; it was a Christmas turkey. That was our favourite picture.'

Just maintaining the camp involved constant work.

Sylvia Muir: We had ourselves beautifully organised. We had squads for everything. We had a ration squad. If you were on that you went down and helped with the rations. Then there was the wash-up squad. We had the nursing squad. You'd go around with the doctors and try and help. We had the hygiene squad which used to go round and see that people kept their camps clean, and sweep out the drains.

One of the civilian internees, Edith Leembruggen, remembers the hard work and expertise of the nurses. When everyone was sick and weak, the nurses, she says, were still giving their time and energy to help others.

After the first months Dutch and some Eurasian women and children were forced to join the British women in Palembang. The nurses and other women who had come ashore from bomb-wrecked boats were at a disadvantage. They went into prison physically weakened and with almost no money and no possessions. One nurse had walked into camp wearing only a man's overcoat and her corset; her dress had been used as a sail on a raft. The nurses' advantages were their long term health, their professional skills, their conditioning to hard work, and their group strength.

Iole Harper: The Dutch had money, and we didn't have any. Some of them had suitcases full of clothes. The Dutch were very good, and some of the British gave us clothes, and some didn't. They used to come out looking like they were going to a garden party in the afternoon. They weren't very well thought of, but nobody did or said anything. What was the use? Three of those that dressed like that didn't last the course, so it availed them but little.

The nurses, Bullwinkel says, worked to redress the imbalance in wealth:

> As time went on women became weak and they wouldn't or didn't want to do their camp chores. And those with money were prepared to pay. So that's when we came in. We said, right, we'll do the chores and you can pay us. Then when the Japanese allowed a trader to come in we were able to buy some fruit and things. Other girls used to cook the rice, make it up very attractively, and sell that.

Betty Jeffrey says: I was the local hairdresser. Somebody had a pair of curved nail scissors, about two and a half inches long. Curved nail scissors trying to cut hair! I used to charge ten cents. Very cheap!

When one of the nurses became ill, and they all did at times, then one of the others took over, 'keeping the job in the family'.

As with the nurses captured in New Guinea, the fear of rape was most intense in the first weeks of imprisonment; and it could not completely disappear where guards slapped women, pushed them around and gave them no privacy. 'It was,' Micky Syer says, 'very unpleasant to be continually on the alert. They used to walk in and out and leer at you.' The fear and revulsion of the nurses was intensified because they knew the Japanese as the compatriots of the men who killed their colleagues on the beach at Banka Island.

In 1942 they faced an explicit threat.

Sylvia Muir: They moved us out of two houses and took the rest of the civilian women and men round the corner, just away from us. Under Japanese orders we cleaned out the houses and put in beds. All being young and full of fun we promptly called it Lavender Street, which was the brothel area of Singapore. And then we found it wasn't fun. That was what they intended it for.

The houses were to be the officers' club, and the nurses were to be the 'entertainers'. When the nurses refused, the Japanese told them they had no choice. An Englishwoman and fellow passenger from the *Vyner Brooke* increased the nurses' sense of insecurity by acting as procurer for the Japanese. The officers demanded six women for the night, and the nurses countered with group solidarity: all who could get away from other duties arrived at the club.

Vivian Bullwinkel: We sat there for about an hour because I think they were absolutely overwhelmed by so many women coming in. Of course we'd all dragged our hair back, we had no makeup, and we looked ghastly. After an hour they said we could go. We all got up to go, bowed, said goodnight, and all marched out again. We were all much taller than they were, and the whole thing became a fiasco.

The next day the nurses asked the Dutch Red Cross representative and the senior British officer in the men's camp to protest on their behalf. Whether it was the result of official intervention, or intimidation by female mob strength, or other reasons the Japanese did not repeat their demand for entertainers.

Other women in the camp were ready to trade sex for favours.

Iole Harper: There were plenty there who were quite happy to have it on. So why bother about haggish looking nurses? You've got 500 or something women, and at least fifty of those who are only too anxious. They'd be given food and money, and if that was their scene, why not? It didn't matter to them whether they were Japanese or anything else.

A young woman who was a recent arrival in the camp told the nurses that they looked like 'a lot of withered peas'. If that saved them from being molested, then it was some compensation.

Shock and physical deprivation solved another problem. For some of the women menstruation 'stopped when they jumped into the water'. Others were able to give up 'pinching bits of curtain material' as they lost weight on their inadequate diet. They greeted the end of an inconvenience: 'As we used to say, ain't nature grand'. After they had been in camp for three years and all had long since ceased menstruating the Japanese Commandant made one issue of cotton wool and voile-like material with the explanation, 'Ladies require them'.

Dirt and lack of privacy went together.

Nesta James: As we were on a rice diet, we practically lived in the toilets. You'd go to the toilets at night, and you'd find somebody had fainted into one. You'd have to get her out, and try and get some water to wash her. There was no privacy whatsoever in the camp. You just had a small portion of bamboo that you lay on, touching the other person all the time. It did become very awkward. You had to control your tongue so that you didn't say unwise things because you were irritated by the lack of privacy. You were never away from everybody.

A woman in another camp wrote how she longed for a smooth-tiled rest room equipped with Kleenex, Cutex, Kotex and scented soap.

In the first years of imprisonment the nurses maintained their morale by celebrating birthdays and holidays. At festive meals 'everything was rice', Sylvia Muir remembers, 'but what we called it was nobody's business. On each plate were Parachute Drop

Scones, Ack Ack Puffs, Palembang Pastries and Prefreedom Sandwiches'. At Christmas 1942 they even served a powerful draft of home made chilli wine. Having rescued a piano from some Dutch women, the nurses 'dragged it past six houses up a slope'. With the shortage of space someone had to sleep on the piano at night, but even its polished surface was warmer than the tiled floor. Soon all the camp could sing Waltzing Matilda.

Betty Jeffrey: We started having concerts with this piano. We used to have sing-songs, and put on silly plays that were hilarious. In the end we had to get out of the house, and just have concerts every night out in the street in front.

At one concert, Beryl Woodbridge says, a 'very little guard was sitting at the back and when we sang "There'll Always be an England" he was humming and beating time'. Three talented civilian women helped transform the camp concerts into art. Margaret Dryburgh, an interned missionary, composed music and Marjory Jennings and Norah Chambers could write and arrange. With Norah Chambers as conductor the women formed an orchestra of voices. Individuals imitated instruments and additional sound came from a chorus of humming.

Betty Jeffrey: At night we would come together in the Dutch kitchen with the one little bare globe over us, and with our scrappy clothes. In these awful, awful conditions Norah would conduct us, and we'd put the sounds together. It was just out of this world. Absolutely beautiful. You weren't in the prison camp any more, you were in a concert hall somewhere. The sound was really excellent. When we gave our first concert everybody dressed up. It was in a little shed in the middle of a quadrangle where we had school for the kids, little concerts, meetings, gatherings and funerals—forget the funerals. We had our first concert there and the Japs tried to stop us. They came running up because we were never allowed to be in large groups. When they saw the people on this evening in their best rags, and little kids with bows in their hair, gathering at this place they immediately became suspicious. But we were ready to start, and as they came rushing up saying, 'You! Don't do this!' Norah started the concert and they just stopped in their tracks. I think the first thing we did was the Largo from the New World Symphony which was absolutely gorgeous. They just stopped. They were human beings, they were away from home, we were away from home, and I think that's about the first time we ever saw eye to eye with them.

When they shifted camp they lost the piano, and their capacity for concerts receded with their health. Margaret Dryburgh died in April 1945; she was an extraordinary woman revered by the survivors of Banka and Sumatra. She had written their anthem, 'The Captive's Hymn'.

On their arrival in Japan the nurses captured in New Guinea were placed in the Bund Hotel on the Yokohama waterfront. Food was adequate and, Mavis Cullen says, 'our hopes were high. We saw the ships in the harbour and we thought any day we'll be going home'. They attached their optimism to a particular vessel marked with white crosses; that was the ship that would carry them south. After a few weeks they were shifted to a screened-off section of the Yokohama Yacht Club. They got less food, but from their seafront quarters they could sometimes use a bamboo pole and wire, not to catch fish, but to hook edible vegetable refuse from the water. The forced inactivity of the first months did not last.

Tootie McPherson: They started us making envelopes. Well, we made millions of envelopes, but we found that we could eat the glue. When they discovered we were eating the glue they decided we couldn't make any more of those. So then we had to knit little bags. They put images of their gods in the bags. We were never allowed to see these, but we made millions of the bags. During that time, except if we were on duty downstairs, we never put foot on ground for nine months; we were kept upstairs. We had plenty of water. There were three showers, cold water of course.

Once a month some of the gold-braided officers used to come and bring up soap and toilet things, and always a roll of toilet paper. They lined us up, gave it to us, and we had to bow forward: we were happy to bow to get it. On the eighth day of every month we had to go outside with the gold braid, and bow towards the Emperor's palace. We didn't mind doing that. The flag went down the line of the nineteen of us and we were supposed to kiss it. Instead of kissing it we spat on it and we all said, 'Bugger the Emperor'. The gold braid stood there and smiled and thought we were simply wonderful. Then up went the flag and upstairs we went. That was a real outing because that happened every month. But once the white ship went and we weren't on it, then we knew that we were prisoners-of-war and we were treated like prisoners-of-war that were never to be released. They put us to hard manual work. Occasionally we had to go out and sweep the streets and help cart the coal. Any work at all that needed doing, we were sent to do.

Unlike the women in Sumatra, the nurses in Japan had a woman as their head gaoler. Known as 'Mama San', she was a matron from a home for delinquents and her presence did not protect the nurses from face slapping by angry male guards.

In their last year in captivity the women were moved to a disused hospital at Totsuka on the edge of Yokohama. The chance to get out into the open, to look at Mount Fuji, did not compensate for the hunger, cold and hard work in the gardens. They became expert thieves, carrying home vegetables which they often had to eat raw. At one stage they obtained a dog.

McPherson: We thought that if we could feed the dog up a bit, when it was big enough we could have some dog meat. The time came and Kay Parker, who was the wonder of the world, said, 'I'll kill the dog.' I said, 'I'll help skin it, but I can't kill it.' Three days before the dog was to be killed it produced pups. So we didn't have the dog.

Only people who have been starving, McPherson claims, could understand their 'terrible disappointment' when they declined the meat.

From conversations with their guards and what they could learn from newspapers the nurses in Japan had some idea of the progress of the war. They learnt of the advance of the Allies, they saw the evidence of Allied strength in the planes overhead, and they heard and felt the massive raids on Tokyo and Yokohama. During their last winter in captivity the nurses, Mavis Cullen says, were at their worst:

We were losing weight and we were hungry and it was cold. And we were all sick. I escaped malaria, but we all had dysentery, beriberi and tapeworm.

After the Japanese admitted that they had surrendered, the guards became more generous and a few days later supplies floated down on parachutes. Relief came too late for Sister Eileen Callaghan. She had contracted tuberculosis, and without medical attention and suffering from malnutrition she declined beyond the recovery point.

The nurses on Sumatra also shifted camp in 1944. With the usual confusion, waiting and crowding, they went back to Banka Island. The quarters in Muntok were adequate, but water was scarce and fever rife. Sylvia Muir remembers the frightening pattern of malaria: 'if you felt well one day you knew what was going to happen; you'd be down with fever the next day. It seemed to work like that.' The effects of chronic malnutrition were visible everywhere:

> Sores wouldn't heal. Your hair was getting thinner. You were so thin that you'd scratch and you'd get your finger caught in your ribs. And what used to fascinate me—my sense of humour—you'd go down to the ablutions and instead of seeing nice rounded little buttocks there would be all these little wrinkles hanging down, in quite young people.
>
> But towards the end you'd get an attack of malaria and you wouldn't be interested in anything for about three days. You'd wake up and say, 'Where's so and so?' 'Oh, she died.' It became just so routine.

Muntok drained life from the women.

No nurses had died in the first years of imprisonment, but by 1945 they were vulnerable.

Vivian Bullwinkel: I think the worst was when our girls commenced to die. This was so harrowing. You felt that it shouldn't have happened, and there was nothing you could do; nothing could be done. It was just soul-destroying.

On Banka Island a lethal fever killed quickly. It was, Wilma Oram says, like a cerebral malaria: 'they would die in twenty-four hours'.

In April 1945 the women were harried into another shift. Again they went by ship across Banka Strait, but this time they went by train and truck beyond Palembang to an isolated rubber plantation at Lubuklinggau in western Sumatra. Eight women died on the journey. Still living in a malarial area and having to work hard to subsist, the nurses continued to decline. Four of them had died on Banka and four more now died at Lubuklinggau. The last death took place three days after the Japanese surrendered, but the nurses were almost completely cut off from news of events beyond the wire. They had not heard about the Allies island-hopping through the Pacific or of the end of the war in Europe. When they were told that the Japanese had surrendered the messenger and the message were unexpected, and both were hard to believe.

Betty Jeffrey: A little Chinese girl who lived with the Dutch nuns next door went past and said, 'War is over. War is over at six o'clock'. It was about four o'clock then. 'War is over at six o'clock.' We just laughed, and went on with what we were doing. Then our girls came back. I remember Flo Trotter was one of them, Blanche Hempsted was another one. Sister James and I were sitting out on the step in front of our place. I don't know what we were doing, picking over rice or something, we were always working. They said, 'It is. It's over, the war's over.' We just couldn't believe it. It made us all numb, dumb. It was all fairly flat for a couple of hours. Then it sank in: war is over, we are free! But where can we go? There was nowhere. So we stayed put. But the message was that the war was over and the Allies would be here soon to take you all home. So come on the Allies.

There was, Sylvia Muir adds, a significant piece of news still missing:

> We were all sitting deciding what we would do when we got home. It was all most exciting, and somebody said, 'I suppose we did win the war.' Nobody had bothered to ask! They just took it for granted.

The forlorn demeanor and the changed behaviour of the guards told everyone who had won. The Japanese released food and medicine, including life-saving quinine.

Now that release was near the anxiety of the girls to leave their camp of mud and death increased. But the Australian authorities had great trouble finding the missing nurses; it was three weeks before paratroopers, including two Australians, arrived at Lubuklinggau.

Vivian Bullwinkel: They were no more than nineteen or twenty. One was from Perth and one was from Melbourne. We took them into our hut and sat them down. Now there we were half our hair falling out, half our teeth falling out. The two kids sat down and we plied them with all sorts of questions: Who'd won the grand final? What about the Melbourne Cup? What were they doing about permanent waves now? One of the boys said they had cold waves now. We thought, 'Oh isn't he sweet. He knows nothing about permanent waving and he's just trying to please us.' They told us about jeeps and B29s and it was quite a foreign language. Although we were exalted at seeing these two boys when they left we all sat down and thought, Lord, can we face it when we go out? It's a different world. For five split seconds we thought we'd better stay where we were.

The nurses' desire for the comforts of the outside world was stimulated when an aircraft from Cocos Island dropped fresh bread on the camp.

With as little warning as their guards had given them of major shifts, the nurses were told through a tenuous line of command to assemble at a nearby airstrip. They waited in their patched grey dresses through most of the day.

Betty Jeffrey: Then the plane came in, a little DC3 which we thought was magnificent. It looked like a splinter on the horizon, just coming, just coming, and it got bigger and bigger, and it came in and landed.

Micky Syer remembers the door opening and her disappointment: 'We'd hoped that perhaps there'd have been a woman come to meet us'. Then suddenly they realised that three of the figures in trousers and safari jackets were women. 'Pants,' Sylvia Muir explains, 'weren't heard of. Not long pants like men wear.' One of the women was Matron A M Sage, Matron-in-Chief of the AANS. But many of the nurses did not recognise her.

Micky Syer: We said to her, 'Who are you? You've got an Australian badge on.' She said, 'I'm the mother of you all.' And she just held out her arms and we flopped around her, everybody weeping copious tears. 'But', she said, 'where are the rest of you?' She was hoping to see sixty-five. And there were twenty-four of us. Nobody spoke.

CHAPTER SEVEN

THE LONG CARRY

'It was one of those things that creates a mental scar. Those mental scars never heal. They never come good.'

In December 1941 the men of the 2/21st Battalion and attached troops became Gull Force and sailed on three small Dutch packets for the south Moluccan land known variously as Ambon or Amboina; but it was Ambon to the Australians. 'There was no man' Roy Harris says, 'who didn't want to leave Darwin.' The 2/21st had been formed largely from men of the Riverina, country Victoria and Melbourne: they were Bourke Street and the bush. Fred Perrin thinks that 'maybe twenty blokes were from Deniliquin'; and Fred eventually got back there again. Bill Cook, one of the youngest members of the battalion band, remembers the home towns of his fellow bandsmen: Mildura, Yarram, Colac, Terang, Geelong and Melbourne. The battalion made the long train and truck journey from Bonegilla in Victoria through Alice Springs to Darwin when other units with less training were sailing for overseas. Drawn from the sort of men who won acclaim in other units in two world wars, they were bored by much of the camp building and garrison duties of Darwin, and found it difficult to keep out of 'a bit of strife'. Many had never heard of Ambon; but at last they were getting overseas and, perhaps, closer to war. Nine days after the Japanese attacked in the Pacific the 1100 men of Gull Force marched to the beat of drums and the flourish of brass into Tantui barracks near the town of Ambon. They had gone to their exposed defensive position when the Japanese were already on their way south.

Ambon, a rough, heavily timbered island only fifty kilometres long, was closer to Darwin than Darwin was to Alice Springs. The Dutch had 2600 European and Indonesian troops to defend this minor part of their empire in the east, and the Dutch commander, Lieutenant-Colonel J R L Kapitz, took seniority over the Australians. Uncertain where the Japanese would land, Kapitz divided his forces. Over 300 men of Gull Force were sent to defend the Laha airfield on the west of the gash of water that almost cuts the island in two, and the rest of the Australians were deployed on the east of the gulf, and south of the town of Ambon. The men of Gull Force faced an impossible task, and their commander, Lieutenant-Colonel L N Roach, knew it. Gull Force had no air or naval support, and almost no heavy weapons. The troops were not on Ambon long enough to co-ordinate their training with the Dutch. The Force could not fight off a large landing force: it was not trained or equipped for guerilla warfare, and the land area of Ambon was too small to support an independent force. Unsure whether he should plan a delaying action, fight to the last, or expect to be lifted from the beach, Roach wrote for specific instructions. He was told to 'put up the best defence possible with resources you have'. The headquarters staff officer, W J R Scott, who received Roach's misgivings, recommended that the commander of Gull Force be recalled and offered himself as replacement. Scott was appointed immediately. The new commander of Gull Force had a distinguished record of leadership in the First World War, but at fifty-three he was older than other battalion commanders and he had no time to win the support of the troops. The men resented that Roach, 'a gentleman', had been 'top-hatted out of the army'—'we suffered a kick in the arse'—and many of them knew about Roach's pessimistic reports. The confidence of the troops, Roy Harris says, was not increased when the last of the departing airforce men said: 'If you could see what was coming to meet you, you'd start swimming for Australia tomorrow. You haven't got Buckley's hope.'

On January 31 the Japanese attacked in strength. At Laha the fighting was close and intense. One group of nine wounded, cut off in the fighting, escaped in an Ambonese *prau* and eventually reached Australia. Another three men, also separated from the main force early in the battle, joined the rest of Gull Force on the east of the island. Perhaps half of the Australians at Laha were killed in action and all those who surrendered were killed by the Japanese within two weeks of fighting. A total of 309 Australians died in defence of Laha airfield. The Australians at battle south of Ambon heard the sound of gunfire across the water, saw the Japanese flag raised above Laha, but did not know what had happened to their comrades until after the war.

On the eastern peninsula the Japanese landed on undefended parts of the coasts and moved rapidly overland. The Australians immediately lost contact with the Dutch. The sounds of gunfire, Japanese ships in the bay and Japanese aircraft overhead told the Australians that they were at war; but how many enemy soldiers they had to fight and where they were was unclear. Roy Harris, a cook, was in what was supposed to be a rear position near Amahusu:

> We were camped on the road. When we saw the Japanese riding their bicycles up towards us, that's the first notice we had. We had no idea what a Japanese looked like, but we woke up. We fired the first shots of the Australians in our section. Then we scampered up to D Company lines. We did shelter halfway up and the Japanese landed a rifle grenade on the pill box and killed one chap and injured three of us. The rest of us got back up to headquarters. From then it was on properly.

Private John Devenish was on higher ground: It was difficult to know what to do. All we had were 303s and a certain amount of ammunition. When they got close enough we got orders to fire at will. So we just opened up wherever we could; wherever we saw a body move we fired at it. I suppose we were shooting anything from one to two thousand yards. Of course off the side of a mountain you could set the trajectory of your weapons to get the maximum distance and we were managing to land slugs right in amongst them. We later found that we'd killed quite a big number. We battled on and belted slugs into them for the three or four days that we were there.

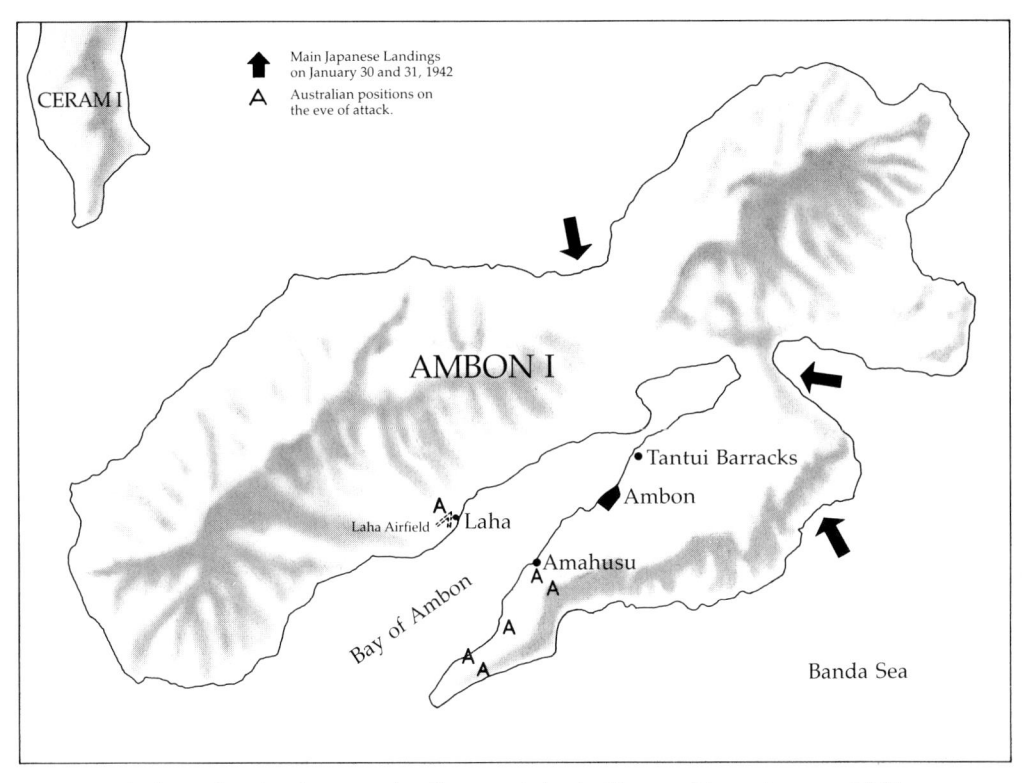

Ambon, showing Japanese landings and Australian positions, January 1942

Dutch and Ambonese troops escaping from the fighting further north moved back through the Australian lines; and some Australians, knowing that the position was hopeless, decided to 'toss it in'. The majority, forced to retreat through their own barbed wire because the Japanese had come the 'wrong way', pushed south.

The Dutch surrendered on February 1 and by February 3 the main force of Australians was surrounded. Having gone through three days without sleep and with little food, they did not have the energy let alone the equipment to counter attack. The men of Gull Force faced heavy casualties from shelling and strafing without being able to inflict significant damage on the enemy. Captain William Aitken, a medical officer, went forward to negotiate with the Japanese, and Scott assembled his men for captivity. Bill Cook said to himself, 'Cookie, you're mad, you bastard', as he tried to stop a Japanese soldier seizing his watch. But a Japanese officer came up, slapped the soldier, the soldier bowed, was slapped and bowed again. The officer said something incomprehensible; but his action had been encouraging. About 800 Australians marched under Japanese orders past the waiting photographers and into Ambon town. At a brief halt men snatched bottles of drinks from a shop: the unlucky Jimmy Duncan grabbed and gulped a bottle of mosquito repellant. The men went as prisoners into their old barracks at Tantui.

In the first weeks of captivity morale was 'fairly high'. The men, Private Jack Panaotie says, believed that because they were so close to Australia and Ambon was 'such a vital island' they would be the first to be liberated in the Allies' massive counter advance. And conditions in Tantui were about as good after surrender as before.

Private George Williamson: Things were that easy. You could have your own little vegetable garden, keep your own chooks, have your own eggs, and all that sort of business. You could buy soap and sugar off the natives as they went through the camp. The first three months were like a holiday. There was nothing to do but just get up in the morning and play cards or basketball; you could play anything. It got that monotonous that men were asking to go out to work. When the work parties started there used to be a scramble to get on them. And to finish up it was a scramble to get off. If you had watches, pens or rings the Japanese would buy them off you, and then you'd have money to play with. The main road used to go through the camp and the Japanese would stop people going into market. If you were lucky enough they'd let you buy off the women taking their fruit and stuff to the market.

And the three strand barbed wire fence which the prisoners put up was no barrier to those who wanted to trade and explore in the night.

About 300 Dutch soldiers, and later Dutch women and children, lived in separate wired-off areas within the camp. Fourteen Americans who had escaped from the Philippines and washed up on western New Guinea were imprisoned with the Australians. The Japanese, after they had helped themselves to most of the sugar and canned fruit, let the Australians use their own stores, and the prisoners tipped the familiar contents of tins with familiar labels into their rice. In contrast with the tents they had lived in near Darwin where there was 'only scrub and more scrub' the *atap* roofs, wooden walls and concrete floors of Tantui barracks sited on the slope of Ambon Bay had attracted the men of Gull Force in December 1941, and they still had their comfortable huts. But now they were centres of inactivity. The Australians broke the boredom with their own peculiar humour; and in doing so did more to separate themselves from the Dutch than any Japanese orders.

Williamson: The game of pretend went on all the time, with leading a dog around on a string, telling it to sit down and behave itself, kicking it, and all this sort of business. That went on much to the guards' delight. They'd be looking and they'd reckon we were all nuts. They'd reckon we'd all gone stir crazy or something. But there were lots of funny little things went on. We used to put on some good concerts early in the piece. They'd make up plays or skits, mostly about the Japanese, and about us and about everybody. There was nobody left out, put it that way.

Panaotie: We used to have a fellow named Pat Balmer, and he was a drover. During the concerts he'd bring this fellow in with a rope around his neck, he'd be stripped off naked, and he'd have his behind painted red, white and blue. He'd take his dentures out and he had the two tusks of his own teeth. Pat would crack the whip and this bloke, he was pretty active, he'd run up the rafters, scratch himself and run around like a monkey.

The Japanese's most frequent request to the band was for 'Blue Heaven'.

Six weeks after the Australians surrendered Lieutenant Bill Jinkins and six other men escaped, took a *prau* and sailed island to island to Australia. Jinkins reported that on Ambon 'The treatment by the Japs was as fair as it could be'. The daily routine, he said, began with physical training; during the day the men played sports; they did courses in shorthand, law, motor mechanics, English literature, solo, whist, bridge and other subjects; and the battalion band could practise until 6.30 at night. That was the last authoritative account that Australian headquarters was to hear of the men on Ambon until September 1945. In fact conditions began to get tougher in response to the escape, but the real end to the days of casual imprisonment came in the form of a brutal drama. In July 1942 thirty-four Dutch prisoners were accused by the Japanese of sending messages to their wives in a neighbouring camp. The messages had no military importance. The Dutchmen, assembled on a slope in full view of the Australians, waited for their punishment.

Panaotie: They had them stand out in the sun from early in the morning and then when we came back they were still there. That was a Sunday, I remember. Then out came two truckloads of drunken Japanese marines. They were armed with baseball bats and pick handles and all that sort of thing. The ones that didn't have them were getting star pickets.

John Devenish: The commandant would blow a whistle, and he'd give his troops three minute rounds, just like a heavyweight boxing championship, bashing the Dutchmen up with these posts.

Lieutenant John van Nooten: I was some one hundred yards away. It went on for two hours or more; at the time it seemed to go on all day. There were terrible screams of agony, and the Dutch eventually quietened because a lot of them were unconscious.

Panaotie: And then they sent out fellows with stretchers to bring them down. They had broken arms and legs and fractured skulls. We'd never seen anything like it.

Van Nooten: This I think was the first occasion on which we realised how the Japanese could react. It was a kind of butchery for a Roman holiday with those who were performing the acts doing so to show how good they were, and the onlookers egging them on and thoroughly enjoying it. It was sadistic and quite horrifying. Three Dutch officers were either killed or died of injuries, eighteen or twenty were stretcher cases. A shocking state of affairs.

Devenish: It was one of those things that creates a mental scar. These mental scars never heal. They never come good. There's some damage to the brain, and the scar tissue never repairs itself. All you could say was that the men more or less from now on just acted like zombies or robots. They just did as they were told and didn't bother to talk much to one another. They became things, not people. We never ever thought that we'd get back. Never ever thought we'd get back.

The prisoners remembered the incident as the 'Dutch garden party'.

After the first two weeks the prisoners on Ambon came under the control of the Japanese navy. The guards, wearing similar loose fitting green jackets and trousers to the ordinary soldiers, were drawn from the marines. From mid-1942 and through the following year Captain Ando was commander of the marine garrison. Where other Japanese officers rarely visited the camp, Ando was zealous in his supervision, and the prisoners suffered from his intervention. It was Ando who spurred his men to a frenzy as they battered the Dutch, and it was Ando who next day attended the funeral of the murdered men, placed a wreath on the coffins, and bowed. Major Ian Macrae, as second in command to Scott, had frequent dealings with the 'indescribable' Ando: 'He behaved like a maniac, foamed at the mouth and jumped up and down on the spot'. His 'mouthpiece' was Ikeuchi, the interpreter who remained at Tantui until the end of the war. Lieutenant Van Nooten as camp adjutant communicated with Ikeuchi:

> He spoke English reasonably well. His family were booksellers, and he used to go to America to buy books. He made himself out to be quite a benign gentleman. He had the honorary rank of a major in the Japanese army, but he was a civilian. He was referred to as the *tsukan*, which is interpreter-manager, as near as I could translate. He tried to give the impression he was working for us; in actual fact I

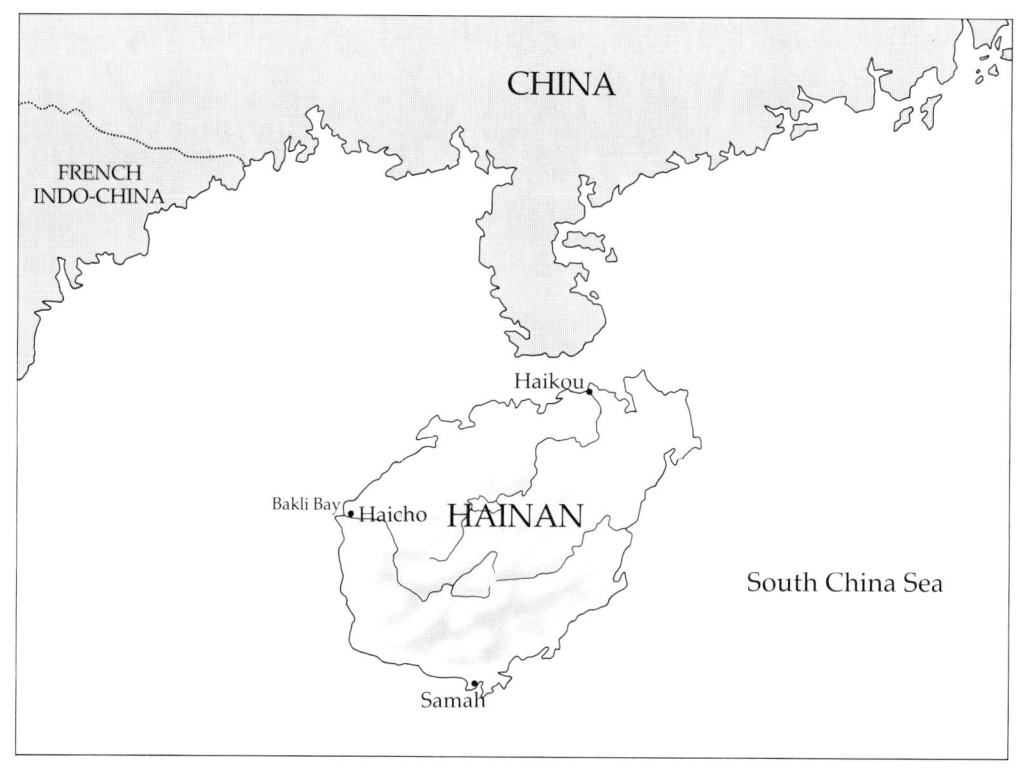

Hainan – sand, prickly pear and forested mountains

could lay almost every piece of bestiality at his door. He either started it, goaded it, reported it, or he certainly did nothing to stop it. For instance at the Dutch mass beating he personally, to show how he was a member of the Japanese nobility as far as bashing was concerned, beat one of the Dutch officers to death. He was in on every bit of nastiness.

Ando and Ikeuchi released their full fury on the Australians in November when four of them were caught trading for food outside the camp at night. Then the beating and questioning started. The men being interrogated were out of sight in the guard house, but the other prisoners 'could see the rise and fall of the iron bars and sticks'; and they could hear the screaming. The madness went on for two days for some men; for a week for others. Finally eleven of the battered prisoners were taken away and never seen again. About a month later Ikeuchi reported that all had been executed with the sword.

In October 1942 the Japanese told the prisoners that 500 men were to be shipped to a special convalescent camp. The sick and weak were selected to make up the 263 Australians and 233 Dutchmen who sailed with hope. They landed at the end of a six-week voyage at 'a godforsaken barren hole called Haicho', in southern Hainan. In the background were high forested mountains; but in the foreground were sand, prickly pear, scrubby trees, scrap-built barracks and crowds of emaciated Chinese labourers.

John Devenish: The first thing, naturally, was to go to the wharves and unload their supply boats. That was a pretty tough sort of a job because it was mainly rice. The bags of rice were pretty heavy, they weighed 250 pounds. We weren't well at the time, but we had to carry these things. One man, one bag. You'd stand up and they'd put this bag of rice on your back, or your mates would, and then you'd walk 100 yards maybe, dump it on the track, and go back for another one. You did this all day. If you went down under a bag, and a lot of us did collapse, you got belted by a Jap guard until you stood up under it. That wasn't humanly possible. So a couple of your mates who were coming back empty handed from the loading trucks, would get each side, lift the bag so you could stand up under it, and you'd stagger off again. And they'd get a whack under the ear for giving you a hand.

We had to build a viaduct across a deep creek bed. All the pylons were telegraph poles. There was no mechanical way of carrying the poles. So many men, twelve or fifteen, depending on the length of the pole, would get alongside it, pick it up, and put their shoulders under it. Like a caterpillar. So off you'd go. You had a bit of undulating ground so of course somebody would find that their feet weren't touching the ground. They'd hold the pole with their hands and the bloke next door would get twice the weight. But you're running like a caterpillar carrying these telegraph poles.

Jeez, they worked us like slaves. There were constant jobs like building a roadway through clay pans. I don't know if you've got any idea what it's like digging clay out of a wet paddy field. You get your shovel into the clay and there's a suction there, and you just can't shift it. Now we had to shovel all this stuff, pick it out of the clay pan, and take it to a particular point to build a roadway right through the middle of the clay pan. Boy, do you think we weren't happy when that job finished. It must have taken us a year to do that. My God, that was a hard job.

Another endless task, Roy Harris says, was shovelling sandhills into the sea to reclaim land: 'we reckoned we were building our way back to Australia'.

During 1943 the prisoners on Hainan were suffering from deficiency diseases, and in their last year in captivity they were starving. The prisoners who saw the livestock and the grain crops beyond their camp believed that the Japanese were deliberately cutting their rations either to kill them or to have them pathetically weak should there be an Allied landing or a Chinese uprising. The daily food issue, Harris remembers, was reduced from three cups to fourteen dessertspoons of cooked rice: 'you could please yourself how you ate it, breakfast, dinner or tea'. The prisoners picked the camp clean.

Devenish: Early in the piece the place was infested with rats, big water rats. Within twelve months you couldn't find a rat on the island. I tell you they're good too. They're like chicken, taste beautiful once you get the fur off, skin them and gut them. Put them in the pot and they are delicious. But they eventually ran out. Then we had to rely on the local natives, coolie types that used to mix and work with us sometimes, as to what sort of plant life we could eat. They'd tell us and we'd pick a certain amount of green grass of some sort, stick that in our pocket, and take it home. We'd get our rice, mix in the grass and let it cook.

Roy Harris: We had the advantage of a good doctor. Captain Bill Aitken always said to us, 'Now boys don't eat anything until I've tried it. If it makes me sick I've got enough medicine to cure myself. But I haven't got medicine to cure a hundred men.' And no matter if it was snails, lizards, snakes, anything at all we brought in, he'd try a bit first, and then he'd say, 'Right, it hasn't killed me so you can go ahead'. The mangiest thing I ever struck was grasshoppers. I couldn't get anything out of them at all. But lizards; I've seen one chap, he was in hospital, sit the whole day with a string over a hole. As soon as the lizard would poke up its head he'd pull the string, and he'd be down to the kitchen to cook it.

Devenish: Any sort of residence where there were Japanese guards on duty there was always a rubbish hole of some sort out the back. We'd walk past and we didn't miss anything. If there was such a thing as a radish top with some green leaves on it or a hard carrot top or something, we'd pick it up, take it home, and make some sort of food out of it. The odd cigarette butt, if there was one there, we'd roll in a bit of newspaper and smoke it. Anything at all that you could see on the ground that was edible, you didn't care about dirt and diseases, if it looked like you could eat it, even a bit of pumpkin skin or something like that, you'd grab it and eat it. In many cases you'd just eat it raw wherever you picked it up, you got that hungry.

Aitken and the quartermaster, Captain Phillip Miskin, tried to make a written complaint to the Japanese area commander. The camp commandant belted both men with his fists, tore the protest up, and thrust the pieces down Miskin's shirt. When Aitken wrote 'starvation' as the cause of death in the camp records the Japanese medical officer told him to change his opinion or he would be taught what death from starvation really meant. The Japanese doctor's threat was about the speed of death; not about its cause.

By scrounging and trading men added to their rations. One enterprising group tunnelled through the loose sand under a Japanese store shed, shoved a piece of pipe through the floor boards, and tapped a steady flow of rice. They stopped before the top bags of the rice stock slumped absurdly, and escaped detection. On work parties men found trading partners among the Chinese and arranged to swap clothes for food. Bill Cook and others went under the wire at night and worked as professional traders. They took ten per cent: if they sold a shirt for ten eggs they kept one. The most valuable and dangerous scrounging was done by the wharf parties who lifted emetine, quinine and vitamin tablets from Japanese ships. Scrounging, for food or drugs, was connived at by some officers and condemned by others who feared the general wrath of the Japanese. In mid-1943 the jubilant guards assembled about 120 Chinese labourers close to the camp fence, forced them on trucks, drove them over a kilometre away, and executed them. Bill Cook had time to recognise one of the Chinese: his trading partner, Syd Fuk. The Australians themselves suffered no brutal penalties for theft: their guards, unlike those on Ambon, were not so determined to catch and kill the traders.

Pulled by a team of prisoners this invention carried the rations in and the dead out.

Under sentence of slow death from starvation, the Australians still had to maintain discipline within their own group. Some prisoners used the methods they had known from stern fathers to punish men who stole from their comrades.

Devenish: I saw this done on several occasions, at least six, maybe eight. Our own Australian boys, sick and all as they were, were made to drop their strides, lean over the end of the mess table, and take anything from six to ten belts on the buttocks administered by our own Australian vigilante committee. This staggered me, to see our own boys inflicting this sort of punishment on their mates in that camp. God knows they were in enough trouble without having to suffer that sort of thing. The vigilante squad was made up of other ranks only; there were no officers.

Harris: One sergeant and a couple of other men were organising it. There was another sergeant, myself and a few others who formed an anti-vigilante committee. We put a stop to it because they were killing men for paltry things. We did have some kleptomaniacs there that used to pinch things, definitely, but no matter how much they got belted it wouldn't stop them. But most of these chaps were the cleanest living blokes you could have got. It was their pride, the hurt on their pride, that killed them.

In their postwar report on Hainan the senior officers said that they encouraged the men to use corporal punishment and they believed the beltings 'proved a success'. But two of the men who joined the vigilantes say that the initiative lay with the men. Just as conditions got tough, thieving broke out and the prisoners had to stop it before suspicion and arguments spread poison through the huts. The cases that the vigilantes dealt with were minor: the stealing of tomatoes from the prisoners' own gardens, or the taking of a rat from someone else's trap. In the postwar one man found guilty before the vigilantes' 'court' was grateful that his fellow prisoners had punished him; they had ended the guilt [and shame] that had worried him from the time hunger drove him to steal. The thieving stopped; but the vigilantes' main justification is that if the other ranks failed to sort out their own problems they faced more unpredictable and savage punishments.

On Ambon Colonel Scott had warned the prisoners that if they violated Australian army regulations and rejected the discipline of their own officers he would hand them to the Japanese for punishment. On Hainan he carried out that threat. The last and worst case was in October 1944. There are several versions of the offence, but whatever the details, an Australian private was charged with insolence to an Australian officer.

Harris: George Roy was a chap from Deniliquin. This day George had gone into the showers. The officers had so long for showers, then the hospital patients had time for showers, and then the showers were left for the workers when they came home. The hospital patients used to fill up a great big trough of water; you had a jam tin and you poured water over yourself; that was your shower, no soap or anything. George happened to go in five minutes before the officers' time was up and there was a lieutenant in there, and he said to him, 'What are you doing in here, Roy?' 'Well,' he said, 'I didn't know what time it was. None of us have got watches. We've already traded all our watches for food. We've got no idea of the time.' 'Well,' the officer said, 'you should have looked into that.' Anyhow one word led to another and George said to him, 'Look, sir, you cleared out and left your men during the action. I happened to be one of your men. And we couldn't find you when the action was on, so don't talk to me.' Anyrate the lieutenant said, 'I'm going to report you to the colonel.' Which he did. The colonel held a court and sentenced Roy to Japanese punishment.

At the time he was sentenced Roy was a hospital patient. On the first day that he went back to work an officer met him at the gate in the evening and asked him if he was ready for punishment. Roy said that he was, and he went to the Japanese guard house.

Harris: Roy had three choices. One was the old punishment standing in front of the guard house holding a dish of water straight out in front of you, and if you dropped it, well, you got belted. The second one was they tied you by the thumbs to a horizontal bar and each guard, there were eight or ten guards there, each one would belt you as long as he could with a pick handle. The third was they'd tie a wire to your thumbs and to your toes, pour water over you, and turn the electric current on. George said, 'I'll take the horizontal bar.'

I was one of them that went over to bring him back from the guard house. We took him to the doctor. Aitken took one look. He said, 'I can't do a thing for this man, they've pulped him from the kidneys down. He's got Buckley's.' Anyrate he put him in hospital. George got over it. He got back to Australia. He was in Heidelberg hospital for quite a while. But he went through Royal Park to be discharged, and they said to him, 'How do you feel?' He said, 'I feel rotten.' Well, they said, back to Heidelberg. He died at Heidelberg.

Major Ian Macrae: We all wished to God it had never happened, most of all Scott. I think in this case he misjudged the reaction of the Japanese. Nothing like that would ever happen again. Scott didn't think that anything as bad as that would happen. He was broken.

Two of the men who became vigilantes were among those handed by Australian officers to the Japanese for punishment.

Scott wrote that Roy's offence was all the greater because it had taken place within sight and hearing of a Japanese guard. In another incident on Ambon Major George Westley was struck on his ulcered leg by Ikeuchi. Westley later told the inquiry into Japanese war crimes: 'The part that hurt me was that it was done in full view of the troops. He never lost an opportunity to humiliate me.' In other units officers hit by the Japanese sensed rage in their men; and they had to act quickly to defuse the anger in the ranks in case the men retaliated. In a close knit unit the officer's position relative to his men was strengthened by the violence of the guards. But in Gull Force some senior officers seem to have been acutely sensitive about their status, and they were not confident that they had support from the men. On Hainan the terrible conditions could warp the slightest defect in the prisoners' own disciplinary system and turn it into brutality. One of the tragedies of Gull Force is that some of the anger of the survivors was directed against other Australians.

Scrap-built barracks, hospital hut, Hainan.

During 1944 a group of forty Australians were shifted fifty kilometres from Haicho to a road-making and timber-cutting camp at Hoban. Because the men were living rough and had no doctor only the fittest prisoners were sent. As they were being driven to work one morning, the men standing crowded on the back of a truck, Chinese guerilleas fired a single shot, sounded a bugle blast and loosed a chattering fusilade. Nine of the prisoners were killed, three wounded, and ten captured. Later the prisoners in Haicho received a message that the ten men taken from Hoban were living in the hills with the Chinese communists. After the war few traces could be found of them. They were presumed dead, but when and how they died is uncertain. Nineteen prisoners had died in a random sideshow of war.

In March 1945 the Japanese began to enclose the Haicho camp in electrified wire. The guards searched the prisoners' huts for any food. The little peanut oil, rice and sugar that the men had obtained at great risk were lost. Bill Cook made his last trip through the wire and came back with ketchup and tobacco for Corporal Righetti. Old Clem 'loved his bloody tobaccy' and he reckoned a smear of Chinese ketchup would help him get a few more cups of rice down his throat. Fearing that it was the last opportunity for any men to get away, Macrae and five other men escaped to take their chances with the Chinese. The Japanese stopped sending the men out to do heavy work. Crowded in leaky huts made from odd scraps of wood and iron, the prisoners waited to see which would come first: their death or the end of the war.

The men left on Ambon faced sudden destruction. At the end of 1942 the Japanese put a dump of 1000 pound bombs close to the camp hospital and between the quarters of the Australian officers and the Dutch civilians. In February Allied aircraft raided the camp. Few prisoners were hurt in the attack, but wooden bomb crates and the hut covering the dump were set on fire. The men rushed to shift the hospital patients and clear the area.

George Williamson: Nobody heard the actual noise of it going off. It was too loud to hear. But you felt the blast.

Jack Panaotie: I don't know whether I fell down with fright or I was knocked down with the blast. All I remember was one sheet of flame and this terrific explosion. The whole place was on fire and all the huts were flattened. We were trying to put the fires out. Under the debris somebody yelled out, 'Help,' and we got him out. The flames were coming across where we were and all. I said to a fellow, 'Look, there's somebody there,' and we could see two hands. It was the padre as it turned out. We didn't know. Chewing Gum Charlie they used to call him. He got burned to death. Over in the Dutch quarters, that was blown to pieces, and there were twenty-seven women and kids killed.

John van Nooten: That particular day we lost six officers, four other ranks killed directly, and a large number injured, many of whom died later. We lost not only our men, but a lot of equipment, and the few personal effects we had. Ninety per cent of the camp was destroyed in a huge blast that was just beyond your powers of registering. It left a hole in the ground some 350 feet long, 200 feet wide and 40 feet deep. How it did not kill more we will never know.

The dead possessed skills needed by the prisoners: they included the only Australian doctor, Peter Davidson, and an engineer and bomb disposal expert, Charles Patmore. The men who were too sick to go out on work parties salvaged what they could of the flattened camp to rebuild the huts.

As on Hainan the prisoners on Ambon were starved. Men were executed for stealing food from the Japanese, but they still had to take whatever they could. On work parties they scrounged edible scraps and shared them with officers and others who could not leave the camp. The informal groups dividing up the spoils could not be any bigger than five; if they were then the extra food disappeared without trace in the rice.

Panaotie: One dog we got, me mate killed it and fixed it up. He said, 'All I lost was the bark and the skin.' He put the blood and everything in. At the finish we were getting about two and a half ounces of rice, a bit of boiled up sweet potato leaves and some blue lagoon soup. We used to call it that because it was boiled up banana flowers and they used to be purple. And it made you very crook in the guts, too. In the finish there was no barter and of course there were no cigarettes, no tobacco, no rice or nothing, sort of thing.

When the war ended the Japanese were holding a reserve of rice sufficient to feed the troops and prisoners on Ambon for a further year and a half.

From the start the prisoners had the sympathy of the Ambonese. Roy Harris says, 'Those Ambonese took belting after belting to get food to us. I cannot speak more highly of anyone than I do of the Ambonese.' When eleven Australians were executed for being outside the camp in 1942 one Ambonese was beheaded, and others were severely bashed. The Ambonese continued to take risks to pass food to the prisoners.

The Japanese kept forcing the men to go out on work parties. Where in Burma and Thailand the prisoners could see that the Japanese had a reason for demanding 'speedo, speedo', on Ambon the work was punishment.

Van Nooten: We called it 'the long carry'. It was carrying bags of cement from Paso across indescribably difficult country, up hills, down hills, through a jungle, and around a track that goats could just walk on, for about eight miles. Japanese soldiers would beat the men with pick handles and sometimes they had to get down on all fours to carry a bag of cement up the hills.

Panaotie: After we'd finished two or three carries with cement they would give us a 200 pound bomb between two men to take over the same track. We'd put it on a pole; and we used to have a hell of a job to get over with that. After blokes had done that, that really put most of them on the skids.

Van Nooten: This task went on for several weeks. It showed the magnificent spirit, because some of our stronger survivors volunteered to do the task rather than let their weaker mates be forced into doing it.

Panaotie: At the finish, the last work party that went out, they could only rake up twenty, and one of those fellows collapsed on the road, and so there were only nineteen of us. But one morning Ikeuchi went through the huts and there was a fellow, as he thought, in bed asleep. He started belting him with a stick and saying, 'Get up'. And the bloke was dead. He'd go through the hospital where the blokes were dying like flies, and he'd say, 'You get out of bed! You get out of bed! You're all right, nothing wrong with you!' And all that sort of thing. The mongrel bastard.

The bombs and cement, which could so easily have been moved by barge, were dumped on the south-east coast, and never used.

Each month the Australians presented a requisition for medical supplies and received nothing, or perhaps one bandage and a few grains of the antiseptic, iodoform. But suddenly a Japanese medical officer took an interest in the health of the prisoners. He selected nine groups of ten men graded from the very weak to the fittest. The 'guinea pig parades' began.

Panaotie: Me and my mate, Chucker Goodwin, had to go up to the Jap headquarters, and the bloke there he'd inject some stuff into us. We didn't know what it was. After about three injections I said to Chuck, 'I don't know how you feel, Chuck, but I'm starting to find it hard even to walk up to get it.' He said, 'So am I.' We got a few more injections, and I think it was lucky for us they cut them out. They tried something out on us. But it didn't strengthen us, that's for sure.

The Japanese claimed that the men were given blood tests and injected with vitamin Bl and casein, the protein of milk. But Van Nooten says that the vitamin injection did not have the smell of yeast usually associated with Bl, and he did not know what it was. About fifty men died during the course of the injections. Most, and perhaps all, would have died in that time anyway.

The death rate on Ambon was far worse than for any Force on the Burma-Thailand railway: less than a quarter of the men left on Ambon in October 1942 were still alive three years later.

George Williamson: They were really dying at the finish. In the hospital they had a room out the back for the sick. This Dutch doctor he used to say, 'Well, I'll take him out'. And he'd just pick him up and take him out to this room and leave him. The men themselves knew they were dying. They'd just leave them there and they'd be dead within an hour or something. Wrap them in a blanket, sew them up, take them up and bury them. And that'd be the finish of them.

They were dying at the rate of six, eight, ten a day, and I was on nearly every burial party. We'd go out and dig the graves, and then bury them. And by the time we got back from one there'd be another one ready to go out, and so we'd just have to start again. You couldn't keep up with it. You'd wake up through the night and you'd hear them, you'd hear the death rattles going on. Not only in the hospital, but in the huts themselves. It got that common that you couldn't take any notice of it. You didn't know who it was; it just went on and that was it. The next morning you'd find out who it was. Then you just used to have to bury them.

Funny part of it was, I think it was comical anyway, this chap, you couldn't shut him up. He died, and we took him up to bury him. When we were lowering him into the ground, with the ropes around him, he bent, the wind came out over his sound box, and as he was going down he went 'Oooorrr'. One of the chaps then said, 'You can't even shut the bugger up when he's dead.'

Yes, you used to think to yourself, I wonder if I'm going to be next. And when is it going to happen to me.

After the padre was killed Van Nooten read the burial service, 'starting off with the usual thing, "Man that is born of woman has but a short time to live and is full of misery. . ." I think, having said it some 428 times, I could still remember it'. Just before a man died Ikeuchi would sometimes give him letters from home. The mail had arrived on Ambon at the end of 1943. The prisoners did not know whether Ikeuchi acted to soothe, or tease, the dying.

At the end of the war 182 prisoners were alive out of the 263 who had gone to 'convalescence' on Hainan. Five of the survivors were living in the interior of the island with Chinese nationalist guerillas. On Ambon the prisoners knew nothing of the surrender of the Japanese on August 15, 1945; but after six days the Japanese announced that there was an armistice. They did not admit defeat; they said that fighting might break out again; and they remained in command. The stalemate continued for a fortnight with the confidence of the prisoners growing, and the Japanese making concessions. The work parties ended, the rations increased, and some medicines were handed over.

Van Nooten: I then got very game and said, 'I want to use your radio telecommunications centre'. It was underground. We knew where it was because we'd worked on it. I had an American radio operator in the camp. So he and I were taken by the Japanese to the communications centre and he was allowed to twiddle the dials, and after about two hours he got through to Morotai which happened to be Allied headquarters. He passed the message that we were prisoners-of-war on Ambon. The operator said, 'Ambon, where's that?' Which didn't make me feel really good. Anyhow we got onto clear language and the operator quizzed me, 'Your name?' I said, 'Van Nooten' which didn't sound particularly Australian. 'Where are you from?' I said, 'Sandringham, Melbourne.' He said, 'How would you like to see Chloe again?' I said, 'Lead me to her.' He said, 'Where is she?' I said, 'Young and Jacksons.' He said, 'You're a bloody Australian.' We then received instructions to maintain radio contact. About four hours later we were quizzed as to numbers and condition, and told that a squadron of corvettes would be coming down to recover us, ETA such and such a time on September 10. Could we get to the wharf? I said yes. I then put a requisition on the Japanese for ambulances, staff cars and trucks. We never had very many walkers at that stage in our 123, mostly stretcher cases. We arrived at the wharf about half an hour ahead of the corvettes.

Panaotie: We were very excited. We were looking out the heads and couldn't see anything, and then suddenly we saw this tiny little ship coming in, and then another one, and another one. The first that came in was the *Glenelg*, then the *Cootamundra*, *Junee* and *Latrobe*. And each of us was allocated to a corvette.

About five men had died after the end of the war and before the corvettes of the Royal Australian Navy sailed into the beautiful Bay of Ambon. Of the 528 prisoners on Ambon in October 1942, 123 sailed to Morotai, and 121 lived to reach Australia. After taking into account the men who escaped early in 1942 and the prisoners on Hainan, one third of the men of Gull Force had survived.

'We'd go out and dig the graves... then you just used to have to bury them.'

CHAPTER EIGHT

YOU COULD FEEL YOURSELF DYING

*'You'd lie down of a night and you'd say,
"This is it".'*

Still raw to captivity, Private Keith Botterill of the 2/19th battalion was working at Pulau Bukum, an island just south of Singapore:

> Me mate says, 'This is no good, Keith, working on a Saturday. Let's go back to Changi.' I said, 'I'll be in that. Blow this working Saturday. Blow working at all.' We just said, 'Oh, we're crook'. The doctor repeated, 'These men are sick', so the Japanese put about ten of us on a little boat, took us to Singapore about ten miles away, unloaded us, and put us on a truck. We went about half a mile down the street and there's a flaming head sticking on a post. A fresh head. A warning: this will happen to you if you try to escape or betray us or cause any mischief. This is lovely! Next corner, another head. And a head on every corner. We get back to Changi. 'Well, this is good', I said, 'what did we come off the island for?' And they said, 'There's a draft going away tomorrow, another working party'. So I got on B Force. That's how I came to set off to Borneo.

Botterill, at twenty years old and already eighteen months overseas, had taken two decisions: to leave Pulau Bukum and join B Force. He had set his own course to nightmare. Prisoners-of-war were always making choices in ignorance, and the results could be the difference between ease and horror. Most prisoners usually decided it was better to stay with their own 'mob'; and defied illness and all signs of impending disaster to stick together. Don't buck fate, they said.

In May 1942 A Force sailed for Burma, and in July the Japanese demanded that the Australians allot another 1500 men to B Force. Packed in the stinking holds of the *Ubi Maru* they sailed east for what had been British North Borneo. It was now one more part of the Japanese Greater East Asia Co-prosperity Sphere. In April 1943 another 500 Australians of E Force followed. On their suffocating voyage the men of E Force had one compensation: they broke into the Japanese stores and left a trail of empty packets and tins in their wake. The evidence of their crime, and of their carelessness, was unnoticed. Soon after E Force landed the Japanese sent 750 British prisoners to join the Australians in North Borneo.

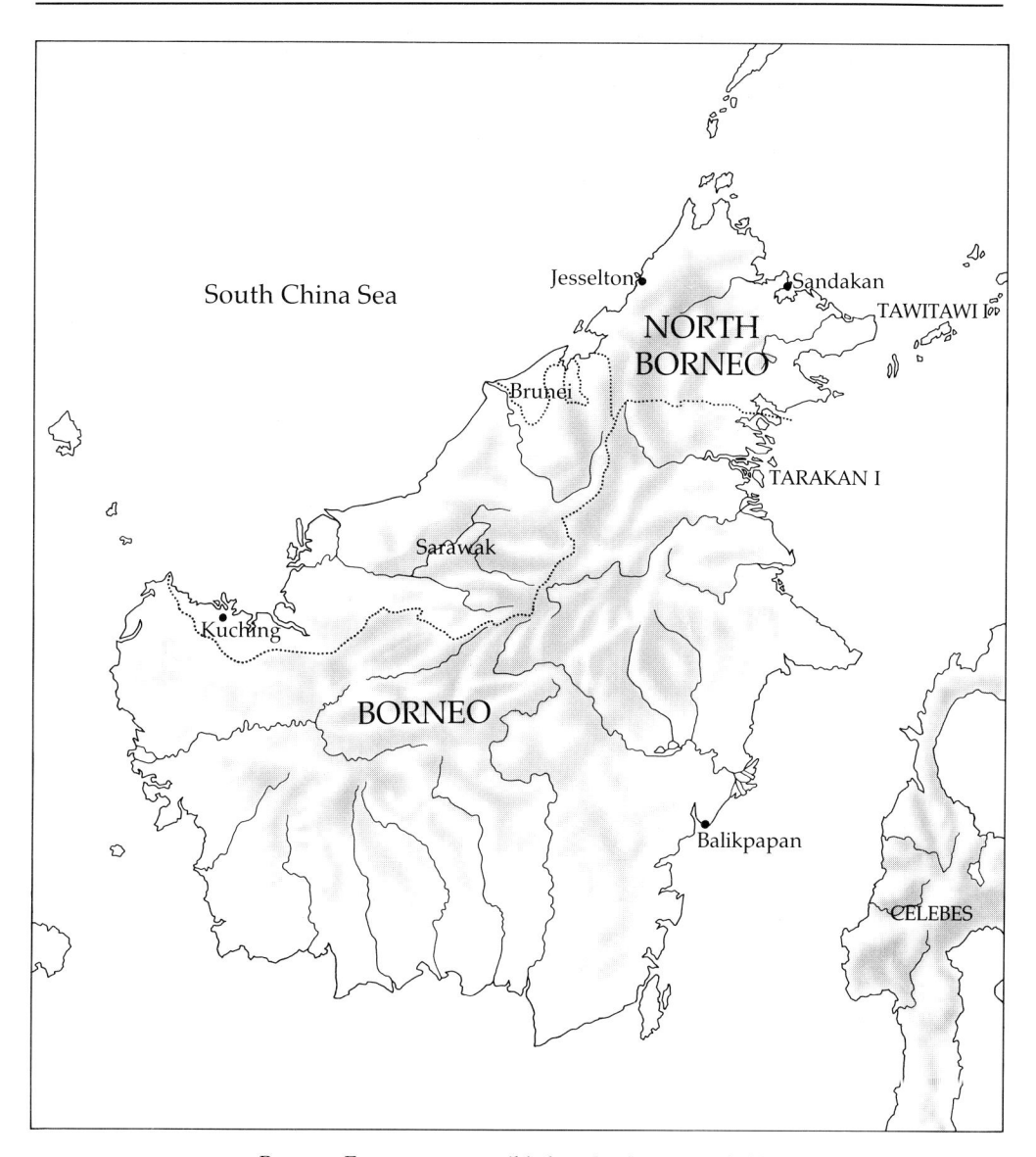

Borneo. Escape was possible but death was probable.

The 2000 Australians of B and E forces were drawn from a variety of units: they were infantrymen, base workers, signallers, machine gunners, and many wore the red sloped over blue of the artillery colour patch. Most of the 2/10th Field Regiment's rugby team went to Borneo, and the 2/15th Field Regiment was to suffer more deaths in Borneo than anywhere else. By the time they sailed from Singapore the troops of B and E Forces had already served several months as prisoners-of-war, but many were still troubled by having taken part in the greatest defeat suffered by British men at arms. They looked for the means to their own rehabilitation. Some nurtured ideas of escape or resistance; and they hoped that both might be easier away from Singapore. Two men of E Force who met on the wharf at Singapore were Lieutenant Rex Blow and Sergeant Jock McLaren. As they waited for the Japanese to herd them on board the tiny *de Klerk* they shared a seat on a box holding Blow's personal gear, parts of a radio, a revolver, forty-five rounds of ammunition, and a map. McLaren also carried with him a small ten-centimetre-square map of South-east Asia. Blow and McLaren, spoke of their hope of getting away, and 'from then on we were friends'. McLaren, who had already risked execution in a failed escape, helped Blow carry his gear on board.

On July 17, 1942 the *Ubi Maru* with the men of B Force lying in pools of sweat came south along the east coast of Borneo and into the port of Sandakan.

Lieutenant Rod Wells: From the sea it's lovely. With the red chalk hills on the side of Berhala Island it really is very impressive. I suppose for a split moment we thought, with a sigh of relief, that here's some beautiful, peaceful land where there may not be any Japanese. It was subconsciously thought, and then immediately dispelled by the white flags with the red blobs in the centre flying over the town. And as we moved into the harbour there were Japanese on the shore. We came back to reality very quickly.

The men were unloaded, counted, and marched to a central *padang*. Fed the same distasteful limed rice that had sustained them for ten days on the *Ubi Maru*, they lolled and stretched until they were formed up in groups of about forty to march to the Catholic mission school on the edge of town.

Men slept where they could find floor space. From where he rested Wells could see a steep slope with six electric light poles, each standing in its own circle of light. To him 'they were Daylesford in Victoria' where he had holidayed as a youth; and he went to sleep wondering about that quiet country town of guest houses, mineral water and gentle bush walks.

The next day the prisoners marched inland. It was 'hard going' but the Japanese took the worst of the sick and some of the heavy gear out by truck. As the prisoners passed a slowly moving cart pulled by a water buffalo a digger stepped from the ranks and gently turned the animal around and sent it back the way it had come. The driver, asleep in the cart, did not stir. Even the guards joined in the laughter. At the eight-mile post the prisoners turned, went through the gate in the tight strands and loose coils of barbed wire, and halted in what the sign told them was the 'No 1 Prisoners-of-War Camp, British North Borneo, HQ Kuching'. The camp had previously been used by the British to house Japanese and other enemy citizens interned after the attack on Malaya in December. Built to house 300, it now held 1500; but its space was luxury compared with the *Ubi Maru*.

The Japanese demanded no labourers for the first few days, and even when the early work parties went out the conditions could be endured.

Keith Botterill: We had it easy the first twelve months. I reckon there'd be only half a dozen died at the top, and I don't think there was that many. Sure we had to work on the drome, we used to get flogged, but we had plenty of food and cigarettes—roll your own, you know. The officers, I think they even volunteered to work at the drome for something to do. They had their own garden. They used to do the gardening for something to do, you know. We actually had a canteen in the prison camp. We were getting ten cents a day, about eight cents in fact because you'd give two cents for the sick. I think a coconut was about one cent, and a turtle egg one cent. Cigarette papers without glue were about a cent a packet. Tobacco was three cents an ounce. And a fair sized banana went for a cent. Yeah, we had it pretty easy. We had a two-up game. We had lights in the huts, boxing every Saturday night, concerts. It was a good camp.

Pay, Captain Ken Mosher says, was the incentive to work: no work, no ten cents.

As on Ambon the prisoners were unlucky in their Japanese guards. The most puzzling was Colonel Suga who had responsibility for all camps on Borneo. At Kuching he took biscuits to the children in the internment camp, and he even gave them rides in his car.

Bombadier Dick Braithwaite: I've heard varying stories about Suga. As a matter of fact he had British Imperial Service ribbons from World War One. I feel that he did have sympathy for us to a degree, and he did as much as he could because whenever he visited us from Kuching rations seemed to suddenly improve. As soon as he went, they went back again.

Gunner Owen Campbell: Old Colonel Suga, he was a bit like an old kewpie doll. He'd come down and address us through an interpreter; and he could talk English too, don't worry. Colonel Suga lined us up this day. I'll never forget it. We were out on the roadway. He stood up on this platform and he said, 'Look at me, I am Colonel Suga'. Everybody was screaming laughing and he said, 'I'll give you three days' holiday: yesterday, today and tomorrow.' Of course you could hear everybody roar and clap. And one bloke yelled out, 'What about a holiday for Ned Kelly, King of Australia?'

Colonel Suga, who promised food, clothes and medicines, who wanted to be thought of as cultured and humane, and who may have been both in other circumstances, cut his own throat in 1945 as he waited for judgment on events that had taken place within his command.

In their day-to-day activities at Sandakan the prisoners were under the control of Captain Susumi Hoshijima.

Botterill: He was almost six foot; a very kind and vicious man, depending on his mood. He gave the officers permission to build a garden outside the camp, and then he'd turn around and gouge a man's eye out.

Hoshijima was seen by the men with relief in the distance as he 'rode round on this old horse', and with fear as he came to deliver an order.

Owen Campbell: I think he must have come from a fairly well-to-do family because he kept himself aloof from everybody. Then he decided he'd put on a sports day. I think it was just a ruse to see how many fit men were in the camp. And of course a lot of our blokes fell for it. They had boxing competitions, wrestling and foot races. They had a race round the camp and back again, and a lot of them went in for that, like fools. The winners got a big basket of fruit; but the next day they were on a working party.

Hoshijima stayed in command at Sandakan until April 1945. For the last two years his guard troop were the 'kechi', the 'small soldiers'. They were young Formosans who, like the Koreans on the Burma-Thailand railway, 'were certainly treated with contempt by the Japanese'. They tried to show that they were worthy of a place under the rising sun by the intensity of their hatred for the Emperor's enemies.

The men at Sandakan had to build a two-runway airfield and its service roads. Each day gangs left the compound at 7.30 am, marched about eight kilometres to the aerodrome, cleared rubber plantations and scrub, burnt off piles of dried bush, filled swamps, dug gravel, and pushed the 'tumbling tommy' trucks along the light railway to where the gravel was dumped and levelled. 'Coffee Dan', George Batros (Peterson) remembers, gave the diligent a ticket to present at lunch time and be rewarded with a cup of coffee. At about five or half past the prisoners marched home. With Johnny Morrison leading the singing they could ignore the guards.

Early in captivity the prisoners staged two musical reviews, 'Radio Rubbish' and 'Let's Boong It On'. Captain Claude Pickford, with his tenor voice to lead and his enthusiasm to organise, trained a choir among the officers, and it was 'Claude's Coons' that presented 'Let's Boong It On'. Performed on a wooden stage in a natural amphitheatre, the shows were a memorable extension of the Changi concerts with their interlocutor, the sextet and sketches. But from the end of 1943 the Japanese raised successive petty objections: they refused rehearsal time, they allowed a show to be planned and then suddenly cancelled it, and they objected to all the scripts shown to them for censorship. Entertainment came to depend on individuals rather than organised groups.

Nelson Short: There were impromptu shows. Men that were fit enough to try put on acts. I had an improvised ukulele which I'd made out of three ply, signal wire and part of a comb for the frets. The pegs were whittled out of glass. When you're put to the test you can make anything, I think.

Men recited their own poems and Short wrote songs:

> If that Harbour Bridge was spanned across the causeway
> And old Fremantle came to Singapore
> If Adelaide bells rang out at Bukit Timah
> And Bondi Beach was lined around these shores
> If the River Yarra flowed into the harbour
> And old Rockhampton on this island did appear
> Then we wouldn't want to roam
> We would always feel at home
> If we only had Australia over here.

In spite of the barbed wire that circled the camp, the men at Sandakan had better contact with the outside world than other prisoners. Some of the civilians in the town had not been interned, including Dr Jim Taylor, an Australian working at the Sandakan hospital. Many of the British North Borneo Constabulary were loyal to their old masters, and, as elsewhere, the Chinese took risks to help the prisoners. In the early months men 'could stroll out through the wire any time they liked. Home from home it was.' Botterill's casual understatement reflects the laxity of 1942, but not the dangers of crawling under the wire and being caught with red scratches on shoulders and back.

Taking advantage of the ease of movement Captain Lionel Matthews, as the prisoners' intelligence officer, arranged for Borneo policemen to collect medicines from Taylor and bring them to the camp. Lieutenant Rod Wells, out on wood-collecting parties, picked up the life-saving vitamin B1, iodine, M and B tablets and surgical instruments. The police also delivered the basic parts for a radio. Lieutenant Gordon Weynton and Wells, using aluminium foil and other makeshift components, got a radio receiver working.

To pick up a BBC news broadcast on the headphones of their primitive radio took fine co-ordination. The electricity for the camp came from a generator driven by wood-fuelled steam engine controlled by a Chinese engineer, Ah Ping. But the power that gave a dull glow to the light globes was insufficient for the radio. On the promise of being given news of his homeland, Ah Ping agreed to build up the revolutions of his ancient engine each night at about ten o'clock until the wiring of Sandakan sang with unaccustomed power. The wood party delivered extra wood each day to the power station; the 'cockatoos' took up their lookout positions; and the radio operators retrieved their set from a bore-hole and plugged it in. The first attempts to tap international news were unsuccessful. Wells and Weynton found the BBC frequency, but heard over thirty minutes on hop growing in Kent. And Ah Ping fired his boilers with such enthusiasm that he blew nearly all the lights in the camp. He was persuaded to increase revolutions gradually, and Wells and Weynton learnt the news schedules. The wireless gave service for nearly a year, from August 1942 until July 1943. Ah Ping was never punished for his services to better communications and lighting.

A secret group among the prisoners began working on more ambitious schemes. The same team that built the radio receiver now made a transmitter which they developed to the point where they made test broadcasts. Matthews also found that through Chinese-Filipino traders he could pass messages through the Sulu chain of islands to the American guerilla forces in the Philippines. Given time, he hoped to be able to send information to, and receive it from, Australia. The guerilla leader on Tawitawi in the Sulu islands could even supply arms to be hidden and used by the prisoners in the event of an Allied landing. But the number of people now involved, including the courageous Funk brothers in Sandakan, Alexander, Johnny and Paddy, various policemen and traders, and the European population, made all operations increasingly risky.

The Japanese did not gradually pick up scraps of information; the evidence was given to them as a gift.

Wells: Some time in the early part of July 1943 an Indian blackmailed a Chinese who was helping us in our general intelligence work. The Chinese refused to help the Indian—I think he wanted money—and the Indian told the Japanese. As a result of that two or three of our trusted Asian helpers were arrested. During the interrogation, unknown to us, Lionel Matthews' name was mentioned.

Japanese troops arrived suddenly in the camp. Most of the prisoners were working at the aerodrome, and the sick and those engaged on camp duties were driven outside the wire while the huts were torn apart and gear scattered in a frantic search.

The Japanese found neither radio nor transmitter; but they did take, Wells says,

some notes that I was to take to police sergeant Arbin the next morning. They were hidden in some socks I had. There were two or three sheets of this material. They called for Lionel Matthews and took him off. The next two nights weren't very happy for me. On the third day they stopped all work parties outside the camp, Hoshijima got up on the back of a vehicle, and I thought he was about to address everybody. He just called out those two words I'll never forget, 'Lieutenant Wells'.

Hoshijima signalled Wells to come forward and accused him of having a radio. When Wells denied the accusation Hoshijima hit him twice under the chin, then grasped the rag around Wells' neck and began to throttle him. Eventually Wells decided it was better to give up the parts of the transmitter and leave the radio intact. He gambled correctly that the Japanese would not recognise that they were holding the valves of a transmitter rather than of a receiver. Hoshijima called a parade.

Wells: He took me to the top of the platform where the *tenkos* were held. He asked the whole camp to look at me, and said they would not see me again. And that was the last time I saw my lovely friends who went on the Ranau death march.

Sitting on the back of a truck with two silent guards, Wells was driven off into the night.

In Sandakan Wells was forced into cells under what had been a beautiful old bungalow. It was now the headquarters of the *Kempeitai*, the Japanese military police.

Wells: It was a horrifying place because you would hear the groans and the cries from people being interrogated. Every morning the *kempeitai* would have their meeting for the day, and always there was a quietness. Then all the chairs were pulled back. You'd know the meeting was over, and you'd think, 'Who's for it now?' You'd hear the clumping down the stairs and in would come one of the *kempeitai*. He would just signal with a gesture and you knew that you were in the box that day. That was horrible. And this went on for months, from July to November.

Wells, who had just begun his career as a school teacher before he enlisted, was twenty-three at the time of his arrest.

Isolated from all other prisoners in the first weeks of his imprisonment and untrained in intelligence, he could only guess what the Japanese already knew and what points he could concede without further incriminating himself and others. The *kempeitai* were exquisitely professional. They used the standard interrogation techniques of reward and punishment. He was offered a cigarette and he was belted. His freshly bathed and scented captors pleaded, then screamed. And when the *kempeitai* chief lost patience he turned to tougher methods.

Wells: He asked whether I was hungry and I said I was. With that they brought in a container of raw rice. I thought it was cooked rice. He said, 'Eat', and I thought he was joking because he smiled when he said it. I said I would, but I only ate a little bit because it was raw rice. With that, two of their bullies came in, held my hands behind my back, opened my mouth, poured it in by spoon, and kept tapping my head till I swallowed it. I don't know how much of it I had. Probably three or four cupfuls they got down my throat. Then they brought a garden hose in, held me, pushed the hose down my neck, and turned it on. They kept going until the water came gushing up.

    They threw me back in the cell. You can imagine the rest. About three or four hours later the pain became excruciating as the rice swelled within the stomach. I didn't know much about human anatomy then, but the rice must have somehow gone through the pylorus, the outlet from the stomach, into the small intestine, and the pain for about a day and a half was intense. Part of the bowel came out; but there was no medical attention. It bled for a while; it was very painful and gradually it got better. I managed to push it back by hand. Then the interrogation continued.

    On another occasion the interviewer produced a small piece of wood like a meat skewer, pushed that into my left ear, and tapped it in with a small hammer. I think I fainted some time after it went through the drum. I remember the last excruciating sort of pain, and I must have gone out for some time because I was revived with a bucket of water. I was put back in the cell again after that. The ear was very painful; it bled for a couple of days, with no medical attention. But fortunately for me it didn't become infected. Eventually it healed, but of course I couldn't hear with it, and I have never been able to hear since.

Wells had, he thought, little chance of getting home alive. In that 'bleak existence' it was just a case of 'get whatever nourishment you could today, keep out of as much trouble as you could, and hope that there wouldn't be any more interrogation until tomorrow'.

After the first weeks Wells was sometimes held in the same room as Matthews and Weynton. As signallers they had an advantage:

We were placed in triangular formation, all facing the sentry whose instructions were to watch and make sure there was no talking. Matthews commenced using morse. He would come back from interrogation, sit down, cross his legs as we were instructed to, and tap his fingers on his chest casing. I could read the message. It was a laborious way of communicating, but anything's better than nothing. He would go through the topic on which he'd been interrogated that morning and the answers he'd delivered.

The exchanges not only enabled the prisoners to avoid accidental incrimination; but they boosted confidence. One sentry, noticing the persistent tapping, indicated to the relieving guard that Matthews had gone a little crazy and might turn dangerous.

The *kempeitai* interrogated twenty-two Australian prisoners. One died during over four months of questioning, one was acquitted, Matthews was executed, and the rest were sent to the punishment prison at Outram Road on Singapore. Eight Asians were executed and other civilians, including Dr Taylor, were imprisoned.

At the Sandakan prison camp the Japanese responded vindictively to the underground movement, to Allied victories in the Pacific, and to four escape attempts. One group of escapers succeeded in crossing from Berhala Island through the Sulu islands to guerilla-held territory on Mindanao in the southern Philippines. Rex Blow and Jock McLaren were two of those who got away. The Japanese decided that the prisoners at Sandakan would be less trouble without their officers, and they shipped all except five to Kuching in Sarawak. At Kuching survival was probable; at Sandakan it was an act of defiance.

Botterill: No more talking to the natives. Double the guard around the wire. Put out trained savage dogs to guard around the wire. Cut the rations and medical supplies. And we were still doing it hard at the aerodrome. The work parties were bashed along all day for no reason whatsoever.

Short: They were watching you all the time. They were walking around with sticks like swords, and if you weren't working hard enough you'd be getting whacked. Or you'd stand for an hour or two holding up a weight and looking into the sun, which I did and got solar burns in both eyes. There'd be beatings every day.

Braithwaite: One fellow that was stood up outside the guard house for an unknown misdemeanor had his eye knocked clean out of the socket. There was no sympathy given for that at all. He was still kept standing there and he didn't get any treatment till he came back into the camp about six or seven hours later. There were numerous incidents of that nature. You tend to live with them, and they don't stick in your memory because they were commonplace. As with the deaths. It was a way of life that you learned to accept, and expected.

When Dick Braithwaite finally decided to sell his watch, he traded it for thirty quinine tablets. Whether to ask for food or drugs was always a tough decision.

The Japanese punished men by putting them in the *ishō*, the cages. Built of slats of wood, the cages stood about a metre above the ground, the roof was too low for a man to stand, and they were too crowded to allow all the prisoners to lie down.

Short: I saw one chap come out of there. We watched him come into the camp. He was bent over, walking on a stick; and he died about five hours later. He'd be a bloke only about twenty-five years of age. Keith Botterill's been in it.

Botterill: The time I was in for forty days there was seventeen of us in there. No water for the first three days. On the third night they'd force you to drink till you were sick. For the first seven days you got no food. On the seventh day they started feeding you half camp rations. I was just in a G string, never had a wash, and covered in lice and scabies. We were not allowed to talk, but we used to whisper. We had to kneel down all day. There wasn't really room to lie down at night, but we all lay side by side, squashed up, and had to sit up again at dawn and kneel. Every evening we would get a bashing, which they used to call physical exercise. They'd bring us out at a set time at five o'clock every night. They had English cooks working for them because they wouldn't trust the Australians anywhere near the cookhouse. The Englishmen knew that we got out at five so they'd come down then to feed the dogs with swill, the kitchen rubbish. They'd pour it into this trough. We'd all hit together, the dogs and all of us, and we'd fight the dogs for the scraps. If you've ever tried to pull a bone out of a starving dog's mouth you'll know what it was like. The dogs would fasten on to your wrist to take the bone off you, and you'd still be putting the bone into your mouth. And you'd finish up the better.

Keith Botterill could exploit an animal instinct to survive, and still remain human. Other prisoners could not bring themselves to fight with animal fury. Or if they did, they could not sustain their rationality and sensitivity.

In October 1944 Allied planes flashed across the camp. The prisoners had never seen anything like the 'split arses', the twin fusilaged P38s, and they took them as a sign of imminent invasion. But as in other camps the planes were a prelude to further disaster.

Short: The Japanese allowed us to put a big POW sign in black and white on the highest point. But the planes continued to bomb and strafe the camp. So the Japanese made us take up the POW sign and give them an open go. Bombs left craters right in the camp, and there was one just outside the camp that went right under a hut and killed twenty or thirty blokes. I can't understand it. When we had the POW sign there, anybody could see it, and they just continued to strafe and bomb. The Japanese opened up on us as well. They were putting rifle fire into the camp. They were having a go too. They wanted to get rid of as many as they could.

Other survivors think there may have been an easing of the raids while the POW sign was on display. Those Japanese officers who suddenly appeared in the camp during the first raids apparently thought they were safer inside the perimeter than out.

Perhaps anticipating invasion, the Japanese began shifting the men from Sandakan. In January 1945, 470 Australian and British prisoners, split into groups of fifty, marched out of camp and turned west. They were on their way to Ranau, an isolated camp 250 kilometres into the rain-forested interior of North Borneo.

Botterill: For the first five days we were going through mangrove and jungle swamps, and they made a path of logs. But we kept slipping off them into the mud. So we decided to walk through the mud. The Japanese guards were doing that too; we were waist high, pushing through the mud. We thought if we fell from the logs and broke a leg they'd shoot us.

You'd lie down of a night and you'd say, 'This is it.' Just in the swamps. The poor Japs were doing the same, you know. You lay up against a tree in the driest spot you could find, and you were that weary with aches, and 10 000 leeches as big as pencils were climbing all over you. Off to sleep. Sort of sleep. Big baboons were screaming, wild pigs were making a noise, and crocodiles. And I was twenty. I said, 'This is it. I'm going to die.' You could feel yourself dying. You'd sort of give up, and then you'd say, 'Oh, no.' But you couldn't snap out of it. You just automatically got up, and away you'd go, you know. I never had a great will to live; I just put it down to luck. If you were all right in the morning, well, that was it. You would take the day as it came. Don't let the day beat you. Say, 'Well, it's going to be a good day today. I know I'm going to get a couple of thumpings, but that's all right.' Just cop it. Don't let nothing get you down. That's how I found it.

I've seen men shot and bayoneted to death because they could not keep up with the party. We climbed this mountain about thirty miles in from Ranau, and we lost five men on that mountain in half a day. They shot five of them because they couldn't continue. But I just kept plodding along. It was dense jungle, I was heartbroken; but I thought there was safety in numbers. I just kept going.

The march took seventeen days. Thirty-seven of the fifty men who had started out with Botterill reached the desolation of Ranau.

The fittest men were immediately forced to carry rice forty kilometres back towards Sandakan. The rice, in forty-five pound bags, was to feed the Japanese and other prisoners coming through from Sandakan.

Botterill: We'd get through the flats of Ranau and start up the mountains, and then men would start to get sick and sit down. The Japanese would shoot them and divide the rice up amongst the fit men. The killing would start about five miles out of Ranau, and the second day there'd be more killing of a morning. We'd arrive at Paginatang on the third afternoon, rest up there, and head back on the fourth day. There'd be more killing on the way back, and on the fifth day, within sight of the compound, they'd still be killing us.

No effort whatsoever was made to bury the men. They would just pull them five to fifteen yards off the track and bayonet them or shoot them, depending on the condition of the men. If they were unconscious it would be a bayonet. If they were conscious, and it was what we thought was a good, kind guard, they'd shoot them. And there was nothing we could do.

On the last rice carrying trip, we refused to carry the rice, and this Captain Nagai, the Japanese commander, came out, and he said, if you don't carry the rice I will march you all back to Sandakan. Well, we knew that ninety-five per cent of the men could never get back to Sandakan. So twenty of us decided to carry the rice for them. And only five returned on that trip. We lost fifteen. So that was the last rice carrying trip.

Because only half the men could eat curry, they would just give it to you in a small tin and you'd please yourself what you did with it. Well, we used to trade our curry to the Japanese twenty-five miles back at Paginatang. Now to double the quantity, we used to get the borer droppings out of the bamboo. It just looked like curry. We used to mix it, fifty per cent borer droppings and fifty per cent curry and trade it to the Japanese for rice and salt. They thought they were on a good thing and we knew we were on a good thing.

The survivors of the march and the rice carrying lingered on the edge of life in a dirt-floored hut at Ranau.

Botterill: We were fairly well crowded when we first moved in. But as the time went by the person next to you would die during the night, and his place would give more space. You'd wake up of a morning and you'd look to your right to see if the chap next to you was still alive. If he was dead you'd just roll him over a little bit and see if he had any belongings that would suit you; if not, you'd just leave him there. You'd turn to the other side and check your neighbour; see if he was dead or alive.

There'd be a burial party every morning, approximately nine o'clock, which consisted of two men to each body. We used to wrap their wrists and ankles together and put a bamboo pole through them and carry them like a dead tiger. We had no padre. And no clothes on the bodies, just straight into six inch deep graves. The soil was too hard to dig any deeper. We'd lay the body in and the only mark of respect they got, we'd spit on the body, then cover them up. That was the soldier's way.

Death was just as common among the men left at Sandakan: about 230 British and Australian prisoners died in March 1945 alone. On May 29 the Japanese suddenly ordered the prisoners to assemble on the road outside the camp. Only 566 prisoners were fit enough to muster; and they watched the guards belting the sick to see if any more could be forced to join the parade. But always there was the hope that this was the last horror.

Short: The men thought the war was over, and we were going to the boat at Sandakan. That was the strong rumour. So any man that could get on his feet and march got on his feet. When we came down to the bitumen road men said, if we turn left we'll be going home, we'll be going to Sandakan. If we turn right, well, we don't know where we're going. So when we got there we turned right. We went to the eight mile peg and it was straight into the jungle, and that was 156 miles, and mush and slush and jungle.

Like the men who left the Sandakan camp in January, they marched in groups of fifty with guards at the front, flank and rear. The Japanese burnt the camp behind them.

Braithwaite: It was a strange, sad sort of feeling to see those huts going up in flames. Knowing also, of course, that any records of our friends that had died, things that we'd made and cherished, the little bits of wood that had become more or less like the family jewels, they were going up in smoke. It was a feeling of great loss. Although we wouldn't allow ourselves to give up hope of ever being rescued or getting out, it must have been in the back of our minds all the time that this was it for us. Where were we going from here? Maybe nowhere.

Short: Before the eight mile peg they started to drop out. And they marched us right through the night and in mud up to our waists, up to our necks. The guards would be singing out, '*lakas, lakas*', go faster. We'd be marching all night till about three o'clock in the morning or something, then when they wanted a rest, they rested. When the time came to go on again, after three or four hours' rest, the men couldn't get to their feet. They became paralysed in the legs. The ones that couldn't get up, they were all put together. We went on for a distance, and all we heard was the rattle of a tommy gun; and that's what they did with them. And that's at every resting place. Blokes fell over, couldn't go on, and they just machine gunned them. It was a killing off party.

Braithwaite: We were issued with rice to carry. Some of them kept it in a bucket, but we split it up so that if anything happened and it was spilled, it wouldn't all be lost. In the conditions that prevailed later, this was very wise.

Campbell: The Japs of course had staging camps all along the road and they used to get fed. And we were carrying some of the food for those staging camps. If the Japs got a bit tired of carrying their own packs, they'd give it to you and make you carry it.

Braithwaite: We were a bit lucky one time. We caught a python lying in the sun—which we had to share with the Jap guards of course. It was very nice, a bit like chicken.

Short: We were marching on nothing. Bamboo shoots, banana shoots; you'd grab whatever you could see. Eat whatever you could. Survival.

Braithwaite: I became aware it was a one-way trip when we started to hear shots, and you felt that there was no hope for anyone that fell out. I was going up one of these slippery slopes one time, and not making much headway when I got a crack across the back with a rifle swung by the barrel, and I got a bit of a kicking. That's why I'm deaf in one ear now as a matter of fact; I got a rifle butt in the ear. Then another one came straight at my face, and fortunately I just turned otherwise it would have caved the front of my face in. The butt just skidded off my mouth and mashed up my lips, but I didn't lose any teeth. I'm sort of semi-conscious, as I recall, and I felt this fellow riffling through the old pack that I had. But they'd used my rice so he couldn't get any of that, if that's what he was after. I was just lying there. I don't know whether you've had the experience of being in the water and becoming absolutely had it. You can't get your breath and you're gasping. You're just heaving, trying to get your breathing going. Well that's how I was. A group came past me, and Bob Sykes, who was a WO in my unit, said, 'Come on, son, you can make it.' And I said, 'Yes, Bob, I'll be there.' Anyway after they'd gone past I struggled up on my knees, then up on my feet, and staggered on. Well, the problem was that if you fell behind your own party and they stopped for one of the infrequent rests, you had to keep going until you caught up with them. By the time you got there they were on the move again, and you missed out on that ten-minute break.

Short: We'd only go on for a few yards and we'd hear the killing off party coming behind. And if blokes just couldn't go on, we shook hands with them, and said, you know, hope everything's all right. But they knew what was going to happen. There was nothing you could do. You just had to keep going yourself. More or less survival of the fittest. There was nothing you could do.

After the officers were shipped to Kuching there were about 2000 Australian and 500 British prisoners left at Sandakan. In 1945 just over 1000 were fit enough to attempt the two marches to Ranau. All the sick left at the burning camp at Sandakan, nearly 300 men, were killed or died before Allied help arrived. Only six men who set out for Ranau, all Australians, survived to learn of the Allied victory.

That was six out of 2500. They were Gunner Owen Campbell and Bombadier Dick Braithwaite who escaped from the second march; and four men, Warrant Officer William Sticpewich, Lance Bombadier William Moxham, Private Keith Botterill and Private Nelson Short who escaped into the jungle before the final killings at Ranau.

For two years Borneo had been horror after horror.

Short: To think that a man was going to survive. You saw these men every day when you were getting treated for ulcers. The dead were lying there, naked skeltons. They were all ready to be buried. Day after day they were just dying like flies in the camp, malaria, malnutrition. And you thought to yourself, well, how could I possibly get out of a place like this? Then when it came to the death march, you thought, how can I get out of this? And even after escaping, you'd say to yourself, well, right, we've escaped, now what are our chances, where are we going? Nowhere. We're in the middle of Borneo, we're in the jungle. How possibly could we ever survive? Sydney was a long way from there.

CHAPTER NINE

TO ESCAPE WAS TO LIVE

'There was no option left: die in the camp or die in the jungle. So we decided then and there to go.'

Successful escapes from prisoner-of-war camps were rare. Even in what became known as The Great Escape from Stalag Luft III in Germany only three men reached England. From the thousands of German prisoners held in Britain, not one got back to Germany. The desire for freedom was always intense, and men planned and dreamed of ways to escape. Through a bold and imaginative scheme they hoped to outwit a clumsy enemy, end all irksome restraints and regain their standing as soldiers. But the reality was that many of the plans were the same as dreams: they were substitutes for escape. Prisoners were often relieved when they were forced to postpone or abandon their plans. When American, Australian and British prisoners of the Japanese wanted to take their own track home, they faced greater problems and greater risks than the men in the stalags of Europe.

Under the Geneva Convention of 1929 the harshest penalty that could be imposed on a prisoner who escaped and was recaptured was thirty days in solitary confinement. If in the course of escaping the prisoner bashed a guard or stole then he was liable to suffer other penalties. The Germans generally followed the Convention with prisoners captured on their Western front. The Japanese were harsher and less predictable. Perhaps through inefficiency or the attitude of a particular Japanese officer some escapers were treated lightly; but most of the time the Japanese dealt with their prisoners as though they had entered the Japanese army. The army could deploy them as labour units wherever it pleased, and it would treat them as deserters if they attempted to escape. The Japanese executed Australian escapers in Malaya, Singapore, Burma, Thailand, Borneo and Ambon.

Out of nearly 15 000 Australians who marched into Changi in February 1942 none escaped from Singapore and reached home. But Captain Ray Steele of the 2/15th Field

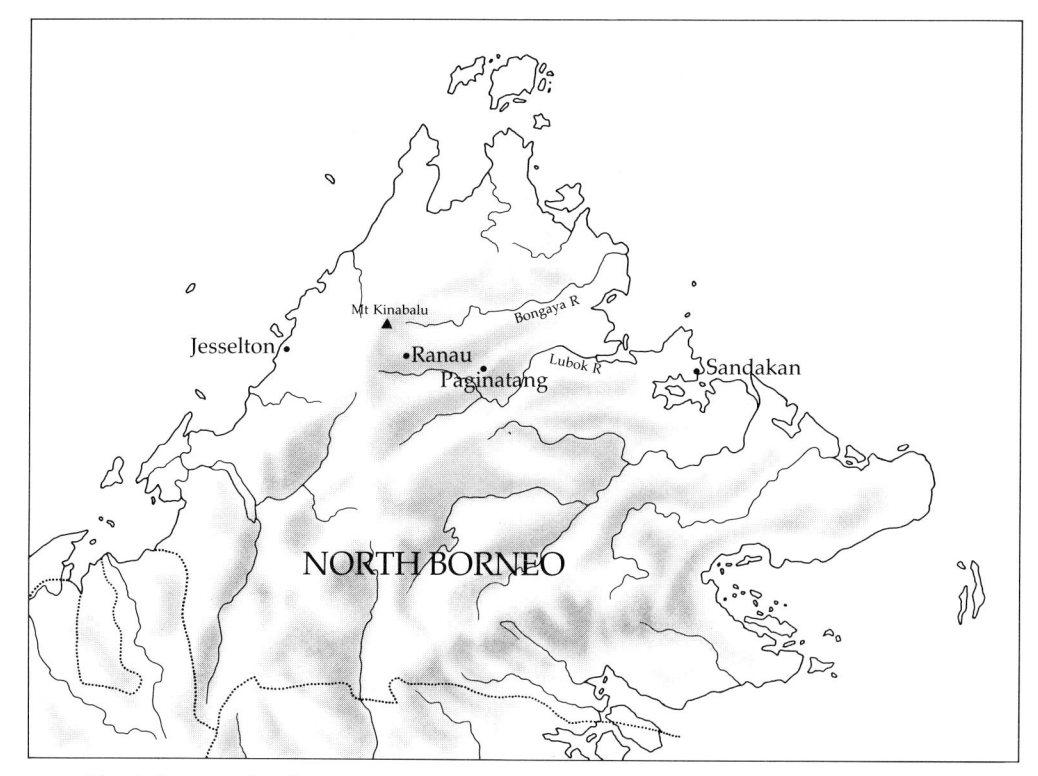

North Borneo. Sandakan to Ranau was two hundred and fifty kilometres of 'mush, slush and jungle.'

Regiment was determined to try. In the middle of 1942 he was sent with a working party to Bukit Timah on the north-west of Singapore city:

> I very soon found out that Rex Blow and Miles Gillon, who were both in the camp but from a different unit, had the same idea. We started to talk about getting away and very soon it became known amongst the other fellows that there was an escape being planned. They started to call us the Escape Club, or the Dit Club, dit being Morse for E and E being for Escape.

Lieutenant Rex Blow and Miles Gillon were fellow gunners from the 2/10th Field Regiment.

Blow: We had a little map. Rumours would go around that such and such a party was going to such and such a place so you'd immediately have a look at your map and say, where could we get to from there? We heard about this Borneo party and we thought that probably we could have a go at getting away from there.

Steele: We thought this could be it because at least we were getting a bit closer to home.

In March 1943 they arrived at Berhala Island off North Borneo as members of E Force.

The members of the Dit Club, now joined by Lieutenant Charles Wagner of the 2/18th Battalion, wondered if the lush and tranquil island could be their take-off point.

Blow: A few of us always used to volunteer for wood parties. You'd go out sawing wood for cooking and you could always have a poke around and you might pick up something you could use. We also did a very good reconnaissance of the island; and we found where we thought we could hide.

Steele: Escape was uppermost in our minds at this stage because we realised we weren't going to stay on Berhala for long. As a matter of fact we were told very early by the Japs that Berhala was only temporary while they erected more huts on the mainland where the original Borneo party was building an airfield. We knew that once we got over there, this was going to reduce our chances: it gave us further to go and it put us on the mainland instead of on the island. We realised that if we were going to escape at all, it was no good putting the day off.

The guards, who allowed the men to swim twice a day and play baseball on the open ground between the camp and the shore, gave the prisoners less immediate incentive to leave than they did nearly everywhere else.

The prisoners gradually learnt that Berhala was a better place to begin an escape than they had expected. A string of islands, the Sulu Archipelago, stretched between North Borneo and Mindanao, the main island in the south Philippines. They also met Corporal Koram, 'a fantastic young fellow', who was a member of the North Borneo police and already carrying messages between Matthews in the Sandakan camp and civilians in the town. After a week of cautious conversation, the prisoners on Berhala decided that they could trust Koram and they told him they were planning to escape. Through Koram they learnt that Filipino and American guerillas were operating in the Philippines, and a group was in action on Tawitawi, one of the closest of the Sulu islands. Following their traditional trade of exchanging dried fish for rice, men in the guerilla force still sailed between Sandakan and Tawitawi. Suddenly the prisoners knew that the distance they had to travel was short and that there was traffic between them and Allied forces. They also realised that had they known of the guerillas in the Sulu islands they might have tried one of their wildest schemes. As the *De Klerk* turned south down the Borneo coast they debated seizing the boat at dusk and seeing how far they could get under the protection of the night. In fact, they now knew, they would have had a reasonable chance of reaching the guerillas before the Japanese could have mounted an effective search. Their ignorance having caused them to reject trying the war's most dramatic dash to escape, they had to wait while Koram slowly and carefully passed messages and arranged for a Tawitawi boat to pick them up from a beach on Berhala.

But there was a complication. With so many factors beyond the control of the prisoners all escape plans would suffer from the unexpected.

Blow: We heard through Koram that a group had escaped from the mainland, three of them, that two of them had been caught and shot, and Wallace was still alive. So we suggested to Koram that he bring Wallace over to the island, which he did. Then we hid Wallace on the island just outside the wire, and we used to take him food.

Steele: We had no alternative but to take him with us because if he'd been left there he would have died or been discovered. There was no point in taking him into the camp because he wasn't on the rolls. He was a fellow that had had a fairly mixed life; he was a permanent coastal soldier for some time, he was a prison warder, and you know what Australians think about policemen and prison warders. He was a blustering type of fellow. But let's face it, he was an Australian, he was a volunteer soldier, he was with us, and he needed help. And we took him.

The two men who had escaped with Walter Wallace were not shot while trying to get away; the Japanese executed them. The prisoners now knew the penalty for failed escapes in North Borneo.

There was another disruption to the plans. The four officers learnt that another group led by Private Jock McLaren was preparing to leave. Born in Scotland, McLaren was a Queensland veterinary surgeon and over forty years old; but he was tough, fit and flamboyant. He had first talked to Blow about escaping while on the wharf in Singapore, and now they debated their plans in detail. McLaren had two companions: Driver Rex Butler and Sapper Jim Kennedy. As all the prisoners knew, once one group escaped the guards would be strict and vigilant. If all eight men were to get out, they would have to go together.

They planned to leave camp on the night of June 4, 1943. That day the Japanese suddenly announced that everybody was going to the mainland in the morning. They had to 'shoot off that night'; there might not be another chance.

Blow: As it happened when we did tell our commanding officer of the camp in Berhala he threatened to report us to the Japs. I think we had to threaten him. He was worried about repercussions. Maybe they'd cut the rations, which weren't very good, for a week. Or give extra work.

Steele: We got out of the camp fairly simply. Right on the water's edge there were the usual native toilets. The only way to get out was to wait till as near dark as possible, wander out to the toilets, drop through the floor onto the mud underneath—and what else was there. It was all a bit hazardous: it wasn't quite dark and there were guards on the gate forty or fifty yards away. We had already taken our gear out during the day and planted it close to where Wallace was; we only had a tiny pack each. All we had to do was drop into the mangroves and run like hell.

'Here we were, sitting ducks, right in the middle of the Sibutu Channel.'

All crossed the beach without being seen, scrambled into the dense bush, and met the waiting Wallace.

The escapers planned to divide. Eight, they thought, was too many for one party, and difficult to feed and hide on Berhala. McLaren, Butler and Kennedy carried with them rough paddles they had shaped in secret, and they were to seize a canoe and leave immediately. On their reconnaissance excursions Blow and Wager had sighted a sea-going canoe anchored off a leper colony. Normally the main residents of the island, the lepers had a village on a beach opposite the prison camp, the lepers' gardens spread into the rough forested country behind them. Blow and Wagner, both strong swimmers, crept through the village, waded into the sea, and swam into the dark.

Blow: We were picking up the anchor. It was three lumps of metal joined together with a bit of wire or something, and of course when we put them in the canoe there was a hell of a clang that woke the lepers up. They came down and wanted to know what we were doing. We told them we were just going fishing. They obviously didn't believe that, and they raised a bit of a din. But we realised it would take them some time to get the Japs. We took the boat in and by the time we got there the lepers had found Jock, Kennedy and Butler on the beach. They were haranguing them: You mustn't take our boat. We just said to Jock and the other two, 'Come on. Hop in quick.' We all jumped in and paddled along the coast. As we went around the big overhanging cliff Charlie and I jumped overboard and swam back. We actually had to go up that cliff at night. We didn't get back to the rendezvous until next morning. The others were a bit worried about us, but we had to shake off the lepers first.

Blow, Gillon, Steele, Wagner and Wallace settled to wait for the intensity of the Japanese search to die and for a *kompit*, an inter-island sailing boat, to pick them up.

The escapers were now under more restraint than they had known in prison.

Steele: It was a difficult three weeks because it wasn't such a big island and therefore we couldn't sing out, and we couldn't light a fire for obvious reasons. We had to talk in a whisper for practically all the time because the Japs, as well as circle the island in boats, landed with dog teams.

The lepers, who were extending their gardens, were likely to catch sight of the Australians, and after the loss of their canoe they would not have any sympathy for the prisoners. The *kompit* did not come at the arranged time, forcing the escapers to return to the beach rendezvous each night. The glow of cigarettes was to be the only signal the prisoners were to give.

Steele: We used to make our way down of a night—this was the only exercise we had—and we'd get down there with our packs and sit around. On this particular night we knew the launches had stopped. Every other night we would hear them going round and round and round. We said, well, it's likely if the boat's coming, it'll come tonight. We had these gosh-awful native cheroots which Corporal Koram had provided, and they knocked the top of your head off. They were shocking things; but we were all smokers in those days.

We heard a boat in the distance. We could hear the sail flapping and the oars going. We said, this has got to be it. So we all lit these awful cheroots, and we smoked and puffed until we were nearly ill.

Blow: By midnight we were really sick of these bloody cigars.

Steele: But it did the trick. It brought them in, and we all clambered aboard.

Blow: I can tell you, it was a great relief. We were all aboard in ten minutes flat. By morning we were away along the coast.

As they had waited for the Japanese search to taper off, Koram had ferried food across to Berhala. Before the escapers left Blow tried to express the gratitude of the Australians by giving him his watch, the only object of value the prisoners possessed. Later in the year when the Japanese arrested the civilian supporters of the Allies, they overlooked Koram. He was there to help the invading Allies in 1945.

The five escapers left Berhala on June 26, 1943. The *kompit*, a broad, eight-metre-long craft with a square sail, moved with leisurely speed. The five Australians had no reason to mistrust the Filipino captain and his four Moro crewmen, but they decided that one of them should always be on guard.

Steele: Rex Blow was on watch. And he discovered, much to his horror, that we were heading in the wrong direction, back towards Borneo. He shouted out and the rest of us woke up. We thought that they'd sold us out and were taking us back. These fellows didn't have such things as compasses; they'd been navigating by the stars for hundreds of years. But their navigator went to sleep, or made a blue, or he must have been the biggest dumb navigator in the Philippines because he certainly headed in the wrong direction. Rex pulled his revolver and threatened this bloke. Of course he didn't know whether Rex had anything up the spout or not. But he smartly turned the boat round, and we had no more trouble. We never did discover whether this was purely accidental or whether it was deliberate.

In another incident a small Jap naval vessel approached smartly. When we saw it hit the horizon there was a great old panic from the Filipinos. They got some floorboards up—there were big bags of rice underneath—and all we could do was lie on this rice with the floor boards pressed down on us, and hope to goodness that these fellows were all right. It was just after the incident of heading back towards Borneo and we still weren't sure whether they were fair dinkum or not. And we could do nothing.

Blow: This little bloke sat up the back and he kept relating what was happening: 'They are still approaching us.' 'How far are they away?' 'Oh, about a mile or two miles.' 'Are they still coming our way?' 'Still coming our way, Sir.' 'Oh God!' After all that, here we were, sitting ducks in the middle of the Sibutu Channel. Anyway they came right up and had a look in. The Filipinos had a sort of junk cover over the boat, and then it was just planks on top of the rice. We said, 'Open the cover. Give them a wave, smile, laugh, do anything!' The Japs just came up, sort of looked into the boat, didn't get down from their warship, and kept on their way.

When the boards were finally lifted from them, the five men lay wet in their own sweat and too stiff to move until they relaxed and their blood flowed again.

McLaren's party, after ten days of hard paddling, reached Tawitawi and the guerillas. After another fortnight of waiting, McLaren and his two companions had almost given up hope of seeing the men left with the angry lepers. Then the *kompit* was sighted off Bangoa in southern Tawitawi. As the *kompit* drifted in light air, the people on shore organised a reception.

Steele: They all descended on to the beach. They were all yelling and waving and going on. We thought, this is good, this is better than we've had for quite some time! This looks like the real thing! And of course they wanted to carry us ashore and hang garlands round our necks. They're mad on fiestas. All they ever want to do is play guitars and sing and dance. That night there was a big fiesta. And everybody got very full.

Blow: We had bamboo tubes of this stuff they call tuba. They call it toddy in Malaysia. It's from the coconut tree. And we had quite a bit of tuba to celebrate the reunion.

Steele: We certainly had one hell of a time. I personally felt that a weight had been taken from my shoulders. We were prisoners for only sixteen months, but sixteen months was like sixteen years to us fellows. And all of a sudden we hit this beaut place with not a care in the world, and everybody dancing and singing and eating and drinking. It was tremendous. It was just as though we had new life. Lovely.

The eight Australians recovered quickly to meet Lieutenant-Colonel A Suarez, commander of the 125th Infantry Regiment of the United States Forces in the Philippines.

The men of the AIF agreed to take temporary positions under Suarez to convert the enthusiastic Tawitawi irregulars into a disciplined company of the 125th Infantry Regiment. They named their headquarters hut 'Anzac House'. To the surprise of the Australians the name was familiar to the islanders.

Steele: We hadn't been there long when they were very proud to sing us an Australian song. And we thought, where will they have learnt this? There'd been no other Australians up there. And you wouldn't want to know: they beefed out the old Anzac song, 'Anzac, Anzac, Oh what a glorious name'. It's an old World War One song. I'd heard it many years ago; I heard my father sing it. And all these kids were singing this old Anzac song. Where they got it from I never did discover.

The Australians responded by singing for the islanders. And they took another step into the culture of the Sulu Archipelago. They bought fighting cocks, matched them against the prized birds of the area, and supported them in the betting. They built up a 'stable' of four cocks, then in a counter move mounted by the Tawitawi the Australians were 'completely wiped out': on the one day they lost their punting money and the cocks lost their lives.

The fighting between people on Tawitawi was constantly confused. The conflicts of a world war overlay older divisions between Christians and Moros, and a long tradition of independent piracy. But the Australians mounted one efficient guerilla raid against the Japanese. On August 1, 1943, a Japanese submarine chaser, heavily armed and carrying about thirty crew, put in at southern Tawitawi. Runners brought the news to the Australians at Batubatu. Wagner, McLaren, Kennedy and a troop of Filipinos caught the Japanese in intense small arms fire as the Japanese, standing idly on the deck and bridge, pulled away from the jetty.

More often the Australians were in conflict with other groups on Tawitawi who were looting, intimidating and sending challenges and insults. A fortnight after the attack on the submarine chaser Blow led a force against pro-Japanese Moro:

> We attacked them from the rear. We hadn't quite realised by this time how wily the Moros were, and of course they let us go through. We couldn't find any of them anywhere. It wasn't till we started back that they ambushed us. Butler was killed and Miles Gillon was hit. Rex Butler was obviously dead and we decided we had to leave him there. But we brought Miles back.

Steele: They lopped the poor devil's head off and took it back to the Jap headquarters to claim their reward.

During the shooting one of the guerillas trained by the Australians tried to change sides. He was shot dead. Later they learnt that he was a relative of the Moro leader. McLaren used his veterinary skills and sharpened bamboo to cut gunshot pellets from Gillon's left arm and legs.

Japanese planes bombed guerilla camps, and Japanese landing parties burnt and looted villages of the Tawitawi who supported the Allies. But another group of about thirty Japanese came ashore powerless; they had been drifting in lifeboats after their ship had been torpedoed.

Steele: They were an embarrassment to us. Under normal circumstances, and according to the Geneva Convention, these fellows should have been fed properly and housed and made prisoners-of-war. But we all knew the type of treatment we'd had, and we all realised that there was no such thing as Red Cross or Geneva Convention as regards the Japanese treatment of our blokes. So that eased our consciences a bit.

> We got what information we could from them, which was nothing, and then we had a great old argument as to what we were going to do with them. We were hundreds of miles from anywhere; we had no chance of getting off the island; and we had no chance of keeping them, half the people were starving to death. We had nowhere to keep them. So we decided we'd just have to dispose of them. I realised this was dead against the done thing, and if anyone was going to stick his neck out I guessed it was up to me as the senior bloke. I just gathered a few Filipinos, we put these fellows into boats, took them out to sea, and we disposed of them. Mainly with parangs. Pushed them overboard, then just cleaved their skulls in. Anyone that looked like he wasn't dead or was going to get in again, I shot him. That was all we could do. The Japanese knew we were on the island, but they didn't know any facts: who we were or how many of us there were. And we didn't want these facts known. What else could we do with them?

Through American servicemen manning coastwatching stations, the Australians sent radio messages for retransmission to American and Australian bases. In October 1943, after four months on Tawitawi, the seven surviving escapers were told to sail to Mindanao. The first *kompit* leaked so badly they were lucky to get back to shore. On the second attempt they sailed for six days through seas patrolled by Japanese ships and planes. On Mindanao they again joined the guerillas, and suffered their second death: Lieutenant Charles Wagner was shot by a Japanese sniper. In March 1944 three of the Australians, Steele, Kennedy and Wallace, were picked up by an American submarine and taken to Darwin. They were the first Australian prisoners from Changi to reach home. From their combined knowledge, the written statements of the men left in the Philippines, and from what they had learnt from other prisoners passing through Singapore, they were able to report on a wide variety of units and camps. McLaren had been in Pudu; the prisoners in Changi had talked with Major John Wyett who had been in Outram Road; they had first-hand knowledge of nearly every work camp on Singapore; they had met men from Java; they had seen A Force leave; some of them had been in Selarang when the Japanese had forced prisoners to sign the no-escape clause; a Dutch officer had told them that Australian nurses had been shot on the beach, and the remaining thirty-three (in fact it was thirty-two) were in Palembang. But the ex-prisoners could not persuade senior Australian army officers to mount an operation to rescue the men left in North Borneo. Blow, Gillon and McLaren stayed on with the guerillas. Moving between tranquil villages and world and communal violence, they were in an active battle area for longer than almost all other Australian servicemen.

In his report completed in Australia, Wallace wrote of the punishment cages and the bashings at Sandakan. But he knew nothing of the dying that began at the end of 1943. In fact the men left at Sandakan were soon in conditions so desperate they were beyond the imagination even of those who had spent over a year as prisoners of the Japanese. When the marches to Ranau began most of the men knew that if they stayed as prisoners they would die: to escape was to have a chance to live. In all other camps the odds favoured those who waited. Owen Campbell made his gamble for life in June 1945 while on the second march to Ranau:

> About six days out, I think it was. I had made arrangements with these other four chaps that we'd go at the first opportunity so we were all together on the march, one behind the other. I said to the fellow at the back, when you see the Japs out of sight

on your side, and they're out of sight on my side, we'll go straight down the bank, just slide straight down. They won't know what's going on with all the noise around. If anyone saw anyone escape they made a big racket so as to hide the sound of the blokes getting away. So we slid down this dirt bank, about 200 feet, into the bracken and rubbish, and we just lay doggo until all the Jap parties went past. We took a compass bearing. We decided to move on toward the coast because we knew the Yanks and guerillas were out there somewhere. Through the jungle it was heavy going. In some places you couldn't even crawl. We carried on for four days until this one fellow got sick. Then we decided to split up. I said I'd stay with him and the others said they'd go on. They'd leave marks the way they'd gone so I'd know where they'd gone.

The sick bloke had beriberi and dysentery. I used to go down to the creeks and get these little freshwater crabs, and tiny fish, and certain fungus you could eat. When I came back from one trip I found that he'd cut his throat so as not to compel me to stay there any more. Which took a lot of guts to do, you know. He did it, and in the long run we appreciated what he'd done because I suppose if I'd stayed there I would never have got out. I buried him, as best I could, in the circumstances. The ground was soft and I dug a hole down a foot, and rolled some logs on him, and some stones.

I pushed on. I was looking for those signs left by the other fellows, marked trees and things like that. I caught up with them; they were camped, and they'd used their groundsheets as a bit of a lean-to. But they were very close to the water's edge, which I couldn't understand. They said to me, 'There's a fishing boat comes up and down here every day. We'll hail it.' I said, 'Are you sure they're Malays?' They said, 'Yeah, there's only two Malays on it, and they have nets.' I said, 'It's a bit dickie.'

They heard the boat coming and took off. I thought, I'll just hang back a bit, see what goes on, you know. So they ran right down to the boat and were singing out. The boat swung in, the Jap popped up from beneath the awning with a machine gun, and opened fire. By that time I was burrowing holes in the ground, believe you me. Funny thing, they never came ashore to look or anything; they must have thought that's all there was. They just went out into the stream and went on. I thought, that's funny. I went back and one poor bloke was lying there. He said, 'What happened?' And I told him. He said, 'We thought they would help us'. I said, 'The poor old Malay couldn't help you with a Jap sitting there with a machine gun'. Anyway I stayed with him for a while, then he died. I scraped a hole, buried him, and then I pushed on myself.

I was sitting down raiding this fish trap which was in behind some overhanging branches, when the branches parted and this Malay bloke looked in and said, 'What are you doing?' I said, 'Pinching your fish'. He said, 'Stay'. And I crawled back into the jungle.

Owen Campbell had met Orang Tua Kolong, one of the local guerilla leaders. The guerillas took Campbell, fed him, and hid him from the Japanese. By early July strong Australian forces had landed on the east of Borneo at Tarakan Island and Balikpapan, Allied guerilla and reconnaissance units were operating in the interior, and the American navy dominated the seas between Borneo and the Philippines. Kolong and his men decided that they could get Campbell through to the Allies by taking him down the Bongaya River.

Campbell: There were eight or nine canoes there. They were cunning. They had an Australian flag on a pole, and they had a Japanese flag, so if American planes were over they put up the Australian flag, and if a Jap plane came over they put up the Jap flag. I don't know how many days we were on the river. But they gave me a tin of Log Cabin tobacco, so I knew they were in contact with Australians.

We went into this jungle hideout, and Kolong said, 'You stay here'. I said, 'Why?' He said, 'Oh, we make sure first, see'. We knew there were Japs in the area. And he came back with this big tall fellow, Jock Hollingsworth. I'll never forget it. It was a fantastic feeling to see him, you know. He picked me up and carried me into this hut they had built, and said to the fellows to get a hot meal ready. There must have been thirty or forty fellows, natives and that, there with him. He said, 'We've got to get you out because the Japs are pretty close'. And I said, 'Well, what are we going to do?' 'Oh,' he said, 'we'll have to wireless for a seaplane or a PT boat, get them to land, we'll most likely have to move in a hurry, see.' And he said to me, 'Do you want some money?' I said, 'What good is money?' 'Oh,' he said, 'when you get to Morotai and those places you'll want money.' So he gave me a handful of notes. And they wirelessed these Yanks, and they came and picked me up in a seaplane.

Owen Campbell reached safety in July 1945, three weeks before the end of the war.

Dick Braithwaite's strength was failing. On about the sixth day on the track to Ranau his mates had to hold him up during *tenko*. Struggling through attacks of malaria, he was soon so far back he was just out of sight of the rearguard shooting the stragglers: he knew he had to make a break then or never. After the marchers crossed the greasy log bridge over the Lubok River he took advantage of a gap in the line to drop into the jungle and lie motionless beside a fallen tree. Ants running across his mess gear seemed to make enough noise to attract the guards.

Braithwaite: At dusk I decided to head back to the river because I had to have some sort of guide to the coast, and I ran into this Jap. I think he must have been pretty sick too. He didn't have a rifle or bayonet or anything. We more or less ran into each other on the track. Before he could sing out I grabbed the branch of a tree and clobbered him, killed him, dragged him down into a gully, covered him up, and left him there. And he didn't have any food either. I found a few water snails and a few flat fruit, a bit like Brazilian cherries. But they affected the old bowels so that I thought I might have blackwater fever; it was just running out of me in a loose black, viscous stream. There's not much food in the jungle unless you know where to look.

I just slept at the base of a tree and it rained heavily most of the night. I didn't hear many animals. Pigs mainly. But I kept going, and finished up in this swamp, which was very gloomy. And it was full of snakes, scorpions and centipedes and so on. I just couldn't see any way to get through. When I turned and tried to work my way out, I had no where to go because of the gloom, and the surrounding vegetation was all heavy jungle, thorny. I just sat down on a log there and watched these reptiles, insects, crawling past, thinking, well, this is where it happens, mate, you're finished. After about half an hour just sitting, all of a sudden I thought, no, you're not finished. You're not going to die in a place like this. And I became really angry. I just put my head down like a bull and charged that jungle, and, I don't know, it just seemed to part. Maybe someone was looking after me, I don't know. Eventually I came through into sunshine which gave me direction.

I thought, well, I'll have to go to the river and see if I can build a raft and float down. I spent a very uncomfortable night there, attacked by ants and hearing the old crocs coughing in the river. As I was trying to get away from these ants I came

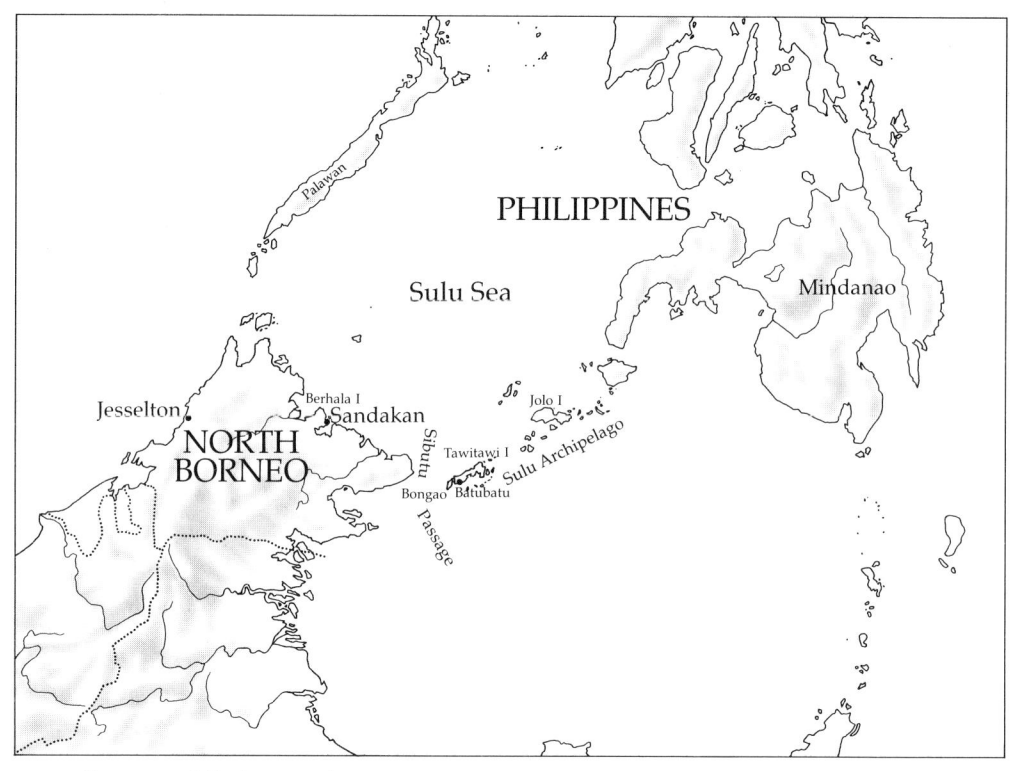

Borneo to Mindanao. The Sulu Islands stretched between Japanese Borneo and the Allied guerillas in the Philippines.

very close to falling in because it was pitch dark and raining most of the time. I heard a couple of motor boats go up the river. I could hear the Japs talking on them and I was tempted to throw in the sponge. Then just on dawn I heard the noise of paddles and I peeped through the bushes at the edge of the river and it was this lone Dusun [one of the Dayak peoples]. I called out, '*Mari sini*', which in Malay means, come here. I said, 'Australian', and it probably didn't mean much to him. But he was a bit scared, he wouldn't come over to my side, and he hung out. He eventually did come over and motioned me to get into this little outrigger. His name was Abing, and he was an elderly man. I understand he died before the end of the war. But he took me down river, I suppose about three quarters of a mile or so.

Like Campbell, Braithwaite was taken to a village where he was fed, nursed and hidden.

A Filipino, Abdul Rasid, who worked on the coast, arrived in the *kampong* and joined in the discussions. The people wanted to help Braithwaite, and they had a self-interested motive: they wanted him to tell Allied pilots to stop strafing their village and canoes. But to reach the guerillas on the coast, the villagers had to pass Japanese patrols and a camp. When Braithwaite volunteered to go alone, they told him he was too weak; they would take him down the river. With a pile of banana leaves to cover Braithwaite and a small canoe to act as a decoy if they were challenged, they set off down the river at night. Braithwaite remembers seeing the shape of trees illuminated by swarms of fireflies, and he awoke when they were out at sea. They had taken him down the river in twenty hours of non-stop paddling to land on Liberan Island. The people of the island were to hand him on to Allied troops.

Braithwaite: Just on dusk we were sitting on the island and they said it was too dangerous to go at night because they might get shot out of the water by anyone. In the distance you could see a naval task force. It was a beautiful sight; it was obviously American. Next morning, first light, I'm up to have a look. Not a sign of anything. The horizon's clear. The old heart dropped a bit. I thought, they've gone without me! But I think it was the next day we saw this PT boat come through. We hopped into the small boat, paddled out with a white flag and we got up alongside. They hove to; they thought that I was a Jap that the natives had captured. We got up alongside, and I see this giant hanging over the side. He said, 'Good Christ! It's an Aussie!' And he said, 'What would you like, Aussie?' I said, 'A pint of beer'. He said, 'Not a so-and-so doubt about you Aussies.' Then they hit me with seven pound cans of bully beef, you know, and all sorts of stuff.

The Americans said that they would be back. Braithwaite distributed the goods to his Borneo companions, and the PT boat continued its patrol into the mouth of the river. On its return Braithwaite collected a dozen cartons of cigarettes and gave them out 'in a few tearful embraces'. When he climbed on board Braithwaite asked the skipper the date. It was June 15: Braithwaite's twenty-eighth birthday.

The Americans dropped Braithwaite at Tawitawi. After he had had a week of debriefing and sick bay care, an Australian colonel came in and announced, 'We're going in now to look for your friends.' Braithwaite: 'I can remember this so vividly. I just rolled on my side in the bunk, faced the wall, and cried like a baby. And said, "You'll be too late".'

The prisoners who completed the march to Ranau found not relief, but more horror. Men who tried to escape were recaptured, tortured, then killed. But on July 7, 1945 Keith Botterill, William Moxham, Nelson Short and Andy Anderson decided that they would take their chances in the jungle.

Botterill: We picked the moment when we knew that death was a sure thing. There was no option left: die in the camp or die in the jungle. So we decided then and there to go.

Nelson Short: That night there was pouring rain. We could see the Japs sitting round this fire under shelter and we said, right, we'll make our way. Sticpewich was there then; he escaped later on. I said to him, 'Well, we're making a break for it'. So I shook hands with him, and he said, 'Oh well, good luck'. The four of us, away we went. And we passed right by the Japs. We made our way towards this hut where the rice dump was, and Moxham said, 'I think it would be about here'. So we turned in, and we ran right into it in the pitch black jungle. There was a lock on it, but it was only done up with wire, so I got a stick and put it through the wire and just turned it and turned it, and it busted. But we didn't know whether it was going to be guarded or not. We carried away as much rice as we could. We put it in billy cans and bits of sack and carried it away with us.

We must have got about three miles out that night, and it started to break daylight. We hid in the long grass close to the track. I said, I don't think we'd better stop here, it's too close, there'll be Japs coming along here, you know. We'll push on down the mountainside. This was right at the bottom of Mount Kinabalu, the highest mountain in Borneo. So we made our way down. Still raining. All we had to light fires was a little magnifying glass. I said, 'I can do it. Wait till the sun comes through.' We had a jack knife with us. 'We'll scrape the bamboo and it will soon dry out with the hot tropical sun.' Which it did. I put the magnifying glass on it and we got the fire going. There was plenty of water there. And we boiled up some rice.

Botterill: The essential things you needed over there to escape were a billycan and a magnifying glass. You could go with that; but if you never had the billycan and the magnifying glass, you were just wasting your time.

Short: So then we continued on down the mountainside, and we came to a river right at the bottom of Mount Kinabalu. And we ran into a cave. So we stopped there for about three or four days. We ate little bits of rice, not too much. And we had clear water there from the stream. Then we decided we'd make our way back up the mountainside. Moxham had a map, and he said, 'I think we'll make our way towards Jesselton if we can'. But we'd never have reached Jesselton in the state we were in. Anyrate, he said, we'll do that. So we made our way back up the mountain. We were as weak as anything after three days; and we got worse. Got terribly weak.

Botterill: We came out of this gully, and started along the Jesselton track, and we saw this small hut. It was a Japanese police hut. Tied up to a post was a horse, and we tried to undo it. Our idea was to ride it for the first few nights and then eat it. While we were trying to unhobble it and untie it, this Japanese policeman looked over the veranda and shouted out through the darkness in Japanese, 'Be quiet, you stupid fool', to the horse. And he never saw us. But we had to leave the horse behind, and we were counting on it. As soon as we saw it, we thought, that's ours, for sure.

After a night in the open, their fleshless bodies huddled together for warmth, the four escapers found a hut. Botterill, who was ill with malaria, lay down while the others scavenged for discarded scraps of onions and potatoes.

Short: All of a sudden I hear, 'Heh! *kotchi koi* (come here)'. I look up and here's a Jap and he'd got his rifle over his shoulder. He sang out to me,' *Arpi*'. I want a match. I said to the others, 'I'm spotted. There's a Jap up there and he's got his rifle and all.' He didn't see them. I made a dash over the top of the mountain and fell down and down through this long grass, tumbled and tumbled down the mountainside. I waited there for about an hour in the long grass.

Botterill: I got off my bunk and walked to the Jap, and when he saw me he just turned and ran for his life. I went back and called the other two up from the side of the hill. I said, 'A Jap has just seen us. I think we'd better get going.' So we grabbed our gear, and Nelson Short returned then.

Short: Away we went down the mountainside, and then we came to another little hut. I said, 'Stop here, and I'll see if I can get a bit of water'. There was plenty of water around there. I filled the billy and said, 'Righto, we'll boil up some rice'. Got a fire going. Moxham looked up and said, 'Hey, look, coming right down.' And there's another Jap coming straight towards the hut. 'What'll we do?' And he said, 'I've got the jack knife. If there's any trouble, you keep talking and I'll get him with the jack knife'. So anyrate he walked right down, looked in the hut and said, 'Oh!' he got a surprise, you know. 'You got a watch?' No, we got no watch. '*Pisang?*' [Malay for bananas]. No, we got no *pisang*. Food, *makan?* No, we've got none of that. We said, '*Hancho pigi obak*. The Japanese officer's gone to get medicine. All got malaria. Sick, *sakit*, sick.' He said, 'Oh'. We had a fire going, and at that time our planes were strafing anything at all. Anywhere there was smoke, they'd strafe. And at that particular time a plane was coming across. We could hear him coming low. This Jap looked up, and he could see we had the fire going. So he went for cover. He ran. When he ran, we ran. And we ran into Bariga, the bloke that found us.

He had a big bunch of bananas on his back in a basket. He said 'Oh, *Japoon djahat* [bad]. There's Japanese round here. You come with me!' But we didn't know if he was a friendly native or what he was.

Botterill: We said we were four escaped prisoners from the Japanese. We thought it best to tell this chap our story. We put all our trust into him. And he said, 'Right, I will bring you some rice and tobacco tomorrow. Just stop here; I will look after you.'

The prisoners knew that the Japanese promised rewards to villagers for returned prisoners and terrible punishments if they helped them. But Bariga slashed jungle to make a shelter; and when he returned he was alone and he carried food.

Anderson's health continued to decline. When Bariga told them that Japanese patrols were close and they would have to move, Anderson said that he did not think he could travel any further. But he dragged himself to another jungle lean-to. Soon other villagers were coming into the Australians' camp, sitting and watching while the men cooked, ate and fought against sickness. Anderson, wasted with chronic dysentery, died at the end of July. Bariga brought a chunkel and they buried him in the jungle.

Soon after Anderson's death a village man mentioned that there were many *orang* (men) from an aeroplane in the area. The Australians wondered if they were paratroopers. Bariga, who knew nothing of the strangers, said to wait and he would find out. After two days he came back with a packet of life savers, a bottle of vitamin B tablets and a note telling them to stop where they were. Bariga had found a small Australian force which could do little more than provide material evidence of its own existence. By now all three were close to death: Botterill was swollen with beriberi, Moxham was incapable of walking and Short thought that as for himself it was 'bye bye blackbird'. A week after he brought the first message Bariga arrived with momentous news: the war was over, the Japanese in the area had not acknowledged the surrender, and they were to march out if they could. Taking a wide circle to avoid the Japanese and villagers eager to take their last reward for handing in prisoners, Bariga led them on a long trek. For days the Australians suffered the frustration of knowing that they were close to safety, but still in danger of recapture or death from illness. They lived with postponed celebrations.

Short: We marched all the 24th August 1945. And in the afternoon about four or five o'clock we hear this trampling, crash, bang, coming through. We said, 'Hello, what's this? Is this Japs coming to get us? They've taken us to the Japs, or what?' But sure enough it was our blokes. We look up and there are these big six footers. Z Force. Boy oh boy. All in greens. They had these stretchers, and they shot them down. 'Have a cup of tea. Some biscuits.' You could see that they had seen the state we were in. This is it. Boy oh boy. This is really it. I cried, they all cried. It was wonderful. I'll never forget that as long as I live. We all sat down and had a cup of tea together. I couldn't eat, biscuits or anything like that. The stomach was shrunk, you know. Anyrate, we made up for it later on. Big Lofty, about six feet seven tall, boy oh boy. They said righto, hop on the stretchers, and we'll take you up to the camp. They put Moxham and Botterill on, and I said, 'No, I'm right. I'll walk the rest of the way if you just put your arm around me. I don't want to get on a stretcher.' So I walked the rest of the way into camp.

The doctor with Z Force, a reconnaissance and guerilla group from the Allied Intelligence Bureau, looked at Botterill and said, 'Keith's going to die tonight. You'd better shake his hand.' In fact all three, Botterill, Moxham and Short, recovered.

The men of Z Force rescued one other Australian prisoner, Warrant-Officer William Sticpewich who had stayed at Ranau till the end of July. By then there were not enough fit men to bury the dead. Warned by a friendly Japanese guard that the surviving prisoners were to be shot, Sticpewich looked for other men still able to struggle out of the camp, and that night he and Private Algy Reither escaped. A headman from a *kampong* close to Ranau fed the two Australians and sent men to contact Z Force. Reither died on August 8, just before help arrived.

Twelve prisoners had escaped from Borneo and reached home. Eight men had gone from Berhala Island, and two of them had died while serving with the guerillas in the southern Philippines. Owen Campbell was the only survivor of five prisoners who broke away from the Ranau march. Dick Braithwaite went alone from the march. Four men were picked up in the jungle near Ranau. The prisoners who sailed or paddled from Berhala had carried out a rare, successful, planned escape: the men who escaped in 1945 went in desperation. And they went just in time.

Short: When Bariga took us away, and we were making our way to Z Force, we heard this tat, tat, tat, tat, tat. 'That's machine gun fire', I said. 'Wonder what it is? Our blokes might be coming through or something. Might have been an attack somewhere.' We found out that was the killing off of the last of the men in the prison camp at Ranau. They killed the lot of them.

Six of the twelve men who escaped from Borneo were alive in 1984; Rex Blow, Dick Braithwaite, Keith Botterill, Owen Campbell, Nelson Short and Ray Steele.

LONG ODDS TO LIBERTY

'They dug a hole for me about three times. But I managed to pull through. I was just one of the lucky people, that's all.'

When General Gordon Bennett escaped by small boat from Singapore in February 1942 all the Australians in the area learnt of the legal and moral problems to be faced by those who 'shot through'. At first many of the men who marched into Changi resented the fact that their commander was not there to share their humiliation; but gradually their attitude changed. It was a strange reversal of popular opinion which happened in the absence of radios and newspapers, and of any organised advocates of change. By the time the released prisoners reached Australia at the end of 1945 they were displaying banners in praise of Bennett: he had become one of their heroes. In the eyes of the 8th Division Bennett was associated with their battle success on the Malayan Peninsula; he was believed to have been more aggressive and astute than his English counterparts; at the last moment he outwitted the Japanese; and he had been badly treated by his fellow senior officers in Australia. But the immediate result of Bennett's escape in 1942 was to make many Australian officers oppose other plans to get away. Their first duty, they thought, was to the welfare of the majority of the prisoners, and not to the daring or foolhardy few. Their values were to affect Chris Neilson's second attempt to escape.

Signaller Neilson's first try to win his freedom from Singapore island ended in machine gun fire and the death of his mate. Two months later he was again looking for the chance to escape. In April 1942 he was sent to Adam Park to work on roads and build the Japanese monument at Bukit Timah. The guards bashed men in the first week, but prisoners found it easy to leave the camp at night and scrounge for food or anything that might be useful.

Neilson: We were out scrounging for parts to build a radio. We used to go into private houses. For two or three nights this young Chinese bloke used to be, not talking to us, but following us. And then one night I thought we'd better pull him up. Speaking in Malay I asked him what the game was, what was he following me for. He said, 'What are you after?' We told him. The next night he said he was

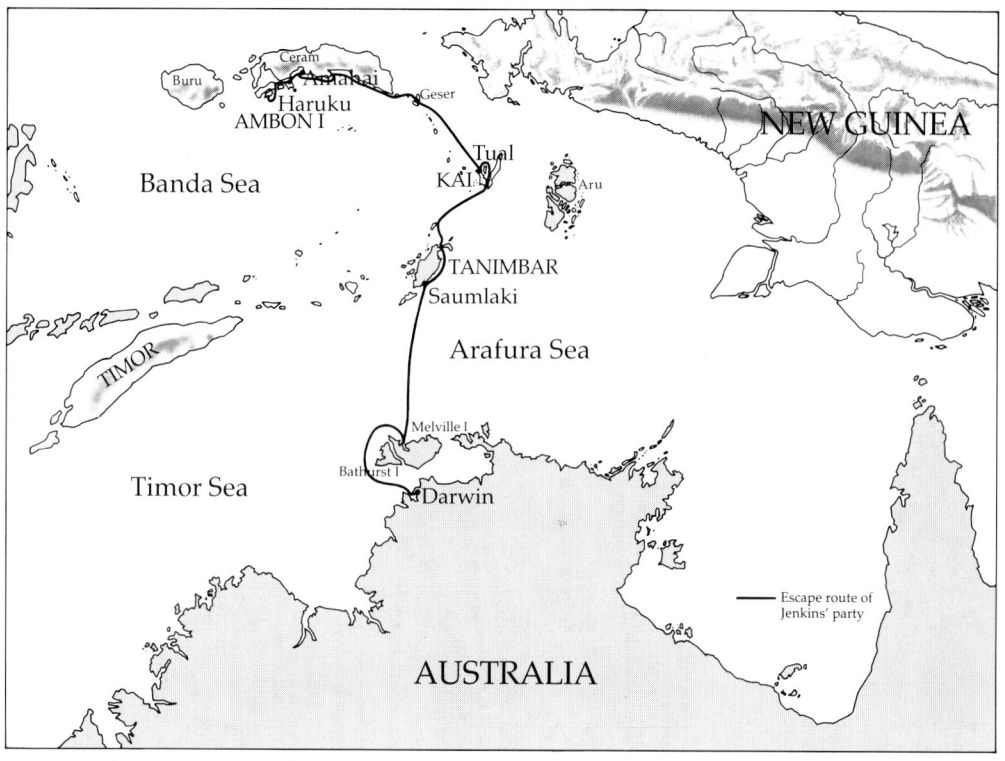

Ambon to Darwin. There were stepping stones of islands and then the long crossing of the Arafura Sea.

representing people that turned out to be the Communist guerillas. They weren't then, they were an assortment of British, Australian and Chinese, all sorts, working outside Malacca and a bit towards Kuala Lumpur. He said, 'Well, you're looking for radio parts, and we want a wireless operator and a technician'. That was Bob and me; but he also wanted three mechanics to drive and repair trucks.

Signallers Bob Green and Neilson recruited three drivers, Ken Bird, W Goodwin and Reg Morris of the 2/2 Reserve Military Transport to go with them.

The men at Adam Park knew the risk they were taking. Captain Fred Stahl, the camp adjutant, had already gambled with his own safety to intervene on behalf of men caught outside the camp. The Japanese warned that in future prisoners caught beyond the camp would be shot; but Neilson and the four others wanted the chance to 'wipe out the shame of being taken'. On June 4, 1942 they left Adam Park, heading for the jungle behind Seletar aerodrome where they would wait for the Chinese to arrange for them to cross Johore Strait.

It was easy to get down to the jungle camp. There were really no guards as such, only on the main road coming in. We just skirted round them. He was that good, this Chinese boy, that he took us on the main road in single file dressed like Chinese; and he clip-clopped and bowed to every sentry along the road, and we walked right past the big guard post near the ammo dump. We had a tommy gun and grenades, everything under the sarong, and of course the Chinaman in the front to do the talking. And he wasn't challenged once. It was so brazen. I suppose that at times we'd only be ten feet off the guards. And we just had blackened faces. He led us all night, and at daylight we were pretty well on the Johore Straits. He said, 'We'll stay here; we'll be contacted.' Anyrate, at 4 o'clock in the afternoon Green, the technician, went down with amoebic dysentery. The Chinaman went into a village where he was known, and he couldn't get any drugs whatsoever; the Japs had everything. We stayed there for five days trying to get him right. The only stuff the Chinaman could get was acriflavine and Condy's crystals. We had to give poor Greenie an enema with a bike pump because that was the only way of treating dysentery at that time. You had to retain fluid; it was what they called a retention enema. Anyway, after five days it was obvious Greenie was delirious, and it was no good going without him.

About the sixth or seventh night we decided to pull it off and go back to camp and swap him for another technician. Well it took all night to carry and drag him, and keep him quiet because we had to follow the trenches alongside the road. It was near the Nips but it was still the shortest way back. Greenie was delirious and we had to clobber him a couple of times, knock him, shut him up, and then carry him past these guards. We go back to camp and straight away the word came over from the Australian colonel in charge. He came along and more or less abused us for going, pointing out the risks not only to ourselves, but to the whole mob, and that he and the whole mob might be punished. Anyway we got some quinine and a bit of stuff together through our mates; another bloke was going with us to replace Green; and we were going through again that night.

We decided we'd go to sleep while the work parties went out. Well, I was awakened with a boot into the ribs. The Nips had been informed that we were back and the next minute we were gathered up. Handcuffs and hobbles went on. You couldn't ask anything. If you went to open your trap to speak you got slapped. But I said to an Australian officer, 'If anything happens to me will you drum my brothers, I've got four in the Army, what happened to me?' And he said, 'Yes, for sure.' Because they expected I'd be lopped.

The colonel admitted that he had notified the Japanese because, as he put it, he wasn't going to risk his life and the lives of all the others for the sake of the few that would try the impossible. Quite as plain as that he put it. And then I said to him. 'If you'd have waited, we'd have told you we were going through again tonight and that would have left your numbers balanced because Green's place would have been taken by another technician. He'd apparently rung the Japanese the minute he knew we were back. For a start I couldn't believe it. This fellow turned me in for doing my duty.

Neilson's story is supported by Driver Reg Morris in a sworn statement made in May 1946. The colonel, Morris said, questioned us, and 'saw fit to hand us to the Japanese'.

The five Australians were driven to the *kempeitai* headquarters in the YMCA building. Their first encounter was with 'a quiet little bloke' who smiled and 'passed a few lollies across'. They went into another room and there were 'these three muscle men, and were they good!'. An opening whack across the mouth cost Neilson the lolly he was eating, and 'then it started: questions over and over again'. Through bashing and interrogation the five escapers tried to maintain that they had just been out of the camp looking for food. The *kempeitai* sent them to the punishment cells in Outram Road gaol.

Other British and Australian troops cut off in the fighting on the Malay Peninsula were able to link up with the Chinese guerillas. One was Sergeant Arthur Shephard of the 2/

29th Battalion. Although wounded at Muar he followed the small bands of troops trying to force their way through jungle and Japanese fire to rejoin their units.

Shephard: We took refuge in a swamp to try to get away from a machine gun nest that was taking heavy toll of our troops. It was a little bit disconcerting. We were up to our lips in water with tracer bullets just whistling over our heads. After a while the tracers died down and we slowly, quietly made our way to the north, and then struck out in the general north-west direction trying to link with troops that were still fighting at Parit Sulong. From there we hoped to get to Singapore.

Another Australian, Lieutenant Bill McCure who had commanded the 4th Anti-tank gunners at Muar, was also in the swamp with men clinging to branches, wounded crying to be put out of their misery, and the whole scene lit with dazzling flashes of light.

A large force of men, perhaps 200 strong, struggled through the swamp to assemble in a clearing. Hoping to by-pass the Japanese they set off; but the Chinese told them that Yong Peng, forty kilometres to the south, had already been taken by the Japanese. The officers held a meeting and told the men to break up into small groups. McCure, who had argued that they should stay together as a single force, left with one of the groups hoping to get to the coast and seize a boat, or even walk all the way north to Burma. As they wondered whether they could build a raft to cross a river, a Chinese man came up and offered to guide them. He led them to an isolated *kampong* where the Chinese were beginning to set up their guerilla units. As they waited for the Chinese to provide another guide to take them on the next stage, Jock Smyllie came into the camp. A member of the prewar civil administration, Smyllie was the leader of a small British special operations group left behind to sabotage Japanese communications. McCure joined the British at their base at the edge of the Soc Fin rubber estate near Chaah in central south Malaya. Arthur Shephard and a companion, Gordon (Bomber) Wainwright, wandering between *kampong* and jungle, risked a bold approach to a house and met a friendly Chinese. He passed them to others who debated what they should do, then guided them to Jock Smyllie's camp. About twenty troops from a variety of units were now at Soc Fin.

Operating separately from their isolated *kampongs* the Chinese were unwilling to commit themselves to a full alliance with the British saboteurs. They constantly promised guides and support, then delayed on the excuse that they had to have the authority of some distant party official. After Singapore had fallen and uncertain how long they could survive, the British and Australian troops again divided into small groups to try to trek and forage their way to safety. Some were captured by the Japanese and sent to Pudu gaol; others disappeared; none escaped. McCure, Shephard, Wainwright, Corporal H R 'Bluey' Ryan of the 2/29th Battalion, Smyllie and three other Englishmen were the last to leave Soc Fin. After days spent in swamp and mud they abandoned their plan to find a boat on the west coast, and struggled back inland. Befriended by an isolated Chinese community, they did what they could to help the village sick, and began building their own camp, just upstream from the *kampong*.

Shephard: There were two of us left in the camp one day: I because I had malaria, and Bomber was cook. He was cleaning a chicken, a little weeny thing. When the Japs came in they surrounded the camp and started shooting. We took off like startled hares up the creek, and fortunately they missed us. I think I passed one bullet twice, once when it passed me and once when I passed it. That's how fast we went up the creek. We stayed in the jungle overnight, wondering what to do, and went back to the camp next day. Everything was just ripped apart, and all our possessions gone.

The Chinese who had helped them had been slaughtered. Knowing that escape by boat or long march was near enough to impossible, Australian soldiers and British saboteurs debated what to do. There seemed no alternative but to live off wild bananas, sweet potatoes and berries while they made their way back to reserve rations buried at Soc Fin.

Shephard: We flipped a coin to see whether we'd go by jungle or by rubber. Walking through the rubber estates was much easier, and more dangerous, than walking through the jungle. And the coin came down and it showed that we'd go through the rubber. We went just a short way and we came across Chinese carrying rice. Jock was a police superintendent of a place called Kedah before the war, and he wanted to buy some rice from this Chinese, but the Chinese said no, he would give us some because he was a communist. The upshot of it was that he said if we followed him, he would lead us to a safe place. We decided to follow him, and he led us through the jungle to a Chinese guerilla camp. After a long discussion we decided to stay with them.

At least two other Australians, Privates T J H Percival and R J Roach, were in the scattered guerilla *kampongs*, and there were rumours of other soldiers in isolated jungle camps. The Australians with the Chinese Communists of the Malay People's Anti-Japanese Army had entered a world of extremes in physical hardships, cultural differences, and violent political warfare.

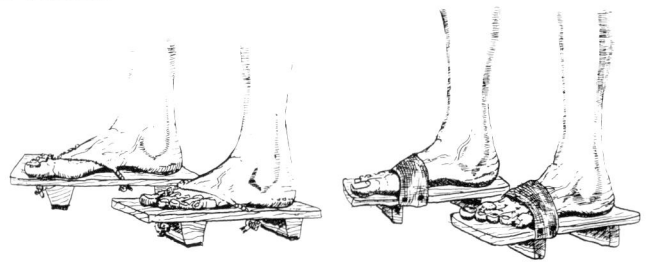

Some men had camp-made klompers.

On the island of Ambon the 800 Australian prisoners in Tantui barracks were less than 1000 kilometres from Darwin; and between Ambon and the Australian coast were convenient stepping stones of islands. Some troops who avoided capture got away in small boats and eventually reached Australia; but the men at Tantui knew nothing of what had happened to those not behind the camp fence. Lieutenant Bill Jinkins had been reluctant to surrender in the first place, and he was determined to get away from Ambon and its prison compound. He began planning an escape on his first day in captivity. From a school atlas he traced maps at a scale of 1:25 000 000, and they were to be his guide through complex sets of islands and across open ocean. He gained the support of Major Ian Macrae and the senior Australian officer, Colonel Jack Scott. But the details of the plan, Jinkins says, were his alone: 'I told Macrae, I suppose, about forty percent of my plans'.

Alec Chew had an abrupt invitation to freedom:

I was sitting in the camp and Bill Jinkins came up. He said, 'Coming out? You know, get over the wire?' I said to him, 'What for?' And he said, 'I'm going to get out of this bloody place'. So I said, 'Yes, all right.' At that time I was his batman.

Jinkins also approached Lieutenant Gordon Jack who helped with the early planning. Like Blow and Steele on Berhala, they arranged to go on parties working outside the camp to become familiar with the country and to contact friendly Ambonese. Within the camp they looked for men with appropriate skills and temperament. Private Cliff Warn says he was asked 'because I was supposed to have a reasonable amount of knowledge about the salt water, sea work, handling a boat in the sea'. Warn was a fisherman from the south coast of New South Wales. Lieutenant Rowland Rudder, Private Harry Coe and Arthur Young completed the seven-man team.

The men left Tantui soon after dark on March 17, 1942.

Warn: At the appointed time we met on the northern side of the camp. And we had to go under the wire and watch for the Japanese guards who were patrolling outside. We didn't all go in a bunch; we went in ones and twos which doesn't take long with only seven people. The atmospheric conditions helped us a lot because it was raining fairly heavily. But we wouldn't have been more than a couple of hundred yards away when the cloud lifted and the moon came out. That didn't help much.

Ambonese carried gear and lit the slippery track with burning torches.

To keep the Japanese in ignorance of the escapes for as long as possible, three men from the ranks took the place of the missing officers. And they continued in imprisonment under their assumed names. As far as the Japanese were concerned Lieutenant Jinkins died in an air raid in 1943 (in fact it was Sergeant C McK Wilson); Lieutenant Rudder died of illness in 1945 (it was Private G A Waring); and Lieutenant Jack (Sergeant S C Piggin) sailed home at the end of the war.

In four outrigger *praus* manned by Ambonese the escapers left the south coast.

Warn: It was blowing reasonably well, and we decided we'd go off in the dark and hope that everything was right. But when dawn broke we were still only a few hundred yards off-shore. It was a tropical storm, and it was just impossible to make any headway. With men rowing these *praus* we thought we were doing really well; and it was amazing to wake up next morning and find that we were only a few hundred yards off-shore, and the Japanese were still there, looking at us, sort of thing. We had a lot of luck; I think anybody has in any of these sorts of circumstances. I'm not a religious man, but I do think that sometimes the Lord does look after you.

They sailed on in daylight. Peter, their Ambonese guide, said it was better to keep going than to wait on shore where they were likely to be seen by Japanese informers.

Jinkins: When day broke we were, I suppose, three miles off the Bay of Paso, which was on the eastern end of Ambon Island, and heading across to Haruku Island. I think we got to Haruku somewhere about 3 or 4 o'clock. We landed and we were taken into the reception hall of the Rani of Haruku, the princess of the island; and she was a lovely person. We were endowed with fruit and a whole lot of other things to eat; much more than we could manage. The paddlers felt that they'd done their share, and they asked permission to go back. So I arranged with the Rani of Haruku that she would get us a suitable craft to go across to Ceram, the objective being Amahai.

Peter, the Ambonese guide, stayed with them until the last stage to Darwin.

They set out on a series of remarkable voyages for 300 kilometres along the south coast of Ceram. In whatever boats they could beg, borrow or buy, they paddled, sailed and wrestled cranky diesel engines. One week after leaving Ambon they were bailing constantly as their leaky motor launch tossed in a storm.

Jinkins: And it was there we saw the seamanship that Cliff Warn knew all about. He took that ship through giant waves, six and eight feet above us at deck level. He just rode up on the face of the wave at an angle and then down the back edge of the wave at another angle, ready to pick up the next one and go over. We did this for hours. And he was at the helm all the time. He showed remarkable seamanship.

Warn: We were almost shipwrecked one night. We were pulling into this bay and there was a fairly big sea running. You can always find an opening between a reef somewhere along the line, but things were getting a bit desperate so we took the plunge and went straight over the top of it. That gave everybody a thrill. So we got inside and anchored there for the night. But the biggest problem was we knew that the following day we had to make Geser. We'd only got one anchor. And just prior to leaving—we'd got the motor going again—we went to pull the anchor up, but the line had chafed through overnight, and we lost it.

Jinkins: We headed away again and got to Geser which is a little island on the south-east tip of Ceram. When we put in there we found a Dutch controller with a German wife, a very amiable Dutchman. He was jovial; he was pleasant at all times; and a heavy drinker.

Warn: For some unforeseen reason, I don't know how, we could always have a few drinks; and occasionally we might go a little more than a few, and end up in a singsong. And the food was excellent. Everybody was very happy; you wouldn't think there was a war on.

At Geser Arthur Young noted in the log of the voyage: 'We have now travelled 200 miles–more than 700 yet to go'.

At various ports the Australians arrived just before or just after Japanese patrols. There was always a moment of tension as they strained to see what flag was flying from mastheads near the jetty. But in most of the small islands the Dutch colonial officials still held power in the confused international situation. Unable to start the motor on the boat that got them to Geser, they bought a traditional islands sailing *prau* called the *Java*. It was, Warn remembers, about thirty feet long and 'roughly nine feet in the beam, very shallow draught, with a small jib and a mainsail; just one mast'. The Australians could manage the sails, but they lacked the skills to handle the peculiarities of the *Java*'s tiller. Peter engaged the services of a Malay seaman to help him keep the *Java* on course. They listened to a Chinese orchestra play 'The Beer Barrel Polka' and 'South of the Border', and took advantage of fine weather. The next morning it was too fine, and they lay becalmed. They sat below still sails, and savoured the scenery and scent of the Spice Islands.

Warn: Bill Jinkins used to say it always reminded him of a lady's boudoir. Well, we innocent ones, having never been in a lady's boudoir, wondered just what it was like; but he would never enlighten us. The perfume was exotic; it was fantastic.

When the wind picked up on the second day the Malay at the tiller trailed a line, and pulled in two fish. They cooked them and ate them in the moonlight as the *prau* made steady way south.

After another fortnight's adventurous sailing and chancy navigation they arrived at Saumlaki. They just made it: the *Java*'s rudder broke away as they pulled alongside the jetty. Saumlaki was their last port before they faced the long crossing of the Arafura Sea to Darwin. The resident Dutch official, Controller Leenartz, was generous with help, and they also talked him into letting them take the government's diesel-powered schooner, the *Eleida*. But the crew refused to go with the boat.

Jinkins: We got the crew to give us a run round the harbour to show us how to drive it. The only trouble was it only had enough fuel to do 250 miles, and directly from Saumlaki to Bathurst Island was 250 miles; and that was still about eighty miles short of getting into Darwin. We couldn't find any more diesel, but we decided to

> head away. On the basis of doing eight knots in a calm sea we could make the 250 miles. If the sea was not calm and we couldn't make eight knots, we would finish half way across the Arafura. We decided to take this chance in the hope that the RAAF Hudsons, which we saw flying over every second day, would see us and pick us up.

They cleared the harbour on the evening of April 22. They had seven men, most of them inexperienced, to replace the *Eleida*'s normal crew of eighteen.

Out of Saumlaki harbour they struck heavy seas whipped up by the monsoon. Worried that their precious fuel was being consumed too rapidly they still pushed on hoping for better conditions. But, Arthur Young says,

> This storm hit us. There were huge waves and we were just hitting them head on and not getting anywhere. Again this was where Cliff Warn's seamanship came in. But we decided to turn back, and in turning we were broadside on. Somehow we turned and washed around. And it was pitch black of course. We ran back on the same course as we came out. We'd been going for two or three hours, but we ran back pretty quickly with a following sea.

Warn: Unfortunately we miscued, and ran aground on a reef.

Young: We stuck fast; we couldn't get off. We tried, but it was high tide, she just went over on her side as the tide went down, filled with water, and that was that.

They were back onshore, and boatless.

The day after Jinkins and Warn told Controller Leenartz what had happened to the government schooner four more Australians arrived in Saumlaki. Three were escapers from Ambon, and one had decided during the fighting that he would serve himself and his country best if he 'shot through'. Jinkins' group had helped stage them through the islands. Now they agreed to take them to Darwin; if they could.

While the Australians searched for another boat and tried to make radio contact with Darwin, a forty-tonne trading schooner, the *Griffioen*, carrying Dutch refugees sailed into Saumlaki. Although Jinkins couldn't persuade Leenartz to let the Australians take the *Griffioen*, he was determined to have a boat, fuel and a crew. He wanted to get to Australia and arrange relief for the stranded civilians collecting in the islands, and he felt a particular responsibility for the men left on Ambon. As the Australians schemed and debated, Japanese planes flew overhead every day, and an Australian aircraft bombed and strafed the *Griffioen*. Fortunately it did little damage. Leenartz remained sympathetic.

Jinkins: We didn't have enough fuel for the *Griffioen* to get to Australia safely. But we were able to persuade Leenartz that it didn't matter who was going to sail it, us or the Dutch, there had to be enough fuel. He gave the order that every village within the area of Saumlaki had to produce coconut oil, and we had hundreds of natives coming in with large six- to nine-inch diameter bamboo stems with the centres knocked out, something like seven and eight feet long, full of coconut oil. About a week before, during the negotiations to get the ship, we had started the engines on diesoline. After the engines were well warmed up we switched to run on coconut oil, and they functioned quite well. But this was not a strange operation to the local people. They had been using this method for some time. The coconut oil was poured into forty-four gallon drums, filtered or strained through hospital bandages.

They found a little aviation gasoline to add to their cocktail of fuels.

Jinkins finally cut through the negotiations by declaring martial law, commandeering the *Griffioen*, and marching the crew on board at gun point. Leenartz, who did not want to be seen to be assisting the escapers, was untroubled by his temporary loss of power.

Jinkins: We ordered the forty-four gallon drums to be brought alongside and they were poured into the fuel tanks of the *Griffioen*. At the same time the four men that were armed and had the crew on board stood guard at strategic points on the ship to see that these fellows didn't dive overboard and swim away. There was some weeping at the end of the jetty because by now their families had come down, and there was some hardship about it; but I was determined. In fact I told the skipper that he had to navigate us to Darwin, and if he deviated from the course more than five degrees either way he would be shot and thrown overboard. It so happened that the engineer did not take a wink of sleep for seventy-two hours, nor did Harry Coe. Harry stood alongside the engineer; he helped him with every chore that he had to do with the engines; he kept the oils up; he kept the bearings going; he did everything. I took post alongside the skipper at the helm. The rest of the crew were posted around the ship to see that there were no untoward happenings from anyone. I didn't move from the helm from the time we left till we knew where we were in Snake Bay. I had the fear that in the night the skipper might have been able to turn the ship into reverse and go back on a 180 degree course, and it would have been very difficult for me to know where we were. But the sky was cloudless and I was able to mark our course on stars. When we realised where we were, after being able to orient ourselves from the small maps we had, we had to reverse course from Snake Bay and sail fifty miles north-west to clear Melville Island. We then sailed down the west coast of Bathurst Island, till we crossed to Darwin.

Young: The first thing we could see was Point Charles lighthouse. We were home. The intention then was to go and have dinner at the Hotel Darwin as soon as we got in. When we sailed towards the bay and through the boom we couldn't make out what we were looking at; we could see these sticks in the bay. They were actually sunken ships from the bombing raid on February 19. And as we went in we looked up and saw the devastation of the Hotel Darwin and the Post Office and everything. So we knew that our dinner at the Hotel Darwin would not be on.

Warn: Everybody was terribly thrilled. It was something I didn't expect to succeed because the elements were against us, particularly on the long trip across the Arafura Sea. At the end it's just one of those feelings that, well, we've done it, where do we go from here? It was a long shot, but it was worth trying because if we'd stayed in the POW camp we possibly would not be here today.

They came into Darwin Harbour on May 4, 1942. It was seven weeks since they went under the wire at Tantui camp on Ambon. The Australians on the *Griffioen* had escaped being prisoners, but they were still soldiers and they had over three years of war to fight. Jinkins went to Melbourne to help plan a rescue mission to Ambon. At the last moment the mission was aborted: all Australian prisoners were to wait until the general surrender. Unlike the Americans in the Philippines, and the British in Burma, they would not be liberated by battle.

In October 1942, Ian Macrae, who had helped organise the escape from Ambon, was shipped with other Australian prisoners to Hainan Island. There, in April 1945, he joined five other men who were taking their chances with the Chinese guerillas in the interior of the island. When they left they thought they might be the only ones who would live to say what happened to the 263 Australians who had landed on Hainan.

Macrae: We were helped somewhat by the fact that an air raid was going on, and we got out with a bit of difficulty. The fence was electrified at that stage, and getting underneath that and crawling over prickly pears was not my idea of a pastime. But we got out. We made for what we thought was the right direction, crawled under some bushes about 4 o'clock in the morning, and went to sleep. Miles Higgins woke up, crawled around, then told everybody for God's sake to keep their heads down because we were only about fifty yards from a Japanese fort. So we kept our heads down. And it may have been a good thing because the Japanese probably gave us credit for sufficient intelligence not to be as close to a Japanese fort as all that.

The following night we took off. Before dawn Tommy Lockwood and I were wandering around looking for water. By this time we were short of water, and we'd got away with just a few handfuls of cooked rice. When we came back to where the other four were we found them surrounded by the wildest looking lot of brigands you've ever seen in your life; muzzle loading muskets, bows and arrows, and a sort of bow thing around their heads. They picked us up and took us into a Chinese village that was completely surrounded by a double palisade. Fortunately for us it was a Nationalist village, and the Nationalists apparently had orders from Chungking to succour escaping prisoners-of-war. They looked after us for quite some time; I suppose a week.

I kept agitating to move on because our condition wasn't getting any better, and I could see beriberi starting. Eventually the headman of the village got some cove to start a party, and after a lot of wanderings and dodgings—I was never quite sure whether we were dodging the Japs or the Communists—we eventually got to the Chinese headquarters. At that stage they were very aggressive to the Japs. If they got hold of a Jap they'd torture him to death, and invite you to come and see it, something I was never very keen to do. But I think on the whole the Chinese tactics served a purpose. There were a couple of Japanese divisions on the island, and they were held there by the Chinese policy. I think that the Communists did as much damage to the Japs by blowing up bridges and tearing up railway lines as the Nationalists did.

I did my level best to get a move to the mainland. First of all to get arms so that the five or six of us could do something about the bloody Japs. But the Chinese would never give us any arms. They fed us pretty well. We had the same sort of food as Chinese headquarters had: buffalo meat, beans and vegetables. Actually we were infinitely better off—we didn't know we were alive compared with the chaps left in the camp.

The Chinese heard of the end of the war on their pedal radio and the escapers celebrated with rice and Chinese whisky. It was a false alarm; but a second and accurate report of the Japanese surrender followed; and they celebrated again. The Chinese brought in leaflets telling them to take any Allied servicemen to the United States forces that had landed on the island. Fred Perrin, reluctant to take risks with his freedom, asked how could they be sure it wasn't a Japanese trick. Macrae said that if Americans were on Hainan they could come and get them. They did. The five surviving escapers who were driven to the coast by American paratroopers were Macrae, Perrin, Stewart Campbell, Ron Leech and Tommy Lockwood. Miles Higgins had died of malaria at the Chinese Nationalist headquarters.

The other Australians who took long shots to liberty by joining independent guerillas were still active soldiers in the early months of the war. While with Jock Smyllie's group in southern Malaya, Bill McCure was in action when most other members of the 8th Division were becoming used to the impotence of being prisoners:

> We set to and started to lay charges on the railway line. We did this with quite a deal of excitement and a lot of fun. A lot of worrying times, a lot of panic. You'd get caught unprepared by Jap patrols or Tamils. They were quite active days, and I would say fruitful days to a point where we caused havoc on the railway line.
>
> Who suffered? Well the Malay suffered because as soon as we were successful in doing something they'd send in patrols. We'd leave our area and go into the jungle on the far side of the line. Their patrols would just go through the Malayan villages and slaughter the whole lot of them. Which was so sad; but this was war. I think, even if I say so myself, we did a damn good job.

When the Australians first joined the Chinese Communist guerillas they had tasks in combat units.

Arthur Shephard: I and the others with me were training the guerillas in all sorts of military things: aiming rifles, throwing hand grenades, and using machine guns and dynamite and all that sort of stuff. Their idea of rifle fire, for instance, was getting out a rifle and madly going bang, bang, bang with it; they had no idea of any military training whatsoever. Most of them could speak Malay, and I learnt Malay, and could converse with them and instruct them.

> During the first weeks of the war the price on my head was one bag of rice, about eighteen dollars. In the last years of the war the price went up to about 500 000 dollars. Of course the Japs could do that because they printed the money.

McCure: We were raided on one occasion; the Japs got through and raided our camp. And Les Taylor, who was the ex-manager of a tin mine and who was on guard, was shot by the Chinese for neglect of duty. There was no court of enquiry, no nothing, he was just shot. His Chinese guard companion was demoted and sent to another camp somewhere.

Shephard: We made a monopoly set out of memory, and we made cards. We used to play a lot of cribbage. And we told stories to one another. So we filled in our time pretty well.

But for most of the time the few British and Australian soldiers were scattered in different jungle camps.

The Chinese gradually imposed tighter restrictions on the foreigners in their guerilla units; they rarely let them out on operations and they took away their arms and much of their private property. The Australians were told that if they tried to leave the camps without authority they would be shot. The guerillas probably feared that any white soldier attempting to escape would be quickly picked up by the Japanese and tortured to reveal the location of camps, names of guerillas and methods of operation. After a time, McCure says,

> We felt that we were their prisoners, but we didn't think the word prisoner. We felt that each day our troops would be back. You go along with the system with the expectation that you will be saved in time. Certainly we did not expect to have to go on for three or four years. After a while we felt that it was only a matter of whose turn it was next to die.

You start to fail a little bit healthwise. You get to a point where you've got nobody to talk to, and at night times in particular, night times and early mornings, you just wander off to the outskirts of the camp and you squat down. You'd pray; you might weep. I'd be thinking of Mum and Dad. And I suppose it comes to a situation where it doesn't matter what the circumstances are, even if you're crook, if you've got somebody to talk to it's half the battle. Not to have anybody to talk to was difficult. It was difficult.

Shephard: The other people in my party died over a period of about four years through malaria, beriberi and other things. They just died. I nearly died also. They dug a hole for me about three times. But I managed to pull through. I was just one of the lucky people, that's all.

McCure: I can't single out any incident where a given day stands out: by Jove, that was funny, or, I really enjoyed that. I can't. All I can think of is swamp, moving over that swamp. All I can think of is leeches, snakes, mosquitoes and sickness. There was no way of sending a note to Bluey Ryan or Shephard who might have been at a camp, and you were not to know what he was doing. You just knew that somewhere around the circuit there were other camps.

Shephard: I attended a People's Court one day where two traitors were being tried. As they spoke in the Chinese dialect of Hainan, and I couldn't understand Hainan, I wandered back, and there was a fellow guarding more traitors. I asked him if he would like to attend the meeting, and he said he would, and so I said, well, I will take over guard while you go.

During the day a water buffalo was brought into camp. When they brought a buffalo in they generally cut it open, took out the heart and liver, did it up with herbs and made it very nice. They gave it to a chosen few. Some time after the trial was over I smelt beautiful meat cooking in the kitchen. A Chinese wandered up to me and said in Malay, 'Have something to eat.' I took it and ate it, and it was very nice. I asked him for some more when he came back, but he said, 'No, we only had two.' I said, 'Two? I only saw one water buffalo come into the camp.' He said, 'Oh, that wasn't water buffalo, that was traitor!'

Well, it was the heart and liver of a traitor. It tasted nice anyway. I was most reluctant to bring it up. But it's only mind over matter. In the jungle we ate anything that was edible: rat, cat, dog, snake, bear, elephant. To eat elephant it took twenty-four hours boiling to make the meat tender enough to eat.

McCure: The normal practice with prisoners was to put them through torture. They'd be tied down to the ground, ants would be put on them, they'd be cut with knives, leeches would be brought; they'd have water poured into their mouths, they'd be kicked, hit with rifles, hit with sticks, hair pulled, finger nails pulled. And the individual might be so innocent. You never knew this. The conclusion would be, when they couldn't get any more out of him, he would be made to dig his own grave. He would be placed up against a small sapling, four or five inches in diameter, and a loop of cane would go around that and then around his neck. And half a dozen fellows would pull on each end of the cane, and so there would be slow strangulation. We witnessed this. We saw a lot of it. We saw them opening up the individual while still alive. They'd open up the chest and get out the heart and eat it because it gave them courage, it gave them strength. They ate it raw.

The gap between the young Australians and the Communist guerillas was as great as between the Australians and the Sakai, the frightened, shy aboriginal people who sometimes left their jungle homes and came into the camps. Moments of compassion between a lone Australian and a guerilla, expressed in a hand on a shoulder, or a shared laugh, were rare. The Australians were as isolated by the customs and the fervent, primitive politics of the guerillas as they were by the jungle and the Japanese. And the rain forest overwhelmed the camps, cutting out all sunlight.

At the end of the war the Chinese took Bill McCure, who was ill with malaria and scarcely conscious, by stretcher and canoe to hospital in Muar. Bluey Ryan and Arthur Shephard were the only other Australians to survive with the guerillas. While still in the jungle Shephard heard rumours of a big bomb dropped on Japan, and that the war was probably over. In August 1945 he walked out of the jungle at Segamat. He had a haircut and a shave, and went off to find the British special unit that had parachuted in just before the Japanese surrender:

> They were loaded to the teeth with all sorts of arms, automatics on each knee, big machine guns, and everything like that. I happened to walk into the camp the back way. And I just walked up to them and said, 'Howdy fellows.' They couldn't make it out. They wondered where I came from. They thought there was no white man there.

McCure stayed on with the paratroopers as an interpreter. In the turbulent aftermath of war at Batu Pahat the small British force tried to reduce communal murders as they moved between road blocks, crowds of parang-wielding Malays, and isolated Chinese *kampongs* where the people feared extermination. In peace McCure saw a continuation of hate and violence as intense as he had known in war.

Arthur Shephard went down to Singapore to re-enter the army's bureaucracy:

> I was interviewed by a young lieutenant sitting at a desk underneath a coconut tree in the open. He had piles of papers everywhere. He had just come from Australia. I walked in, saw this lieutenant, and he said, 'What do you want?' I said, 'I've come round here to be interrogated.' He said, 'What's the story?' I said, 'I wasn't taken a prisoner-of-war; I've been in the jungle for three and a half years.' 'Oh,' he said, 'I've got no forms like that to fill in. I've only got prisoner-of-war forms here. I'll have to take it down in longhand.' So off he went: 'I Arthur Frederick Shephard, VX 39088, sergeant, 2/29 Battalion . . .'. He went right through the whole details: 'I have lived with the Chinese gorrillas ...'. I looked over his shoulder and said, 'Break it down, I wasn't one of those!' And he said, 'Oh yes, how silly. It's spelt with one 'r' isn't it.'

Shephard, Ryan and McCure met in Singapore before they came home. Although they had never surrendered to the Japanese they had suffered hardships and constraints equal to those in the toughest camps; and the death rate for Europeans living with the guerillas was higher than the general rate among Australian prisoners-of-war.

The only Australians to break out of Japanese prison camps and reach Australia escaped from Ambon and Borneo. And there were only about twenty-five of them. In all cases they were dependent on acts of courage by local peoples. Around the same number of prisoners escaped, were captured and executed; and others died while trying to escape. The Japanese punished the prisoners remaining in the camps by reducing food and imposing other restrictions; but they did not, as they threatened to do, kill others in reprisal. Only in the last year at Sandakan and Ranau was escaping the best way to survive; and then it was the only way.

TRAVELLING IN CAPTIVITY

'So when we were going up the gang plank one of the chaps near me said, "We'll see if these are life preservers." So we dropped one and it went straight to the bottom.'

An irony of being a prisoner-of-war was that men travelled further in captivity than at any time before in their lives. Only in retirement as they caravan around Australia and take packaged tours back to sites of young manhood and horror are they again travelling so far. Australian servicemen captured on Singapore went north to Burma, followed the railway into Thailand, crossed to Saigon, back to Singapore, and took ship to Japan. Prisoners travelled by truck through the mountains of central Sumatra; they marched nearly a thousand kilometres into the interior of Thailand; they went by barge down the Mekong River; by train from Phnom Penh to Singapore and from South Korea to Manchuria; and they sailed in all kinds of sea-going craft. The prisoners became experts at travelling under duress.

Travelling dispersed units. The 2/6th Field Company of Engineers was captured in Java. By the end of the war only ten men were still in Java. Others were scattered in Sumatra, Borneo, Singapore, Indo-China, Thailand and Japan. The 2/29th Battalion suffered in the fighting on the Malayan Peninsula and on Singapore; but it lost many more men after the surrender. The battalion dead were separated by thousands of kilometres. Men died with the communist guerillas in Malaya, with A Force in Burma, with B Force in Borneo, with F and H Forces in Thailand, and others were buried or cremated in camps as far apart as Java and Japan. The prisoners were like debris in a flood. Some were dumped in backwaters; they were caught in eddies, detached from one group and linked with another; and they stayed in the mainstream while all around them sections were impeded and diverted. When prisoners met an immediate task was to trace movements of different groups and speculate on the whereabouts of other men from the unit.

Travel by sea was one of the most dangerous experiences imposed on prisoners-of-war. Before the Japanese entered the war ships carrying prisoners had been sunk in European waters, and the International Red Cross called on the warring nations to protect prisoners-of-war at sea. Germany and the Allies could not agree on a way to give free passage to prisoners' ships at sea; the Japanese would not consider the matter at all. Throughout the war prisoners had to take their chances against the planes and submarines of their own side.

The Japanese attempted to ship over 4000 Australian servicemen and six nurses from the Pacific and South-east Asia to Japan. The prisoners were exposed to a long and hazardous journey. The risks increased as the war went on and Allied naval and air power increased. Donald Stuart, a machine gunner captured in Java, was shipped to Singapore, went by train to work on the Thai end of the railway, returned to Singapore, and early in 1945 he was one of hundreds of prisoners crowded on a cargo boat bound for Japan. On some previous voyage the prisoners' ship had been sunk and resurrected; but it was not the least seaworthy craft in the convoy.

Stuart: We had two Co-Prosperity Sphere ships which were rather like the Yank Liberty Ships, thrown together out of sardine tins and welded with chewing gum, and three Japanese sloops. We always prayed for night so that the recce planes couldn't see us, and then we prayed for daylight so the submarines couldn't get us. One night, we didn't know where we were going, one of the Co-Prosperity Sphere ships went with a whoomf! And we said, 'Oh Jesus, that's good!' Someone said, 'Good! If those bastards are about, the Yanks or whoever they are knocking them off, they could knock us off too!' Someone else said, 'Shut up. All those Japs on that ship have gone down. That's good.'

A bit later the other Co-Prosperity Sphere ship went down just coming on daylight. The following night one of the sloops went. Coming on daylight the second sloop went. And I tell you straight, it's a bloody great thing to see them go. Whoomp! The third one, just after daylight, they must have hit him fair in the magazine because he was a real bloody Guy Fawkes show. Our blokes were packing it a bit that we'd be next. I mean, we were last out of six, and the odds were agin us. And yet we were so bloody pleased to see these bloody Jap ships go down, taking the Japs with them. Then we ran out of bloody coal so they're breaking up the interior fittings, feeding them into the boiler. Of course there's sparks and smoke and everything and when it come on night time, you could see half of the South China Sea or whatever it was with our bloody flare from the funnel. But we got through.

Stan Gilchrist, who kept a diary on the same convoy, noted that a 'pretty hard-bitten old Aussie' called Brum steadied the panic in the holds. Brum, who had worked in shearing sheds and on whalers, shouted in his commanding voice, 'Have some bloody sense!' and the rush for the deck became orderly. The Javanese prisoners refused to go back into the hold, and found places for themselves in every topside corner. A Japanese destroyer packed with survivors escorted the prisoners past dozens of sunken boats and into Saigon. To the relief of the prisoners that was the end of their sea travels.

Another draft of Australian prisoners leaving Singapore in July 1944 saw their ship and knew that their chances of sinking were high, even without Allied bombs or torpedoes. Ray Parkin, a survivor of the *Perth*, looked with the eyes of a professional seaman:

She'd been called the *Potomac*. She was a Blue Funnel ship, but she'd been in Singapore and apparently bombed. Her bridge was burnt down, her number two hold had been burnt out, the deck had dropped about fifteen inches under the heat of the fire and she was just a wreck. Some of our fellows had to go down to the wharf one day to do a bit of loading and they worked on this ship. They came back and very facetiously said, 'We've just been working on the ship we're going to Japan in.' They didn't know how right they were. When we were finally marched into the ship they nearly collapsed. This thing, she was virtually a derelict.

Reg Newton: Petty Officer Horry Abbott, he looked her up and down, and he said, 'Well, I've never seen a ship in all my life like it. It's an absolute wreck. It's got to be *Maru*, to finish with, but the only thing I can think of, it's *Byoki*: it's a bloody sick ship. From them on, that ship was called the *Byoki Maru*.

Others say Don Moore drew a cartoon and labelled it the '*Byoki Maru*', and that gave the ship its new name. Apart from being the *Potomac*, the same ship had also been during her undistinguished career the *Canadian Prince* and the *Rashin Maru*.

Gordon Maxwell: Well, I guess it wasn't a great deal bigger than a Sydney ferry. We just couldn't believe that we were going to Japan in this tub. We thought we must be going somewhere to tranship to a vessel of bigger proportions and more seaworthy.

Parkin: Her engines were I suppose sound enough, but right on the poop they had rigged a jury bridge. We reckoned we were the terror of the China seas. We were armed, and the arm was a brass, wheeled cannon like you see in the old fashioned pictures of battlefields, and a heap of cannon balls alongside it. So we were a defensively armed merchantman. They marched us into this ship—there were 1200 of us went and she was only about three or four thousand tons. There were no number one or number two hatch covers; she was open right down to the lower hold. Well, anyone that's been to sea knows that it's a bit risky going to sea with uncovered hatches.

Hugh Clarke: Major Newton was in charge of us, so we were marched down, and there was a big pile of rubber lying on the wharf, and each man was told to pick up two of these twenty pound bales of rubber.

Newton: Lieutenant Tanaka, the Japanese officer was there. I said, 'What the hell are these for?' He said, 'They are your life preservers. You will carry them on board with you and look after them.' So when we were going up the gang plank one of the chaps near me said, 'We'll see if these are life preservers.' So we dropped one and it went straight to the bottom. That was the life preserver.

Parkin: The people that went into three and four hatches were under cover. But we were open to the sky. The tweendeck was only a shelf around the edge really, with a coaming in the middle. And I think there were about 400 of us packed down into that space.

There was literally standing room only. But I sat on a couple of bales of rubber with my back up against a bulkhead, and I sat like that for three days without being able to move. There just wasn't the room to move, and we weren't allowed on deck much. Your first thought was that this is impossible. But then the impossible somehow becomes possible. You think, this can't be, it can't last. But it does, and you adapt to it somehow. We were seventy days in that hatch.

Maxwell: We treated the old *Byoki Maru* as just another camp. Men were assigned to cook the rice. It was all steam cooking. The rice used to come out in a great four-gallon tin sort of thing and be apportioned out.

Cliff Moss: Two feeds of rice pap a day, and there wasn't much of that. They had a lot of dried fish like a sort of herring which we called Modern Girls. You know about the modern girls no doubt. Two faced and got no guts. Finally they went rotten, these bloody Modern Girls.

Frank Baker: The food had maggots in it. It had, well, you name it and it had it in it; but of course it was stewed up with rice and we ate it. And it stunk. You were sick from it, but you got over that and you ate it again because there was nothing else.

Parkin: It wasn't a comfortable voyage, we'll say that much about it. The weather was relatively good until we got to Manila, but we were cursed with flies. So the Japanese with great practicality said right, each man kills ten flies a day. Of course in the beginning this was easy, there were plenty of flies. We had to produce bodies at night and they were counted and then thrown overboard, so that you couldn't bring them into the next day's tally. But eventually it became a game of great skill to catch your ten flies for the day. Even the Japs had to give up eventually. We killed nearly all the flies. But we went down in the lower hold, we went everywhere. If a fly landed on a fellow it was more than his life was worth for him to move until someone had got the fly. I remember on one occasion a bloke had spilt some tea or coffee or something, someone that had a little bit of *gula*, sugar. This spilled on the bloke and he cursed the bloke who had spilled it on him, but the other chap said, 'Don't move! The flies are coming!'

Clarke: The sanitary arrangements on the ship were two wooden boxes which held two men at a time, on each side, so there were four boxes. These were slung over the side. And no one was allowed on the deck except to get into the toilet, which meant you had to take your turn, and when the bloke got out of the box, and came back, well, you could take his place.

The sanitary arrangements were two wooden boxes which held two men at a time, on each side. The boxes always had a tremendous queue.

David Thompson: There was always a lot of diarrhoea and dysentery on the boat, so the boxes always had a tremendous queue. And there was never any toilet paper provided so one had to do the best one could, even if one's favourite book had to be used for toilet paper, bum fodder, as it was called more colloquially. Now this old Herb McNamara was a very devout reader. While we were on the boat he learnt one book of the Bible, I think *Revelations*, completely by heart, and he'd set off to learn one of Shakespeare's plays. Somebody had the book of Shakespeare and Herb was reading it lying on the deck one afternoon and he came to a place where there was one page missing. He was most concerned because it stopped him learning the rest of the Shakespearean play. When a gust of wind suddenly brought a piece of paper past him, Herb quickly recognised it as a page out of the book that he was reading.

He grabbed it with great joy and said, 'You wouldn't believe that, it's Scene 2 Act I; it's just the page that was missing'. He turned it over on to the back and here was a very nasty big brown smear on the back of the page! Obviously the wind blowing from the side of the ship had wrought that miracle for Herb.

Newton: We had nothing at all to entertain the blokes. They had singsongs and things like that, but probably the most successful thing that I started was to give them the one exercise: how much would it have cost you in peace time to have travelled over the area that you have travelled since you have been in the services? And from then on, for seventy days until we hit Japan, it was the longest journey ever of a ship to Japan, you could hear them saying, 'What's the bloody second class fare from Bathurst to Sydney? What's the fare from Quilpie to Brisbane?' And it was all mental arithmetic. I told them, whoever gives me the best ten answers will get a carton of cigarettes each.

Maxwell: You know, you'd have great arguments, terrific arguments. I remember one particularly: it was whether when you made a sponge cake, you put butter in it. No, butter's no good, you know, that's fat, that wouldn't let the sponge rise. No, somewhere, you've got to put butter in a sponge cake. So this argument would rage for an hour or more.

Parkin: In our gear we'd brought a lot of nits. We tried to do away with all the bugs we could, but we still had the nits, and in the hot, humid conditions these bugs bred like mad. They got into the bales of latex where you couldn't possibly get at them. Before long we were almost being carried around the hold by these bugs, and of course they were biting us and keeping us awake. At night we would sneak up on deck with a couple of bales and drop them in the wake of the ship.

Lice was another thing we got there. A louse is a fairly transparent thing, and against the skin he's not noticeable. But once he's had his breakfast you can see the little blood spot in his stomach, and that gives him away. We used to sit on deck in friendly conversation in a little lice-catching circle. I remember one bloke, they were hunting them, and he was going 'Tally ho, there goes the bastard'. He'd say, 'I think this one is Will o'the Wisp out of Dracula'. Well, all that ironic sending up of ourselves was going on. That was just part of the deck sports we had on board.

The voyage, rarely out of sight of land, was uneventful until the *Byoki Maru* was off the entrance to Manila Bay. Just as the prisoners thought they were about to reach safety they heard heavy crashes against the hull; the Japanese were dropping depth charges. The rest of the transports in the convoy steamed into the Bay while the *Byoki* turned in a slow circle. The prisoners feared they were the bait to trap an Allied submarine.

The *Byoki* waited three weeks in Manila. The prisoners were hot and ill-fed; and the guards bad-tempered. The number of torpedo-ripped and distorted Japanese boats in Manila Bay did not increase the confidence of the prisoners. On August 9, 1944 the *Byoki Maru* joined a convoy of thirty vessels for Japan.

Clarke: Well, we wouldn't have been a mile outside the harbour when there was an enormous explosion and the tanker behind us vanished. There was just flecks of oil and pieces of debris on the water. You couldn't see any people. Of course, then our own guards came and belted us down into the hold.

Don Noble: The ship in front was a freighter; the ship behind was the tanker. And those two were blown out of the water. And I can still see in my mind the mast of the freighter which would have been a 5000, probably 10 000 tonner; she was a big freighter. And to see the whole foremast, just going up like a lazy thing, just going up and up, turning as it went, and coming down. By the time it hit the water there was nothing left of the ship. Now God only knows what was on that ship, but it just disappeared. We drove through the rubbish that was left, and the next thing of course, the tanker at the back went up too.

Clarke: In the hold I was in there was a bugler from the 2/19th battalion, Tich someone or other. But he started to play 'Rule Britannia'. And instantaneously everybody in the hold started to sing. There was nothing premeditated about it, we found ourselves all singing 'Rule Britannia'—of course it was an American submarine, but that didn't matter. The Japs were going crook on top. But we wouldn't shut up, we finished it. And then they called the man with the bugle. So Tich went up on deck, and he got a terrible thrashing; they broke his arm and threw his bugle overboard and he eventually came down. I think Reg Newton got a hiding at the same time, trying to stop them belting the bugler. And to belt Newton, who was over six foot, to get at Newton's face, they'd stand him near the steps and the Jap would go up about two steps to hit him with ease.

Maxwell: We always took some comfort in the fact that no self-respecting submarine commander would ever waste a torpedo on the *Byoki Maru* when there was a tanker or something else in the convoy.

Baker: Then this typhoon hit us. And it was a most shocking thing. In a vessel of any kind, but a ship like that, well, I just wonder that I'm talking to you now because I didn't think that ship would survive even a ripple. The waves I would say were fifty or sixty feet high, and if you were in the bow of the ship you looked directly up at the stern. Then the next minute you were looking directly down at the stern.

Maxwell: On the deck there were two huge girders, and these went from the fo'c'sle, right through as far down to the stern as we could see. They were spot welded to the deck. There was a crack right across the ship, about amidships where the bridge superstructure had originally been. Obviously the girders were holding the ship together. When we hit the typhoon and these mountainous seas and you couldn't see any other ship in the convoy, the old *Byoki Maru* started to sway and creak and groan, and various bangs—not quite as loud as a rifle shot—started to occur and we wondered what the devil was happening. And we suddenly found out because all the spot welds were breaking along the girder. Some mates and myself got ourselves at a spot near the old bridge and we were sort of astride the crack that ran across from side to side, and the crack started to open up and close as the ship went over waves. The welds were parting. We wondered how long this was going to go on.

Parkin: Of course with open hatches it was bad. But the one thing that saved her was she had such a high freeboard. She had little in her, and all the weight was bottom weight. Now when you stick bottom weight in a ship, what you do, you exaggerate the rolling, it goes like a pendulum. It swings about very violently. But with the high freeboard, she was keeping clear of the water. But I remember on one occasion she gave five violent rolls. And I thought she was going to go straight over. I was lying down athwartships on my back and one of the rolls actually threw me up on to my feet from a lying position. I just grabbed a stanchion and saved myself from being chucked down into the middle of the hold. But a mate of mine was thrown out into the centre of the hold. One of the hatch beams was loose and every roll it was careering across from one side of the ship to the other. Now these things weigh over two tons; a huge beam about twenty feet long. And this chap was being chased by this thing across the hold. He was running across the tops of barrels of latex. As the beam went across, it was knocking the tops of the barrels, and he was in great danger of stepping into one. If he'd stepped into one and the beam had come after him it would have cut him in half. The footwork he got up to was fantastic; it was just like a diabolical sword dance with this two ton beam careering after him.

Newton: I've read a few books about the soul of a ship and I will say that ship did have a soul. There was something there that nobody could ever fathom. That typhoon scattered and sunk ships in the American Fleet, yet that old hulk, without any hatch covers, and the water coming in all over the place remained afloat. Coupled with the fact that the Japanese skipper was superb. He was good, without the slightest, slightest doubt.

Parkin: Men were in the last stages of seasickness; they were almost turning inside out. There was nothing there; they were just heaving and retching. I think some of them were in fear of disembowelling themselves through the mouth. And of course there was this awful vertigo with the ship moving. We had christened this ship *Byoki Maru*. You see, you never said you were sick. You'd say 'Oh, *byoki, byoki*.' So we had named her the Spirit of Sickness. And she was one of us, you see, we had a great fellow feeling for her.

With rivets popping under the stress and loose drums thundering about the deck, the captain pulled the *Byoki* out of the convoy and sheltered among the Mabudis islets north of the Philippines.

After a day in refuge, the *Byoki* sailed in smooth waters to Taiwan. With the normal confusion, the Japanese and their prison labourers provisioned and coaled the *Byoki*. The prisoners raffled the few extra packets of cigarettes that came aboard. After a false start in which the convoy sailed and returned to the starting anchorage, the *Byoki* was under way to Japan. The prisoners provided their own passenger comforts.

Parkin: The fellows noticed that there was a leak in the bottom of the ship—she was only single plating. This leak was like a minor spring; there was a trickle of water coming in. One of the chaps got a bright idea. He got a bit of three-by-three dunnage and gave it a good whack, and it came in like a little fountain.

Don Moore: A fellow said, 'Oh, you'll have to report that to the guards'. I said, 'No. Just hang on for a while; we'll all have a wash first.' And so we had about three or four hours of this beautiful water laid on. We had a lovely time playing and frolicking underneath that water jet.

Newton: It was about a two-inch hole and the water was taking a bit more of the rusted flaked steel off. Obviously the Nips had to find out because their bilge pumps could not handle the water, and they came up and found out what was happening.

Parkin: So the captain and the chief engineer and a couple of carpenters came around searching, and when they found the leak in the lower hold, of course they bashed us and sent us out of it. The carpenter sharpened a huge plug and drove it into the leak to stop it. But that finished the business as far as our washing was concerned. Well, to do a thing like that he had to be a farmer, not a sailor.

Clarke: The captain was a very humane sort of fellow. We had no complaints about the crew or the captain; when people died he always slowed the engines and there was a ceremony as the body went overboard.

Maxwell: We finally made land at Kagoshima in Japan on September 3, which was an odd date: five years after the outbreak of war. We were there for a day and then we went on to Moji.

The men stood to attention in sight of terraced hills as they conducted their last burial at sea. Warrant Officer Ned Turner, who had done more than his share on the railway, died two days out of Moji. His body was wrapped in his blanket, weighted, and slid under the flag and into the sea.

Noble: When we got to Moji the Japanese crew all lined the decks and waved farewell to the POWs. It was an extraordinary thing.

The captain and crew of the Byoki Maru were merchant seamen. With their experience of the ports of the world they were less aggressively patriotic than most Japanese servicemen. They sometimes stopped guards from bashing prisoners, and when talking to prisoners they agreed that Japan would probably lose the war.

At the same time as the prisoners on the Byoki were taking their first look at the rocky outline of southern Japan, Able Seaman Arthur Bancroft sailed from Singapore on the Rokyu Maru. She was one of two transports taking another draft of 2200 British and Australian prisoners to work in Japan. 'Blood' Bancroft, who had already survived the sinking of the Perth, was as sceptical as earlier prisoners of the value of the hard block of rubber that he lugged on board. He guessed that the Japanese aimed to carry in the one ship both the raw materials and the labourers to sustain the war for their homeland. Outside the harbour the Rokyu Maru fell in line with three other merchant steamers, two tankers and four escorting destroyers. A week later the Royku Maru was steaming in convoy off the south China coast.

Bancroft: One of the tankers got hit. That went up with a terrific roar and flames, so we knew straight away that there was a submarine attack. I think it was only a matter of minutes later another one went up, and we thought, when is it going to be our turn? We didn't have to wait too long. We would have been silhouetted against the burning ships, so we were a sitting duck. Now when a torpedo hits, the whole ship seems to go up in the air and then down again. So that first torpedo hit and just lifted the ship. We started trying to get out of the hold. There were only two ways to get out: up a small companion ladder, which would take a long time to get people out, or to get the covers off and throw ropes over. You can get a lot up that way. That's when the second torpedo hit. But that actually just went straight through the bows and we could hear the water coming into the holds forrard of us; but as we found out later, it had just blown a great big hole through the ship. So luckily neither torpedo hit where there were any of our troops. Nobody got killed or injured in the torpedo attack.

    Then it became clear that we could be drifting towards the burning vessels; the water was alight around the tankers. That was when it was decided that we may have to abandon ship. We didn't know exactly what damage had been done except we were sitting dead in the water. But with two torpedoes in the ship we knew we couldn't stay on board too long. Up till that stage it was suggested nobody jump over until we could assess the situation. When we started drifting towards the burning oil on the water, it was decided, by whom I don't know, it will be abandon ship and just take whatever you can to float with and every man for himself. By the time we got everybody out of the holds and decided on what action to take, the Japanese had taken the lifeboats and they'd gone. They had abandoned ship very quickly. As far as we were concerned we could do what we wanted. We were free for the first time for two and a half years. So that's when we abandoned ship, throwing ourselves in the hands of fate again.

When we jumped from the ship there still wasn't any indication it was sinking. And as things turned out it didn't sink for about twelve hours or so. But our main concern was to get away from the burning tankers with oil alight on the surface. Once we got into the water we struck out in the opposite direction, and it didn't seem to take long before we were quite a distance away. By the time dawn came— and I think from memory it was around about five o'clockish in the morning—we seemed to be a quarter of a mile away from the ship. At that stage we were in little groups, and I think the group I was with might have been a hundred or so, all gathered round, just hanging on to whatever there was to hang onto. We had one Jap officer in amongst us, he had his sword and full regalia on. We thought he might be our meal ticket. Rather than hold him under the water, we got him up, balanced on one of these rafts, to signal to the Jap destroyer that was whizzing around, and eventually the destroyer came over and dropped a lifeboat off. They came over with an officer in the bow with a revolver holding us at bay, and got the Jap officer to swim to the boat. They hauled him in, went back to the destroyer, took the boat back on board. And then off it took.

After the destroyers had rescued the Japanese crew and guards the prisoners took over the abandoned lifeboats. The destroyers, continuing to patrol among the debris, picked up the Allied prisoners in one lifeboat; but the men scattered in the water heard firing and believe that the prisoners in other lifeboats were killed. Late on the same day, and beyond the hearing of the men from the *Rokyu Maru*, the second transport, the *Kachidoki Maru* was also torpedoed, and nearly 1000 British prisoners were forced to abandon ship within twenty minutes of the first strike.

While the hulk of the *Rokyu Maru* was still afloat prisoners climbed back on board and took whatever they thought would be useful. Bancroft was too far away to battle the currents back to the *Rokyu Maru*, and he had to make do with what he had when he jumped.

Bancroft: When we got into the water, my particular mate said, 'We'll stick together and we'll see this out'. And the next morning we had oil all over us, in our mouths, ears and eyes. I had my water bottle which I'd protected very jealously just in case this happened. Lofty said to me, 'Hey, let's have a little swig of your water and that'll help keep us going'. I said, 'OK'. Uncorked the bottle and handed it to him. Of course having oil all over his hands and all over the bottle, it just slipped through his hands. And by the time we got it back, the salt water had gone in and mixed with the fresh water so it was useless.

We seemed to settle in to several groups of a hundred or so. But after the ships had disappeared and night time came we found the groups were starting to get a bit disjointed. Some men were starting to drink salt water, some were starting to go a bit berserk, so much so that a fight developed between a couple of the English troops on one of the rafts. The next day these army fellows said, 'Look, this is no good to us, what about we break away from this main group? You're the sailor, where's the nearest land?' I said, 'Oh, I would think the Philippines would be the nearest and that would be over in that direction'. They said, 'Well, let's paddle towards the Philippines.' I said to Lofty, 'Come with us, we're going to break away from this group.' Lofty was sitting on one of the rafts up to his waist in water, and he said, 'No, I think I'll stick it here because I've got a seat on the raft'. And I said, 'No, come with us'. But he wouldn't. That group was never seen again.

But we broke out. There were a lot of these little rafts around, so we gathered them together until we had one each and we tied them together; we tried to get one on top of the other to get us out of the water, but that was pretty difficult. We paddled for an hour or so until we were out of sight of the big group. And we were just on our own out in the middle of the ocean, just the six of us. The sixth one, we picked him up as he was floating past. He had some sort of life jacket on, but he was in fairly bad shape from drinking oil and salt water. We swam over, grabbed him, tied him onto one of the rafts and stopped him from drinking any more salt water.

We decided that we weren't making much headway paddling with our hands and we thought well, we'll have to just let the current do whatever it wanted. We just sort of settled in there. It was all a joint effort. We decided that we had to stop being dehydrated as much as we could because the sun was hot. One of the Army blokes had a long-sleeved jacket on, I only had a short-sleeved jacket. And he said, 'Blood, you'll get sunburnt too much,' and he took off his long-sleeved jacket and gave it to me and took my short-sleeved one. Because he was a big bronzed Queenslander, he said, 'I don't burn like you bloody Western Australians!' And that was a help.

Whenever we got too hot, we slipped into the water. That's how we spent the day, just trying to stop dehydrating. We had a straw hat, from an old Dutch army hat. That helped later on when it rained, and we caught a bit of water in our hats. But that was not until, I think from memory, the fifth day. Nothing to eat, and nothing to drink. In one of the rafts they had a little water tank. We took all day and we eventually got it out and it was full of salt water. So that was that, but it gave us something to do. We saw a melon floating past, swam over and got it. That was just covered with oil and full of salt water, but we cleaned as much as we could off and it gave us a mouthful, just to provide a change from salt water. When we felt it necessary we rinsed our mouths out with salt water and then allowed a little to trickle down our throats. I'd always read a lot as a kid, and I'd read the *Mutiny on the Bounty* and remembered one of their lifesaving tactics. Captain Bligh allowed salt water to trickle down their throats when they ran out of water, and I couldn't see why if it worked for them it shouldn't work for us.

The attack by American submarines on the Japanese convoy had not been the result of a chance sighting. The Americans had intercepted Japanese radio signals; and the submarines were waiting. But the Americans did not know prisoners were on board.

Four days after the sinking of the transports carrying the prisoners, two American submarines were moving slowly back through the attack area. They were looking for information about the boats sunk and for crippled ships to destroy.

Bancroft: I suppose I was a fatalistic person. I never thought anything serious was going to happen to me. I just felt that I was indestructible I suppose. But youth is a great thing. I never thought for a minute that I wasn't going to get out of it. And I was with a group of fellows that had the same outlook. As we lay on the raft, we'd talk about the food that we hadn't eaten. We'd say what will we eat when we get home? We went through menus. We said one of the first things, we'd go to a hairdresser and get our hair cut and we'll have a facial massage—we used to talk like that, you know. I think this helped to get your mind off what was happening around us.

There was nothing happening around us. We just couldn't see anything; there was just water. And water and more water. The weather was calm, the sea was very flat, no wind to speak of in the first four days. And it was on the fourth day that the submarines started coming around. We knew they were there. We didn't know who they were, we didn't know whether they were Japanese, whether they were German or American. Two of them came along, and they were on diesel, and you could hear this diesel motor before you saw them. Up till then a couple of aircraft had gone over, and this was quite a different noise to aircraft. And so we tipped it must have been a submarine, because it was not the noise of a ship, it was this diesel noise. If you have ever heard a diesel motor at sea, it carries for miles.

When it was getting late afternoon, we could see this one submarine. We saw that it was heading towards us, then it would head away, then come back towards us, and head away again. So we were up, waving and yelling and doing all sorts of things.

Eventually it turned away from us and went out of sight. We found out later what had happened. They'd picked up so many they couldn't pick up any more. We were the next and they just couldn't get to us. Darkness settled in. I think that would have been our lowest. We looked at each other and thought, well, is this the end? Then the next day we said, you know, there must be others around; if there's one submarine around there must be others.

On the fifth day a bit of a sea started building up and the wind started rising. It rained and we caught some. Up till then the first lot of rain we experienced I think was on the fourth day. It was raining on the starboard side of us and raining on the port and we just drifted down the middle and didn't get any, not any. We were getting pretty dry by then. When it rained on the fifth day we had an old bucket that we'd picked up. We were scavengers: anything that was drifting past we'd grab it in case we needed it, and one thing was an empty rice bucket. We grabbed hold of that. So when it started raining we could channel some of the water into the bucket. And we caught some in our open mouths and whatever we could—in our hats. We ended up with a bucket full of water. It was salty, it was oily, because there was oil over everything, but that kept us going then for the fifth day. On the sixth day of course we lost the water because the seas had come up so rough that we had to eventually tie ourselves onto the raft. We each had a raft, we tied ourselves on, and the rafts were tied together so they wouldn't drift apart. We set out to ride out the storm, which we didn't realise was the edge of a typhoon.

Then we heard this noise again. It was in the afternoon and we heard the beat of the diesel. When we saw the submarine we weren't too certain whether it was there or not because it disappeared. Then we'd see it and it would disappear. But what happened was that we were floating on the surface of the water and of course the waves would have been ten or fifteen feet high; they were rough. We were going up and the submarine would go down. And of course we'd look out and we couldn't see the submarine, and the next time we'd see it. So we weren't too certain how far it was from us. But it was gradually getting closer, zigzagging round and looking for people. When they got to within hailing distance they called out. That was the first indication we knew it was an Allied sub. We didn't know if it was Japanese or what—but when they got close we could tell who they were. They looked so clean and so white. They were Americans, and they just told us, 'Take it easy, guys', and threw ropes to us. It was a fairly dangerous operation from their point of view. Some

had already dived overboard and were helping us out. But they were hanging over
the side of the submarine and getting hold of us by our arms and sort of lifting us up.
I suppose it was the old navy training, I jumped on board, turned to the captain,
who was up on the conning tower, and threw him a salute. The Yanks reckoned
that was pretty good. But it was purely reflex. If you join a ship of war, you salute the
quarter deck. So that's what I did.

Arthur Bancroft had jumped on board the United States submarine, the *Queenfish*. He was one of the last of the prisoners from the *Rokyu Maru* to be rescued. Nearly three-quarters of the prisoners on the two transports had been killed or drowned. The Japanese rescued 520 British prisoners from the *Kachidoki Maru*, and 277 British and Australian prisoners survived from the *Rokyu Maru*. American submarines picked up 141, and the Japanese destroyer took on board 136.

The Americans on the *Queenfish* were anxious to talk to Bancroft: he brought the first eye-witness account of the sinking of the *Houston* which had gone down with the *Perth* two and a half years earlier. The rescued prisoners also gave the first detailed accounts of the Burma-Thailand railway. The *Queenfish* arrived at the American island base of Saipan on September 25, 1944. Bancroft left the generous Americans, their food and nightly movies, and sailed via Guadalcanal for Australia. Ray Steele, who had reached Australia from the Philippines only seven months earlier, was one of the reception committee that met the *Rokyu Maru* survivors in Moreton Bay.

On June 24, 1944 the *Tamahoko Maru* carrying over 700 American, Australian, British and Dutch-Javanese prisoners was one day out of the Japanese port of Kure. With the lights of Japan in sight the guards drank and sang to celebrate their deliverance from the torpedoes that had shattered so many of the boats in the convoy. Down below Lieutenant Lance Gibson and a senior NCO were hiding the empty sugar bags and other evidence that the prisoners had consumed much of the *Tamahoko Maru*'s cargo of sugar and pumkins. Gibson went back to sleep in the 'tweendecks wondering how the men with every pocket of their clothes and kit crammed with sugar would get through the next day's searches. Suddenly everyone was awake as a ship in the convoy exploded. They had hardly scrambled to their feet when the *Tamahoko* was almost blown apart: men were killed and water poured in the gaping hole.

Gibson: The first thing I knew the water was coming in, and I was bumping against the
roof of the hold. I managed to kick towards the hatch cover which was blown off.
We had eighty men sleeping on the hatch cover and not one of them survived, the
blast was so bad.

I surfaced to see the back of the ship towering above me: and I went down with
it for quite a way. I thought it was half a mile, but it wouldn't be very far. I surfaced
again and swum around. I thought I was the only survivor because it was pitch
black. Then gradually I could see something in the water: it was the floor of the
bridge of our boat or another. The compass binnacle was still standing on it. It was
a bit of a help, and we gradually got other people on to it. Luckily they didn't depth
charge as much as they had done when there'd been an attack before because we got
badly jarred from the ones they did drop.

At daylight a destroyer picked up the Japanese and, Gibson believes, it was only because of the intervention of a Korean interpreter that a whale-chaser later gathered the prisoners from the water and took them into Nagasaki. A total of 560 prisoners had died, and they had reached the mouth of Nagasaki Bay. Only seventy-two Australians out of the 267 on the *Tamahoko Maru* survived. No seas were safe for Japanese ships: prisoners were even killed and drowned in the Straits of Malacca while making the crossing between Sumatra and Singapore.

The sinking of the *Rokyu Maru* was not the worst disaster suffered by Australian prisoners-of-war at sea. In 1942 the *Montevideo Maru* had been sunk off the Philippines, and over 1000 civilian and military prisoners from New Guinea had died. By the end of the war nearly twenty percent of all Australians who died as prisoners-of-war of the Japanese had died at sea. A total of over 10 000 Allied prisoners died at sea. That was the cost of the warring nations failing to agree to give free passage to transports carrying prisoners, and of the persistence of the Japanese in shifting captives when they were completely unable to protect their shipping.

After he had been debriefed and taken leave, Able Seaman Bancroft returned to the navy. The survivor of A Force on the Burma railway was given his assignment to speed an Allied victory.

Bancroft: I walked into Flinders Naval Depot with another sailor who knew what had happened. They were working on the depot railway line. I said, 'Hey, wouldn't it be funny if we got on that.' We went down and had to report to the petty officer. He said, 'Righto, you two, go and get a pick and shovel from the store and go down and report to Petty Officer Soandso on the depot railway line.' I said, 'You'd have to be joking', but I reckoned he was right, so off we went, picked up the shovel and went down.

The Petty Officer said,'You fellows have to re-ballast this and do that.' And I said, 'I've got news for you too.' And he said, 'What?' I said, 'I'm not going to do it.' He said, 'You're not going to do it, eh?' And I said, 'I'm not going to do it.' A naval officer who'd been selected to look after returning prisoners-of-war from Germany came down to see how I was making out. I was called up in front of him and he said, 'How are you making out—is everything OK?' And I said, 'Well, not really. Actually I'm supposed to be down re-ballasting the depot railway line.' Oh, boy, all hell cut loose. I was in a staff car and straight back in the convalescent home. He ripped shreds off somebody. But I think it was all through lack of communication.

In November 1944 the Allied leaders made public statements on the Japanese treatment of prisoners-of-war. In Australia Frank Forde, the Acting Prime Minister, told the House of Representatives about the sinking of the *Rokyu Maru* and gave a summary of what had happened on the Burma-Thailand railway. He spoke of the forced labour, the starvation, the hospital camps, the ulcers and amputations. An early estimate, he said, was that 2000 Australians had died, but he hoped that this figure 'was too high'. In fact it was too low. Forde could not avoid speaking to the people of Australia, and he and the other Allied leaders thought they might persuade the Japanese to be more humane; but from then the friends and relatives of all Allied prisoners wondered if their soldier or nurse was dead, or still suffering.

CHAPTER TWELVE

FROM TIMOR TO MANCHURIA

'. . . they didn't practise any sort of designed brutality. They just allowed us to die from starvation, disease and things like that . . .'

With the Burma-Thailand Railway, Changi and the Sandakan-Ranau death march dominant in popular knowledge, the men and women who were in other camps sometimes feel that their part in great events has been neglected. It is as though they took part in sideshows, something less than the main event, when in fact conditions were likely to be extreme on the frontier of the Japanese empire. That had been the case for the men left on Ambon.

The experience of prisoners differed from camp to camp, not just because terrain and climate varied from the hot wet tropics to the snow-covered plains of Mukden, but because the surrounding cultures and the combinations of prisoners and guards were different. The amiable ineffectiveness of a guard such as 'Useless Eustace' could make a camp a haven; the 'Black Mamba' could transform it into a place of torment. 'Useless' was an asset to be treasured, to be protected from his superiors who might shift him to less onerous responsibilities. A Japanese commandant recently brought into the army from a civil post had no hope of obtaining supplies for his prisoners against the competition of other sections of the Japanese army. A commandant determined to be vindictive was immeasurably worse. The prisoners might be a close-knit group with strong appointed or natural leaders; or they might include more than their share of the bad citizens of camp life, such as the gunner whose final gesture was to pinch all the new sheets put on the beds for the returning prisoners on their first night ashore in Australia.

In February 1942 just over 1000 Australians of Sparrow Force were captured near Koepang in southern Timor.

Don Noble: On Timor the treatment was reasonable. I can remember one fellow walking back into camp after being on a working party carrying a kapok mattress. They didn't worry about taking it from him, but if anybody carried a knife or something weapon-like, then he was dressed down properly.

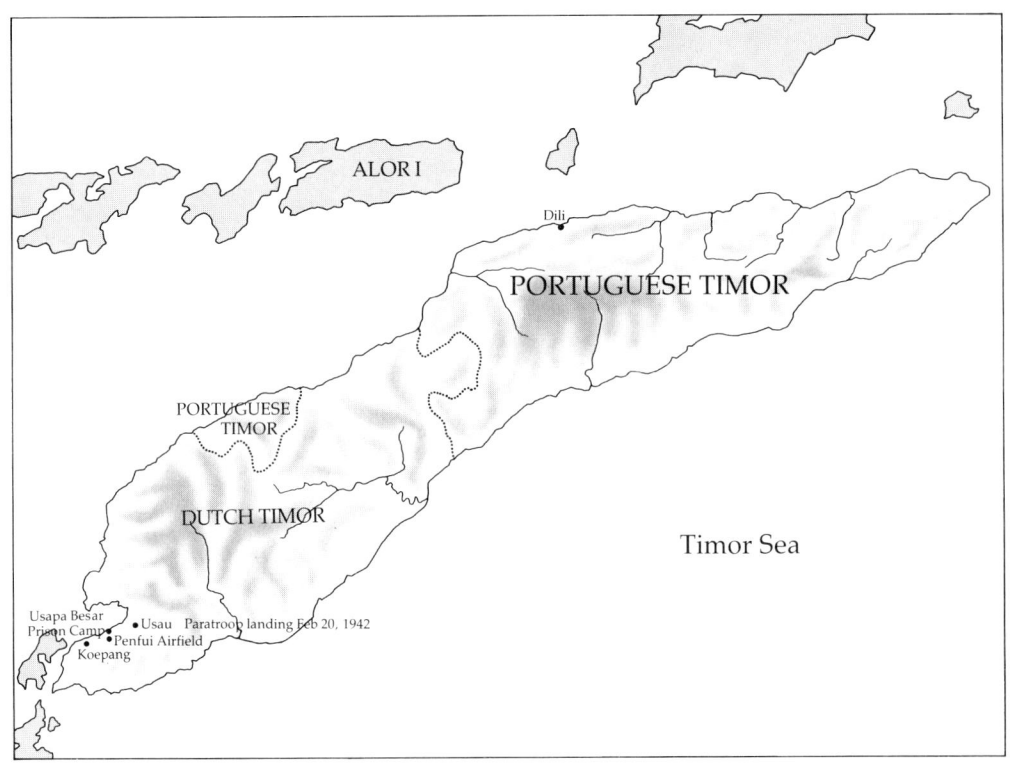

'Timor... only 400 miles from Australia, surely the Navy could do the job and bring home a few men.'

I think that we played the game as far as we could because we fully expected that we would soon be repatriated. We thought that the Navy would come steaming in the heads one day, pick us off the beach, and away we would go. As it turned out they didn't know much about us.

We stayed in a coconut plantation right on the beach, and we had the freedom of the beach. Of a night time we could sit out there and be quite free. I can remember one night we were sitting out on the beach just swapping yarns; we were right opposite the heads. We used to think what a wonderful night it would be for the Navy to come in and get us. That was our one thought: we were only 400 miles from Australia and surely the Navy could do the job and bring home a few men.

The men lost weight on Timor, and they buried a few comrades under carefully carved wooden crosses, but they were to look back on the *atap* huts in the coconuts as one of their best camps. After six months on Timor the Japanese shipped the prisoners to Java. There were already about 3000 Australian prisoners on Java. Cut off by the swift advance of the Japanese and left aimless by the surrender of the Dutch commanders, some groups of Australians saw no Japanese for several weeks. They settled into camps, scrounging stores where they could, and trying to cross to the south coast where they hoped to be picked up by the Navy or seize boats for themselves. At Bandung in central Java, Weary Dunlop was in charge of an Allied general hospital housing over 1000 patients. When the Japanese finally arrived in April 1942 they entered the city in a formal parade, the Japanese troops were disciplined, and the officers were correct in their behaviour towards Dunlop, although they were obviously displeased that he persisted in flying Allied flags. The Japanese changed suddenly.

Dunlop: We were told to disband the hospital in ten minutes. They actually walked up to blind and paralysed patients poking bayonets at them with the intention of proving they really could move, and I found myself obliged to stand between the soldiers and patients. I stormed off to the commandant and told him that I would like to know who gave these outrageous orders because I had every intention of having someone hung. When he said that he gave the orders I said, 'Right, one ruddy day I will have you hung. This thing you have done will be transmitted to every power on the Allied side'. He said, 'Good, you lead the march to the gaol.'

We went into a really clinking gaol. We got there somewhat exhausted by a ten-mile march. I had done operations on the wounds of some of these fellows within the last two or three days, and the neck wound of one man opened on the march as he was trying to carry his pack. So we weren't in very good shape and we went into just four or five small cells, a verandah and a courtyard. We were massed humanity with one hundred people standing sodden in the tropical rain taking turns to change with others who were under shelter.

Two days went by without food. On the third there was some food, and this didn't quite get around. Then there was an inspection, a thorough military procedure by the Japanese to see what was happening in the gaol. It wasn't the Japanese fault actually that we had done so badly in that we had come in under a Dutch administration. There were misunderstandings and we got the thin edge of the wedge. But my troops failed to understand this, and although I told them they were meant to show good discipline and do the best under the circumstances they just stood in a group and sang, 'Bless them all'. [The Japanese took particular exception to the men replacing 'bless' with a much stronger verb.] And someone kicked a football at the Japanese inspecting office. Oh God, all hell broke loose. He marched his guard out, and they fixed bayonets, filled their magazines and came back for retribution. We had to stand on parade and we just had screaming hurled at us: what terrible people we were, accepting the bread and the loving kindness of the Japanese and then behaving in this terrible fashion. We were the scum of the earth. We were told that we would be shot on the spot if there was the least indiscipline or resistance to the Japanese.

When all this seemed to be over the interpreter, a Dutchman, said that I could dismiss the troops. I dismissed them in the British fashion, everyone turning to the right and me moving forward to salute; but the Japanese took offence and I got a hay maker in the teeth. This really upset me and I threw my hands up and gave him an old-fashioned look. At this stage he just ripped his sword out like a panther and sprang at my neck with the intention of running me through. I had done a fair bit of boxing and I just avoided the point of the sword but the shaft hit me in the larynx with a resounding crack that you could hear all over the gaol. There was an awful moment when I realised that the troops were breaking ranks and would try to attack the Japanese. I couldn't speak with this smack in the larynx, I could hardly breathe, but I was just able to put up a hand and say, 'For God's sake don't move', and turned to the Japanese, pointed to his sword in a way to say you are the big boy, you have got the sword, and stood to attention. This seemed to calm him a little. He did an exhibition of samurai swordsmanship around my head, flicking my hair and my ears, then sheathed his sword, and poked about half a dozen people flat on their backs with his sword in its scabbard. At that stage we had another lecture and then finally we were dismissed in a rather salutary way.

In November about 1000 Australians were shifted from Bandung to a barbed wire enclosure around *atap* huts in a coconut plantation at Makasura. It was a dangerous camp: when wind gusts turned the palm fronds inside out the heavy nuts crashed through the thatch with the force of cannon balls.

From the end of 1942 most of the prisoners on Java were shipped north to work on the Burma-Thailand railway. One who remained in Java was Yeoman of Signals, Jack Willis. Separated from his shipmates on the *Perth* when he became sick at Tjilatjap he spent nearly a year as the lone Australian among thousands of Dutch. By the time he reached Bandung he was wearing a Dutch uniform and he was so unused to speaking his own language that the Australians thought he had been planted among them as a spy. Willis was relieved to find an officer from the *Perth* to testify for him. After a relaxing fortnight in a propaganda camp Willis spent the rest of the war in the Cycle camp at Batavia; he used his sailor skills on a sewing machine to give himself an edge in survival.

No Australian unit was fighting on Sumatra at the time of the Allied surrender in 1942, but men in transit were trapped there. Air crew, sailors and troops trying to escape from Singapore were gathered in by the Japanese who quickly cut off any further movement south through the islands or west across the Indian Ocean. Frank Robinson, close to the Singapore waterfront when he heard the order to cease fire, joined a group of British and Australian troops who commandeered a Chinese junk. They sailed through the islands at the south of the Malacca Strait and into the Kampar River on eastern Sumatra. By sampan, foot and truck they crossed to Padang on the west coast where they were captured in March 1942. Often angry at the way the Dutchmen in the camp jealously guarded their riches in cash, tinned food and clothing, the Australians were surprised to find Dutch women endangering themselves as they tried to help foreign prisoners. On one work party Robinson saw a Dutch woman drop her handkerchief; he tried to return it; and she signalled that he keep it. He found that it enclosed a guilder note. By midday he had so many handkerchiefs in his pockets he could not think what explanation to give if the guards searched him. In June the prisoners were driven north by truck for five days, exclaiming at the beauty of Lake Toba and with choked emotion at the lines of white-limbed Australian gums. At Gloegoer camp near Medan, Robinson remembers lying back on the seventy centimetres of boards allotted to each man and listening to the soft lilt of a Welshman reading *How Green Was My Valley*. Robinson transposed the scene to his green homeland in northern Tasmania.

Conditions for the prisoners in northern Sumatra became harsh in 1944 when they were forced to build roads. The job ended with an exhausting one hundred and forty-five kilometre march to the trucks that carried them back to the dust of Medan camp. After a week the prisoners were again compelled to labour. Trucked back to central Sumatra they began laying a narrow gauge railway across the island. Ironically the 230 kilometre route was close to the track followed by the footsore soldiers in their escape bid two and a half years earlier. They began months of constant work.

Frank Robinson: This I suppose was the very, very worst thing that happened to us in
> Sumatra. We weren't too good healthwise. I was down to roughly six stone and I would be one of the fittest there then. Everybody, including the cooks, had lost a terrible lot of weight and all became very weak.
>
> The main job in the first place was to build a bridge that had to go in a semi-circle. It went down one side of a huge gorge, across the gorge and back up the other side. Several men lost their lives here. One was on the other end of a saw from me. His name was Jack Stapleton. Jack had borrowed my old boots on this particular day and we were on the felling gang, felling a particular tree. When we started to go into the back of it with the crosscut saw, we went in say about six to eight inches when the tree went off like a shot gun and broke about twenty-five to thirty feet up. Had

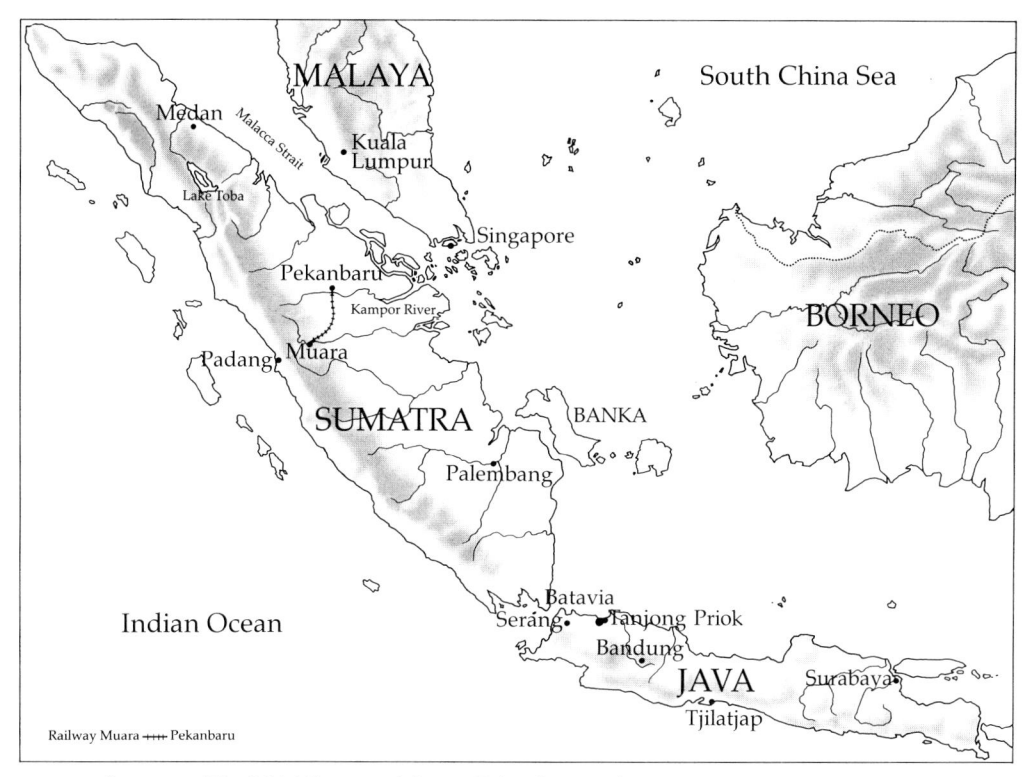

Sumatra. The 230 kilometre Muara-Pekanbaru railway was built for no purpose.

it have come down my side of the stump it would have been OK because I had already cleared a patch for me to escape if something like this did happen; but Jack was on the top side and when the tree split he tried to move and found he had these boots caught up in a piece of rattan. He was stuck. He only had seconds, and I can still see to this day how that tree toppled over his side and came straight down on top of Jack. This was the closest I had been to any man being killed accidentally. I even wished it had been me instead of Jack. I couldn't fell trees after that for quite some time. I asked to be taken from that particular gang.

I went on to a squaring gang where we squared trees for the bridge. We smoothed them off with tomahawks and they were almost as smooth as if you had planed them. They used the Australians all the time for these particular jobs because they seemed to know exactly how to do them whereas the Dutch and the English who had never had any experience at all in that type of thing were hopeless. The poor old Englishmen and the Dutchmen were used more or less as animals to pull logs into position on the bridge. Then the Australians took over again because they knew how to fasten trees and what have you to this bridge without a great deal of roaring and shouting from the Japs. We had the happy knack of being able to do it.

Frank Robinson had his twenty-first birthday on the Sumatran railway. He caught a chook and his mates cooked it for him. In spite of their intentions the starving men could not resist the cooking flesh: Robinson celebrated with what was left of the watery broth, and his mates suffered remorse for actions they could not control.

As on the Burma-Thailand railway the men were vulnerable to diseases in combination; and they had few medicines.

Robinson: The only thing that we ever had issued for malaria was the raw quinine bark from the tree itself. This we would pound up with a couple of stones, make a powder, mix it with rice and make it into little balls. We would swallow these; it was hit and miss. We didn't know exactly how much to take and I remember when you did take a rice ball with quinine bark in it, it was about as bad as the malaria. Your ears would really buzz and you would almost become unconscious.

I will never ever forget the first time I had malaria. I was sitting with three or four of my friends and we were talking. The next thing I thought they were whispering and talking about me. I just jumped up and abused hell out of them; I had got my first bout of malaria. But after that malaria seemed to come to me about every fourteen or fifteen days. I had malaria twenty-six times altogether and once when I came back home.

I felt, whether it was right or wrong, that while I was working I sort of got something hard inside of me. I don't know how to explain it. But I felt that if I worked I would survive but if I didn't work and I sat down and had a fortnight's holiday that would be the end of me. I think something went soft inside of you, and this fact was born out on several occasions when different ones wanted to have a spell. Especially one particular case where there was a New Zealander. I remember him so well because he had a beautiful beard. He wanted to have a spell, and he said to Stan Jackson, 'I want my finger cut off'. He laid his finger on a stump and said, 'Cut'. Well Stan thought he was joking and he half-heartedly tried to cut it and the chap pulled his finger away. He said, 'I don't think this stump is solid enough, we will find another one'. So after several attempts at this Stan realised that he was fair dinkum, that he did want his finger cut off. The next time he put his finger on the log to test it, he never even got his mouth open when the axe came down and the finger was off. He didn't feel anything of course and he bled. He said to Stan, 'Thanks, mate.' 'She's alright,' Stan said, 'any time.' He is a funny man Stan Jackson. So anyway this New Zealander went back to camp and within a fortnight he died, not because of his finger being cut off, but I think even now that had he stayed at work he probably wouldn't have died. They wanted a spell and they sort of lay down and they didn't get back up.

Once when we were pretty down they took us a little further up the mountain than we were usually working. We were actually cutting off little hillocks on the road and flattening them out, making them a little bit less of a steep pinch for trucks to go up. It was raining. Actually we liked this because it was usually warm monsoonal rain. We went over a bank to get a little bit of shelter and here was a Japanese camp containing some twenty or thirty. It looked to be a camp big enough for the engineers, but there was only one or two there plus the cook. The cook looked at us and said nothing, but after about an hour he came out. He must have counted us because he gave each one of us a ball of rice a little bit bigger perhaps than a cricket ball and it had salt laced through it. This was absolutely heaven for us. I remarked at the time, you can't hate them all, perhaps only 999 out of 1000. Actually I would possibly hate one or two individuals but you can't hate a nation for what went on in northern Sumatra. To have a Japanese cook you a rice ball—and he did it again the next day—gave you a feeling, well they can't all be bad.

Over 500 Allied prisoners, and many more Indonesians, died in the construction of the Muara-Pekanbaru railway. About forty Australians, including men sent from other islands, died there. They died for no purpose: the railway was never used.

The men in Sumatra were still working on the railway when the war ended. After the prisoners linked the two ends of the Burma-Thailand railway in 1943 many of the survivors were brought down to base camps in Thailand. They were, the men said, put in 'fattening pens'. Early in 1944 the guards began selecting the fittest men to go to Japan, and some prisoners began their journey by going east into French Indo-China.

Arthur Bancroft: We left Tamarkan by rail after our fond farewells to the others who were staying behind. Again we were going on a great adventure. The Japanese guards weren't very enthusiastic: they kept saying that we were going to be fish *makan*, fish food. We were taken by rail through Bangkok and to Phnom Penh. Phnom Penh was a beautiful place on the banks of the Mekong River.

Our first contact with the French was when we went from the railway station to a little camp next to a big pagoda. We marched through the streets of Phnom Penh. We had French women coming out and we thought they were beautiful. They were the first white people, other than ourselves, we had seen for a couple of years. They were coming out and waving to us and we thought we were film actors. Well we didn't have a chance to talk to them and they had no chance to come amongst us.

When we got down to Saigon on the working parties, we did talk to some of the French. They would try and get close to us to pass on news or provide us with money, food or clothing. They had to be very careful because the Japs were keeping an eye on what they were doing and they took personal risks.

When the Japanese failed to get Bancroft's group through the American blockade of Saigon, they sent them by barge and train back to Singapore. But other Australians, off-loaded from Japanese convoys in Saigon, stayed in Indo-China for the rest of the war.

In Thailand and Singapore the prisoners had lived in a world of uniform madness and deprivation. In Indo-China the French colonists were not interned. The prisoners could see a French woman cycle past with long loaves of bread sticking from her basket; they could glimpse people sitting at boulevard cafes in Saigon; and if they chose to take the gamble they could sneak out of camp after *tenko*, and go to the pictures. In Saigon and Phnom Penh the prisoners had to accept that not all the world was full of venom; suffering was for the few; and they were among the few.

All of the Australian military prisoners captured in Rabaul, New Guinea, early in 1942 were shipped north, either to Japan or to drown. But as the Japanese captured more Allied servicemen in the south-west Pacific they held them in the Rabaul area. Most of the prisoners were American airmen who crash-landed or bailed out over Japanese-held territory. Captain John Murphy of the Australian army's M Special Unit was an exception. He landed on the south coast of New Britain in October 1943 to set up a coastwatching station. The two other Australians with Murphy were shot in ambushes; he was wounded in the wrist, and washed down a flooded river into the middle of the pursuing Japanese. They sent him to Rabaul by submarine:

The ride was smooth enough, except between Gasmata and Rabaul we had fourteen crash dives due to American or Australian aircraft overhead. That was a bit unnerving because that klaxon used to put the breeze up me every time it went. It went suddenly and down we would dive. I was supposed to be tied up but it was easy to slip the bonds off. At meal time the cook or somebody would come around with a great bowl of rice balls inside of which was a bit of meat, a pickled plum or something. Nobody pushed me around much. I managed to slip my hands into a

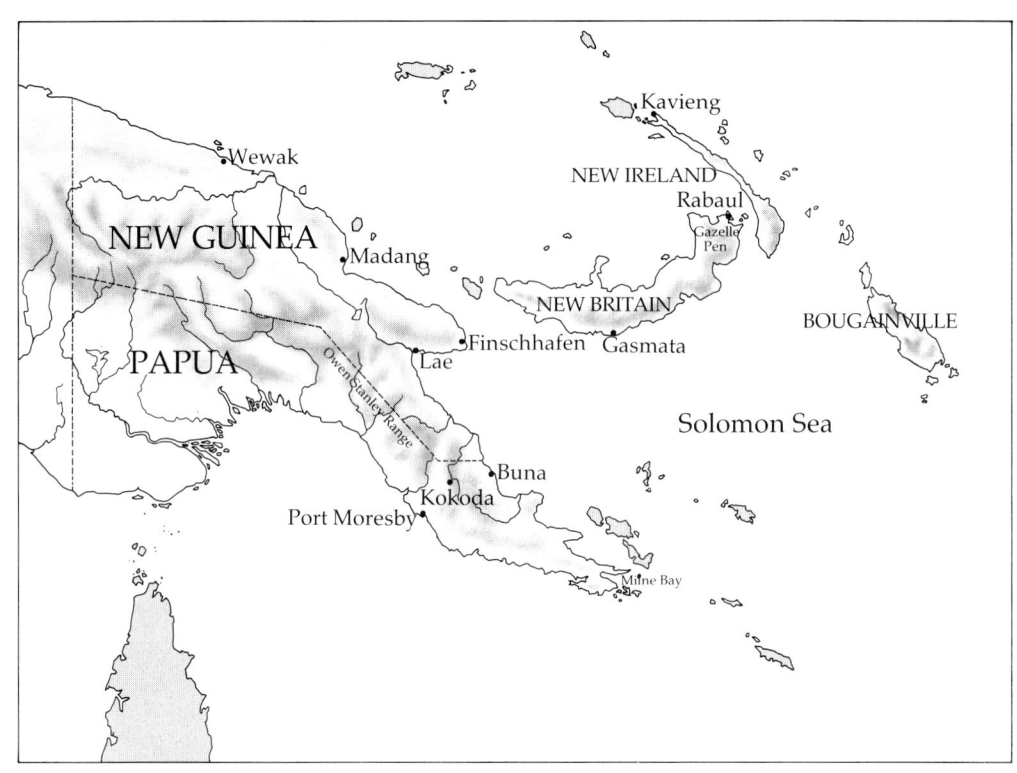

Papua and New Guinea. In Rabaul the Australians were prisoners in what had been their own administration's headquarters.

drawer which I was leaning up against and pinch a packet of cigarettes and slip those in my pocket. Every now and again an officer came, I would indicate I'd like a smoke, and he would take me down to a bamboo cupboard thing that had a little flame like a petrol cigarette lighter. I could stay there and smoke, put out the butt carefully, and go back and sit down. Now that was the life of Reilly until about midway through when we hove to and took on maybe a dozen or more oil-covered Japanese sailors. They must have been sunk on a barge. That was the end of me; I was tied up in a disused lavatory and the Japanese sailors got them hot tubs of water and washed and bathed them. But I was tied up in this blasted Japanese dunny all the way into Rabaul.

The Japanese had over 100 000 troops and auxiliaries in the Rabaul area, but with the advance of the American forces through the islands their enormous land strength on New Britain was isolated and powerless.

Before the war John Murphy had been a patrol officer in New Guinea. In Rabaul he was a prisoner where he had once been a *masta*:

I was standing outside something or other for a hell of a time with my blindfold on. Then I was taken inside, questioned very briefly for a bit and taken into a cell where there was a long skinny American bloke and a short American bloke; and lo and behold it was Ah Teck's tailoring shop where I had had my last pair of pants made. The Japanese had made it into a sort of prison camp and the headquarters of the *kempeitai*. They started to jeer at me and call me spy boy. One dirty greasy moustached sort of bloke told me I was for the big chop, 'You know what we do with bloody spies, eh?' That sort of approach. Well that was the wrong tack because it made me defiant. I thought, well if I am for the big chop there is no use trying to win friends and influence people around here. I got a bit anti, and they were sort of frightened of me in that they didn't want to lose face. They thought I would let one go at them, and so they were very stand-offish. I didn't know why at that time. I thought it was just my belligerent attitude; and I was belligerent. I found out later that they had no intention of doing me mischief. Cripes, in retrospect, I had a hell of a fright.

What had really happened was this. The Japanese had published that they had caught the great Australian spy—Captain John Joseph Murphy. The German papers had it and the British and American papers picked it up and it was printed in Australia. My mother took a fit, my wife took a fit, my uncle hopped into his car and drove down to Sydney. He got in touch with the government and the cardinal of our church and they sent representations both through Switzerland and through the Vatican that I was not a spy, that I was captured in uniform, and they wanted to know about my whereabouts and welfare. And this is what caused the Japanese to think that they had a great hostage that they could trade later. I remember once the interpreter asked me, 'Give me the names of your influential friends in Australia'. I said that I had none, but I think that the Japs thought they had a real catch. They treasured me and this led me to believe that they were frightened of me; and this in turn led to a situation where they were frightened of me. They didn't want to lose face if I hauled off and cracked them. Obviously they were forbidden to push me around too much by their superiors, and I wouldn't let them anyhow. I made them call me Captain Murphy; I was the only bloke they gave a title to in prison. I wouldn't answer; I would ignore them if they didn't address my by my proper title. This started at the beginning and then it became a habit with them. 'Murphy-tai', it is so easy to sound—Murphy-tai—'Captain Murphy'.

The occupants of the building across the road provided a diversion for the prisoners waiting to be interrogated by the *kempeitai*. The women of the Eighth Consolation Unit charged with providing a moment of delight for the Japanese troops in Rabaul would raise their skirts, beckon and mock. A bare-foot 'frumpy lot', unlike the neat dolls the prisoners expected, the Eighth Consolation Unit was more interesting than enticing.

With his quick wit, aggressiveness and local knowledge, Murphy became the leader of Allied prisoners. One of the American pilots wrote of Murphy: 'There was a dynamism about him that commanded respect'.

Murphy: I started entertainments, concerts, and this was great because everybody could do something. Then I asked the Japanese if we could have religious ceremonies on Sunday mornings. They said, 'Oh yes'. So we took it in turns to give a sermon, and I introduced the rosary and everybody, Catholics, Protestants, atheists, pagans all took a turn in reading the rosary. I encouraged them to eat all the weeds and grass they could when they got out, but somebody said it gave you malaria so they knocked it off. I pretended I was a mesmerist of the first order. I put the mesmerism on James MacMurria, a friend of mine. He'd stiffen and fall back flat, somebody would just happen to be there, and they would catch him still stiff as a ram-rod. Well from that we worked into little entertainments. The Japs thought it was great because they were in the audience too.

It got to the stage where the Japs would let me punish any small misdemeanors. This was how I would do it. Nason is a particular example. Nason was caught trying to smuggle a small bunch of green bananas into the cell. Ishimora was about to nearly kill him, and I said, I will deal with it. I said to Joe, 'Go and sit in the corner there and hang your head, mate, and look as shameful as you possibly can. You other blokes move away from him and shake your heads in disgust.' So I went back to my corner and I thrust my finger out to Joe and I said, 'The boy stood on the burning deck . . .' I went on like this, and Nason hung his head lower and lower. He won an Oscar that day. The Japs were so sorry for him that they gave him a half cigarette because of this terrible ordeal. And Joe, plenty *bushido* (warrior spirit), he asked the guard if he could give me a few puffs because he had no resentment against me for punishing him so much. We had a lot of laughs with things like that. This bloke Nason said that the one thing he was thankful for was we were able to keep our sense of humour.

At one stage we were let out to do a bit of gardening but the new commandant came along and he said no, inside, stay inside. Then one bright bloke taught us how to make coconut rope and we made coconut rope sandals for ourselves and the guards. I told them I was a terrific expert in cigarette manufacturing and if they would give me some old whiskey, sugar, paper, the tobacco, some cloth and twine I would make them the best cigarettes that they had tasted. Well they couldn't get me any whiskey but they got me sugar, paper, native leaf tobacco and scissors, so I set up a cigarette manufacturing place. I sat down there and I was turning out packets. I told the bloke I was making them for, now you can't expect us to make all these fags and not have a smoke, it would be too much to ask any human being. Yes, we could smoke while we are making them, so we smoked our heads off and he got about one to every ten but he got enough. The cigarette-making gave me a great hold over the guards because they had to beg some; they couldn't bully me for them. I would just say, now look righto, everybody out. I threatened to knock the workers off when the commandant came down if they tried to steal the cigarettes. But I could trade a few out of the cell for food, sweet potato nicely cooked, a bit of extra rice. So that did us very well until the next commandant came in, then boink, a sudden stop again.

The mixture of nationalities in the Rabaul prison added interest to the talks that prisoners gave to pass the time: My Favourite Movie, My Hometown, and—inevitably with starving men—My Favourite Meal.

The American airmen in the camp, Murphy believed, faced a particular disadvantage:

Before they were captured they had a hazardous life but they got back to great comfort. This is our foot soldiers' point of view. Once they were back, debriefed and went to their mess, they had icy cold beer, canned turkey and ice cream. In prison they came slap bang into a small ration of rice and thin soup. They just couldn't eat the rice. For days and days they couldn't face it. And we old timers in the clink gained. But finally hunger would catch up with them. Sometimes we would try to swap them. If we had say a bit of pawpaw or banana somewhere we would let them have our share for their rice. Prison was a terrible shock to them. I think malnutrition, as much as anything, probably accounted for all but seven of them dying. There were one or two pneumonia cases, there was certainly dysentery and beriberi. But their big setback at the beginning meant they never had anything to build on. I think that they didn't give themselves a chance by that abhorrence, that distaste, for the rice meals.

A 'dozen times' Murphy thought about escaping. After the Allies occupied southwestern New Britain he was confident that he could get through, but few of the others had the skills and none had the knowledge that he had gained on prewar patrols. When the Japanese threatened to kill the remaining prisoners if any of them escaped, Murphy decided he would have to 'hang on' till help came to him.

While carrying out his duties as a New Guinea field officer, Murphy had made a particular study of Pidgin English, the *lingua franca* of the north of the island. Before he was captured he completed a book on Pidgin, and it was published in 1943 while he was in prison.

Murphy: If the *kempeitai* in our area had a native prisoner he would be thrown in with us. He would be very frightened and the Japanese would take him out, beat him a lot, and give him no food for a couple of days. They would put him in a good mood to be questioned. I was the only one in the prison who had lived in New Guinea and could speak Pidgin English. I could get to them and find out a lot that was going on outside the prison. In the first day or two, meagre as our rations were, we would make sure that they had a mouthful by taking a bit off everybody's plate. This cheered them up and made them feel friendly towards us.

    I let one go once, his name was Gandov. A bright lad, he used to be a policeman at Salamaua when I was there. The Japanese had sent him home to Japan for a short course in something or other, had taught him Japanese which he could speak, but somehow or other he must have been fed up with them and their treatment. He assaulted a couple of Japanese, was caught and imprisoned. He got away and killed a Japanese soldier, was caught again, and arrived at our camp tied with electrical wiring to a pole like a pig. He was put against the wall of our camp. At the time an air raid occurred and the Japanese ordered us all into our hole and they themselves beat it into their air raid shelter. I came out to this fellow and that is when I found it was Gandov. He told me quickly his short history and I briefed him on a couple of things while I undid his wiring. I told him where to go and he took a month but he arrived at Major Fairfax-Ross's camp. That was the first real news that came out that I was alive and gave the location of the POW camp.

Gandov reached Fairfax-Ross's coastwatching camp on December 29, 1944 bringing detailed information about the prisoners, the location of defences, dummy positions and the effects of Allied bombing. At the end of the war the ex-prisoner and American pilot, Joe Nason, was delighted to see 'little old Gandov' sitting in the back of a jeep and smoking a native cigar.

After Allied aircraft destroyed most of Rabaul in a series of heavy raids the Japanese shifted the prisoners out of the town area to Tunnel Hill. At first their new camp was so crowded that all men could not lie down at the same time. But it was better at Tunnel Hill than to be in the groups selected to move.

Murphy: Then one day the Japanese took twenty prisoners out. A few minutes later we heard shots. We thought, 'Cripes!' Up to that time we had been clamouring to go on work parties and get out. Then a day later they took another twenty out, that left twenty-three, including the Chinese, and again we heard shots. We thought they are doing us over, party by party. I worked it out there were not enough shots to do twenty people. But at that time they were great on saving shots and using bayonets. Anyway I told the blokes, 'Don't worry about it. We only heard about six shots and there were twenty of those blokes.'

>They were taking them down to the north coast to be shipped across to Watom Island where they had a group of British prisoners from Singapore. And they never got there. They were all assembled on the beach near Nordup when they were attacked by Allied aircraft and many of them and some Japanese were killed and a lot wounded. The Japanese then turned on the prisoners who were wounded and alive and bayonetted the lot of them on the beach. My information comes from some prisoners of the Japanese from Formosa.

After the killing of the forty prisoners on the beach at Nordup, the survivors in the crowded tunnel were sixteen Allied servicemen, three Chinese civilians, two mixed race men and two New Guineans.

Late in 1944 the prisoners moved to a slightly more spacious camp: a wooden-frame shack hard against a hill and extending into a damp tunnel. The stress on the prisoners increased when a badly wounded New Zealand pilot was dumped in their midst. The guards ignored pleas for medical aid, and the men tore up their shirts to bandage the new man's suppurating upper thigh where a bullet was embedded. Every four or five days a Japanese orderly unwound the bandages, and when he stopped laughing at the swelling and the virulent infection, he put the rags back again. As the infection spread the new prisoner became delirious. He would crawl to the door calling, 'Hurry, we will be late. The car is waiting and all is set.' The other men would carry him back to his space on the floor. After three weeks the harrowing drama ended; the young flying officer died.

The prisoners at Rabaul suffered a death rate higher than at most other camps. But the reason is difficult to find. They were not worked to death; they did not have particularly vicious guards; and they were not being punished for real or imagined crimes.

Murphy: Apart from a few welts with a rod the individual guards used only a bit of a slap
>for disciplinary purposes but they didn't practise any sort of designed brutality. They just allowed us to die from starvation, disease and things like that; they didn't hurry death with brutal kickings or bashings. They had no work for us so they couldn't push a program like the Burma Railway. The guards were with us all the time and they would sort of get to know us. It was like having a herd of fowls. You know the fowls individually, but you don't worry about them. That seemed to be the guards' attitude to us. It was their superiors who denied us the food and medical treatment that caused the death of fifty-six out of our group of sixty-three. Fifty-six died from plain disease and starvation.

Murphy was the only Australian survivor; the other six were Americans. About ten days after the Japanese surrendered a Warrant Officer guard came to the Tunnel Hill camp, took the lock off, and threw it in the bushes. It was the prisoners' first definite sign that it was all over.

At the end of the war John Murphy was one of the few Australian prisoners to be arrested and charged with giving information to the Japanese. In fact he had not been the source of the information. The six Americans who had survived with Murphy were surprised and angry when they heard about the charge. They made sworn statements in his defence saying that he had been a buffer between them and the Japanese, and that he had gone out of the camp to steal fruit and medicine for sick men. Without Murphy, they said, none would have lived. Murphy was completely exonerated by the court.

As a prisoner John Murphy was always in familiar surroundings, when he left the camp at night he was finding his way by starlight along roads that he had travelled in peace time; sometimes he heard reports of missionaries, Chinese or German nationals that he had known; and infrequently he would see and talk to one of them. But Spud Spurgeon travelled beyond the range of experiences of nearly all Australians:

> As soon as we got to Korea things seemed to get a bit better. We were put on a train, quite the most magnificent train I think I have ridden on. Korean trains are outstanding, great big five feet three inch gauge, magnificent locomotives. If you are a Hornby train fan it would drive you nuts. Double deck sleepers we had. The only trouble was that most of the journey was done with the blinds down. We would sneak them up between stations or when the guard was out, and when we got up country a bit they didn't worry. The food was good. We were told continually, 'You are going to a very special camp for officers', and the people on the train were almost pleasant. We were allowed on the platform for meals. They had cookers on the platform, plenty of hot drinks and some fruit. They grow beautiful apples in Korea of course. And the thing that struck me were the women. By that stage they were looking like Greta Garbos or Rita Hayworths I suppose; but the place looked prosperous and clean until we got up on to the plains, and then of course it gets dreary all the way to the Yalu River.
>
> We got to Mukden about a day and a half later. The train appeared to have no other passengers; it was an express—if you can call it that—especially for us. We were taken out of the train in Mukden and put on another train and driven to a siding alongside Hoten Camp. When we got out, it was cold, by jeez it was cold, no vegetation, just flat uninteresting Manchurian plains. Then we saw the camp barracks. They had these big Russian pachika stoves inside them, decent double decker bunks, blankets, and each of us had an issue of clothes on the bed. Our blokes had fixed that up; but it was a better organised camp. We didn't see the Nips. The Japanese were on one side, and we were on the other, and they only came near us for *tenko*.
>
> The ground was part frozen and they couldn't even bury the guys that had died. The crappers had a big trench underneath from which the honey carts would take away the refuse and put it on the vegetables. In the winter everything froze. And each time you crapped, you built a spire which eventually came up to the floor level. So they had a crow bar that you had to use to knock the top off this thing. Of course some unlucky guy would drop the darn crow bar in the hole and he would be made to go and get it. An officer I know well put his washing in the basin one night and he didn't get it out for two months. The whole thing froze. They are the stupid stories; but it was cold, really cold.
>
> I didn't go outside the camp until we were released, except to a funeral. There were plenty of books to read. Apparently the prisoners had brought books with them and they formed a library so you had access to books. There were plenty of extra curricular activities: you could learn horticulture, you could learn astro-navigation. I did my astro-nav and astronomy up there because the skies were great for star-gazing. Other than that I suppose all that we did was spend a lot of time surviving.

Lance Gibson, another young Australian officer sent to Manchuria, took a farmer's interest in the speed with which the black soil plain 'burst into life' in the short spring. At the height of summer stifling dust storms swept across the camp blocking visual escape into the countryside. But the prisoners would be out before the next winter.

CHAPTER THIRTEEN
OUTRAM ROAD

'They can give you hidings, they can break your hands, they can break your skull, but only you can beat yourself.'

For all Allied troops captured in Singapore Outram Road was the most feared prison. It was a place of punishment. Anyone judged by the Imperial Japanese Army to have committed a grave offence was sent there whether they were Japanese soldiers, Asian civilians, European internees, Allied prisoners-of-war, men or women. People seized by the *kempeitai* from the local communities and accused of espionage or insurrection always outnumbered the prisoners-of-war. It was a harsh place for those Japanese soldiers sent there to be instilled with proper attitudes; and it was horrific for everyone else. An Australian lieutenant, Penn Dean, sentenced to two years for attempting to escape, wrote that when he arrived there in April 1942 'it was like Bedlam. People were screaming all day from pain from their wounds and their beatings'. The men of F Force were on the worst of the Burma-Thailand railway for six months; Outram Road went on and on.

Outram Road was 'concrete', 'cold', a 'forbidding place'. It was three storeys of cells opening on to a central passageway: it was a place of thick walls, small high windows, iron bars and a steel gate. An 'old fashioned' gaol built by the British, 'dynamite wouldn't have blown it up'. The high exterior wall was embedded with glass and strengthened with barbed wire. But Private Stan Davis, arrested in Sandakan because of his association with the underground movement, recalls an impression, not of a building, but of inmates:

> The day we went in there the boys were out for their wash. It was revolting. The whole of their bodies were covered with scabs, and they were so thin there was no muscle anywhere. They were pure bone. Even the cheeks of their backsides had gone. When they turned to walk away from you, you could see their backside; there was just no flesh on the bone at all. It was frightening. Just looking at them, you wouldn't know how they could still live.

The irony was that the Japanese, by sentencing Davis to two years in Outram Road, had saved him from almost certain death in North Borneo.

Chris Neilson, arrested for attempting to escape from Singapore, was one of the first Australians to enter Outram Road. Like many others in the cells he was under threat of execution:

> When they were going to execute one of their own blokes they always came around, and every one of us got a gift of a piece of banana or a little cake in a paper fold like we used to have when I was a kid. Penny cakes they were. Nice little cakes with a few sultanas and things in them. And then they'd take the bloke out. They always had their holy man with them. He was like a Catholic priest. He dressed like one only that he had no crucifix; there was just all these beads. But he was in full black, and he went out with this bloke. But you have to give the Japs full marks for this: not one of those going out to be executed ever cried or asked for anything. He went out like it was his duty to go and get lopped. So did the Chinese.
>
> The only one I saw executed was a Dutchman. I put the boards up to look out the side window. And the way that blood gushed out of that bloke. He was on his knees with his hands behind him. And a swish and it was off as quick and as easy as you could cut a little carrot. And the body just stayed motionless there squirting blood out of the stump of his neck. That was enough for me, I got down, I didn't want to see any more.
>
> We were certain that we were going to be done because this bloke used to come along. We called him Very Special, and he used to love having a shot at me. He used to try and make me say I was Nelson. I said, 'No, my name is Neilson. That's Danish, Danska. Nelson was English.' 'Well', he said, 'doesn't matter.' He could speak fair English, he'd been round the world on ships. He said, 'Doesn't matter anyway, Nelson, I will do the honour for you and you will be very happy, because I am very good'. '*Satu patong*'. He was always saying '*satu patong*'. It means 'one cut' in Malay, one hit and your head will be off. And I thought, bugger him. But I said, 'Thanks very much. I'm glad I'm getting you, because you do a good job and that's good because,' I said, 'I'll go straight up to heaven to my mother and father and grandma and granddad.' He didn't know how bloody frightened I was.

After a return to the court Neilson's sentence was fixed at three years. He no longer had to dread the footfalls of the execution squad and the craftsmanship of Very Special. The threats of beheading were more than sport for the guards. An Australian sergeant brought into Outram Road on a charge of espionage in August in 1943 was constantly taunted by the guards, and finally executed in December.

The three-metre by two-metre cell contained all that the prisoners could see or touch. Private Herb Trackson, another prisoner transferred from Sandakan, was recaptured after a month of freedom and sickness in North Borneo:

> In the cell there was two boards, about eight inches wide and an inch thick that you used to lie on. That was your bed; and there was a block of wood for a pillow and one tattered blanket. And a bucket in the corner for latrine purposes. And that was it. Absolutely nothing else.
>
> The cells were infested with bugs and cockroaches. And the walls were covered in blood marks where fellows had—and we did it ourselves—seen a bug on the wall and squashed it with their fingers leaving all these stripes of blood down the walls. Great big brown cockroaches, they used to walk on their feet like a goanna. Honestly, you'd never see cockroaches in Australia that size, they'd be every bit of two inches long. And you'd squash them, tramp on them.

At one stage a mouse came into Trackson's cell. By saving grains of rice he encouraged its visits but he could not coax it into his hand. One night, 'in a bad mood and depressed' he trapped it under his bed boards and squashed it. The action was, he says, a fair reflection of his attitude at that time.

Major John Wyett, one of the few non-regular soldiers to go to Quetta Staff College, felt that the Australian government had invested heavily in him as a soldier, and he had an obligation to keep fighting. On Singapore he was helping set up a radio transmitter, and he hoped to leave the island in style. Wyett and Flight-Lieutenant Jack MacAllister planned to seize a plane and fly to Cocos Island. Arrested and sentenced 'with great solemnity' to death, Wyett went into the cells of the condemned. On the Emperor's birthday his sentence was commuted to twenty years:

> You literally weren't allowed to do anything, or I wasn't. You just had to sit still. You weren't even allowed to stride up and down your cell to get a bit of exercise; that wasn't allowed. You were allowed to use your slop bucket. But apart from that you just simply sat there and stared into space all day long. You weren't even allowed to twiddle your thumbs. If you moved your thumbs they'd come in and bash you up.

All that the prisoners could see, or touch, was contained in the cell.

When the guards were not around Wyett caught lice, fed them to a spider, and it was 'most interesting to see the old spider getting fatter and fatter'.

Lieutenant Rod Wells was sentenced to twelve years when he was arrested as one of the leaders in the Sandakan underground:

> The latrine bucket remained with us all the time and was emptied about once a week. It contained the excreta for a week and any sickness one had. Vomiting had its phases. It was the body's normal way of rejecting these long tape worms we got into ourselves. You'd feel sick and then this great long, long tapeworm would come out of your throat. That was very demoralising to think that this thing was getting the nourishment that you should have had. And it would stay there for a week or whenever the bucket was emptied.

Neilson: There was breakfast at a certain time. There'd be a yell in the morning to get up, there was a yell at night to go to bed. Each hour, you were supposed to be sitting in your cell to attention, and each hour there'd be a bell, and a yell would come; you'd change position, squatting. If you talked to yourself, well, you'd get a hiding for it if they caught you at that.

Wells: The light stayed on. The light was on the whole night from dusk to dawn for the eighteen months I was there. I did not see any darkness other than by closing my eyes. The time it did hurt me was first thing in the morning, about the time the light was switched off which meant that it would be completely daylight in a few moments. It was just before the roll call which they had every morning. I could hear the birds in the trees outside the cell, but couldn't see the tree. I'd picture there must be a tree nearby. And to hear the birds singing and think, 'Oh, how to be a bird, to be able to move, to not have to remain here'. And I'd wonder where that bird was going to migrate to. He could go down to Aussie if he wanted to, and I couldn't. That hurt a bit. But I thought, well, at least life goes on.

Trackson: The clothes that we came in we had for a while, then they took them off us. They gave us a pair of shorts and a sort of jacket that was patched and patched and patched. That's all the clothing we had. They used to give us a change of clothing about once a week. A hair cut every few months, mostly it was from a Jap prisoner, from their own part of the gaol. And he'd come along and just shear you like a sheep, just cut from the bottom of your chin to the top of your head, and back in your cell again.

Wells: We were allowed to wash about once every week, just with the bucket and our hands. And when they said to start washing, the idea was to get your hands into the water and throw as much of it over yourself as you could, knowing that you only had about twenty seconds at the most.

Trackson: And you had a little piece of rag, about a foot by about six inches. And there were little dippers. You'd just pick this water up and throw it over yourself and then wipe yourself off with this rag if you had time. If they were in a hurry sometimes they wouldn't even give you time to wipe yourself off. You'd throw the water off, and they'd have you back in the cell again. That was your bath. Well, you were always thirsty, and they used to watch you and see whether you'd try and drink a bit of water out of your dipper. If you did, well, they were onto you for that.

Wells: Sometimes before the wash you would have to do these exercises; *itchi ni san si*, one two three four, and if you didn't bend the right way, another chap walked behind with a wooden sword, and gave you a good crack across the back to make sure you did exactly what you were supposed to do. On completion of the washing we were taken back to the cells and stood outside. Then, with legs apart and arms in the air, we were physically searched, naked. There'd be a pair of so-called washed shorts at the cell door, we'd pick those up, we were told to walk in, and then we put them on, and they came round and closed the doors. That completed the activity.

In a world where the senses were cut off from normal stimulation, the movement of the shadows of the window bars became an event worthy of scrutiny.

From August 1942 Outram Road was run by the *kempeitai*—the Japanese military police. The guards were Japanese non-commissioned officers. The prisoners gave some of them names: Jessie James, Churchill, Hitler and Pinocchio. But most of the guards went nameless. Prisoners who rarely spoke had few occasions to create words to identify particular guards. For the prisoners the guards were, and remain, vivid images.

Wells: They were just, as far as I was concerned, arch bastards strictly implementing the rules. They wore their compulsory dress for guard duty. They would take off their boots when they came on to report for duty, put on soft soled rubber shoes, just creep along the passageway from one cell to the other, looking in. You couldn't tell where they were. They ran by strict rules, and providing you kept within those rules you could manage to survive all right, without much trouble. But we didn't want to run within those rules because one of them, the most important one, was no talking of any description to anybody. And of course one of the things for survival was communication with others. And that was the main risk one ran, being beaten for talking.

Neilson: Each hour they changed the guard. It didn't matter what hour of the night, he tapped on your cell. And you had to answer. That's only to prove you're alive, because if the next bloke came on duty and found a dead bloke in there, he'd kick up all hell. He'd say, 'No, this bloke was dead when I come on duty'. So the bloke before, he'd be in trouble. I don't understand why that should be, because they didn't give a bugger whether you lived or died in the first place.

One guard, Trackson says, was an exception. A short fat man, he did not slap prisoners, hit them on the head with a bunch of keys swinging on the end of a chain, or try to trap them in some misdemeanor. At one meal Trackson was served rice and four or five tiny, intensely salty fish. He ate with the usual ravenous speed, and waited for water or weak tea to be served. None came. In the night Trackson's tongue swelled, and in his desperate hunt for fluid he lay on the floor in a pathetic attempt to draw moisture from the cold concrete. The guard looked at him, then Trackson heard the rattle of the tea cans. By emptying each can into a dish the guard collected about three or four tablespoons of water which he gave to Trackson. Without it, Trackson doubts if he would have survived the night. It was one of the rare occasions when the rigidity of the rules in Outram Road allowed a guard to express sympathy.

The meals came on what the prisoners called the 'food train'. The train was a wooden box holding aluminium bowls. Every prisoner followed its progress along the corridors and galleries by the banging of bowls, stamping of feet and shouts of command. In a submission to the Tokyo War Trials in December 1946 Penn Dean said that the basic daily ration was six ounces of rice and one and a half pints of watery soup.

Trackson: The cell had a big two-inch thick wooden door with a hole sawed in the centre where they used to put the aluminium dishes through. One held the rice and another smaller dish had a bit of soup as they used to call it, but it was really a few sweet potato leaves and occasionally you'd find a little piece of squid about as big as the top of your little finger, or perhaps one piece of meat. After you'd emptied your soup you'd hold the dish out and they'd half fill it with very, very weak tea water. Three times a day that used to come around.

Wells: And when they gave the word to commence eating, you could start. Ten seconds probably for breakfast, maybe twenty seconds for the lunch period, if you had that, it would be certainly no more. And then they'd just call out *yame* or 'stop'. You could get some down after that, the sentry couldn't be looking at every cell of course; but that was the order to stop eating.

Neilson: I'd have been in the vicinity of twelve stone when I went in, fit and very hard, very tough, been an athlete all my life. I came out six stone two. But it took fourteen months to come down to that.

Wells: If we were out emptying latrines, and it was a great thrill to be allowed to go out and do that, as you walked past a hibiscus plant, you could put your hand out, grab a couple of leaves, and get those into your mouth. Or a snail, if there was one there, you just crunched him up and chewed him down, raw and everything. Hunger is a bad thing. During the emptying of these toilet buckets, the buckets of Japanese prisoners were emptied also. And the Japanese, of course, had better rations, but like us they had to eat them quickly. They were given lots of lovely cooked rice with big black beans in it, high protein beans. They swallowed these whole and of course they passed through; they were in the buckets. And I've seen our chaps, if the opportunity came, grab a handful, and wash it when they were washing the buckets, and eat it. It was some extra protein. And that just gives you some idea of how hungry we were. I didn't quite do it. I nearly did the day I was out, but some of the other chaps had been doing this job more regularly and one or two of them were indulging in this when the sentries weren't looking.

All the prisoners were forced to the edge of death by the poverty of the diet. They knew that the slightest disruption to their food supply could kill them; they feared having their rations cut more than being beaten.

The cries of those who went mad were terrifying for the other prisoners. Madness was a prospect for everyone in Outram Road. In one harrowing period the inmates listened to constant dull thuds as an Asian prisoner destroyed himself by battering his head against the cell wall. Unlike the Australians in other prison camps, the men in Outram Road could rarely take strength from their group. One survivor said that either the mind went inward and drew on reserves of memory, or it crumbled.

Wells: I kept track of the days by memory. Each morning I would say to myself, well, today is Wednesday 23rd of whatever. And I was not a day out. Someone would say 'What's the date today, what are we?' And I'd say, 'Thursday, 28th August' or whatever. And I don't know whether I was sort of official date keeper, but that's one thing I did do. I seemed to want to know what the time space was. I think there must have been a subconscious feeling that if I didn't I may lose track of reality.

Trackson: When I came back from the war I could relate things that happened at home years before. There were eight of us in the family, and when I went back my father and mother were still alive and we started talking about old things and that. I could remember minute details about when I was just a little kid, things that they'd forgotten all about, and I could tell them more about family history in the time up until the war than they ever dreamed existed. Your mind wandered from one thing to another. Naturally there wasn't much else but back home, and consequently you were thinking of these things over and over again. You came to a self-hypnotised state. You'd sit there for hours with all these things running through your mind without consciously thinking about them. You'd walk round and round your cell and stop and look at the wall, or peer out the opening to see if there was anything you could see outside, but there was just nothing else; there was nothing else to occupy your mind. You studied every inch of the cell and every inch of the boards and every inch of yourself. You could spend your time picking off your little scabs, putting them in a heap and putting them in the latrine bucket. But I suppose you would say we were just like caged monkeys sitting there, and doing a bit of a pick and having a look around and a bit of a scratch and a walk; and that was it.

Wells: Periods of meditation, of imagery of the past were, I suppose, the equivalent to reading a light book for relaxation. More serious thinking was stimulating, but hard work. For example, I was concerned over my health and I decided to try and take my own pulse rate. To take a pulse of course one needs a time reference, so the first problem was to get a time reference. I got a strand of hemp about eighteen inches long into the cell by putting it around the cheeks of my anus. And then a piece of stone was the next thing to bring in for the weight for a pendulum. My plan was to make a pendulum with a known period of oscillation. So I had to put this stone up my anus to get it into the cell. It wasn't a very smooth stone, but well, neither was the anus then so it probably didn't matter.

I was very fortunate. One day when we were washing ourselves and all these shorts—semi G strings, semi shorts—with numbers on them were lying in a heap on the corridor floor. A tape measure was lying across them because they'd been doing some measuring or alterations. They'd been to the tailors, and they'd been washed, or so-called washed. I noticed, because of the position of the tape measure, that the number stamped on the trousers was on a piece of cloth about one-and-three-quarter inches long. Having got some means of measuring the hemp and with the stone already smuggled into the cell, I then made up a pendulum of the correct length to have an oscillation of one second. This is done by the physics formula of the periodicity or the time of a pendulum equals two pi root L over G, where L is the length of the pendulum and where G is the acceleration due to gravity, and by transposing this equation in simple algebra. It was made complex of course by not being able to write anything down, and having to do this in one's head under the sluggish conditions of one's brain. Having calculated the length I made a pendulum which would oscillate at one second. And then merely by finding the pulse in one's wrist and doing a juggling act of counting two things at the same time, that is the pulse and the pendulum, to time the number of pulses for sixty swings of the pendulum. I did this for some time. In fact the bit of stone was in the cell for months, I think. It was never found. It was pushed into a corner where there were a couple of cracks in the cell and it was probably seen, but no significance placed on it. The distressing part over some months was the fact that the pulse rate was getting appreciably slower, which was worrying.

Neilson: I've often wondered about this. We were all totally different. We all had a different education, we came from different sides of the track. Some were brought up, you know, more or less like sissies. And I was brought up rough and tough. And yet, they made it. I think it's got to be some inbuilt pride or something. If you tell yourself you can't be beat. I've always argued this and I told the psycho bloke. They can give you hidings, they can break your hands, they can break your skull, but only you can beat yourself. You decide you're going to chuck it in or you're not. So while you force that will upon yourself, you can't be beaten, you can only be given hidings. You're in charge of your nut, you can't be beat. Take the hidings, cop it sweet, laugh at them because that hurts them. After they've given you a hiding and you grin as they're going away; oh God, that used to drive them crazy. I've said it before and I'll say it again. I'm no bloody hero, I'm just one stubborn bugger, that's all. You've got to put your pride into it. Perhaps you want to make your people think you're a hero. But you're not really. Anyone can be a hero. Depends on how you look at it. It's all right to be frightened. The main thing is, when you're frightened don't let any other bugger see. That's the secret. I was frightened, but I was the only bugger knew it.

As the prisoners themselves saw, education and home background had little to do with survival. Such things influenced the way men behaved, they equipped them to be different within the private world of their heads; but they did not determine who lived and who died. Survival depended on strength and determination possessed by prisoners who came from all social classes.

Prisoners were as desperate to communicate as they were to eat. Some men preferred to provoke the guards and be bashed rather than stay silent and inactive. After the flurry of shouts and slaps the mind of the battered prisoner was full of new images, anger and signals of pain; and the next hour passed quickly. The prisoners exploited every means to link themselves to others. For a time the prisoners wrote brief messages on the bottom of their aluminium food bowls, and news circulated in cryptic scratches.

Trackson: There was a signaller in the cell next door to me, I think it was Chris Neilson, and he taught me Morse code. He taught it to me through the wall without any contact verbally or in any other way, just by the taps on the wall. We used a little stone dug out of the masonry. I got to learn A and B and gradually picked up the lot. I never got good at it, but I knew enough to understand a sentence over a period. It might take him a quarter of an hour to tell me a sentence, but I got to be able to understand what he was talking about. It was only simple sentences. And a doctor was put in the cell across the road from me, an English doctor who had been with an Indian brigade, and he could talk deaf and dumb with his fingers. He taught me to speak deaf and dumb through the hole in the wall across the passage by giving me a signal with his fingers that's 'A', until I eventually picked up the alphabet. I never could talk real fast or that, but we could have a short conversation while the guard was up the other end; good morning, how are you, and that sort of thing.

Neilson: There were all the other blokes that went mad, that were screaming all around the place. John McGregor often said if it hadn't been for the fact that I got the Morse code through to him, we wouldn't have made it either. It's not just loneliness or fear. It's the isolation. There was nothing else but just wait and sit around in a cell all day.

When I got McGregor proficient at Morse, I'd say, well listen, today I'm going to take you for a trip north of Cooktown, fishing. It would take all day to tap through what you could say in half an hour. The next day he'd say, I'll take you for a trip up to the grape country, in Perth, not far from Midland Junction where he lived, Swan Valley. I said, 'Yeah, I've been there'. And he said 'Yeah but you people pick the oranges and peaches and put them in bags. We wait till the school holidays over there and the kids roll down one peach at a time'. And this sort of thing went on all the time.

Neilson says that in 'that filthy cell' he could smell a washed and scented guard from yards away; sometimes he would even know which particular guard was coming. He would have time to warn McGregor and both men would move to the centre of their cells. But John Wyett was not so fortunate. When he was caught using a button to tap on the wall, he was bashed, and his few remaining buttons cut off. In case other prisoners were using the same transmitter, all prisoners had their buttons removed. Late in 1943 and in 1944 discipline was so rigid and the gaol so quiet that, Stan Davis says, 'you could hear yourself breathe': at the slightest tap the guards were 'there in a flash'. The men could do nothing but sit 'facing the bloody wall'.

When Outram Road became crowded two prisoners had to share the one cell. This gave them a greater chance to communicate; but the two men were also rivals.

Wells: You'd have a standing arrangement that at this meal you'd take the right hand bowl and your colleague would take the left hand bowl, or the other way round; but you'd agree on this beforehand. Because even though we were brothers in a way and tried to help each other, there was that tendency to get your hand on the bigger bowl if you could, and that would create a strong tension the whole day. It may have only been ten grains of rice more, because the bowls were flattened off with a spoon, but sometimes there'd be a bit of a knob on one which may have a little bit more rice in the top of it. And you'd eye the other chap off and you'd feel him saying, 'Lucky devil, he's got the bigger one today, I might click next time'. And it was only half a spoonful.

Trackson: Well, I had this young fellow put in the cell with me. He was very quiet; he didn't talk much. When we used to go to sleep at night they used to sing out or blow a whistle. It was generally about nine o'clock, and it was the time when you were allowed to put your planks down and you could lay down. And this fellow, he used to just put his planks out, lie down and pull his tattered blanket up over him and that was it, say nothing. After quite some time, this got nagging at me and one night I really flared up and I said to him, 'Look, there's only the two of us in the cell and we're in the same predicament. If you're not going to even say goodnight to me, I'll fix you up good and proper. I'll bloody kill you. Then I'll have a cell by myself'. That was an example of a typical nervous upset. Afterwards he did at least say goodnight to me. I don't know why, but we never talked very much and he never ever told me where he came from or anything. I think he was English, I'm not sure.

After that we were changed around every now and then and the next cell mate I had was a fellow named Shelley from New South Wales. He was an ex-wheat lumper, but a very very nice sort of a bloke. But later when he wasn't in my cell he got dysentery very bad. When he was with me, we got on well. He taught me a piece of poetry, a long piece, that I could recite word for word right to this day: 'I want free life and I want fresh air, And I long for the canter after the cattle...'

Wells: I remember once not liking the way a colleague scratched his scabies. But my scratching probably was just as ugly for him to look at. Unnecessary time sitting on the toilet. All these things irritated, particularly if the chap that you were with— and I'm not being intellectually snobby—had no conversation except about driving a truck and the food he would eat. And that was a minus as a whole if you didn't have a partner with whom you could have some mental sparring to keep both of you mentally active. It was a plus when you didn't mind putting up with the other person's eccentricities. But to have someone with you who had no mental communication and to have to put up with the physical displeasures of whatever they were, and if they weren't there you made them up, made having someone else in the cell a disadvantage.

At one stage Wells shared a cell with a British civil servant, a 'very wise man', some fifteen years older than himself. The two were able to spend hours in whispered conversations. 'We both', Wells says, 'disregarded each other's bodies, knowing we could do nothing about our appearances'. In the postwar they continued a close relationship, unaffected by long periods when they did not meet.

After a few months in Outram Road all prisoners were physically loathsome: they were skeletons encased in weeping sores and flaking skin. The sores were the obvious sign of their degeneration; and they were a torment.

Wells: They produced in all of us a mental strain in that there was a tendency to want to scratch them. You knew that was only making more pus and tearing more skin off.

So you would resist and resist, probably for a couple of hours. Then something would break mentally, and I mean break; you just couldn't contain it any longer. We'd just go into ourselves and tear ourselves to smithereens, and there was pus and blood from all over the body. We'd just drag it out, just let it come out; these things would be infected completely. After half an hour, with the limited energy we had, we'd be absolutely exhausted, just as if we'd come in from a day's hard work. You'd be absolutely exhausted, in a filthy mess and sore all over, but at least not itching, which was a lovely relief.

What we were doing was digging these things out and spreading them across the rest of the body; but mentally we just couldn't prevent ourselves. One would have a couple of days without any further trouble, and it would gradually begin again as these things were burying back further into the skin. And then the diarrhoea would start; it was just one continual battle. You could do so little about it. At least the mind seemed to be untouched by this. I felt that inside the head was something that they couldn't get at; that was mine and I could exercise it. I could manipulate it and use it as I wanted.

Wyett: I had amoebic dysentery by this time, and they wouldn't empty the slop pail. The cell absolutely stank and I stank. Then I got to the stage where I found I couldn't stand. I was lying on the floor of the cell and I had the most peculiar experience. I was detached from my body, the real me was perched on the wall up there in a corner; and this filthy body that was on the floor was nothing to do with me at all. I was up there, looking down on this thing. I recalled at that time things that I didn't know I knew. I can remember one of them now. When I was a very small child, my parents caught me drinking out of the dog's water bowl. I was severely reprimanded for it. And I thought at the time, how distinctly unfair they were. It was one of those silly little things. I suppose I wouldn't have been more than about three to four years of age at the time. I didn't know I knew it, but this came back to me and it's remained with me ever since. I've remembered it with startling clarity. That was when I got to the stage where they thought I was going to die–I was half dead anyway.

One prisoner says his need for a disruption to the monotony of prison life was so strong that he welcomed a death. It set in train movement and sharp talk among the guards, the coming and going of trusted Asian prisoners who carried the corpse, and speculation about who had died.

Most of those who died in Outram Road were Asian civilian prisoners. Dr Jim Taylor, gaoled for helping Allied prisoners-of-war in North Borneo, witnessed many of the deaths:

In Outram Road I think I counted about 1400 deaths. The Japs had a peculiar mentality. If they had a prisoner about to die, they'd put me in the cell with him. They were cases on their last legs, unconscious mostly. I would be present as a doctor, although they wouldn't let me practise. But they could say that they had a doctor there. It was upsetting: I couldn't do anything, and they wouldn't give us drugs or anything like that. And I'd be taken out again immediately he died.

After a body was taken from a cell piles of scaley skin lay on the floor and gathered in drifts in the corners. The guards protected themselves by wearing masks and only touching things in the cells with gloved hands or sword points.

In spite of the frequency of death in Outram Road, the very rigidity of the system in the last two years of the war gave some protection. In other prisons, Wells says,

Any guard on a work party, if he hit you too hard with a wooden stick and broke your neck, well, it was no worry, he'd just accidentally killed a prisoner who didn't do what he was told. Nobody worried much because there were thousands more and the prisoner was just a number. But once you were arrested and came under the judicial *kempeitai* system —the establishment if you like—officialdom had to know all about you, what you were there for, and what sort of character you were. The trial records were kept. You were more precious as a *kempeitai* prisoner than as an ordinary prisoner-of-war because as an ordinary prisoner-of-war you were one of sixty odd thousand: if a few went, well, it didn't matter. But at Outram Road you were sentenced to a term of imprisonment, and they were going to make certain that you did that. It was skin off their nose if you didn't. They had not achieved their aim, and the aim was to hold you there to serve a prison sentence. So therefore, if you became sick or you appeared to be sick and you could die, well then they would willingly stop your sentence. Their own medical people, whom they had to bring in, said whether you should go to hospital. The commander of the prison didn't take responsibility. Now it was easier for the Japanese to send the sick prisoners to Changi hospital where our own colleagues would look after them than to their own hospitals. So you went to Changi. And while you were at Changi your sentence was under suspension. When you came back you started from the next day that you would have done and that was the system. I'm sure none of us would have been here now had we been put in Outram Road to die.

There was other pressure on the Japanese to account for their prisoners in Outram Road. When the senior Allied officers at Changi heard of the deaths there, and saw the 'absolute neglect' of four of the released men, the Australian commander, Galleghan, 'remonstrated with the Japanese' and warned them of 'displeasure' after the war. Perhaps Black Jack's aggression was the reason why the Japanese sent Dr Taylor to observe the dying Asians; and it may have made the Japanese more willing to have a public record of their gestures of aid for the dangerously sick prisoners-of-war.

The Japanese policy of sending men on the verge of death to Changi gave prisoners one way of getting out of Outram Road. They could injure themselves, or feign illness. But it was a dangerous strategy. The prisoner had to make the attempt before he had declined to the point where recovery was impossible. And he had to be prepared for intense suffering. He was gambling with his own resolve, the durability of his own body, and the fact that the Japanese would intervene in time.

Near the end of the war the prisoners at Outram Road were sent out to work. One job was to dig tunnels where the Japanese planned to make their last stand against the coming Allied assault on Singapore. The prisoners went to work in chains; but they were slightly better fed, and they had more chance to talk and plan.

Neilson: There was a little bloke called Joe Smart, an Englishman. He was working and I says, 'What's the matter, Joe'? 'Oh', he says, 'I'm bloody crook'. It was obvious he was passing blood, amoebic dysentery. Well, as we got back about fifty feet into this hill, there was a slight incline, then it flattened off and the tunnels went T-shaped. As the loaded skips were coming out, I took a ride down with him to empty the skip and bring it back. On the way down I said 'Joe', and as he turned round I gave him a shove. He landed pretty heavy, broke his pelvis. But it saved his life. He got out to Changi and that's where they kept him for the rest of the war. He visited me once in Cairns. He came out to live in Australia, as a shipwright, up near Cairns, but his wife couldn't take it, the heat.

Anyway, after we got Joe out, I decided to do this fall. So I let myself fall; it was the funniest thing in the world. I don't know how these blokes on the movies put on these bloody acts, because it was nearly impossible. They come over and I had to play being unconscious. They were all concerned because the chap in charge, he said, 'Oh, we need this bloke, he's a good mining bloke. We need him bad; got to get him right'. And they're trying to pour coconut oil down my throat and I'm trying to work out how you choke, being unconscious, you know.

After a couple of days they decided they'd take me back to Outram Road. They weren't too sure I might be putting up a trick so they left the cell door open. It was tough, but once you started, you had to keep going. They left the door open, and they put my food on the front step. Now that was the hard part. You're starving bloody hungry, and the food is there, six foot from you, and the *benki* bucket is in the other corner. So when you had a piddle, you piddled yourself. That food stopped there. And when I'd see a Nip, just around the corner, having a look in, I'd kid I was trying to crawl to it, and all of a sudden I'd let out a yell with pain and I'd kid to faint again. After three days they're satisfied that I was crook. So they let a *tobung* they call it, a servant, come in to change my pants, bring me food and help me onto the *benki* bucket. Anyway it must have been a couple of weeks, and this bloke feeding me all the time. They brought the Jap doctor in; he was going to have a look at a few others to see if they could go to Changi. So he had a look, and he went to move me, and of course I threw another mickey and fell back, like as if I'd fainted with the pain in the hips. He was satisfied. I heard him say 'enough' in Japanese. I could understand him say, 'Yeah, he's got something broken there, better send him out'. I'll never forget it. They put me out and left me lying on a stretcher in the yard. And one of the Nips, I have to say it the way he said it, he said *go go ichi* in Japanese means 551, my number. Then he said in Malay 'You're not sick. You want to go to Changi where there's good food'. And out I went.

We came in by truck. They took myself and a couple of others off, dumped us on the ground and the truck went. The first bloke peering over me is Major Clark from Brisbane, he's since dead. He said, 'How are you?' I said, 'Have they gone?' He said, 'Yes' And Professor Glyn White comes along. He said, 'Neilson, you bastard, you cost me ten dollars. I said you'd be out in three months. It's three and a half'.

Dr Glyn White: There was Rod Wells and a lad named Chris Neilson. Well, Rod was unrecognisable. And you could count the surface anatomy of every bone he had in his body, practically, he was so emaciated. And almost too weak to talk. I was only about seven stone myself, but Rod, it was just like picking up a weeny little baby. I can still feel how he just relaxed as soon as I got him into my arms. It was a very very emotional episode. He was almost too weak to speak. But you could see his smile under his whiskers. He looked just awful. Chris was taller than Rod Wells, and being taller he looked even gaunter. And it was exactly the same reaction, when I picked him up and carried him in, his eyes just showed how thankful he was to be back with us in Changi.

Around June 1945 Rod Wells had decided that his health had reached the point where he had to take an immediate gamble on being shifted to Changi. If he waited for the Japanese to make the decision he feared that he would die in Outram Road or within days of going to Changi. Like Neilson he collapsed at work, took the beatings and refused food. After the Japanese doctor made his inspection Wells heard 'the lovely words, "641 Changi".'

Herb Trackson also feigned injury and was taken to Changi. When he recovered the Japanese claimed him and he returned to Outram Road to continue his sentence. Within weeks his body was again a skeleton and scabs. Just before the end of the war the Japanese sent him to Changi, and he was still there, dangerously ill, when the Japanese surrendered. Stan Davis was trucked to Changi with those so ill the Japanese thought they were within hours of death. He recovered and returned to Outram Road and the tunnel gangs. Near the end of the war timber shoring fell across his chin and chest. He remembers a fellow prisoner saying, 'How are you doing Darkie? Keep it up. I think you will get to Changi.' He was thrown on a stretcher and he too heard, the magic word 'Changi'.

John Wyett, almost unconscious and grotesquely distorted by beriberi, was sent to Changi. So ill he did not have to fake symptoms, he stayed under the protection of Changi's doctors.

Chris Neilson's stuntman's fall and feigned injuries earned him his second trip to Changi. Neilson, the 'Reb' as he was known in his old unit, had first gone to Changi when he was so sick the Japanese had thought he would die that afternoon. While in Changi the doctors had trained him to fake an injured back, show the right symptoms, and deceive the Japanese when they tested his reflexes. Neilson was sent to Changi before the end of the war; but too late for Glyn White to collect on his investment in the Reb's ingenuity.

CHAPTER FOURTEEN

RICE NOW FOR RICE LATER

'Somebody that was hungry would sing out, "I'll give you rice and soup on Wednesday night for that rice now".'

From the first weeks of the war the Japanese shipped Allied prisoners back to Japan. By early 1945 nearly 3000 Australians were held in the homeland of the enemy. Most of the prison camps were next to work sites along the industrial strip between Tokyo and Nagasaki; and a few were close to mines and factories scattered north to Hokkaido. No camps were consistently pleasant: but they varied almost as much as those on the frontiers of the Japanese empire. Zentsuji, an old army barracks in northern Shikoku, was one of the best camps. The sixty Australian officers captured in Rabaul were sent there in July 1942, and later a few other Australians joined the British, American, Dutch and New Zealand servicemen in the camp. The Australians were as surprised to find gum trees at Zentsuji as they were at some of the conditions. Early in the war Japanese newspapers, including one in English, were delivered; the officers were sometimes allowed to walk in the countryside; and representatives of the international diplomatic community visited the camp. Mail supplies were more frequent than elsewhere: an American prisoner received nearly all of the daily letters that his mother wrote, and an Australian says that he was handed thirty letters in three years compared to the three or four that went to men in most South-east Asian camps. Zentsuji was one of the first Japanese camps for Aircraftman First Class Ken Parkyns shot down off New Hanover in northern New Guinea in 1942:

> Living conditions were good, food was good. Well, better than anything we'd struck in any other camp. We were allowed to have concert parties. They drew the line at a few things, including some of the sketches the boys used to sing, like 'Ta ra ra boom de ay, we've soup and rice today. We had it yesterday, we have it every day'. And then the chorus comes in with everybody, 'Ta ra ra boom de ay . . .' and away it goes.

Japan. Camps varied almost as much as those on the frontier of the Japanese empire.

John May, padre with Lark Force in Rabaul: Outside the camp there was a bakehouse. At first when we got there we were given a ration of bread which was made of rice flour, and it was very tasty. This bakery operated for quite a long time, and every day you'd get the smell of the new bread wafting over the fence.

We had American cooks and a very good cookhouse. The quantity of rice varied, and sometimes there wasn't any rice, leaving us with millet and poorer quality grains of that kind. We had a few beans from time to time; some stuff called gooligum. I don't know what that was. It was a round, tacky, sweet, custardy sort of thing which wasn't too bad. We had three meals a day, and a reasonable amount of hot water and a bit of tea so we could have brews from time to time. We kept on complaining because the level of rations wasn't anything like what we were used to. To the Japanese it probably wasn't too bad. Quite possibly we were better fed, particularly in the later part of the war, than the Japanese civilians although I've got no proof of that. I think there were only a couple of deaths in Zentsuji that you could attribute directly to shortage of food.

We started off with what we stood up in. Eventually we got an issue of British army stuff captured in Hong Kong and sold to us, including greatcoats and boots. The Japanese issued us with a bit of their stuff, but with cold weather and shortage of food, sometimes you put on your greatcoat and all of your clothes, got on to your palliasse with your two or three blankets, and just lay there shivering.

Flight Lieutenant Paul Metzler was second pilot in a Catalina caught in anti-aircraft fire from Japanese cruisers on January 21, 1942. Two members of the crew drowned and the others were among the first Allied prisoners taken by the Japanese in the New Guinea area.

Metzler: It was an ordeal; but everything's relative. It was nothing compared with what men put up with, or were killed by, on the Burma-Thailand railway. Time utterly dragged, there was a sort of hopelessness, you couldn't see any end to the war, you could hardly believe that you had lived any other life than the one you were living. It was just time, hunger and a miserable poverty. Officers, who weren't detailed to go and work, stayed in the camp and did absolutely nothing. All they had to amuse themselves was each other's company.

John May: On an average sort of day in 1943 or early 1944 there would have been classes going on. People who knew a bit about sidereal navigation or economics or geography or English grammar or Spanish or French or something would be giving classes. One day I counted eleven languages being taught in the camp.

I think we understood that we were in a propaganda camp. This was driven home to us when on one occasion the Japanese made an issue of fruit. They lined up people, cameras were whirring and people were photographed receiving it. Then they were marched round the corner and it was taken away again.

By October 1944 John May had lost two stone in weight. Not much by comparison with the emaciated stick figures that stumbled about in the worst camps, but sufficient to make men depressed, lethargic and have their thinking dominated by food. Punishments were harsh without being hideous. Metzler, confined to a cell just over a metre by a metre, worked a nail loose from his boot, and using his boot as a hammer, expressed his anger by punching unrepeatable anti-Japanese messages into the walls. When some of the men released from Zentsuji heard about a pleasant propaganda camp somewhere in Japan they could not believe it had anything to do with the grey, bug-ridden, two-storey barracks where they had been repressed and restricted.

In the 1940s 'psychological warfare' was a new label, and a new force for nations to bring against their enemies. One reason why the Japanese frequently asked prisoners to fill out questionnaires was so that they could exploit their skills. It was to the regret of the many self-proclaimed brewery and brothel testers that not all occupations were of equal value to the enemy. But men with a higher education or a background in journalism were likely to be forced to work for one of the propaganda agencies. The Japanese invested most effort into radio, and much of the material they transmitted was aimed simply to build up a short wave audience. At the end of 1943 they assembled a group of potential broadcasters in an old Tokyo college closed by the military because of the liberal taint to its courses. The prisoners knew the building as Bunka camp. At one of the first meetings the prisoners were asked if anyone did not wish to broadcast. An Englishman stepped forward and he was quickly hustled away by the guards. An enraged Japanese officer implied that the prisoner had been executed. It was not until after the war that the men at Bunka learnt he had merely been transferred to another, harsher, camp.

Parkyns: There weren't only Australian broadcasters. There were German, Italian and Spanish speakers; they had all nationalities. Naturally it was under the scrutiny of general headquarters. Stephen Shattles refused to do a broadcast to America. He was a civilian. When they put him in front of a microphone a Japanese with a two-handed sword stood behind him and said, 'You broadcast, Shattles!' I saw this myself. He refused. He said, 'I can't read this stuff. It's against my principles.' The guard waved the sword, and they had a gun on the desk as well: 'You read it!' How he could ever read it I don't know. He was trembling; but he read what the Japanese put in front of him. So what can you do?

When I first started broadcasting I was just called in every now and again as a strange voice picked out of the blue. I was still working in the galley, or the cookhouse. I might have three lines playing the batman talking to his officer. And because I had an Australian accent I would sound like a Cockney. I was in 'Journey's End' at one stage. There were a lot of rewrites. There were no restrictions set on these because they were established stories and plays known throughout the world. Everything that was newly written was very closely scrutinised by the Japanese. They were looking for any double meanings that we were putting through.

'If you were sick you had a shushun tag.'

An Australian army lieutenant forced to read Imperial General Headquarters communiques ended with his own unscripted comment suggesting that listeners could have 'their own thoughts about the validity of these statements'. He was turned over to the 'tender mercies' of the kempeitai and then shifted to a camp 'reserved for those who had particularly annoyed the Japanese'.

One achievement of the prison broadcasters was to help transmit messages between prisoners and their families in Australia. At the end of the war Major Charles Cousens was put on trial in Sydney for his part in the propaganda broadcasts. Cousens, who had commanded a company in the fighting on the Malayan peninsula, had been a professional announcer with 2GB before the war. In his defence Cousens claimed that he had had no choice, and that he had attempted to sabotage the broadcasts. The charges against Cousens were dropped. In 1948 Cousens and Ken Parkyns went to San Francisco to appear for the defence in the treason case against Iva Toguri, said to be Tokyo Rose. She was sentenced to ten years' imprisonment, and pardoned in 1977.

As the Japanese military leaders called up every available able-bodied citizen for what they believed would be the decisive battles of the war, more prisoners were needed as labourers in the industries supplying the armed services. Most of the Australian prisoners arrived in Japan between mid 1944 and early 1945. They came ashore, tall gaunt men in a variety of inappropriate clothes, uncertain of their reception. To the Japanese the Australians were the *Goshu*, and they were a people to be avoided. Mothers hustled their children past.

Ray Parkin: It was just like an old-fashioned slave market. There we were on the wharf and blokes came down from the various mines and factories and bid for us.

Reg Newton: The Japanese took the first fifty men which contained the bulk of the NCOs, and gave me fifty Western Australians. Then to my amazement they took the balance of my chaps from the other end. So I got fifty South Australians; and only fifty of my original 2/19th Battalion chaps. I was not amused. I appealed and appealed and yelled and yelled and tried to get the message through. But to no avail, and so we took off for Ohama which was a coal mining town.

Frank Baker: We ended up with all sorts of people from different units. It was a mixed crowd. And we just had to get used to that. It was the first time that we had been separated from the people we'd been with all the time. But there were some of us together still.

We had a train trip on a very nice passenger train, well equipped and comfortable. But we had all the windows blocked out because as soon as you lifted them the Japanese on the platform spat at you.

David Runge: We went from Moji to Omuta, and that was our camp. We got in there in the early hours of the morning. It was dark, and we could hear the Americans saying, 'They're Australians, they're Australians. See the big cowboy hats.' Meaning the Australian slouch hat.

When we were going up to this Omuta, we asked the Japanese what we were going to do and they said, 'Well all Australians are big men and all Japanese are little, so we are going to mate you with Japanese women so that Japan will have big people.' We thought that was a pretty good idea. We didn't know we were going to end up in a coal mine.

The Japanese had certainly had the opportunity to observe the breeding capacity of the Australians. The group with David Runge had stood naked on the Moji wharf while Japanese men and women had commented and laughed. When a Japanese officer announced that their clothes had been de-loused and were ready to be re-issued, the men dashed through a doorway only to be confronted by another row of women. Each had to wait till his number was called then go forward and take his shorts and shirt.

The breaking up of units that had stayed together through training, battle and imprisonment was unexpected. With much of the old unit structures destroyed and camp administration taken out of the hands of their officers and NCOs, the Australians had more direct contact with their gaolers; and they were more conscious that they were prisoners. The enforced short haircuts and numbered Japanese uniforms made it even harder for the men still to think of themselves as soldiers.

Ray Parkin: When we got to Japan we were suddenly confronted by wooden buildings with windows and doors and all sorts of things. And of course Japanese rooms have *tatami* mats. That was something. Our rooms had twelve mats, each about six feet by three. That was our sleeping place. We found neatly rolled at the head of each mat there was a mattress and a thing like an eiderdown. This was like the Ohama Hilton. We thought, well, this'll do us. But of course that was only the top dressing.

Cliff Moss: We also got a brand new suit of Jap clothes. Some of them were made of proper cotton material, but the one I got was hessian, green hessian.

Ray Parkin: You had to report the state of the room: how many present, how many sick and how many were here and there. And all this had to be done in Japanese. Well, it terrified us; we didn't have the language. So they gave us an Englishman. We had a Scotsman as a matter of fact; Jock was our bloke. He was very good and he conned us into everything that was going on. He looked after it until eventually we had to do it ourselves.

Jim Richardson: One man told us that as long as you shouted at them and made it sound something like it you would be right. There was one thing that we used to have to say, and I still don't know what it was, but we used to say, 'A few shin bones and a curry at Mersing'. Now if you said that quick and loud, it sounded exactly like what they said. I always got out of it with that. If someone was away, around at the toilet, you had to say there was one man *benjo*, report on the rest of the men, and finish up with 'a few shin bones and a curry at Mersing'. It sounded like the right thing and we got away with it.

Don Moore: One of the most unfortunate things that did happen to us was we had to sleep in numerical order. Your bunk corresponded with the number which you wore on your jacket. And so consequently being M I was with Macs and the Murrays. It meant you were taken away from Smithy, who was your mate. You were with fellow POWs, but you hadn't established any relationship with them. You hadn't shared experiences over the years.

Hugh Clarke: There were all sorts of rules which you could regard as psychological torture. For example in your room you were belted if you were caught wearing your hat. Likewise if you were outside the room without your hat, that was a crime. If you went to the toilet, you had to hang a tag on your bed so that if the guard came round and he saw an empty bed he'd know where you were. For the toilet, you had a *benjo* tag. If you were sick you had a *shushun* tag. If you were in hospital you had a *nuyin* tag. You had to remember all these things.

Parkin: When we arrived at the camp at Ohama, we were admiring the scenery and saying what a wonderful place it was. The men already there were saying, 'You just wait till the weather warms up and we get the fleas'. We said, 'Have you got fleas?' And they said, 'Yes, we've got fleas'. 'But', we said, 'what about bugs?' They said, 'No, we've got no bugs'. We said, 'Want to bet?' Because we knew we'd brought them with us. Anyway the bugs did well there, they thrived. And with the *tatami* mats and all this open woodwork it was a haven for them and they bred like mad.

David Thompson: The trick used to be to get into bed with your pyjamas or whatever you were going to wear at night, and lie quietly for about an hour. When you thought the maximum number of lice had got onto you, go outside into the perishing cold, take your pyjamas off, leave them out there and get back into bed. Then you got a couple of hour's rest before more lice disturbed your night.

Eric Endacott: There were 300 of us put on a train, and we went north up through Osaka bordering the Inland Sea, through the railway junction at Kyoto, to Naoetsu. The snow was beginning to fall then, and being more or less opposite Siberia we experienced some of the biggest snowfalls I've ever seen. The snow was up twenty to twenty-five feet deep. It used to be right up level with the crossarms of the telephone poles, and steps had to be cut down to the doorways of the houses.

We had a sick room with some of our medical orderlies looking after people, and they had the only fire in the building. A little charcoal brazier was burning there, and men could get around it and warm themselves. Quite a lot of people used to die every night. I remember one time I was in the sickroom, and I think they'd sort of given me up. The chap on my right hand died and then they moved me up into his position, and before the night was out the chap on the other side died. It was a case of Old Nick chasing me up and down the room all the time I was there, but I managed to survive.

Dr Ian Duncan was further south in Omuta: As a matter of fact in 1943 they had the coldest winter for seventy years. So our sickness was mainly respiratory diseases, particularly pneumonia. And we had nothing to treat it. But we found if we could take a couple of hundred mls of blood from, usually, the cooks who were the best fed in the camp—and give it to these very sick men they responded rather dramatically. Just to that small blood transfusion.

The mine had a hospital but we found that the men were coming back with broken limbs set without any anaesthetic, and wounds deep enough to cut tendons just sewn up with the coal dust still in there. Always we had to take the stitches out and re-suture them.

Frank Baker was on Shikoku: The conditions in Japan were the worst that I encountered. The living conditions in the camp itself were OK. They even had hot water for us to bathe in. We had clean surroundings, and we had to be clean. All that was good. But the food was dreadful, and the discipline was very, very severe. The work was in a copper mine and it was very arduous. People got their ration at the place of work. Now if they weren't at work there were no rations. The only other arrangement I believe was a third of a ration for a sick person. So when our rations came out, it was assessed on the basis of so many well people, so many sick people. But of course we evened it out and everybody got the same. That didn't necessarily happen with the civilians. If they didn't go to work they didn't eat, and that was the way it was.

Parkin: Three breakfast cups of cooked rice was the virtual ration for the day; that's all. You might get a bit of soup or a few soy beans at times. We got some squid now and again, some crab, and little odds and ends like that came through. Even the chooks got avitaminosis. We had about eighteen or twenty fowls there and they lost all the feathers off their hindquarters and it was only avitaminosis causing that. After the show was over we fed them up and they all got feathers on their bums again.

Dr Rowley Richards was at Sakata, one of the most northern camps:

During the winter the Japanese issued an edict that all pet dogs had to be destroyed, allegedly because they were eating food that could be better eaten by the civilian population. And also allegedly to provide leather from the pelts. There were two or three Australian slaughtermen who'd been working with the local butcher, Takahashi. He became very friendly. He was one of the two very fine civilian

Japanese that I met and in fact went back after the war to meet again. They had the task of slaughtering the dogs. I went up on the particular day to the slaughterhouse to be confronted with literally dozens of yapping dogs, from little poodles up to Great Danes, being brought by the locals. They were weeping, of course, because they were losing their pets. It was a terrible sight, I'll never forget it. After they all left, our fellows despatched the dogs, and then somebody suggested there's a lot of good meat here. We sort of put our horror and abhorrence behind us and took all the carcases back to the camp because the Japanese wouldn't have them. We deep froze them in the snow. Then each day we'd take a few of these carcases out and cook them, and the meat was pretty good. Prior to this we'd learnt that horsemeat wasn't too bad. But the terrible part of the dog bit was that as the snow melted, so we'd see a couple of little paws or a little nose pointing out of the snow at us. But despite our guilty consciences we still saw fit to eat them.

David Runge: Some jokers at Omuta would have a vegetable can. It would have been made by someone like IXL and on the glossy label there would be a picture. If it contained meat and vegetables that would be displayed on the outside. You'd get some of these blokes with one of these cans and they'd be looking at the label and eating their rice, and they'd imagine that they were eating that. And you'd say to them, 'Hey, let me look at your label while I eat my dinner'. 'Go to blazes, you're not looking at my label'. And that sort of thing.

In Japan the prisoners became familiar with the *bento* box. It was a small rectangular wooden box in which they carried their midday meal. It might contain a soggy mass of sago, perhaps some seaweed, a piece of salty plum, or a pickled onion or a mandarin. If the prisoner were tempted to eat early, he starved for the rest of the day.

Scrounging and trading outside the camps had been common in South-east Asia. It gave the prisoners access to essential extra food and it allowed them a moment of independence. In Japan the chance for enterprise beyond the camps was limited; but some Australians were imprisoned with Americans who had established an aggressive free market system within the camp fences.

Don Moore: If you were sick you didn't say, 'I can't eat, fellows. The doctor's put me on a diet so that means you can put an extra spoonful around.' That would happen normally on the line on the Burma Railway or any other camp. But in this particular camp at Fukuoka, no, you hung on to that meal. That was an asset, and you traded your food. You would sell your meal for cigarettes. So they became the basis of the currency. And we joined into the system.

David Runge: You'd get somebody that didn't feel too well, and they'd sing out, 'I've got rice now for rice and soup on Wednesday night'. Somebody that was hungry would sing out, 'I'll give you rice and soup on Wednesday night for that rice now'. When Wednesday night came he'd find he owed about six rations and he couldn't pay them. After a while they'd declare him bankrupt. Nobody would trade with him.

Moore: The Dutch commander came down one night and said, 'Moses is bankrupt'. We were new to the camp. He said, 'Oh, you do not understand. It is impossible for him to pay for the meals that he owes. The doctor said he would starve to death if he had to pay back all his meals at once. So he's bankrupt. So you never trade with Moses'.

Runge: There was an old Dutch padre in the camp that got all the bankrupts. They were starting to get like skeletons because as soon as they came through the chow line with their rice and soup there'd be blokes there that they owed the food to and they would take it off them. They wouldn't get anything to eat. So the old Dutch padre had all the bankrupts sitting down in one place and they had to pay back one ration a day and were allowed to eat two.

Moore: As soon as we got into this new camp, it turned out to be better because we all got back with our own mates again. Then one day one fellow said, 'Look, I can't have my rice, who wants to trade it?' 'Give the bloody thing away'. 'What?' 'Give the thing away. Don't start that bloody racket again. We'll turn this into an Australian camp.' And from there on everything was pooled. The attitude was quite different.

The Americans, by being sent to Fukuoka No 2 first, had the key jobs in the camp administration, the cook house, ration store and sick bay. One of the medical orderlies had a 'good racket'. Before a prisoner could be given a ticket entitling him to light duties his temperature had to be over a certain level. For the payment of the equivalent of half a bowl of rice the orderly would 'see you right'. But in spite of his inflated income the orderly was not a master of the trading system. He spent recklessly, paid above the going rate, and after a brief life of plenty he, too, was declared bankrupt.

Fukuoka No. 2, Nagasaki

In Japan the different national groups often lived close together, and the differences in their behaviour were significant. The trading of the Americans was almost a parody of a free capitalist economy. And in their reminiscences Americans are likely to recall prison life as competitive with survival going to the fittest. Australians, however they behaved, are more inclined to talk about people sharing and surviving as groups.

Compared to the work camps on the Burma-Thailand railway or other major projects, the prisoners in Japan laboured within a tightly controlled system. The hours on the dockyard, Don Moore says, seemed 'rather respectable', but the men had to be up at 5 o'clock, go through numerous *tenkos* and travel before they began work at eight. 'At 4 o'clock in the afternoon the same thing would happen. We never used to get back until about half past six.' The copper miners suffered the same controlled and protracted day.

Frank Baker: We were counted inside the camp, we were counted again outside, and handed over to the mine guards who were a terrible crowd, really nasty specimens. We would march to the railway station; sometimes get on a passenger train where everybody stood up, no seats, just straps; other times we would sit on the ore trucks and be taken to the mine. Again we would be counted, marched around to our point of duty and be counted again. Then we would go down to our drive, about four kilometres into the hill. We used to climb down about 500 feet of ladders to get into the bottom drive where we worked.

Eric Endacott: Some people were employed at the stainless steel factory on furnaces, a very hot job. Later one particular nasty area was where carbon electrodes were manufactured. This entailed powdered carbon of various degrees being mixed with a tar-like substance. It was very hard on the respiratory system. We were covered in black and I remember after I returned to Australia for two or three years I was still having carbon come out through the pores of my skin. I'd absorbed so much.

Hugh Clarke: The first camp was at Nagasaki, on an island in the bay, and the job there was working in the dockyards. The fit men were picked out as riveters and sent to do a course. I was a riveter. There was constant sabotage. And bludging, of course. You'd always use the wrong sized rivet. But they'd detect a lot of them because they always came along and tested. But there were some places they wouldn't go: up high or where it was dangerous—or you could overheat a rivet. If you overheat a rivet it gets crumbly, like stale bread. And the gas cutters cut holes in the plates. There wasn't enough supervision to check every rivet.

Don Moore: There was a code of signs which was common to the Japanese and ourselves. We had a tic tac system of workers in bondage. A *kaigun*, a member of the navy police, was the common enemy of all. And if we saw one we would tap two fingers on our upper arm; that would signify that a *kaigun* was in our area and looking us over. So this became a mutual warning system between the Japanese and ourselves. We got to waving and saying, 'Hi' to them by sign language. You couldn't talk. I think it was something that perhaps mellowed our attitude towards the Japanese.

David Thompson: I worked in the zinc refinery and we used to load blast furnaces. We had hand-pushed trolleys and we used to load the ingredients into these trolleys, push them on rails and tip them into the blast furnaces. We got quite skilled at it. We were lucky with the Japanese shift bosses, the *buntaijos* (*buntaichō*) or whatever they called them. We had some very friendly, quite reasonable, ones. They taught us the secrets of working these materials and then, particularly on the night shift, they used to go off and have a sleep. We used to load the furnace up for them: a truck of this and two trucks of that, and sometimes we used to stuff the whole works up by putting the wrong thing in. Not intentionally, because we rewarded kindness from them with extra effort on our part. We didn't work fast, but there were very few bashings in that job.

Peter McGrath-Kerr: The first time I went to work it struck me as very hard. There were two women mixing concrete with shovels, one with a baby in a thing on her back. Women were doing the labouring work, they were helping unload coal from barges, using a pole and two baskets. There weren't many men about, except some older men working round the factory. Young girls and young fellows worked in the machine shop nearby; they were all school-age kiddies.

After he arrived in Japan McGrath-Kerr spent a week doing nothing because the Japanese were not prepared for the sudden arrival of a gang of labourers. After demolishing an old building to make themselves a camp which became Fukuoka No 14 the prisoners went to work in the Mitsubishi iron foundry. McGrath-Kerr cleaned diesel engine blocks, smashed spurs from castings for re-smelting, repaired motor-tricycles, and made spanners from old truck springs. The work was unrelenting, up to eleven hours a day, and one day in ten was *yasumi*, a rest day. It could have been worse.

Mining was one of the most dangerous jobs. By the end of the war the Japanese were desperately short of raw materials and they were forced to exploit old and almost exhausted mines.

Don Noble: It was a wet mine, drift mine, about 300 feet below the bed of the Inland Sea. If the pumps stopped for a day it took seven days to get back into operation. It was horrific. The one thing that was good about it was that the temperature was even. In summer it was cool, winter time, oh boy was it good, because all we had was a cotton singlet, a cotton pair of black trousers and a pair of rubber soled canvas shoes, and in the snow they weren't terribly warm.

Parkin: At times we were only seven metres from the sea bed. That's not much of a bridge over your head. By this time the Americans had come in and they were dropping mines around the Inland Sea. The tugs towing the barges of coal around would quite regularly go over these mines and blow up. Well, when you're down in the mine it's for all the world like being in a submarine being depth charged. I had eight mines go off during one shift down there. The whole earth would shudder and shiver, and there would be actual spurts of water, just like in a submarine. You'd wonder what was going to happen.

Noble: You had to walk a mile and a half to get to the face, work your eight hours and then you had to walk your mile and a half to come home. We were lucky that some of the English POWs had been miners, particularly the Welshmen. I reckon they saved our lives on more than one occasion. Being experienced miners they had no trouble at all while the mine talked—you could hear these odd creaks and groans and scuffles and shuffles. When we first went down we were terrified because while the thing was talking and moving, it appeared as though at any minute we were going to be entombed. The Welsh miners told us while the mine talked there was no real trouble, just keep your eye on the timbers to make sure that they were safe. When the mine came still, that's when you moved, and as soon as the Welshman said move, we moved. I can remember being the last man out of one gallery and I was hit on the heel with part of the roof that completely collapsed.

David Runge: My whole attitude was to do everything in my power to really cripple that coal mine. I took emery dust down the mine and put it in the motors and chewed out the chain conveyor motors. But down the coal mine I had a very bad name with the Japanese. My number in Japanese was *go haku go ju*, that's five fifty. And the Japs used to say *go haku go ju dani daro*, that's 550 no good. Because every time that I went to work something happened to them. Or something went wrong.

Roy Whitecross: We were faced with mine foremen of very, very limited intelligence. They had never had the opportunity or desire to speak English so we had to speak Japanese. One of the few sensible things that the Japanese did when my party arrived in Japan was mix the working parties. There might be a small party in a lateral, only four or six men. They would take three men from what they called the old Australians and three from the new Australians. So that when the Jap foreman said, *kotchi koi barades*, one of the old Australians would say to us, 'he's asked you to bring him that big drill'.

In return the newcomers provided news of the progress of the war. It was like a 'breath of fresh air' to men cut off for two years from reliable reports of the outside world.

Some prisoners could not endure the hard work, the danger and the confined space of the mines. At Omuta there were men, most of them long-serving Americans, who preferred mutilation to mining. In accordance with the free enterprise system the victim paid the mutilator for his services.

David Runge: If you wanted your leg broken you had to pay eight rations of rice and soup. If you wanted your arm broke, it might be five rations of rice and soup. There was an American there. We called him Jackhammer. We were working together on a chain conveyor. I'm on one side and he's on the other. He said, 'Dave would you break my foot?' And I said, 'Yes, I'll break your foot, Jackhammer.' He said, 'Look, I don't want to see it coming. I just want you to break it unknown to me.' I said, 'OK Jackhammer'. He said, 'I'll give you so many rations'. I told him, 'No, I'll break it for nothing'. I didn't want any food. I wouldn't take food off anybody. They want their foot broke, OK, I'll break their foot for nothing, or their arm, or their leg. So Jackhammer's there, he's got his leg out, and he's shovelling coal. I picks up this jackhammer and threw it right at his foot, he spotted it coming and he jumped about six feet in the air. He said, 'Jesus Christ, I don't want to be killed!' Later on when he wasn't looking I threw a big rock on his foot, and that put him out of the coal mine.

When they were loading coal trucks Private David Runge, Australian Army Service Corps, buried rocks below the surface and used other tricks so the prisoners could fill their quota of skips as quickly as possible. A new prisoner, Runge believes, reported him to the Japanese who took him to the mine head. There they suspended him by his thumbs, belted him, marched him back to camp through the snow, and shoved him into a cell. Each day he was forced to kneel over a bamboo with one of the guards, the Sailor, occasionally adding his weight by standing on Runge's thighs. For the first three days he was not fed and throughout the ordeal buckets of cold water were thrown on him. When he was finally released after six days an American orderly was waiting. He picked up Runge and carried him to the camp hospital. The staff worked to save his life, and his limbs: 'They used to cut my toes off with scissors. Then Dr Duncan and an American doctor, Major Thomas Hewlett, said they would have to take off my legs.' He was given a spinal injection and both gangrenous legs were amputated below the knee. Runge looked at his legless image in a dirty window, said 'Steady there, boy. You can't crack up now.' And he didn't.

The prisoners could not operate radios in Japan; but from what they could see about them they knew that the Allies were winning, and they picked up details of the news in all sorts of ways.

Reg Newton: The Japanese divider in doorways and rooms was a bamboo sliding door. It was a very light construction and they pasted over it with paper. Generally it was a parchment type of stuff with flowers and pictures on it, but they were short of this and they were using ordinary newspapers. But these were the English edition of *Mainichis*. So we were able to follow the course of the war, where their cities were being bombed, and where battles were fought. We all went to these papers very quickly and followed the course of the war from Leyte right up to Okinawa. And once we'd read all those we kept putting our fist through them to get the up-to-date editions pasted up. So we knew that the war was coming closer to Japan.

Parkin: It looked to us as if Japan was going to be invaded. And we didn't like our chances if there was an invasion. We reckoned that they would knock us off, particularly as we were right on the sea front and they hadn't shifted us away. You would have thought they would have shifted, but they might have been going to use us as bait or something, I don't know. But there was only one thing they could have done, and that was to do us over as soon as the invasion started so that we wouldn't be an encumbrance.

By August 1945 many of the prisoners knew that they would not survive the coming winter. And they were right to think that the Japanese would dispose of them on the eve of a land battle. Their lives depended on the course of the war; and they could have no influence on how the war was fought. They were spectators to a contest in which their lives were one of the minor prizes.

When the Allied planes came over in hundreds and included short range and carrier-based aircraft, the prisoners knew that the end of the war was near. Concentrated in northern Kyushu and southern Honshu they were close to the climactic events of August 6 and 9.

Gordon Maxwell: We saw Hiroshima. In fact we reckon we saw 'Enola Gay' coming over to drop the bomb. We were sort of on a direct route to Hiroshima. There was just one solitary single plane which we reckoned must be piloted by a silly bastard to be flying round on his own over Japan. And suddenly this thing went off. You could feel it; it was like a strong wind. It was enough to make the windows rattle, we saw the cloud, and then we got raced into the air raid shelters.

Don Noble: I actually saw it and heard it and felt it at a hundred miles distance, and that was something. Later on the ground shock came, rattled the windows of the building, and the gust of wind hit us.

David Runge: Our camp was twenty-three miles away from Nagasaki, and we thought they hit a gasworks because of the colours radiating from the thing. Like if you seen a dry storm at night going out to sea. You see that flashing going through the clouds. And there was a hell of a wind after it.

Peter McGrath-Kerr: I was up in the hut with Murray Jobling and Bert Miller and Les Prendergast. They were having a smoke, I was reading a book and we heard this plane flying over, but there was no air raid alarm. We didn't take any notice because there were lots of planes flying around. The Japanese flying school wasn't far away. And then there was the sudden change in the engine note. Les said, 'That's no Nip'. And we all started to get out. I remember jumping into a haze. It was like jumping into a shimmery mirage that you see on the road sometimes. That's all I remember.

Sergeant Peter McGrath-Kerr of the 2/40th battalion was less than two kilometres from the centre of the blast at Nagasaki. He was knocked unconscious and suffered broken bones and numerous cuts and bruises; but the shattered camp building had fallen on him and protected him from the bomb. Four Dutch prisoners were among the thousands who died in the second atomic explosion in Japan.

In the postwar the prisoners looked at the evidence of the awesome power that had been the immediate cause of their release.

Runge: We went by train into Nagasaki. It was just burnt; and very, very flat. There wasn't a thing standing. It was like if you went to a world that had been destroyed. Atomic flash, it's that terrific heat; it doesn't set fire to anything, it just scorches everything. It destroys any human flesh that's there.

David Thompson: When we finally left, we got the train to Nagasaki. There was a railway that went right though the centre of Nagasaki to the wharves. And as you approached the city you could see a few trees denuded of leaves, and as you went a bit further the trees had less leaves and they started to lean, and so did the electric light posts and structures. Houses and buildings started to lean away from the centre where the bomb had been, and when you got to the centre there were no trees and no buildings. And then you went through an area that was absolutely flat, where everything had just disappeared.

Roy Whitecross: Some of the big buildings looked as if a giant hand had simply wiped out the ground floor and the whole thing had collapsed into a heap of rubble. But the epicentre was just a plain and all that was on it was twisted pieces of corrugated iron. Nothing else. Absolutely nothing else. It was just a burned area and the only thing on it were these little bits of corrugated iron.

Jim Richardson: I noted that there was a lot of these cement bags that were lying about on the ground as we were going into the station; I found out later on these cement bags were in fact skulls. They'd just burnt them. If you've ever seen a piece of cement bag that's been burnt and left lying there. That's what they just looked like, right along the railway line.

Thompson: And as you went a bit further the buildings and trees started to stand up again, but on a different slope to the ones that you'd seen coming in. Then you ran out towards the wharf, I don't know how many miles, and the trees and buildings were practically untouched. So we went right through the centre of where the bomb fell.

It was interesting, but we didn't realise the import of it. By that time we knew it was an atom bomb. There were enough blokes with scientific knowledge amongst us to say if you ever split the atom it would go off with a terrible bang, and through them we knew that had happened. We just thought that, oh well, Nagasaki was laid waste. We didn't know anything about all the other things that allegedly happened as a result of radiation, or if we did know we didn't take any stock of it. We were just so pleased to be on our way home.

Ray Parkin: To me, the biggest thing was, I knew I'd be alive tomorrow.

CHAPTER FIFTEEN

ARE WE FREE?

'. . . all the guards were gathered around a loud speaker. Some of them were crying. It was the Emperor addressing the nation and telling them that the game was finished.'

Sergeant Clarrie Thornton had gone from a farm in Berrigan, New South Wales, where the family was proud of its prize-winning horse teams, to the forward anti-tank gun at Muar, to Pudu and Changi prisons, to the railway in Thailand, and to a line of marchers leaving Nakom Nayok in June 1945. Their starting point was north-west of Bangkok, and they were heading further north. All of the 700 British and 100 Australians were practised prison-travellers: they carried their billies, mess gear and blankets in the remnants of their webbing or in a rice bag. A few men, looking for night comfort, had packed rice bags with straw. The Japanese issued split-toed boots to the bare-footed, and the smallest men were able to get them on; and they gave out shirts and loin cloths, what the men called 'Jap nappies' or 'Jap happies', to those with fewest clothes; but what most changed the columns of prisoners was the distribution of Thai bamboo hats. They became bobbing pyramids of thatch travelling in heat haze.

The three trucks that carried the cooking gear, the rations and the guards' kit stopped at Lopburi: there was over three-quarters of the journey still to go. The men packed all the heavy material on hand carts and pushed them for the rest of the journey. They covered twenty-five kilometres a day. Sick and exhausted men were bashed and forced to keep walking. Six Australians carried one man on an improvised bag stretcher for 120 kilometres. Men plucked edible weeds from the roadside to stew with their inadequate evening meal. At Lopburi the two English doctors travelling with the prisoners collected a dollar from each man, and went in to town with $800 and bought whatever medicines they could. Whenever they had a chance the men picked up medicines as a side line to their night-time scrounging. Two privates from a Scottish regiment were among those whose enterprise extended often to public benefit. The straggling lines of men, forced to march to a place and for a purpose unknown, could not even be sure whether it was better to prolong the journey or to arrive.

The Thai people were sympathetic. When the men rested at Lopburi the local people left hard-boiled eggs at the river's edge for them to find when they went to wash. By mid-August the prisoners had travelled over 800 kilometres into sparsely populated jungle country. They had lost contact with the outside world; and the Japanese guards under the strict discipline of Sergeant Norojunichi (Baldy to the prisoners) gave no sign that they had heard anything of the Emperor's broadcast of August 15 bowing to the Allies' surrender demands.

Clarrie Thornton: We got into a boong village, and when the Jap guards turned their backs on us they had these signs up, 'You are free'. Well, we didn't sleep, we talked all night, couldn't get over it. Next morning the sergeants and warrant officers—there were no officers left—decided they'd go and front the Japs. They said it was over. We still had sixty miles to go to get to a main town, that was Pitsanulok. We said we'd march under our own steam, not with them belting us along. We got back to the old army drill: ten minutes' rest in every hour, and we'd take the load off the weak bokes. We did it easy in comparison.

When we got there we reckoned we were free, but we were put in a barbed wire enclosure and there were guards with machineguns. That night about ten blokes shot through, came back that full they could hardly move, and brought in heaps of stuff. God strike me, are we free or aren't we? The next night about thirty blokes went, and the third night everybody said, 'Well, this is too much for us, we're all going.' After roll call just on dark we made a beeline for the fence and a ratatat from the machineguns went around the fences. The huts filled in an instant, and in the silence one bloke yelled out, 'Are we free?' The next day a Pommy major parachuted in, walked straight up to the Jap guards with his revolver and took over.

It was another month before the liberated men found transport back to Bangkok, and by then 'all the scrounging had been done and there was nothing left for us blokes'.

Charles Almond was at a camp north of Bampong in Thailand:

We worked a couple of days after the war finished. We came home from work one night and the flags were flying from all the huts. The Japs had finally announced that the war was over. I wouldn't believe it. My mate said, 'The war is over, Chas'. And I said, 'Not again!' He said, 'It is fair dinkum this time'. I said, 'Yeah, I'll believe it when I see it'. He said, 'Well, come out here'. One of our chaps was walking along and there was a Jap walking towards him. As they got close to each other the Jap stuck out his hand, offering to shake hands, and our bloke just hauled back and clocked him one under the chin. I said, 'The war is over, fair enough'.

The mayor of the small town where the men had been building petrol storages came out with 'meat, vegetables, fruit and you name it'. The English, Dutch and Australian prisoners had 'one whale of a party'.

In 1942 most prisoners had believed that they would be out by Christmas. Even in 1944 when men were placing bets on the day of their release nearly all were still too optimistic. But when they finally heard about the end of the war they were reluctant to believe it. Many were emotionally as well as physically frail. They were not strong enough to let their hopes rise and expose themselves to another shattering of hope, another celebration deferred.

In Changi the prisoners had radios, and they knew what was happening in the outside world. But they could not predict how the Japanese would react, and there was evidence that the Japanese were going to be bad losers.

George McNeilly: Towards the end of the war we wondered why they were building big pits just outside the gaols, and we were going out daily to dig them. Then some men finally discovered that the pits were being built for us to be machine-gunned into, so they told their friends and soon the whole camp knew. That's when the suicides became more prevalent. Generally they threw themselves down the bore holes.

Sydney Piddington: The command asked us to run the radio and get hourly reports which we did. As it became more and more dangerous it was a rule not to tune in until right on time, however, I tuned in about five minutes early and heard the last few bars of Paul Whiteman's band playing 'Rhapsody in Blue'. Then I heard the first news of the dropping of the bomb on Hiroshima.

Dick Ryan: No one believed that the war had ended. I was in the 100 metre huts at the time with malaria and we said, 'Tomorrow morning the fellows will come down and they will say, "The war is ended"', and we laughed like one thing about it. Sure enough, the next morning they came down and they opened the door and said, 'She's over'. We said, 'Like hell', and we laughed, and they said, 'What is wrong with you?. The war is over'. 'Don't talk rubbish, those rumours have been going about for weeks', and the blokes were really knocked back when we told them that. Finally we got to believe it, but God, we couldn't understand it for a while.

Jack Sloane: There was a tailor in our hut from Plug Brothers who gathered pieces of red, white and blue material from lord knows where. Before we knew what had happened the Union Jack had been sewn and was hoisted.

Snow Peat: Wonderful feeling, elation, peace of mind and the thoughts of getting home to your loved ones. Just the thought, I made it, and then you think back, oh jeeze what about Charlie, what about Bluey, what about Curley. They are still laying up in . . . You had two thoughts: you made it, but what about the other poor buggers that never had a chance.

Jack Sloane: Not long after the capitulation by the Japanese it was made known that we could venture out of the wire if we wished, but we were not to go far afield nor become entangled with the Japanese. The advice was, we got this far let's make sure that we get home. But with the opportunity to go out I naturally went out. I can remember walking to Changi village which was only a few hundred yards away from the gaol and suddenly wondering what the hell I was doing out there because really there was no reason to be there. Like a bird that had been cooped up in a cage for some time I just went back inside and I didn't want to venture out again.

Fred Brightwell: We're out of the army, out of the army, out of the army
We're all out of the army now.
We've changed our uniforms for some civvy clothes
We got some but we cannot tell you how.
The wife will be excited and so pleased to see me back,
She'll be in my arms before my stetson hits the rack,
We'll have a second honeymoon—and lots more after that,
We're out of the army now.

Fred Brightwell of the Changi concert party had often played the drums while Slim de Grey had sung his own songs, 'Back in Circulation Again' and 'Out of the Army'. What had been wishful thinking was now close to reality. The men were elated, but not all were confident that they could swagger back into civvy street.

At Hoten prison camp on the edge of Mukden in Manchuria the Australian officers knew that something extraordinary was happening. The Americans from the ranks who normally worked in the factories came home early; the guards were agitated; and on August 16 the prisoners saw a large plane make a parachute drop. Lieutenant-Colonel Wilfred Kent Hughes wrote in his verse odyssey of seeing the tear-smeared face of a clerk from the Nippon office staff and that 'Wilder and wilder grew the prison guesses'. Captain Des Brennan had sailed from Singapore three years earlier as medical officer to the senior officers:

> That night suddenly a message came down to us, 'There are Americans in the Jap officers' place'. Several thousand prisoners rushed up to try to peer in. You couldn't see. The gates were all locked, but some guys got up on other fellows' shoulders and looked over the top of the palisades and said, 'Yes, there's an American there and he is laying down the law to Matsuda', who was our camp commandant. So this gave us great amusement and delight.

Spud Spurgeon: We didn't go to sleep at all that night. There was too much conjecture about what was going on, and the lights burnt all night on the Japanese side. In the early morning two of the senior officers were sent for. They went over to the Jap side, and a man came out and said, 'She's finished, mate'.

Brennan: And it was quite a surprise that the dirty great big hole with the machinegun post wasn't needed after all.

Spurgeon: Then for the next week it was sort of ecstatic mayhem. Nobody did anything that anybody told him, nobody got out of bed early in the morning.

Brennan: It was so exciting, you couldn't sleep properly, you wandered around with a grin all over your face and everybody was great mates. You thrilled.

Spurgeon: After about four or five days, time is difficult to put together, there was a hell of a clanging noise outside the front gate and a Russian tank drove straight through. The gate wasn't big enough, and he just ripped out part of the wall.

Brennan: And one very public relations type of guy says, 'We have come all the way from Moscow to release you and now we are here'. We didn't say, well the Yanks have already released us, mate. But he came on with a great to do: you can go out, you can go anywhere, and that is how I got to have a bit of a look at Mukden. We went up town several times for a bit of a walk.

Spurgeon: We found a brewery, a shed full of Kirin beer, and we all got as pissed as newts. I have never been so drunk in all my life. The Russians came in, as I said, through the wall, and the following day a couple of truck loads of them came in and they put on a sort of a concert. They used to meet us in town with bottles of vodka. The whole bloody lot of them were always full.

The convivial relations between the Allies were placed in jeopardy by rape. The perpetrators were said to be Russian soldiers who enticed a handsome young Australian officer into their truck and compelled him to act for their pleasure. The Australian did not press charges against the burly Russian women.

In the streets of Mukden shops were looted and factories stripped. Chinese continued to kill Japanese whenever they had the chance, and Chinese Nationalists, Communists and opportunists competed for spoils and positions. During the day sporadic shooting could be heard, and at night the firing would intensify until the Russian tanks and armored cars quietened things down. The prisoners were safe within their protective brick wall from everything except Russian hospitality. Russians and prisoners shared a desire to drink, and the Russians possessed an apparently endless supply of vodka, but the emaciated prisoners had a limited capacity to consume. In spite of having almost no words in common with the prisoners, the Russians were able to propose toasts to Stalin, Truman, 'wifu', and mother, and insist that the glass be drained each time. Soon prisoners were 'cross-eyed' and the exuberant Russians were firing sub-machinegun bursts through the ceiling. Four Australians in an attempt to obtain some less potent beer hired *droshkies* to take them to a brewery. As they loaded the first crates two Russians strode up, shot the horses and splattered the prisoners with blood. One of the Manchurian drivers panicked, ran and was shot. After searching the prisoners the Russians motioned for them to start walking. They walked the length of the drive wondering if they had been spared as prisoners only to be killed as looters by trigger-happy Russians. Once out of the gate and behind the shelter of the brewery wall they fled. They did not, Lance Gibson says, 'stir out of the gaol for another week'.

In Japan the constant Allied bombing had destroyed ports and driven nearly all the workers from the dockyards, but the prisoners were still sweating in coal and copper mines, in foundries and factories, and suffering from hunger everywhere. The Australian army and mission nurses working in the fields at Totsuka picked up pamphlets warning them of an impending invasion.

Tootie Keast: We knew things must be happening. Then one night when we had gone to bed there was a terrible scream for Parker, and poor old Kay went out to see what it was. They told her that the Americans had dropped this one bomb on Hiroshima and all the damage it had done. She said, 'Oh *takusan takusan*', we've got plenty more of those. She came around, told us and we all shrieked with laughter. We said, poor silly fools, fancy them thinking one bomb can do that. Then they told us that we had three days to live. All prisoners-of-war in Japan were going to be killed within three days. Well a couple of nights later Kay was called again, and they told her that another bomb had been dropped at Nagasaki. Well those two bombs may have done a terrific lot of damage to the Japanese but they saved the prisoners-of-war in Japan. I can't help it, every time it is the anniversary and all the fuss goes on, I can only say thank God they dropped them.

Hugh Clarke: Then one day we got up in the morning and all the guards were gathered around a loud speaker. Some of them were crying. It was the Emperor addressing the nation and telling them that the game was finished. So that was it.

Ray Parkin: What really clinched it was when our own fellow in charge of the shift was reporting to the officer and he said, '*Keirei nai, keirei nai*' which means no salute. The men said, well if you don't have to salute a Jap it must be over. And it was a sleepless night with everyone talking their heads off. The Japanese guards came around and gave us a very friendly request, you know, not so loud some people are sleeping. Then we gradually took charge of the camp.

Don Moore: I never slept for four nights, I got up and I thought, oh well, I'll go into the kitchen, and make myself a brew of tea. There were lots of fellows up there who couldn't sleep. We just sat around and just talked and yapped and yarned and wondered what was going to happen to us.

We were taken on parade and the Japanese officer got up and said, 'Well, I must tell you good news. You can go back to your wonderful countries.' 'Oh Christ', said a bloke at the back, 'listen to the bastard.' 'Me, I am very sorry for the food that has been served to you in the last three months but this is due to the very destitute conditions. There are some Red Cross parcels in the *bokogo* and your officers will be able to distribute them to you immediately.' I think I ate half a packet of Kraft cheese, gulp, gulp, straight off like that.

Cliff Moss: Blokes got real sick because they couldn't sleep. The doctors there had some opium pills and they poured those into them and that put them to sleep for a day. They were all right after that, once they had a sleep.

Clarke: Well, when we realised that the war was over all the national groups in the camp had ceremonies. The Dutch sang their national anthem and put their flag up, the Americans and the British did the same, and we sang 'Waltzing Matilda' and declared our independence of the Dutch commandant. He previously said, now there will be strict discipline and we said, no, we're Australians, we take orders only from Australians. I was the senior Australian in the camp and I said I dissociate myself from all other nationalities, and all my mates agreed. I had some good American friends, so we promptly took off.

For Hugh Clarke the timing of the end of the war had particular significance. Determined to get away from the coalmine at Nakarma he had responded to a call for expert oil drillers. At Fukuoka he found himself in charge of twenty-one men of various nationalities—Dutch, Indonesian, American, Australian and English—all of whom had falsely claimed to be drillers. The Emperor instructed the Japanese to endure the unendurable before the incompetence of Clarke's crew could be tested at a drill site.

The prisoners in the camps in Sumatra saw little of the war: few Allied planes flew overhead and no land battles were fought anywhere in the area. Perhaps the Japanese soldiers were equally ignorant of the fortunes of the nations at arms.

Graham Chisholm: When the war finished our local Japanese didn't surrender. It took them up to ten days before the Emperor's cousin came down and said, 'Hey, you had better surrender'. We were then told that the nations of the world were again at peace. But we had a pretty tough ten days because they brought the regular troops around the camp. They put down their chin straps, and when a Japanese soldier put down his chin strap you knew that something serious was on. They had machine guns ringing us. So for ten days there was hardly a movement, even the birds were quiet. They had vast armies that had not been defeated and they wanted to go on fighting.

But when Count Terauchi came down with the surrender order direct from the Emperor the senior officers in our area, I think twenty-two of them, had a little party. They drank saki all night and put on their ceremonial dress. I don't know whether they were short of swords, but when dawn came they went outside and bowed to the rising sun, went back and had another slug of saki, each one took a hand grenade, and they sat in a circle around the walls. On the word of command there were twenty-two pins pulled out of twenty-two hand grenades, and that led to little brown flecks on the bricks of this place. It was devastated. But they went on to an honourable way of life afterwards, rather than being dishonoured by having to continue living.

In other camps the prisoners noticed that the guards who had been most inclined to goad them for their failure to suicide in 1942 were not among those most likely to offer their lives to atone for Japan's defeat.

At the end of August 1945 Frank Robinson's gang was near the Muara end of the railway in western Sumatra. Robinson himself was under six stone, but he had scored a job in the Japanese cookhouse. Knowing that this was probably his last chance to recover his strength, he stole frequently and inventively:

> I think we were one of the last people to ever be told by the Japanese that the war had ended. We were there some fortnight or three weeks after we heard rumours about these 'atomic bombs'. But the Japanese eventually said to us that the war had ended and with that it was more or less no shouting, there was no cheering, there was no nothing. All that we did was sit on our bunks, lay back and rest. We just talked quietly among ourselves. Well, looks like we have made it. We were in such a condition at this stage that you could see the look of death in people's faces. Men had practically given up, they were about to die and some of them still died. Now had we known perhaps three weeks before when those bombs actually did drop, there would have been other lives saved. None of us would have survived another three months. Nobody.

Frank Robinson's immediate pleasure ended when an officer handed him a letter telling him that his mother had died three years before. The officer had withheld the letter doubting Robinson's strength to carry any more burdens. Later Robinson thanked the officer for protecting him.

During their captivity many prisoners thought about the revenge that they would take against the guards at the end of the war. The day will come, they would tell themselves, and they would imagine in fine and bloody detail the way they would square the account. At times nearly all prisoners thought it would be worthwhile to sacrifice their own lives if only they could kill one or two of the most loathed guards at the same time. The intense hatred that some prisoners felt may have helped keep them alive; hate was a good driving force. But at the end of the war many of the prisoners found that their passion for vengeance had gone.

George Aspinall: There were a number of dead Japanese found at the back of Changi Gaol down at the beach. Whether they were shot by Chinese or by our people, we don't know. But we were so pleased, so elated, that the whole thing was over and we would be going back home, I don't think a lot of us were looking for revenge.

Jack Sloane: It never occurred to me to bash a Japanese just because he was a Japanese. I knew enough of them to realise that their code of conduct was completely foreign to us, but that didn't justify bashing just any Jap because we had been bashed from time to time. If it was a particular Jap, well that was different in my book. We were aware that some of the occupation forces had made it possible for people to take action if they wished. A story going around was that one Australian was given the opportunity and he took it but in doing so broke his wrist. It is debatable whether that was worthwhile.

Charles Almond in Thailand: The padre offered a prayer first and then in a speech he said, 'I know how you feel, you'd like to take the Japs apart but don't let's lower ourselves to their standards. We'll take it like men and decently. If you want to take it out on them, challenge them to a football match.' Well that was one damn fine football match. At one stage there wasn't a Jap standing on the field.

Eddie Henderson: Our old guards that ill-treated us were taken away and new guards brought in. The Japanese knew it was all over and probably wanted to avoid incidents. The Australian attitude, I think, is that you can't kick a dog while it is down and they looked so beaten and so subservient that we couldn't do anything to them. But if it had been the ones that had ill-treated us we probably would have been into them.

Sir Edward Dunlop: Total hate was there, a curtain of hate. You see so many people die in such misery that the hate becomes intensive. But towards the end of the war I began to see something of their point of view. The miserable remnants of the Japanese army were coming out of Burma along the railway line and rough tracks. They were in terrible condition and looked very much like our own fellows.

On one occasion I was confronted with a Japanese who had hopped God knows how many hundreds of dreadful miles with one leg chopped off through the middle of the thigh. The bone was sticking out of stinking gangrenous flesh, and he was still sort of hopping. With his ghastly shrunken eyes he was in terrible shape. When the train started he tried to get up. Bombs were falling in an air raid and people walked on him. I tried to help him, and I found myself with a dead man, and everything else was moving.

The hate drained out. I enjoy going to Japan these days, and I admire many things in Japan.

Gordon Maxwell in Japan: Some of our fellows did catch one of the Jap guards and they put him in the guard room in the little solitary confinement cell for a couple of days, but the novelty wore off and they just let him go.

David Thompson: Our feeling of pleasure covered up a lot of our feeling of hatred.

Rowley Richards: It was quite incredible really. Despite the threats that many of them had made against the Japanese, when they had the opportunity they did nothing. While there were some who claimed that they dealt with a few, I personally doubt it because the bad Japs who knew that they were going to be in trouble just plain shot through; they disappeared. There were also a certain number of Japanese with whom they had been working, civilian Japanese, that they had got to know fairly well. I myself had a little Japanese medical orderly and I was invited to his home, and also to the home of the butcher.

Ray Myors: We were down at the bank of the river in Bangkok and this particular fellow and a couple of his mates were a little bit high and the worse for wear from drinking *lao*. This was the local brew, a type of wine spirit which was apparently the only thing available there. When he saw this party of Japanese coming across the river in a canoe about twenty feet long, this fellow on his own without any assistance from anyone just swam out in the river and tipped it over and one after another he held the Japanese under until they drowned. He got his share of coventry from our point of view because we didn't agree. But there were other isolated incidents where a Japanese was a bit presumptuous with his attitude and a bloke would fall him. Of course that is very natural, but there was no grasping of arms and slaughtering people or anything of that nature.

Donald Stuart in Indo-China: The Japs were all in their own camps and wouldn't come out. A mate and I, a sergeant out of one of the New South Wales New England Battalions, we got ourselves a truck and a Japanese sergeant—well you can't go driving a truck yourself. We told him the rules: he did as he was told or he got his head blown off. He only lasted about forty-eight hours. He either misunderstood something or did something wrong and Frank just shot his head off with a .45 Colt.

I tell you when you get a bullet in the side of the head from a .45 Colt at about twelve inches range there is nothing much left of your head. So we got ourselves another Jap then and he saw the job through.

Apart from isolated violence, retaliation was often on behalf of others rather than being acts of personal vengeance. After the men at Nakarma heard about the killing of the Australian nurses on Banka Island they 'went up the street and did boongs everywhere'. A group of extremely sick prisoners-of-war from Java, including five who were blind, were being flown home early. When they stopped to re-fuel at Balikpapan in Borneo other Australians were so incensed that they shot two Japanese in a prison compound.

Many ex-prisoners still hated the Japanese, they 'felt pregnant with the desire to drop-kick a Japanese', but their immediate need was to distinguish themselves from the behaviour of their former gaolers, and they realised the pettiness and ineffectiveness of any acts of revenge. Even where the prisoners emerged to look upon the sites prepared for their final extermination, there were no acts of concerted revenge. The prisoners were emotionally tired and physically weak and the Japanese were still armed. The most common response of the prisoners was to avoid all Japanese. That was a reflection of both the strength and the feeling of the men.

The end of the war came more quickly than the Allies had expected. And General Douglas MacArthur was determined that no local commanders would take the surrender of the Japanese before he accepted the formal surrender in Tokyo Bay. The prisoners in the camps waited impatiently for food, medicine, news, fellow countrymen and transport home. In Japan the Australians gradually began making excursions from their camps, foraging for food and delighting in their freedom. After a fortnight the prisoners had a delivery service from the Allied air force.

Hugh Clarke: Well the first time they dropped it was a terrifying experience because we were in amongst big pine trees. We saw these B29s fly over very low, they had the bomb bays open and we could see all this tucker and even see the crew looking out. They circled the camp a few times and then came over again and made the drop. Each food container consisted of two forty-four gallon drums welded together, and they dropped them with coloured parachutes, red, blue and green. As we looked up, the parachutes opened with a jerk, half these drums broke off and came hurtling down into the camp. I got my arms around the trunk of a tree. The medical orderly in the camp was a fellow named Joe Truey, an American. He got hit on the head with a case of Spam and was killed instantly. There were broken legs.

David Runge: Another American was standing up with his arms folded. The lid of a drum buried into his chest, cut both his arms off and killed him.

Don Noble: These two double drums came down and they described beautiful arcs very very slowly. We rushed down, because we weren't going to have the Japs get any of this, to find that the control room of the mine had been tastefully decorated and completely ruined by chocolate and tomato juice.

Jim Richardson: They had boots, clothing, chocolate, flea powder, all sorts of stuff in the one drum, and when they came down they just munched the whole lot up. Boots were permanently distorted; you couldn't get them on. Cigarettes, without being broken, were about an inch long. Just concussion. Anyhow, poor little kids came up and got onto some chocolate. Later on they went back and started eating this flea-powder and chocolate and everything. The kids were nearly half dead.

Reg Newton: At the end of a fortnight the prisoners were getting 500 grams of rice, 500 grams of potato, and a ten in one American Army ration box—ten men's rations for one day. Each man got one of those, and they ate the lot and came back for more. Everybody's weight doubled in about two months. I know myself, I went from eight stone six to sixteen stone ten in two months.

Ray Parkin: Within a week of us being on American provisions, all the Campbell soups and that, they were going crook at the sort of soup they were getting. You wouldn't believe it. The fellows had been on nothing for so long, and within a week they were back to their old prejudices. We had all these brands of cigarettes. They could smoke their heads off. And came the time for the second issue and a fellow was given Philip Morris: 'I don't want Philip Morris. I had Philip Morris last time. I want Camels.' Whether it was a reaction or not, I don't know.

Tootie Keast: We said we demand food, and the Japanese said, 'Good, we'll get it for you'. Well we waited a couple of days, and I don't remember all the food, but I do know that ninety pounds of meat—now we hadn't seen meat for over two years— came, a big tin that had possibly two pounds of butter in it, a lot of very coarse sugar, twenty tins of salmon, and I have forgotten the rest. But I got a spoon and I ate the butter and the sugar, and I was desperately ill, but I didn't care. We fixed a roster. As soon as the meat was cooked the bell rang, and whether it was day or night we ate. And our tummies just got fatter and fatter, and all of a sudden it went flomp. Just vomited! And then we were ready to start again.

The parachute drops had been both life-saving and deadly. In Borneo, Thailand, Java and Japan prisoners were killed as excited men ran into the open and drums broke away to become lethal. In Manchuria a Chinese man, stunned by falling fruit cans, was lucky: he was just left 'fruit salad happy'. The biscuit bombers also introduced the prisoners to some of the technological changes that had taken place in the outside world. Among the diverse products of the consumer society that floated down was DDT powder. The men pondered its use, then dusted their *tatami* mats. The fleas, as new to the insecticide as the prisoners, bounced in the air and were dead when they hit the floor.

With their food supply secured, the prisoners in Japan began making forays further into town and country. Some prisoners shifted from indulgence to anarchy.

Ray Parkin: It was about two months before we were evacuated. There were constant warnings coming over the radio to tell us to stay put and stay off bootleg grog. There were a few fellows died of that, and also a lot of fellows were hitching rides all over Japan: getting on to aircraft, getting on to all sorts of things. Some of them were killed as a result. There were a lot of aircraft accidents.

Don Moore: Then we started to go out for walks. We got a little bit more venturesome when we got fatigue uniforms and books dropped from the air. And cartons of cigarettes which were the currency. We walked on to a railway station one day. And the train was so crowded. We travelled for two or three stations, then pulled up. We said, 'Well, there's a good place to travel. Let's give a couple of packets to the driver and the fireman, and let's occupy the cab of the engine.' Then I had a small boy's ideal of travelling in the cab of an engine through tunnels and along the Japanese railway system of Kyushu. It was a wonderful experience.

Gary Hooper: As you'd go along on the train, you'd come to a bombed up section of the track so you'd get out and walk. Further up you'd grab another train, and so it went.

You'd speak a bit of Japanese to communicate, you know. But couldn't speak it fluently. Of course they were all very charming, and bowing and scraping.

Hugh Clarke: Jack and I went and pulled up a truck on the road. We got the fellow to get out, just got in, drove off and left him. I couldn't drive in those days, but that Yank could, he was good. So we found our way back to Nakarma. The first bloke I saw in Nakarma was Lang Fraser, my old mate, trying to swap a parachute for two ducks. I spent a couple of days there, and I learned that the fellows had got a piano, raided the brewery, and they had all their old guards cleaning their boots.

Cliff Moss: A feller called Jack Blythe was one of our notable citizens. He was a good feller Jack, but he was a bloke that had been around in his time. Bloody good man as a POW. He said, 'I've done a lot of things in my time, but I've never cracked a bank'. Thought he'd have a go. He was living it up. He had a Buick with a gas producer unit on it. The thing was as long as from here to the creek. He also had a bloke to carry a chair for him down the street. Another bloke to carry an umbrella. If he wanted to sit down, the bloke held the umbrella over him to keep the sun off.

He got a good waddy in his hand, walked up to the bank, and there was this guard bloke outside the door. So he smacked him over the head with his stick, and he shot through. Jack walked through the door and all the girls inside had disappeared. Jack and the two or three other blokes with him gathered up a pack full of yen and walked out. Well, they were walking down the street with a fair few yen floating about; they were falling out of the bloody pack. They come back to camp with all this 80 000 yen, or however many there were, an immense amount of the bloody things. I think it all finished up back in the bank again, or practically all of it. Anyway, Jack had cracked his bank.

A gunner who kept a diary at Nakarma wrote a month after the end of the war: it is a 'grouse life, eat and sleep and a boong does all the work'. They were recovering three and a half years of debts in food and freedom, and 'everyone was getting a sword'. With a little organisation and much bravado they souvenired swords en masse. They made their best hauls by moving systematically through the carriages of trains demanding the personal surrender of all officers. Perhaps the Japanese recognised the ex-prisoners as a new form of *ronin*, the wandering, masterless samurai of Japanese literature.

When the Australian troops had gone to South-east Asia the Empires of Britain, Holland and France seemed to be dominant. In the battles against the Japanese in 1941 and 1942 the troops had been in the centre of the shattering of the old order. Now they emerged from prison in countries where the war had fostered powerful political movements. The world war may have ended, but from southern Indonesia to Manchuria other violence continued. The ex-prisoners were among the first outsiders to see the new forces that would reshape the region.

Harry Medlin: The Indonesian people, because of their experiences with an Asian colonial power, namely the Japanese, came to think that it is not race that is important but the colonial mentality. That was the important thing that they had to get free of. Those of us who had been in fairly close contact with the Indonesians became increasingly reconciled with their aims as they realised where the issue really was.

Then Indonesia was returned to the Dutch. And of course civil war broke out and it took some five years before it was settled. So how do we get out? A lot of us, because of our sympathies with the rebellion, or the revolution, were virtually put under some sort of house arrest. This was September 23, I think. We were not supposed to go out of the camp inciting the rebellion. It was never put formally like that; but we were really under a state of house arrest until we were flown out to Singapore.

Dutch prisoners, anxious to trace the fate of members of their families, took risks travelling in pursuit of rumours of the where-abouts of wives, children and brothers. The Australians, still within their camps, were sometimes endangered by drunken Japanese guards 'raging round the camp, out of control'.

The beginning of the nationalist revolution in Indonesia almost prevented the nurses making their last journey from their camp in western Sumatra.

Betty Jeffrey: We arrived at this railway station at dawn. There was a train there and we were told to get into it. But nobody took the train away. The local population who were very anti us at this stage gathered and they were very angry. It was beginning to get out of control. Some Japs arrived and it was all very nasty. That's when Haydon Lennard and Ken Brown just walked up and down the station in their uniforms; Haydon Lennard in the uniform of a war correspondent and Ken Brown as an RAAF pilot. They had one revolver each and they just walked up and down, and this sort of kept things under control. They couldn't get the Indonesian driver to take the train away because it never did leave before 8 o'clock or 9 o'clock or whatever it was, but they finally got him to start and away we went.

The train took them to Lahat and they made the journey from the station to the airstrip, sitting on couches on the back of a truck. Out of deference to those who were to meet them in Singapore, the nurses threw their old camp hats into the bushes before finally taking the plane out of Sumatra.

In Saigon Stan Gilchrist saw a march of Vietnamese youths through the streets break into running skirmishes with the French, then shooting broke out. The Vietnamese were 'friendly enough' and escorted the prisoners back to camp. Later when a Vietnamese armed with a knife tied to the end of a stick lunged at him yelling, 'Français', Corporal Gilchrist pointed to the sun-tanned skin and said, 'La prisonaire'. It seemed to work.

After the Americans landed on the coast of Hainan, the Australians loaded their sick on a train, unfurled an American flag, and with two Japanese riflemen sitting on the cow-catcher, set out for freedom. Having passed through valleys lush with crops close to where they had starved, they noticed the telephone poles cut and a village burning. Suddenly the engine was derailed, crashed over and killed the two guards. The carriages remained upright. As Chinese riflemen came from 'all directions' the prisoners said, 'goodbye Australia'; but the guerillas halted, and turned away. Either they had recognised the passengers or they saw the American flag. The Australians were uncertain whether their attackers were bandits, Chinese Communists or Nationalists.

The conflict and flux in the politics of east Asia in 1945 increased the prisoners' sense of unease. They may have known more of these changes than other Australians, but the differences between the worlds of 1942 and 1945 helped tell the prisoners that they were coming home ignorant; they had missed so many of the great events of their time.

The prisoners had become accustomed to the sight of each other. But now men and women who were weak and emaciated confronted white people who were healthy, aggressive and adorned with signs of power.

Stan Arneil was in Changi: There was a young fellow dropped onto the aerodrome and he looked like a pirate. He must have been about six feet three inches. He seemed to be as wide as an ox, in great health, with a revolver and all this sort of thing; and he looked absolutely beautiful.

Chris Neilson: You would have thought he was Flash Gordon. He looked the part; he'd have given Flash Gordon a hiding. He strolled in amongst us and we were all cheering like bloody hell. A Jap raced up to meet him. Evidently they had been told that he would be coming in on his own. This Jap came up, bowed and said, 'I will take you to Takahashi'. He was the head of Changi prison camp. This bloke just went whack and lifted him under the chin. He said, 'You take me nowhere. You bring bloody Takahashi to me.' The Jap ran away and next minute Takahashi came at the double. Oh, it was lovely! You should have heard us cheer. And here is Takahashi rushing and bowing and this bloke upbraided him, slapped his face.

Arneil: It was quite odd. We had gone into the army as kids really, with an average age between twenty-one and twenty-two, down to seventeen, and I remember once two nurses came. They were absolutely delightful and we were sitting in a long 150 metre hut on our bamboo slats. These two nurses walked right through the hut and spoke to every person and I don't think one person replied. It was absolutely lovely to see these beautiful women. They were clean and fresh, they had lovely cheeks and their hair was nice; and we just sat and looked at them.

Leon De Castres: Trying to keep us in the camp was too ridiculous for words. Two or three of us went out, got a vehicle into Singapore and went straight to the wharves. The British Navy had already got corvettes and frigates pulled up there and I can recall standing on the wharf and the boys from the frigates throwing loaves of bread. We hadn't tasted bread and we were tearing into it. Then a few of us were invited on board, and that was a tragedy. They invited us into their ward room and they sat us down to a meal. Of course we just couldn't take this Western food straight off. There must have been a half a dozen of us in that wardroom and one fellow actually died on the wharf getting back. Our stomachs couldn't take it. They had contracted to such an extent that we couldn't take meat. We were actually served up meat!

At nearly every camp the Japanese held ample supplies of food, medicine, mosquito nets and clothes. But what angered many men was the belated release of letters and Red Cross parcels; there seemed to be no reason why they had been withheld. At Ohama, Ray Parkin says, they found among the Red Cross supplies beautifully made wooden cases labelled, 'Detroit Branch, Red Cross Society of USA, Yokahama Earthquake Fund 1923'. Perhaps the force that inhibited the Japanese from using the products of others in 1923 still operated twenty years later.

From his own experiences as a prisoner in Singapore and North Borneo and from interviewing men who came home early, Ray Steele was probably better prepared to meet the ex-prisoners than any other Australian. Immediately the war ended he was flown to Singapore to begin collecting 'the full story'. His main task was to obtain testimony to be used in the forthcoming trials of war criminals; but first he wanted to meet the men from his own unit and those that had been with him on work parties:

> I grabbed a jeep and got straight out to Changi. I remember now walking into the hut. Of course they were pretty drawn, half-starved, worse than I had remembered them. But the reception wasn't that wild, I can assure you. They either completely

ignored me or said very little, just, 'How are you?' But I was a bit uncomfortable. I felt that most of them resented the fact that I looked so healthy and well dressed whereas they had been slogging it out for three and a half years. I don't think there was any great reaction to me in particular. Everybody was apathetic; they just didn't care any more. It wasn't even a hell of a surprise to them that the war was over. They just said, well, it had to end sometime or other.

Ray Steele passed on news of home and families to the men he knew. He confined his interviewing to finding out basic information about when and where prisoners had died: the men in Changi 'didn't have the stamina to talk very much'.

The nurses were flown out of Sumatra a month after the war had ended.

Betty Jeffrey: At dusk we arrived at Singapore and the Red Cross women, reporters and photographers were there. We felt so ashamed of ourselves because we knew we looked scruffy and dirty although we had tried to keep clean all the way through. But seeing them in their immaculate uniforms, we just realised how dreadful we must have looked. They took us into the airport, gave us a cup of tea and something to eat. It was really funny because we had been drinking out of anything: latex cups used by the rubber tappers, coconut shells and tins. We were suddenly landed with a cup and a saucer. We were sitting around a great long table like a trestle table. Half way through I looked down. We would all have a drink from a cup and then we would put it straight down on the table. The saucers were being completely ignored.

One of the reporters said, 'Anybody from Melbourne?' I said, 'I am from Melbourne,' and he absolutely shattered me by saying—no welcome or anything like that—just 'Tell me about the massacre'. I wondered what on earth he meant, and I said, 'What are you talking about?' He said, 'Oh, you're kidding' or something like that. I said, 'What do you mean, massacre?' He said, 'Don't be silly, tell me about the massacre.' This is the Vivian Bullwinkel story. We had never spoken of it as a massacre. That was the journalist's name for it, and it has been called that ever since. I still hate it.

The news of the shooting of the nurses on the beach at Banka was immediate and dramatic news around the world. In a selective and almost sporadic way, the private experiences of some prisoners became common knowledge. Horrific events involving others remained locked away.

One reason why the nurses had stayed so long on Sumatra after the end of the war was simply because no one could find them. Haydon Lennard of the ABC and Flying Officer Ken Brown had chased news of them to Palembang and then on to Lahat.

Brown: Having been in Singapore and seen the fellows at Changi and the condition they were in we had some idea of what we were likely to see when we found the girls. And they were a pretty poor sort of a bunch when we saw them. They had saved their uniforms and they looked as smart as they could, but they were a poor, sore, sorry lot, and they, poor devils, smelt to high heaven. The smell was most objectionable. When I remark to them these days how they smelt they laugh. They just can't believe it. It was quite an experience. But the smell was one that I don't think I will ever get out of my nostrils. I don't know if it was a smell of death or what it was, but it was a terrible smell.

The thing that is in my mind as strongly as the smell was the happiness in their otherwise sad eyes at our arriving on the scene to take them out of all that misery that they had been through for so long. I was the first RAAF officer that they had seen in three and a half years. At that stage I was only twenty-four and a bronzed Aussie, and that was a sight that was probably as pleasing to them as any they'd seen for a long time. Vivian Bullwinkel, I can recall very vividly, had her head shaven and she was very much like a skinhead. They were all very, very thin, doing their damnedest to look courageous in their uniforms that they had put away for so many years for just this very occasion.

While still in Sumatra the nurses had had their first taste of fresh bread. On September 13 'huge planes' came over and made a parachute drop on the nearby men's camp. The men sent them bread made on Cocos Island that day, and with it came butter and vegemite. Frank Robinson was flown from eastern Sumatra to Singapore:

> When we landed on the aerodrome in Singapore they handed some fresh bread and butter to me. That was the beginning of a new life. I felt it was so beautiful. I thought, well, a person was practically being reborn. To me that piece of bread and butter is a symbol of my being liberated. Even today I have never tasted bread anything like that piece of bread; it was absolutely magnificent.

Knocking up a brew of burnt rice coffee.

CHAPTER SIXTEEN

LOST YEARS AND WOUNDED MINDS

'Everyone is cheering. You're with your own people. Everything you always dreamed, you hoped would happen . . .'

Don Moore: We were going home, and it was just really terrific. We were absolutely elated. Even now I think of that homecoming. It is like being born again. Something wells up into you. We saw the islands slip by underneath. There was Timor, and next would be an Australian landfall. The RAAF crew said, 'Well, fellows, it's coming up. Have a look at it.' And there it was: Australia.

Sylvia Muir: We were on the boat and they said, 'That's Australia'. It was Rottnest Island. I just tore up, all the men on the deck stood aside, and they let me go right up to the point of the boat. It was lovely. It was Australia. Well, I just started to howl. I wept on this cove's shoulder; I didn't know him from Adam. I looked around, and half the men had tears running from their eyes.

My hair had grown in four years, and I had no time to put it up. When I went past one man said, 'My daughter had hair like that when I left home'.

Chris Neilson: It was sort of like *Alice in Wonderland*, like a fairy tale. You're finally back, and you're part of the old life again. You can't say elation, it's more than that, it's wonder. There is the contrast from the filth, dirt and torture. Everyone is cheering. You're with your own people again. Everything you always dreamed, you hoped would happen . . .

Snow Peat: We had a lovely trip through Darwin. They turned the town upside down for us. It was absolutely beautiful. As we were coming down the gang plank off the *Arawa* we seen lasses in the army. Well, we didn't know sheilas were in the army. You know, in long pants and that. They kissed us, threw their arms around our necks. It was unreal. When I got off the boat, I kissed the bloody ground. I said, 'You beaut. You'll do me. I'm home.'

David Runge: You always know you're in Australia when you hear a magpie. When I was on the New England bus going home to Murwillumbah I saw this magpie, and I sang out, 'Look at the magpie!' Everybody turned and looked at me: how come this bloke's so surprised about seeing a magpie?

Harry Medlin: I don't think I really started to feel free until we got into Heidelberg Hospital. We had been on a hospital ship. And we were made to feel a little bit guilty, that we had not conducted ourselves properly by capitulating, that we should have fought on and been knocked off—for what purpose eludes me. On the ship there was a broadcast to ex-Japanese prisoners-of-war telling them they should not feel guilty, that their country was proud of them, and this crap. It would have been better not to have said anything. Because all of a sudden you think, hell, am I supposed to be guilty about something?

Fred Stringer: It had its sad moments. One of our fellows passed away and was buried at sea one day before we hit Darwin. You ask yourself a few questions. But can't find the answers. To go though all that and die one day before reaching home.

Forty years after the event there is still a freshness and intensity about the memories of coming home. As they stepped ashore there was a coming together of emotions, from the most personal to the broadly nationalistic. For his first weeks ashore one prisoner found that he could only sleep for a few hours. Well before dawn he would wake, quietly make himself a cup of tea, then wander the streets as the sun was rising. Other members of the family would ask hesitatingly if he was all right. He found it difficult to explain his pleasure as each morning he rediscovered his freedom, and delighted in doing the simple things that confirmed the reality of his return.

In September and October 1945, 14 000 Australian prisoners-of-war of the Japanese came home. The men in Japan were gathered in by the Americans and came through Okinawa and Manila where they made their first contact with the Australian military. Many completed their journey south on aircraft carriers, the fittest playing hockey on the decks, shooting sharks with 303s, and all watching movies: 'Casablanca', 'Shine on Harvest Moon', and 'Heaven Can Wait'. In South-east Asia most prisoners were flown to Changi and then waited to be called to a ship. Priority was given to the sick who were carried on board especially fitted aircraft or hospital ships.

Some of the prisoners had been away from their families for five years. Nearly all had been away for four. In March 1941 Sergeant Ray Brown had learnt that the 2/21st Battalion was being transferred from Bonegilla in northern Victoria to Darwin. He phoned his wife to meet him on Footscray station in Melbourne. At Broadmeadows the troop train looped west, bypassed Melbourne and joined the Adelaide line. His wife and two daughters, aged two and four, waited all day in the cold wind and went home. Sergeant Brown was not given leave before the battalion sailed for Ambon. After the fighting on Ambon early in 1942 Betty Brown received no news of her husband: each week she went in hope to the Red Cross and learnt nothing. After the end of the war a neighbour told her that Ray's name was in the Melbourne *Herald*; she read that he had been picked up in Hainan. Betty Brown did not see her husband for four and a half years and she did not hear of him for three and a half.

The families of most of the men captured in Changi received an official notice that a near relative had been imprisoned, and after long delays perhaps four letter cards followed. They read printed messages such as 'I am working healthily' and 'We have joyfully received a present of some milk, tea, margarine and cigarettes from the Japanese authorities', and a two-line personal note. Some men in Changi received more than ten letters, most less, and some prisoners in the outer camps had none. Most of the nurses in Sumatra were cut off from all news from home.

Prisoners who had enlisted at twenty years of age were coming home at twenty-four or -five. They had missed the years when their vigour was its greatest; when they would have played their best sport; when they would have selected a career; and when they would have married. They were all conscious of the distorted pattern in their lives. They felt a need to try and catch up, and some were uncertain that they could do so.

They were aware of their emotional frailty. Forced to stand in a queue for too long or the victim of a slight error they found themselves flaring with intense rage. Bob Wallace while still in Japan wrote on August 22: 'everyone is jumpy and fed up. Saw a chap drop some of his rice on the floor and he got so temperamental that he threw the balance down'. It was more than a reaction to the euphoria of liberation. The prisoners had emerged from their experiences with a tolerance for the weaknesses and differences of their fellows; but for the rest of their lives many of them would churn with rage at what others would see as matters of little consequence, or they would fall into periods of depression. These were the scars of mental stress.

Many still felt an anger within them. On one of the ships leaving Singapore a hefty rice grower from the Riverina would look down on a group assembled below for boat drill. The officer in charge of the men at the life boat, the rice grower believed, had left before the surrender of the British forces in 1942 and joined the scramble to escape the advancing Japanese. Now each morning the rice grower cupped his hand to his mouth and shouted, 'You want to watch him, he'll go through on yous'. The prisoners had passed through a humiliating defeat and a prolonged, harrowing captivity. Nearly all had searched for reasons why they had been left so inadequately equipped and deployed for the tasks they had been given, and why the world had been impotent when so many of them were dying. The blame, they knew, lay somewhere beyond themselves and their particular group. But they could not locate the guilty men for they were concealed in distant and impersonal higher commands, in conferences of politicians, and British and Dutch colonial administrations. Few of the returning men could express their sense of anger by having a specific target as the one so conveniently located by the rice grower.

On the troopship *Circassia* just out of Fremantle a man threw himself overboard. Another young man who had battled day after day at a hospital camp on the railway to wash and care for patients went home to his mother in central Victoria and committed suicide. The turmoil that churned in the minds of those two men can never be known; but many of the prisoners felt that edge of the blackness that completely enveloped a few of the returning men.

In the excitement of homecoming many prisoners were unaware of their infirmities. One group flying from Manila via Morotai and Darwin put down at an airfield in South Australia. An ex-prisoner whose legs had been amputated was carried piggy-back by his mates. All the men were buoyant and confident.

> Don Moore: We were told we could go out and have a stretch while they refuelled. And there was a group of ladies all lined up with these goodies. There were cups of tea, cream cakes, everything that country hospitality could supply. We went over to them, smiling and happy; and they were all crying, just holding their heads down. We realised what we were in their eyes: bloody scarecrows. We were figures of pity.

In Borneo a football rolled across to George Batros. He went to roost it back to the waiting troops, and suddenly discovered the pathetic weakness of his legs. By their very survival the returning prisoners had demonstrated that they were among the fittest; relative to the men in the occupation forces and those at home they were weak, even pathetic.

An immediate task for all prisoners was to catch up with their popular culture. Nelson Short, rescued in the jungle near Ranau, North Borneo:

> The first thing I asked, because I was a great follower of Bing Crosby, was, 'What's the latest hits of Bing? Sing us a few.' 'Flying Home on a Wing and Prayer', 'In the Bibbidy Bobbidy Boo', and all those songs were new to us. The boys sung them to us when they picked us up.

Another prisoner remembers his incredulity when he was told that Frank Sinatra was more popular than Bing Crosby. But it was Bing and the Andrews Sisters who gave the men the most appropriate number, 'Don't Fence Me In', and they heard it endlessly.

The prisoners were uncertain of their reception in Australia. There was no precedent. They were not like the diggers returning from the First World War, nor the units that had recently paraded through city streets to be honoured for their actions in the Middle East and the Pacific. Many English prisoners-of-war of the Japanese went home almost unnoticed because the war in Europe had been over for five months. The English were already consumed by problems of peace. But in Australia the main groups of prisoners were met by cheering crowds; and that reception boosted the prisoners' own sense of elation. Small boats escorted troopships down the harbour, crowds met them on the docks, some holding notices such as 'Where is Private Harry Jackson?', and city workers and shoppers gave them a boisterous reception as they went by double-decker buses through the streets of Sydney. Those who travelled on to country towns were again greeted at railway stations by local dignitaries, old mates and flag-waving children given time- off from lessons for the occasion.

Throughout their imprisonment most men and women thought constantly of home; and that home was particular. They knew its every detail. As they contrasted their home with the squalor and poverty of the camp they were likely to idealise it and all those who clattered backwards and forwards through its rooms. Now they faced the reality.

Don Moore: I got up and then I saw my brother-in-law, Pat. I'd never kissed a guy in my life before, but I did then. And I looked around and Dad wasn't there. But I didn't say anything. And they said, 'Right, well, Jack's got some extra petrol because you're a POW, so we'll be able to drive you back home. We live in Murrumbeena now.' 'Oh, I see. Where's Dad?' And my sister said, 'Dad died in 1944'.

Sylvia Muir: I walked in, and I thought, that's Dad, because I knew mother wouldn't be there. Now who's that person? We had to place them. And it was my cousin. She had a different hairdo, she was thirteen when I left and was now seventeen.

Patrick Levy: Some men went back happily to the arms of their wives and children, some to their mothers, fathers and sisters, but I didn't. It was not unhappy with my mother and my brother. My wife met me too; and then cleared out.

George Williamson: I got a Dear John letter. She got word that I was missing in action, believed killed. And well, you can't blame her, can you? So then I got a divorce and that was that.

Rusty O'Brien: Before we were sent back home we were going to get letters from home, acquainting us of what was going on. If that had happened there would have been less heartbreak. Lots of fellows came back to broken homes. One fellow shot his wife. Another fellow burnt himself after he shot his wife.

Jack Sloane: When we first came to Greenslopes Hospital from the ship, we were given twenty-four hours' leave. When we met the next day it was so touching. Many of those who had gone home found out things that they hadn't been aware of; the sad stories became evident. Even though we felt we knew each other better than our own mothers and fathers knew each other, we didn't know what to say because we didn't know what news they had obtained.

Nelson Short: All the family was there to greet me at Mascot. And they said, 'Well, you're going straight into hospital.' I said, 'No, never. I'm not going to no hospital.' They said, 'Well, you've got to go into hospital.' I said, 'No, I've been locked up long enough. I'm not going to the hospital, I'm going home.' They said, 'Well, look, you'll have to take this chart, what to eat and everything'. So I went home and I had a great reunion. I was home for about three days, and about three o'clock in the morning I took crook, the ambulance come out and I finished up in hospital. It was nerves. But I didn't take long to rehabilitate myself.

Sir Adrian Curlewis: Our wives and families had all been warned not to give prisoners too rich meals. They were to treat them very very carefully because their stomachs wouldn't be able to take it. But somehow I got quite a good feed when I got home. And champagne. My wife had put a bottle away for three years and kept it for me.

Lady Curlewis: And it didn't seem to affect him at all. And he just looked around and he said with a sigh, 'Oh, isn't it clean!'

Rusty O'Brien: When I got to my friend's place at Oatley, my wife was with me and all our friends, and they said, 'What do you want first, before we eat?' 'Well,' I said, 'the first thing I want is a hot bath, in a bath.' So they ran a bath. We were having a few grogs and I got in the bath and they all came in to have a look at me. Which was very embarrassing because I was as skinny as a rake. And as black as the ace of spades from the sun.

Bob Yates: As far as the opposite sex was concerned, we were told that after our experiences we wouldn't be much good. But that's been proved wrong fortunately.

Daisy Sloane: We'd been told that we probably wouldn't be able to have a family for a while. We'd only been married the nine months and we had a baby boy, and then a couple of years later twin girls. So that wasn't too bad with the rice diet!

In camp the prisoners had helped hide doubts about their virility with the line, 'The second thing I'll do when I get home is take my pack off.'

Even after they had caught up with the major events within their home groups the ex-prisoners were still vulnerable to surprise and irritation at minor changes in what should have been a familiar world.

Spud Spurgeon: I found a lot of things different that sort of pissed me off. I had two young nephews I'd never seen. All my bloody trains and my books had been given away to these kids because you couldn't get toys during the war. And my bike, for crying aloud, my pride and joy, the thing that was to give me wheels when I got home, had been given to some guy because his chemist delivery boy had had his pinched! My beautiful bike.

Stan Arneil: We had some great shocks. I tried to buy a pair of shoes, but I had no coupons. When the lady found out she sold me a pair without coupons. But we didn't know about jet propulsion. Never heard of it.

Jim Richardson: One thing that struck me was the ABC. You'd go to 2BL and you'd get jazz music. You never had that before. You couldn't get Bing Crosby crooning and carrying on on that station. But now you could.

Another thing was the women. I was in the train there and I watched this woman. There was a lot of them smoking now. She pulled a packet of weed out, rolled it, licked the paper, put it in her mouth and said, 'Hey, soldier, have you got a match?' Oh God, I couldn't get over it. Rolling her own cigarette, and just turning round and biting me for a match. I said, 'Here, you can have that'. 'Oh, I don't want all your bloody matches,' she said. And the language of them!

There was also a practical point that hurt many of the other ranks. They received their back pay, and for many it was the biggest single payment they had ever had, equal to well over a year's civilian salary in 1946. But normally a soldier away from his own base and forced to feed himself was entitled to three shillings a day for subsistence. The returned men now said that as the Australian army had not been feeding them for three and a half years they should collect their subsistence allowance. This would also compensate them for the time and money they had spent trying to support themselves. The Australian government did not agree, and the men did not get an extra three shillings a day. As one prisoner said, 'We actually saved the army money'.

All the prisoners had been through extraordinary events. They wanted their friends and families to know what had happened to them. Then perhaps the people at home would understand who these returning prisoners were. For their part the families were anxious to hear what had happened to the prisoners. Yet some prisoners and those who had been close to them found it difficult to talk.

Russell Braddon: When we first got back there seemed to be this wall of almost wilful incomprehension. Subsequently we learnt that the medical experts had advised our parents and friends when we got back not to encourage us to talk about it, to steer us away from it. We were all, they said in effect, as mad as hatters, and it was dangerous to let us rattle on. So we would start talking about what had happened and instantly people were busy changing the subject, looking bored as all hell. They were in fact agitated, thinking you were going to go off your nut. There was this barrier, and there was this need to find people you could talk with.

Frank Baker: We didn't sort of fit in. You can imagine coming back to a place where you knew a lot of people and all of a sudden they had their own interests and you weren't included. You were lost completely, or I was, and I know that others were. The only place we could meet was in pubs; and I drank too much. Everyone was established, their lives were running smoothly, and you were an intrusion. I'd say the first twelve months or so was a very difficult time and would have been for most people.

John Devenish: I was sort of afraid to mix with people. I thought I was some sort of a freak. Meeting other people was very difficult. After being locked away for four years like that, you come back and the world has changed; by jove it changed.

Mickey Syer: We used to write letters to each other, ring each other up and say, 'Do you know anything about such and such?' And they'd say, 'No, but I've just heard about it, and I'll let you know if I find out anything about it.' We had to help each other.

Vivian Bullwinkel: When we first got back we missed each other very very much. In spite of all the closeness that we had to live in, we really did miss each other very much. We felt that nobody talked the same language. We felt that nobody really had any idea. They were saying, 'Yes, how awful, how terrible', but they really didn't know. We wrote to each other, we went visiting each other.

Chris Neilson: I think that's why most of us used to keep together. So many POWs in Brisbane would go down to the boozer together. You couldn't assimilate for a while, you know, you couldn't get used to the way of thinking. It took a good while. I think most of them would agree with that. For the first few months they might have gone out with a woman, but a few minutes later they were back with their mates because they seemed to be the only ones that they could converse with.

Stan Arneil: I used to ring my friend Douglas up six or seven, eight, nine times a day, and he I. That seems odd now. But after you've lived with a bloke for over five years, never separated from him for more than five or six yards, and his thoughts are attuned to yours, it becomes very difficult not to have that opportunity to converse on the only level that you know. So all over the State, these fellows would be ringing one another up all the time, talking, just talking, just sort of comforting themselves or being a little bit more secure, until we got into the situation where we didn't have to depend on a friend. You depended on a man for years.

Jack Sloane: A reunion of POWs is always a very happy event, and it's not that they want to re-live their incarceration, it is just that they know each other so well. No one will take anybody else down, because they know that they are true mates.

Sylvia Muir: Most of our husbands were marvellous. They knew what they were taking on when they married us, I think. My husband said the other nurses were part of his harem. At the reception when we got married he said, 'They tell me I married twenty-four because they've always shared everything. And I suppose I'll get shared too.' It was quite a joke. They'd ring up and say, 'How's our husband?'

Mickey Syer: My mother never asked me questions. I think she was afraid to. And father used to say, I think you need to spend a lot of time playing golf, just taking the fresh air and seeing your friends. Dear old Dad.

Dick Braithwaite: I was resentful that people were complaining about how badly off they'd been through the war when all my friends had starved to death. And I couldn't tell them about it. I thought, well, even if I did tell them, they wouldn't believe me. This has been a block to talking about these things for many years. I just felt that people would look at me and say, 'That couldn't have happened. He's shooting a line. It's just not possible. We'd have known about it.'

Joyce Braithwaite: His whole mental outlook is so much better now, he's so much more relaxed about it. For many years he wouldn't talk about it at all. Most people, even people that we were quite friendly with, knew nothing of his past history and that's the way he wanted it. But now he's quite willing to talk about it.

Dick would smoke incessantly and be uptight and unapproachable, and then he would go into a dead faint on the floor. He never would have the doctor. Dick used to say, I have to fight this myself. And he did. But I used to be concerned. I mean, if somebody passes out, you think there must be a physical cause for it; but he never ever felt there was, and that it was a nervous thing. Well, whether it was or not, they eventually grew less and less severe. After he came round, he would be exhausted, but we would often talk for hours then. And that was useful, I feel.

On their release from medical checks most of the prisoners were on accumulated leave. One prisoner remembers those first weeks being dominated by trying to get back into family life at night and 'chasing a grog here and there' during the day. Beer rationing was strict, and many hotels would open for only two hours a day. A group of ex-prisoners would hear that 'it was on at Liverpool'. They would pile into a taxi, scramble for a few beers, and then go on to somewhere else. It was a month of indulgence and companionship that eased the transition.

Some men found that their jobs had been taken by others in spite of the laws that should have given them security, or their skills were no longer in demand in the postwar economy. Many of the prison-laid plans were irrelevant. Don Noble says that if all the men who had talked about poultry farms had actually started them, Australia would have sunk under the weight of chooks. In the poverty of the prison camp, the poultry farm with its apparently endless supply of eggs and chicken meat, and the absence of bosses (or guards), seemed the answer to all problems. Men devoted hours of meticulous planning to the design of the roosts, the runs and the feed bins. But once the prisoners no longer had to fight for every ounce of protein the chooks lost their attractiveness.

When Sister Nesta James went from Heidelberg hospital to stay with friends they gave her a room of her own. She suddenly found that she was frightened to be alone, and she could not tell her hosts. The minor changes in behaviour were for many of the prisoners signs of complex anxieties.

Frank Baker: When I came back I was horrified to see my mother throwing out the fat off the corned beef. I'd say, 'You're not going to throw this out?' And she'd say, 'Don't be silly, that's rubbish, that's waste'. Waste! It was a banquet, a feast. Now, I think my wife will bear out that I never ever waste anything. I am very reluctant to throw a crust of bread out. I don't think that'll ever leave me.

Sylvia Muir: Often people open my pantry and say, 'What are you going to do with all that?' But you must be prepared, see? And it's become a thing. Because you mightn't get food for a week. So my little pantry is always completely chock-a-block with tinned stuff and I'm prepared for anything.

Chris Neilson: I know this, I couldn't go into a bloody cafe. If I was hungry as buggery, do you think I can go in there and order a meal? Had to find some bugger looked like he was hungry and ask him to have a feed with me. I couldn't do it on my own.

Herb Trackson: You always seemed to be frightened of something. As far as my case goes, I could not bear to be on my own. I had to have someone with me or someone around me, even if it was strangers. To be in a room by myself was just impossible. I'd have to get out or make an excuse to go and see someone.

Sylvia Muir: I have an absolute horror of being shut in anywhere. I know it's silly, but as long as I control the entrance to a thing I'm right. But if anybody else shuts the door, my claustrophobia's up.

Joyce Braithwaite: There was this recurrent thing we had about lice in the bed. We would get up fairly regularly, strip everything off and examine the mattress minutely. He said to me, 'I know you don't ever think there's vermin in the bed but look at my arms.' And he literally had bite marks and raised lumps. I don't know, I suppose it's psychosomatic. One was filled with great sadness that this should have happened and wondered how long this would have to last for him.

Rod Wells: I'm over-fastidious with cleanliness. I shower in the morning and use up most of the hot water in the house. It's very silly when I think of it, because I know I've already washed and rinsed myself once, but I'll soap up and rinse a second time and go through the whole thing again just to make sure.

George Williamson: I always keep two of everything. Never miss. So if I'm buying my clothes, I buy two of the same. If I buy a pair of socks I buy two pairs the same, so if I wear a hole in one I've always got three socks to change with.

David Runge: I couldn't sleep on a bed, had to sleep on the floor. And I'd get up at one o'clock in the morning and drive to Katoomba or drive to Woy Woy or something because I was tensed up, you know. Just couldn't settle down.

Nesta James: I had dreadful nightmares where I had fallen into these cesspits that we had at Muntok, and I would be up to my neck in faeces.

Chris Neilson: The worst nightmare in my book was the one you lived with all the time in Outram Road. The guard would say, '551, today I come to cut your head off'. They played so many tricks, trying to break you. But always the dream seems to end at the door. They don't come in. If you have a bad one, anyone will tell you this, get up and walk around. Don't lay in bed. Get up and walk around and you'll forget about it and go back to sleep. Don't just stay there, because it'll come back again.

Geoff O'Connor: I gave my wife a start one night. She came in and I dreamt there was a Jap outside the window and I thought, oh, I'll throw a hand grenade, that'll fix him. But I grabbed the light on the bed, and I let fly and nearly knocked her bloody head off. She wasn't real happy about that.

Roy Whitecross: Only twelve months ago, I was having a drink with three or four chaps and one of them came round to me and sort of whispered to me, 'Whitey, do you have nightmares? About, you know, the old days?' And I said, 'Of course, I do'. He said, 'How often?' I said, 'Oh, a really bad one, once every couple of months but, you know, might be one a week or every now and then I have them'. 'Oh,' he said, 'thank Christ for that. I have them too.' And I said, 'Yeah, and you thought you were going round the bend'. He said, 'Yeah, yeah, I did. It's been worrying me for a long time.' So I said to the others, 'Righto', I said, 'how many of you blokes don't have nightmares?' And they all looked at me as if I was crazy. And each one said, 'Yes, of course we do'.

When the wives of the ex-prisoners meet they often exchange stories of the effects of anti-depressant drugs, and of ways of helping husbands wake from nightmares that have them bathed in sweat and tangled in sheets. In prison the nights had often been bad, an endless turmoil of insect bites, hunger pains, happy feet, arms and legs lolling on to neighbours, trips ankle deep in mud to stinking toilets, shifting fleshless bones on narrow bench beds, and without the companionship that could make the days endurable. A returned nurse speaks of nightmares in which she is forced to dig a grave. She digs endlessly, but she cannot get it deep enough. Or she is about to be captured again and she knows exactly what she must have with her—everything from clean sheets to tins of corned beef—but she cannot force them all into her suitcases. They are dreams reviving the worst fears and frustrations.

While experiences are re-lived at night many prisoners cannot change attitudes formed at the height of the horror.

Donald Stuart: I don't know how to start earthquakes, but if I did know, believe me there'd be some bloody earthquake in Japan. Twenty-four hours under the sea; that'd fix the whole problem of the Japanese.

Dick Ryan: No use saying I'm angry with them. I used to be, but I'm not now. I wouldn't talk to the buggers. I don't give a damn what happens to them.

Tootie Keast: It is a lovely country, but I have no love for the Japanese. I don't say now I have hate. They were very cruel to us, perhaps it was war, but still I could never forgive them for what they did. Someone said to me the other day, you'd better get a new car, and mentioned the make. I said, it's a Japanese car, I couldn't possibly have a Japanese car. I'm possibly prejudiced, but I'm sorry, that's just the way I feel. I know that we have to be friends with them and they have to be friends with us, but when you've been through what we girls went through, well, you've got that—I don't want to say hatred—but you've got that something in your body and it will never come out as long as you live.

John Devenish: I'd sooner have them fighting with us than agin us, only because of their strength.

Eddie Henderson: I always thought that I would flatten the first Japanese I came across after the war, or try to flatten him. Then in the late 'fifties, early 'sixties, they commenced bringing Japanese parties down to where I worked. The Japanese were coming out and looking Australia over. And I kept well away from them. But I think it was about the mid-sixties, and I had a traveller in my office. He was very difficult to get rid of, and I was wanting to go to the toilet. By the time I did get rid of him it was a case of run. As I came round the corner I ran slap bang into this party of Japanese. I stopped, and turned over in my mind, what will I do. Then I thought, oh, these poor Bs, they weren't born or only two or three years old when their people were ill-treating us. I couldn't do anything to them. And I just went on to the toilet. They were all university students. And that helped me get over it.

Stan Arneil: Well, I hated them of course. We all did, we were taught to hate them. But I changed that very quickly. I got involved with Father Lionel Marsden of the Marist Fathers, and he had a talk to me. He wanted to go back to Japan, to be a Christian and show the people of Japan that Christianity was a forgiving religion. He had a little theme. He said, let's make a Japanese Christian for every person who died on the railway. I realised it's very foolish to hate anybody, there's no point in that whatsoever. If we want the world to go on fighting, well, let's keep on hating. I rather like the Japanese.

John van Nooten: I kind of rationalise it a bit. I looked at it in figures and I say that in any one day of the European war, Germany committed more war crimes than Japan did over the whole period. And it's war; you don't go away to have fun. I don't really think it is natural in the Japanese to be sadistic. I could be wrong, but I think it was in their training. You can whip up anything in people. Australians did some pretty rough things under certain circumstances.

Those of us who'd had the experience of going through Germany were so used to the common reply of, 'We didn't know that six and a half million Jews were annihilated, we were not connected with that'. The Japanese don't say that. They just say, 'We are sorry you had a bad time'. And there's no denial of what went on. But that's typically Japanese. They are basically so honest.

In all theatres of the Second World War Australia lost 27 000 dead. About a third of the dead were prisoners-of-war; they died after they had formally ceased to fight. The suffering and dying of so many men and women as prisoners-of-war is a distinguishing experience in Australian history. Yet by other standards Australia's cost was slight. Over six million prisoners-of-war died in the Second World War, most of them in eastern Europe. It was much worse to be a Russian prisoner of the Germans, or to be a German prisoner of the Russians, than it was to be an Allied prisoner of the Japanese. In the most horrific case about three million Russian prisoners of the Germans were slaughtered or died of neglect. The death rate was sixty per cent, twice the mortality of the Allied prisoners of the Japanese. But to say that some countries committed greater crimes is not to excuse those guilty of lesser atrocities.

In a strange selective application of humanism in the west and barbarism in the east, the Germans were responsible for few deaths among American and British Commonwealth prisoners. Out of just over eight thousand Australians who were captured by the Germans 265 died, including those suffering severe wounds at the time of imprisonment. A pilot was probably safer in a German prison camp than training.

The long term physical and mental costs of imprisonment on individuals are difficult to determine. It seems likely that when the body weight drops by over one third; when conditions are so bad that a third of the inmates die; and when there is intense stress for more than three years, then there will be lasting wounds. Perhaps the extent of recovery is more surprising than the frequency of illness.

Ian Duncan: I would say most of them, at least fifty per cent of them, have some form of nervous trouble. A lot of them have stomach trouble, a lot have gastric and duodenal ulcers, a lot still have chronic diarrhoea. But everyone who worked, certainly on the railway and in the mines in Japan, has some form of arthritis degeneration caused by the conditions under which they worked. I've seen X-rays of the spines of some of these men and they are really shocking; how they get around I don't know. But they do and they make very light of it. The men almost invariably come in and say, 'Well, I don't want to seem to be a bludger, but I've got this trouble'; or, 'I thought I'd come along and see you. I don't think I deserve any pension, we didn't do much fighting.' And this is their attitude. They actually believe that they're not entitled to a lot of the benefits of ex-servicemen. But they are. They fought a pretty hard war. As POWs.

Sir Edward Dunlop: It's quite surprising the achievement of prisoners-of-war all over the country: they've done well in all sorts of occupations and activities. And unhappily, of course, there are men who are damaged psychologically, who went on the booze or smoked themselves to death. I think my major worry has been that the years have found out a lot of them that started off pretty well. They bounded back into civilian life, they didn't want pensions, they didn't want to be cushioned, but they were very tired men and they come home exhausted in the evenings. They didn't go back to tennis, bowls and golf, they put on weight and got a bit flabby. So I think that early heart disease and the diseases which overtake the middle aged and the elderly have taken a lot of them off before their time.

Ian Duncan: At the end of the war I interviewed every Australian and English soldier in my camp; I was the only medical officer in the camp. And I thought it was my duty to record their disabilities. And you'd say to them, what diseases have you had as a prisoner-of-war? Oh, nothing much, Doc, nothing much at all. Did you have malaria? Oh yes, I had malaria. Did you have dysentery? Oh yes, I had dysentery. Did you have beriberi? Yes, I had beriberi. Did you have pellagra? Yes, I had pellagra; but nothing very much. All these are lethal diseases. But that was the norm, you see, everyone had them. Therefore they accepted them as normal.

Geoff O'Connor: My main war was with the young doctors in Repatriation. They know nothing about us, and they don't want to know. They go by the textbooks and there's nothing in textbooks that says what happens to the human body when you're three and a half years working at full pace, starved and suffering from one thing and another. Unfortunately the ones that were battling for us are getting older and they're not in the Repat now. We're getting all the young smartarses.

In the immediate postwar both in the USA and Australia the returning prisoners had higher death rates than comparative sections of the population. The main causes of death were suicides, accidents, tuberculosis and cirrhosis of the liver. The livers were damaged more by malnutrition than alcohol. By the 1960s the death rate of the ex-prisoners was close to that of other people of the same age. But there is no doubt that the ex-prisoners are much sicker. Even when comparisons are made with ex-prisoners of the Germans, the men from the camps of Asia are much more likely to be suffering from a range of illnesses from skin diseases, poor eyesight (a result of malnutrition), impeded movement of the spine, shoulders and knees, and heart disease. And, as American research has shown, the most frequent and persistent damage has been psychological. The ex-prisoners do not have organic brain damage from protracted starvation; they are the victims of traumatic stress. Forty years after the end of the war 8 000 of the 14 300 Australian returned prisoners were still alive.

All the ex-prisoners wonder why they were among the survivors. They can give practical reasons: they were fit, they were at the right age, they were lucky and missed the worst cholera camp, they had a reason which made them determined to get home, and a mate dragged them back to camp through the mud when they collapsed with malaria. But they take the question further. Why them when men of apparently greater strength and talent died? A wife of a returned prisoner says:

He had this feeling, why me? In a way he hated to be the one to be saved when so many were lost. I was inclined to say, well, there must be something very special for you to do. And he never liked that idea. Looking back, I think it was the wrong thing to say. I was young, enthusiastic and wanting to be rather a Pollyanna. He felt it was all so unjust. He found it hard to justify his existence when so many had lost their lives.

Just the fact of being a survivor has its burden. It forces men to choose between sheer chance and a grand scheme. Both conclusions carry frightening responsibilities. And many survivors torture themselves about incidents when they might have taken one small action and saved someone else. Perhaps it required just a word, just a share of some fruit, or the momentary distraction of a guard. Inevitably all prisoners passed through many such occasions, but it is particular and often minor incidents that recur and engender guilt.

To be an Australian prisoner-of-war of the Japanese was not to be the victim of some natural disaster such as a volcanic eruption or a cyclone. It was to be caught in the centre of great political and economic events in the region. For all their apparently uncontrollable sweep, those movements were man-made, and within them people acted and reacted. For the first time in their history white Australians had been caught in a great expression of human callousness; the sort of things that Australians often read about happening in some distant place among strange and violent peoples.

It was not something that was over in an instant of dramatic action. To survive as prisoners men and women had to endure and endure. The prisoners have their own heroes, and they are the men and women who again and again demonstrated that they could lead and help others through persistent horror. The prisoners do not measure themselves against national history; but they are the ones best able to express what being a prisoner did to particular lives.

Graham Chisholm: I'm angry about the futility of it all. I'm angry when I go to the Commonwealth war graves in Singapore and I look at the fine young men there under the pieces of slab, nineteen, twenty, twenty-one and twenty-two years of age, whose lives were sacrificed for no real reason. The slice out of my own life still leaves dark passages because those were vital years, and you're denied everything. But so were other people. We came out of it and we rehabilitated ourselves.

Eric Endacott: Time once gone can never be recovered. Probably in our nightmares we are always grasping for that time. I've always been resentful of that and very bitter. Perhaps things could have been otherwise, but the gap can never be recovered.

Sylvia Muir: Out of my life I lost four years; and very valuable years when you're twenty-five to twenty-nine. They were certainly lost years except for the friendships I made there and the experience it gave me. I think it's made me more tolerant. Things that I used to worry about, now I couldn't care less. *Tidak apa*, as the natives say.

Stan Arneil: Yes, it was the greatest privilege I've ever had. I was so lucky to have been a prisoner-of-war and come to an understanding about things that are important, to live with those people with whom I lived, and to make, in my own tiny way, a token gesture for Australia.

George Aspinall: I can probably understand people's problems a bit better than I would have if I hadn't been a prisoner-of-war. Particularly anybody that's under extreme stress or suffering any social problems. I think a lot of us have got a bit of understanding of that type of thing.

Chris Neilson: It seems a big thing to say now, like big-noting yourself, but it was worth it. The sense of values. I didn't have that before. Got a sense of values now.

Kevin Fagan: It gave me a great understanding of men. And a great appreciation of the ordinary things of life: bread and butter, a bit of jam on your toast in the mornings, a glass of beer when you're thirsty. And, the value of human relations. You know, when it comes to the end, the only thing that really matters are the people whom you love and the people who love you.

Snow Peat: I go to the POW rooms. I enjoy myself. I see somebody I mightn't have seen for years and we've always got something to talk about. You've only got to know so-and-so's been crook or he's in hospital and you duck home, cut his lawn and see everything's going all right. That's nothing, a little bit of effort's no worries at all. You mightn't go out giving bloody ten dollar notes away, but if anyone is having a tough time or he's been sick or anything like that you keep in touch, get on the phone and ring him up, see how he's going. There's a little bond of friendship lacking with a lot of other people. We've got some little thing that nobody else understands.

Jack Panaotie: When we get talking together, we say, couldn't go through it again, but we wouldn't have missed it. An experience that we know that nobody else knows. Not that you want nobody else to know about it, but you cannot explain it to anybody else. Because we are unique.

SELECTED BIBLIOGRAPHY

UNPUBLISHED

Although record keeping was difficult and dangerous most groups of prisoners included at least one diarist, units in fixed locations preserved some papers, and in the immediate postwar many prisoners were questioned and their written testimonies were retained for use as evidence in war trials. Most material is held in either the Australian War Memorial (AWM), Canberra, or in the Australian Archives (AA) in Canberra and Melbourne.

The most useful files from Written Records, 1939–1945, AWM, include: 554/2/1 Report on Burma and Siam 1942–1945 by Brigadier C A McEachearn; 554/7/2 History of F Force; 573/6/1A Report on Ambon and Hainan by Lt-Col J R Scott; and reports by other senior officers on main camps and forces. 1010/3/10 Trial of Lt-Col Nagatomo, and other transcripts of trials of Japanese in the AWM and AA. 1010/4/– Postwar statements by prisoners-of-war filed alphabetically, AWM. 1010/9/109 Sinking of *Rokyu Maru*, and other files on significant events, AWM.

DIARIES AND REMINISCENCES:

BARNETT, B A   Diary March–December 1943, AWM
BLOW, R   Reminiscences, AWM
BROWN, R   Diary of Ambon and Hainan
CHRISTIE, F W   The war diary of VX35135 Gunner F W Christie 4th Anti Tank, roneoed
CLANCY (Turner), Veronica, Reminiscences, AWM
FERRIS, R F   Memories, AWM
FINKMEYER, C   Little food for thought, roneoed
GILCHRIST, S R   Diary and reminiscences, AWM
HARDACRE, J F   The story of F Force, AWM
HARRIS, R   Reminiscences, AWM
JACKSON, F   Diary and reminiscences, AWM
JELLIMAN, V   Reminiscences, Australian National Library
JESSUP, H E   Changi Diary 1942–1945, Australian National Library
KORSCH, J D   P.O.W. Diary of John D. Korsch, roneoed
MORRIS, J G   'Tom', A soldier's reflections forty years on, roneoed
NOTTAGE, S   Diaries, AWM
POIDEVIN, L O S   The 'Potong' Doctor, typescript
SANDILANDS, C E   Burnt rice and bamboo, typescript
STAHL, F E   Autobiography of a P.W.(J), roneoed
WALLACE, R   Diary, AWM
WHITE, J G   Diary, AWM

Diaries and reminiscences located during research have been deposited in the AWM whenever possible. Other diaries not listed here are also held in the AWM, either in the official or the donated records sections.

South to Bataan: North to Mukden, the prison diary of Brigadier General W. E. Brougher, D Clayton James editor, University of Georgia Press, Athens, 1971; Crouter, Natalie, *Forbidden Diary, A record of wartime internment, 1941–1945*, Lynn Z Bloom, editor, Burt Franklin & Co, New York, 1980; and Hardie, Robert, *The Burma-Siam Railway: The secret diary of Dr Robert Hardie 1942–1945*, Imperial War Museum, London, and William Collins, Sydney, 1983, are valuable published diaries for comparative material.

OFFICIAL HISTORIES   Australia in the War of 1939–45:
LONG, Gavin, *The Final Campaigns*, AWM, Canberra, 1963
WALKER, A S, *Medical Series, Middle East and Far East*, AWM, Canberra, 1953
WALKER, A S, *Medical Services of the RAN and RAAF with a section on women in the army medical services*, AWM, Canberra, 1961
WIGMORE, Lionel, *The Japanese Thrust*, AWM, Canberra, 1957, see especially Part 3, A J Sweeting, 'Prisoners of the Japanese'

History of the Second World War, United Kingdom Military Series:
KIRBY, S Woodburn, *The War Against Japan*, 5 vols, Her Majesty's Stationery Office, London, 1957–1969

One of the few professional historians to have written on Australian prisoners of the Japanese is Joan Beaumont: 'Victims of War: The Allies and the transport of prisoners-of-war by sea, 1939–45', *Journal of the Australian War Memorial*, April 1983; and 'Rank, privilege and prisoners-of-war', *War & Society*, May 1983.

BIBLIOGRAPHY   Books by and about Australian prisoners-of-war of the Japanese:

ARNEIL, Stan, *One Man's War*, Alternative Publishing Co-operative Ltd, Sydney, 1980
ARNEIL, Stan, *Black Jack: The Life and Times of Brigadier Sir Frederick Galleghan*, Macmillan, Melbourne, 1983
BANCROFT, A, and ROBERTS, R G, *The Mikado's Guests*, Paterson Printing Press, Perth, ND

BENSON, Reverend James, *Prisoner's Base and Home Again: The Story of a Missionary POW*, Robert Hale, London, 1957

BOWDEN, T, *Changi Photographer: George Aspinall's Record of Captivity*, ABC Enterprises-Collins, Sydney, 1984

BRADDON, Russell, *The Naked Island*, Werner Laurie, London, 1952

BRADDON, Russell, *End of a Hate, A Sequel to 'The Naked Island'*, Cassell, London, 1958

BULCOCK, R, *Of Death But Once*, F W Cheshire, Melbourne, 1947

CARTER, N, *G-String Jesters*, Currawong, Sydney, 1966

CLARENCE, Margaret, *Yield Not to the Wind*, Management Development Publishers, Sydney, 1982

CLARKE, Hugh V, *The Tub*, Jacaranda, Brisbane, 1963, Corgi, 1965 (a novel)

COATES, A, and ROSENTHAL, N, *The Albert Coates Story*, Hyland House, Melbourne, 1977

CORRIE, E C W, *Survival Against Odds*, privately published, Castlemaine, 1983

FIELD, A E, 'POW Diary', *Purple Diamond*, offical organ of the Seventh Division Engineers' Association, vol 2, no 36, May 1979

FIRKINS, Peter, *From Hell to Eternity*, Westward Ho, Perth, 1979

FORBES, G K, CLAYTON, H S, JOHNSON, D S, and BRITZ, J H, *Borneo Burlesque*, H S Clayton, Sydney, 1947

FOSTER, F, *Comrades in Bondage*, Skeffington & Son, London, ND

GREENER L, *No Time to Look Back*, Victor Gollancz, London, 1951. (a novel)

HALL, E R (Bon), *The Burma-Thailand Railway of Death*, Graphic Books, Melbourne, 1981

HAMILTON, Thomas, *Soldier Surgeon in Malaya*, Angus & Robertson, Sydney, 1957

HARRIS, Douglas, *'G' Strings and Bangkok Bowlers*, Globe Press, Melbourne, 1978

HARRISON, K, *The Brave Japanese*, Rigby, Adelaide, 1966

HOWARD, Frederick, *Kent Hughes: Biography of Kent Hughes*, Macmillan, Melbourne, 1972

HUGHES, W S Kent, *Slaves of the Samurai*, Oxford University Press, Melbourne, 1946

JEFFREY, Betty, *White Coolies*, Angus & Robertson, Sydney, 1954

JEFFREY, Betty, *Matron A M Sage 'Sammie'*, no publisher, no date, 55 pp

LAMBERT, Eric, *MacDougal's Farm*, Frederick Muller Ltd, London, 1965

LUMIERE, C, *Kura*, Jacaranda Press, Brisbane, 1955

McCABE, G, *Pacific Sunset*, Oldham, Beddome & Meredith, Hobart, ND

McGREGOR, John, *Blood on the Rising Sun*, Bencoolen, Perth, ND

NELSON, David, *The Story of Changi Singapore*, Changi Publication Co., Perth, 1970

NEWTON, R W, *The Grim Glory of the 2/19 Battalion AIF*, 2/19th Battalion AIF Association, Sydney, 1975

PARKIN, Ray, *Out of the Smoke*, Hogarth Press, London, 1960

PARKIN, Ray, *Into the Smother: A Journal of the Burma-Siam Railway*, Hogarth Press, London, 1963

PARKIN, Ray, *The Sword and the Blossom*, Hogarth Press, London, 1968

POOLE, Philippa, *Of Love and War. The Letters and Diaries of Captain Adrian Curlewis and his Family 1939–45*, Lansdowne Press, Sydney, 1982

RICHARDSON, H, *One-Man War, The Jock McLaren Story*, Angus & Robertson, Sydney, 1957

RIVETT, Rohan, *Behind Bamboo: An inside story of the Japanese prison camps*, Angus & Robertson, Sydney, 1946

ROBINSON, Frank and HALL, E R (Bon), *Through Hell and Bomb Blast*, Frank Robinson, Waverley, Tasmania, 1982

SIMONS, Jessie Elizabeth, *While History Passed: The Story of the Australian Nurses who were prisoners of the Japanese for three and a half years*, William Heinemann, Melbourne, 1954

SPROD, George, *Bamboo Round My Shoulder. Changi: The Lighter Side*, Kangaroo Press, Sydney, 1981

SPROD, George, *Life on a Square-Wheeled Bike: the Saga of a Cartoonist*, Kangaroo Press, Sydney, 1983

STUART, Donald, *I Think I'll Live*, Georgian House, Melbourne, 1981 (a novel)

SUMMONS, Walter, *Twice Their Prisoner*, Oxford University Press, Melbourne, 1946

WALLACE, Walter, *Escape from Hell: The Sandakan Story*, Robert Hale, London, 1958

WATERFORD, John, *Footprints: From Prisoner-of-war days in Singapore and Thailand to Japanese-Australian relations today*, privately published, no date

WHITECROSS, Roy, *Slaves of the Son of Heaven*, Dymock's Book Arcade, Sydney, 1951

Note: Many unit histories have not been included; and they are still being published, eg R W Christie (ed.), *A history of the 2/29 Battalion—8th Division AIF*, 2/29 Battalion AIF Association, Melbourne, 1983; and Cliff Whitelock, *Gunners in the Jungle: A story of the 2/15 Field Regiment, Royal Australian Artillery, 8 Division, Australian Imperial Force*, 2/15 Field Regiment Association, Sydney, 1983

ACKNOWLEDGMENTS

In February 1982 Tim Bowden and I travelled with a group of ex-soldiers back to the sites where they had fought, surrendered and been imprisoned. The oldest in the group was eighty and the youngest fifty-nine. Both had probably lied to the enlisting officers. The men who assembled among the chrome trolleys and suitcases in Sydney airport included ageing larrikin lads and men accustomed to moving a vote of thanks at formal dinners; they were bankers and bushmen, and one was both. Through the following days Tim and I listened to them talk as they scuffed in the ballast of the Burma-Thailand railway, relaxed in air-conditioned motels, looked at the grey walls of Pudu gaol, and held a remembrance ceremony among the headstones of 1362 Australians in the beautiful cemetery at Kanchanaburi in Thailand.

On the tour I shared a room with Lincoln Fixter who, forty years earlier, was captured on the Malay Peninsula, drafted to D Force and sent to the Thai end of the railway. When the tour was half over Lincoln said, 'When I saw that I was teamed with a doctor I thought I could get a free consultation. But a mate of mine said, "You might do better. Perhaps it's a lady doctor." And what did I get? A bloody historian!' All members of the Bamboo Tour gave numerous free consultations; and the historian is grateful.

Tim and I returned to Australia convinced of the importance of the topic, better equipped to ask questions, and in awe of our task. We wanted to give details of the varied and extraordinary experiences of over 22 000 Australians, locate those experiences within national history, and show what they did to particular lives.

After a year of research we had covered much of the basic written material, made some preliminary interviews and were ready to begin the bulk of the recording. Although we had prepared lists of questions all interviews were free-ranging. In some cases eight hours of conversation were taped. Tim Bowden's interview with George Aspinall extended into several sessions and ultimately into the book, *Changi Photographer*. Perhaps another twenty transcripts had such a sustained richness that they could also stand alone. The selection of informants depended on chance, the chain effect of one ex-prisoner suggesting another, the deliberate search for particular individuals, and the aim to cover all the main units and camps. A strict random selection would have given a firm base for some generalisations; but it would have been unlikely to pick up the four living survivors of the Sandakan–Ranau death march, the two escapers from North Borneo to the Philippines, the one Australian soldier left alive in Rabaul in 1945, the two men who fought with the Chinese communists in Malaya, those rescued by submarine from the South China Sea, the inmates of Outram Road Gaol, and a fair representation of the numerically minor services, the Navy, Airforce and the Australian Army Nursing Service. In the event we were fortunate that the strength of the ex-prisoners' network could so quickly locate people. Ultimately 150 men and women were interviewed, and over 350 hours of tape preserved. For every minute broadcast over thirty minutes of recorded material were unused. Inevitably some sparkling anecdotes and strong analytical comments were left out simply because they did not fit the program plan, or someone else made the same point more briefly. The uncut tapes have been placed in the archives of the ABC and copies presented to the Australian War Memorial.

When working on the series *Taim Bilong Masta: The Australian Involvement with Papua New Guinea* Tim and I started with a clear division of labour: he had the skills to make radio programs and I had done some research on the topic. In *Prisoners of War* roles were blurred. Tim became very knowledgeable about the subject, and although Tim and assistant producer Margaret Evans did the bulk of the interviewing, I recorded some informants for broadcast. We collaborated on the planning of the series, but the deft editing skills were Tim's alone. I have turned the transcripts into a book. Because what makes a book is different from what makes a good radio program I have added new material, summarised some sections of the transcript, corrected obvious grammatical errors and omitted repetitions of speech.

When I first spoke to Tim about prisoners-of-war being one of the significant and little understood topics in Australian history, he looked at me as though he had been invited to enjoy battering himself to death with a heavy ABC-issue tape recorder. We were still working on *Taim Bilong Masta*; and he knew that no matter how well we planned another series, as deadlines raced closer he would be working at nights and weekends. He was right. And again we had to inconvenience our families. Although not always treating us with the deference we deserved, they often had to move with caution in case we were recording, about to record, or trying to think of a sentence that might be recorded. Our thanks to Ros, Jan, Barnaby, Guy and Michael.

Don Moore of the 4th Anti-tank entertained his fellow prisoners with cartoons on scarce paper in Singapore, Thailand and Japan. Subsequently his skill has been displayed at numerous reunions, and I am grateful that he has called on his talents and memory to illustrate this book. Associate-Producer, Margaret Evans, recorded valuable interviews, particularly of the nurses, and worked long hours surveying the material and collating it under subject headings. Nora Bonney, assisted by Lyn Carpenter, typed the transcripts and demonstrated a mastery of digger idiom. Karen Haines and Dorothy McIntosh word processed an untidy manuscript into neat clarity. Gavan Daws helped with ideas about the subject and good prose. Courteny Harrison and Tom Morris gave hard-won knowledge.

Many of the team associated with the production of *Taim Bilong Masta* were again at work, and although they run the risk of being labelled recidivists, they are certainly to be thanked: Wayne Chapman was responsible for technical production; Helen Findlay and Nina Riemer edited the manuscript with flattering restraint; Leigh Nankervis designed the book; Susan Crivelli checked, signposted and indexed the tapes; Suzanne Ridley compiled the index for the book; and Glenn Hamilton has given his general support. The staff of the Australian War Memorial, always seeming to operate through builders' debris, gave frequent and valuable aid. Janine Walker and Daniel Connell conducted two key interviews. The recorded comments of Sir Frederick Galleghan, who died in 1971, are from the ABC archives.

The most important acknowledgment is to the informants. Many talked of harrowing events for the first time. And they spoke with moving, almost poetic, eloquence. They were generous with their memories mainly because they felt an obligation to themselves and their comrades to set down their part in an extraordinary piece of history. Often we went back to informants to check and enlarge on points. We were met with unfailing courtesy. The men and women interviewed were:

Sumio Adachi, Bob Adolphson, Charles Almond, Dick Armstrong, Stan Arneil, Berry Arthur, George Aspinall, Eric Bailey, Edna Baker, Frank Baker, Arthur Bancroft, George Batros (Peterson), Claes Bjerner, Rex Blow, Jack Boardman, Keith Botterill, Geoff Boreham, Russell Braddon, Joyce Braithwaite, Richard Braithwaite, Dr Des Brennan, Colin Brien, Fred Brightfield, Arthur Brown, Ken Brown, Ray Brown, Vivian Bullwinkel (Mrs Statham), Dr Lloyd Cahill, Owen Campbell, Leon de Castres, Peg de Castres, Alec Chew, Gregory Clark, Hugh Clarke, Graham Chisholm, Bill Cook, Mavis Cullen (Mrs Cation), Sir Adrian Curlewis, Lady Betty Curlewis, Okuyama Daijiroh, Ted Date, Stan Davis, John Devenish, Alex Drummond, Dr Ian Duncan, Sir Edward Dunlop, Eric Endacott, Nancy Endacott, Dr Kevin Fagan, Sir Frederick Galleghan, Albert van Geffen, Lance Gibson, Ross Glover, Slim de Grey, Murray Griffin, Ben Hackney, Iole Harper (Mrs Burkitt), Douglas Harris, Roy Harris, Hiroe Hasegawa, Eddie Henderson, Dr David Hinder, Chew Tiong Hoe, Gary Hooper, Ken Ishii, Max Jagger, Reverend K. Jambunathan, Nesta James (Mrs Noy), Betty Jeffrey, Bill Jinkins, Tootie Keast (Mrs McPherson), Edith Leembruggen, Patrick Levy, Bill McCure, Peter McGrath-Kerr, George McNeilly, Ian Macrae, Toshiro Matsuura, Gordon Maxwell, John May, Harry Medlin, Paul Metzler, Alf Michell, Don Moore, Tom Morris, Ken Mosher, Cliff Moss, Alan Munro, Sylvia Muir (Mrs McGregor), John Murphy, Ray Myors, Akira Nagazumi, Chris Neilson, Clive Newnham, Reg Newton, Don Noble, Sulaiman Mahomed Noor, John van Nooten, Geoff O'Connor, John O'Brien, Rusty O'Brien, Wilma Oram (Mrs Young), Jack Panaotie, Ray Parkin, Ken Parkyns, Snow Peat, Fred Perrin, Sydney Piddington, Samuel Pond, Dr Rowley Richards, Sybil Richards, Jim Richardson, John Robe, Frank Robinson, David Runge, Dick Ryan, Murray Sayle, Arthur Shephard, Nelson Short, Robert Shoobridge, Daisy Sloane, Jack Sloane, Cuthbert de Souza, George Sprod, Spud Spurgeon, Lee Tian Soo, Ray Steele, Keith Stevens, Fred Stringer, Donald Stuart, Jack Sue, Micky Syer, Nagase Takashi, Hanzawa Tamotsu, Dr Jim Taylor, Jusuke Terai, Alec Thompson, David Thompson, Pat Thompson, Clarrie Thornton, Vern Toose, Francis Trackson, Herb Trackson, Ray Tullipan, George Vafiopulous, Bob Wallace, Cliff Warn, Rod Wells, Dr Glyn White, Roy Whitecross, George Williamson, Jack Willis, Ian Wingfield, Donald Wise, Beryl Woodbridge, John Wyett, Robert Yates, Arthur Young.

INDEX

Bold figures indicate quoted matter

Aitken, William 86, 90, 91
Almond, Charles 19, **192**, 197
Ambon 4–5, 15, 20, 84–9, 94–7, 129, 151
Ambonese 130
Americans 63–4, 134, 147–9, 160, 184–5, 194
Ando, *Captain* 88–9
Arneil, Stan 7, 12, 23, 27, 30, 33, **39, 40, 48, 52, 53, 56, 59–60, 68,** 203, 211–2, 215 218
Arthur, Berry 28
Aspinall, George 11, 22, 25, **29,** 31, **40, 42, 60, 68, 197, 218**

Bailey, Eric **25,** 56
Baker, Frank 29, 48, **62–3,** 141–3, **181, 183, 185, 211, 213**
Bancroft, Arthur 21, **42, 44, 63,** 145–9, **150, 157**
Banka Island 74, 77, 81–3, 199, 204
beatings 45, 49, 77, 88–9, 105, 164
Bennett, Gordon 11, 17, 20, 125
beriberi 52, 81, 134, 176
Blackforce 13, 15–16
Blow, Rex 99–100, 105, 111–17
Boardman, Jack 28
Boreham, Geoff 24

Borneo 4, 38, 98–109, 138, 199, 200
 Kuching 105
 Ranau 106, 109, 117, 121, 124
 Sandakan 100–2, 105, 109, 117
Botterill, Keith 29, 98, **100, 101,** 105–6, **107–8,** 109, 121–24
bowing 19, 77, 201
Braddon, Russell 6, **21, 26, 34, 211**
Braithwaite, Dick 101, **105, 108–9,** 119–21, 124
Breavington, R. E. 31
Brennan, *Dr* Des 17, **194**
Brien, Colin 33

INDEX

Brightwell, Fred 28, **193**
British, the 64–8, 155
Brown, Claudie 16, 17
Brown, Ken 202, **204–5**
Bulcock, Roy 16, 63
Bullwinkel, Vivian 71, 72, **74–6, 78–9**, 82, **83**, 204, 205, **212**
Burma 37–8, 41, 44, 46–57, 98, 138, 198
  Tavoy 37
  Thanbyuzayat 38, 42, 54
Burma–Thailand railway 46, 58, 67, 96, 150, 151, 154
Burmese 64
Butler, Rex 113, 114, 116

Cahill, Lloyd 33, **42**, 50, **53**, 66
Campbell, Owen **101, 108,** 109, **117–19,** 124
Chambers, Norah 80
Changi, see Singapore—Changi
Chew, Alex **129**
Chinese
  assistance 20, 22, 91, 102, 134
  Communists 20, 93, 126, 128–9, 135, 194
  labourers 64, 89, 91
  refugees 72
Chisholm, Graham **196, 218**
cholera 53–4, 65
Christie, Frank 22, 24, 39
cigarettes 19, 100, 114, 121, 144, 158, 184, 200
Clarke, Hugh **28, 39–40,** 41, **44, 46–7, 49, 56, 59, 67,** 140–4, **182, 186, 195, 196, 199, 201**
classes see education
coastwatchers 157, 161
Coates, *Dr Sir* Albert 18, 42, 49, 50, 51
Coe, Harry 130, 133
concerts
  Ambon 87
  Changi 27–8, 193
  Palembang 80
  Rabaul 159
  Selarang 31
  Zentsuji 177
Cook, Bill 84, 86, 91, 94
Cousens, Charles 180–1
Cullen, Mavis 77, 80
Curlewis, *Sir* Adrian **9,20,26,**49, **210**

Davis, Stan **17, 164,** 171, 176
De Castres, Leon 30, **203**
de Grey, Slim 27, **28,** 193
de Souza, Cuthbert **12**
Dean, Penn 164, 168
death rates 4, 96, 108, 150
Devenish, John **85, 88, 89–90, 91–2,** 212, 215
Downer, *Sir* Alec 26
Drummond, Alex 29, **32**
Drummond, *Matron* I. M. 74
Dryburgh, Margaret 80
Duncan, Ian 50,55,**56,**183,**188,**216
Dunlop, *Sir* Edward 8, 26, 50, 54, 67, 152–3, **198, 216**

Dutch, the 63, 78, 84, 87, 131, 155
dysentery 23, 30, 50, 51, 81, 141,173

education 26, 87, 163, 179
8th Division 9, 11, 69, 135
Endacott, Eric 183, **185–6, 218**
escape 30–2, 37, 105, 109, 110–24, 125–37
executions 31, 165

Facey, Barney 6
Fagan, *Dr* Kevin 38, 46, **50, 55, 61, 65, 67, 218**
fertility 32
Filipinos 115
food 22–3, 29, 42, 51, 59, 65, 78, 90, 94, 100, 140, 183, 200
Formosa, see Taiwan
French Indo-China 157

Galleghan *Sir* Frederick G. (Black Jack) 31, 33–4, 68, 174
Gandov 161
Geneva Convention 28, 110
Gibson, Lance **149,** 163, 195
Gilchrist, Stan 139
Gillon, Miles 111, 114, 116
Glover, Ross **14,** 64
Griffin, Murray 23, 32
Gull Force 12, 15, 84–5, 93

Hackney, Ben **16, 19**
Hainan 89–94, 133–37, 202
Harper, Iole 73, 74, 78, **79**
Harris, Roy 12, 84, **85,** 90, **92**
Henderson, Eddie **37, 197–8, 215**
Higgins, Miles 134
Hinder, David 50, 62
Hiramatso, *Sergeant-Major* Aitaro 62–3
Hobbs, Alan 50, 53
Hooper, Gary **200–1**
Hoshijima, *Captain* Susumi 101, 103
Hughes, Wilfred Kent 194
Hunt, Bruce 50

Ikeuchi 88, 93, 95, 96
Indonesians 201–2

Jackson, Stan 156
James, Nesta 72, **79, 213–4**
Japan
  captives in 4, 77, 80–1, 139, 145, 177–90, 199, 200
  Fukuoka 184, 196
  Hiroshima 189, 195
  Nagasaki 186, 189–90
  Naoetsu 183
  Omuta 183, 184, 187
  Sakata 183
  Shikoku 183
  Totsuka 195
  Zentsuji 177, 179
Japanese
  convoys 13, 139, 142, 145, 149
  prisoners 116–7
Java 4, 13, 15–16, 117, 138, 152–4, 200
  Bandung 152–3

Makasura 153–4
  Serang 21
  Surabaya 63
  Tanjong Priok 14
Javanese 64, 139
Jeffrey, Betty 71, **72, 73,** 74, **78, 80, 82–3, 202, 204**
Jennings, Marjory 80
Jinkins, Bill 87, 129, **130–33**

Keast, Tootie **195, 200, 215**
Kennedy, Jim 113, 114, 117
Kingsley, *Private* 75
Kolong, Orang Tua 118–19
Koram, *Corporal* 112
Korea 4, 138, 163
Koreans 45, 48

Lark Force 12, 15, 76, 179
Leembruggen, Edith 78
Lennard, Haydon 202, 204
Levy, Patrick 18, 32, **45,209**
Lockwood, Tommy 134
looting 29–30

MacArthur, Douglas 199
McCure, Bill 128, 135–37
McGrath-Kerr, Peter 186, **189**
McGregor, John 171
McLaren, Jock 99–100, 105, 113–17
McNeilly, George 17–18, 26–7, 33, **193**
McPherson, Tootie **76–7,80–1**
Macrae, Ian 88, **93,** 94, 129, 133, **134**
malaria 30, 48, 51, 156
Malaya 4, 11, 69, 138
  Bakri 16
  Gemas 20
  Kluang 71
  Kota Bharu 13
  Kuala Lumpur 20
  Malacca 71
  Muar 16, 20
  Soc Fin 128
  Tampin 71
Malays 64, 118, 135
Manchuria 4, 33, 138, 163, 194, 200
Mant, Gilbert 6
marches 40, 95, 100, 103, 106–7, 151, 191
Matthews, Lionel 102, 103, 104–5
Maxwell, Gordon 43, 140–5, **189, 198**
May, *Padre* John 76, **179**
Medlin, Harry **15, 201–2,** 207
Metzler, Paul 179
Michell, Alf **52–3**
Moore, Don 6, 11, **12,** 22, 39, 43, **45, 59, 60, 144, 182, 184,** 185, 186, **195–6, 206, 208, 209**
morale 24, 30, 79, 86
Morris, Tom 7, 19, 24, 26, 56
Moses, Charles 20
Moss, Cliff 12, 18, **22,** 59, **62,** 182, **196, 201**

223

Moss, George **45**
Moxham, William   109, 121, 123
Muir, Sylvia   **71, 72, 73. 77–8, 79,
   81–3, 206, 209. 212–3, 218**
Murphy, John   157–62
music   26–7, 80, 102, 142
Mutaguchi, *General*   46
Myors, Ray   **57, 198**

Neilson, Chris   20, 125–27, **165,
   166, 168,** 170–1, 174–6, **203,
   206, 212–4, 218**
New Britain   4, 20, 157
   Rabaul   12, 15, 76, 157, 158, 160–2
New Guinea   11, 76, 157, 177
Newton, Reginald   **39–40,** 49, **62,**
   67, 140–5, **181, 188**
Noble, Don   **15, 151–2, 186–7,
   189, 199**
nurses   69–83, 195, 202

O'Brien, Rusty   52, **209–10**
O'Connor, Geoff   23, 38, **43–4, 54,
   57, 62, 63, 214, 217**
officers   24–5, 33, 34, 58–63, 68,
   92–3, 105, 179, 194, 197
   British   67
Okasaka, *Lieutenant*   31
Oliver, Jimmy   22
Oram, Wilma   72, 82

Panaotie, Jack   9, 86, 87, 88, **94, 95, 218**
Parkin, Ray   45, **48, 50, 53, 57,** 64,
   **139–44, 181–3, 187, 188,
   190, 195, 200**
Parkyns, Ken   **177, 180,** 181
Paschke, *Matron O. D.*   69, 73
Patmore, Charles   94
Peat, Snow   8, 22, 23, 32–3, **39, 42,
   56, 57, 59, 68, 193, 206, 218**
pellagra   51–2
Perrin, Fred   84, 134
Perth, *HMAS*   14, 139, 154
Philippines   115, 124, 142
Pickford, Claude   102
Piddington, Sydney   28, **31,** 193
Pond, S. A. F.   17
Pulau Bukum   98

Quittendon, M. W.   37

rations   *see* food
Richards, *Dr* Rowley   23, 50, **51–2,
   54, 55–6,** 67, **183–4, 198**
Richardson, Jim   23, **35–6,** 37–8,
   182, 190, 199, 211
Rivett, Rohan   6
Roach, L. N.   85
Robinson, Frank   **7, 8, 19, 154–6,
   197, 205**
Roy, George   92–3
Runge, David   8, **181, 184, 187–8,
   189, 199, 206, 214**
Russians   194–5
Ryan, Dick   19, **193, 215**
Ryan, H. R. (Bluey)   128, 137

Sage, *Matron A. M.*   83
Saipan   149
sandflies   40
Scott, W. J. R.   85, 92, 93
2/2nd Independent Company   15
2/4th Machine Gun Battalion   6
2/6th Field Company of Engineers
   138
2/10th Field Ambulance   76
2/10th Field Regiment   6, 8, 99, 111
2/15th Field Regiment   99
2/19th Battalion   17, 62, 98, 143,
   181
2/21st Battalion   84
2/22nd Battalion   6, 12, 76
2/29th Battalion   16, 17, 61, 128,
   138
2/30th Battalion   16, 68
2/40th Battalion   6, 189
7th Division   13
sex   25–6, 78–9, 159, 194
Shattles, Stephen   180
Shephard, Arthur   **127–28, 135–
   37**
Short, Nelson   102, **105, 106, 108,
   109,** 121–24, **209–10, 212**
Singapore   4, 11, 17, 72–3, 203
   Bukit Timah   28, 111, 125
   Changi   22, 24–34, 68, 98, 125,
      151, 174, 191, 192, 197, 203
   Outram Road   105, 117, 164–76
   Selarang   30–2
   work camps   30, 117
Singer, Geoff   49
Sloane, Jack   **19, 193, 197, 210, 212**
Smith, Harry   27
Smyllie, Jock   128, 135
Sparrow Force   12, 15, 151
Sprod, George   27, **56**
Spurgeon, C. H. (Spud)   **13–14,**
   21, **163, 194, 210**
Stahl, Fred   126
Steele, Ray   **18, 22,** 110–17, **203–4**
Stevens, Keith   27, 28
Sticpewich, William   109, 121, 124
Stringer, Fred   28, **31,** 68, **207**
Stuart, Donald   41, 49, **52, 65–6,
   139, 198–9, 214**
Suarez, *Lt-Col* A.   115–16
Suga, *Colonel*   101
Sulu Archipelago   116
Sumatra   4, 8, 138, 154, 196, 204
   Gloegoer camp   30, 154
   Lubuklinggau   82
   Medan camp   154
   Muara-Pekanbaru railway   156–
      7, 197
   Palembang   77, 78
Syer, Mickey   71, 73, **74,** 78, **83, 211–2**

Taiwan   4, 144
Taiwanese   101
Tamils   64, 65, 135
Tawitawi   115–17, 121
Taylor, *Dr* Jim   **173,** 174
Taylor, John   40

Thailand   38, 41, 68, 138, 191, 200
   Bangkok   192, 198
   Hellfire Pass   41, 49
   Hintok   48, 50, 54, 55
   Kanchanaburi   54, 68
   Kinsayok   58
   Konkoita   55
   Konyu   44, 45
   Nakom Paton   68
   Pitsanulok   192
   Songkurai   48, 58, 66
   Tamarkan   68
   Tarsau   43, 67, 68
   Three Pagoda Pass   43, 58
Thais   64, 192
theft   29, 32, 81
Thompson, David   182, **186, 189–
   90, 198**
Thornton, Clarrie   **16,** 17, 21, 191,
   192
Timor   4, 15, 151–3
   Koepang Bay   15, 151
   Portuguese   15
Toguri, Iva   181
Tokyo War Crimes Trial   51, 168
torture   104, 136
Trackson, Herb   **165, 167, 168–76, 213**
Trotter, Flo   82
Tulley, Hughie   39
Tullipan, Ray   28
22nd Brigade   9, 17
27th Brigade   11

ulcers   52, 109
University of Changi   26, 28

van Boxtel, *Captain*   53
van Nooten, John   88, **94, 95, 96, 215**
VD   16, 40
Vietnamese   202

Wagner, Charles   111, 113, 114,
   117
Walker, Gordon   20
Wallace, Walter   112, 114, 117
Walsh, *Padre* Paddy   40, 48
Warn, Cliff   129–33
Wells, Rod   24, **100,** 102, **103,
   104, 166, 167–8, 169–70,
   171–5, 214**
Westley, George   93
Weyton, Gordon   102, 104
White, *Dr* Glyn   8, 23, 72, **175**
Whitecross, Roy   37, **57, 187, 190, 214**
Williamson, George   9, **86–7, 94,
   96, 209. 214**
Willis, Jack   **14,** 154
Wise, Donald   29, **64**
Woodbridge, Beryl   **74,** 80
work   28, 41–2, 51, 64, 93, 154, 183
Wyett, John   166, 171, 176

Yates, Bob   43, **210**
Young, Arthur   130, **132**

Z Force   123–24